Ducati

First published in Great Britain in 2000 by
Virgin Books
An imprint of
Virgin Publishing Ltd
Thames Wharf Studios
Rainville Road
London
W6 9HA

First published in 1999 by Le Lettere, Florence

Copyright © 1999 Le Lettere, Florence
Publishers: Giovanni Gentile and Nicoletta Pescarolo
Graphic design and making-up: Laura Venturi
Coordination: Daniele Casalino
Translation: Huw Evans
Photolithography, printing and binding: Conti Tipocolor,
Calenzano (Florence) Italy

A catalogue record for the book is available from the
British Library.

ISBN 1 85227 893 5

Printed in Italy
January 2000
by Conti Tipocolor
Calenzano (Florence)

Bibliography

AA.VV., *Ducati Motoleggere monoalbero, istruzioni per le stazioni di servizio*, Ducati, Italy 1960

AA.VV, *Ducati: istruzioni per l'uso e la manutenzione 250/350/450, Mark 3 250/350/450 Desmo, 250/350/450 Scrambler*, Ducati, Italy (n. d.)

AA.VV, *Ducati: i monocilindrici 1946-1977, dal Cucciolo ai Desmo*, AAVE, Italy (n. d.)

AA.VV., *Ducati 750cc. Manuale d'officina e catalogo ricambi, 2° parte, ciclistica*, Ducati, Italy 1973

AA.VV., *Ducati 250, 350, 450. Catalogo ricambi, 1° parte, motore*, Ducati, Italy 1974

S. Eke, *Ducati Tuning V-twin with bevel drive camshaft*, Lodgemark Press, Great Britain 1986

AA.VV., *Cycle World on Ducati 1962/80*, Brooklands Books, Great Britain 1987

C. Cathcart, *Ducati Motorrader*, MBV, Germany 1988

M. Walker, *Ducati Desmo*, Osprey Publishing, Great Britain 1989

R. Bacon, *Ducati V-Twins 1971-1986*, «Motorcycle» Monographs no. 19, Niton Publications, Great Britain 1991

B. Cavalieri Ducati, *Storia della Ducati*, Editografica, Italy 1991

M. Walker, *Ducati Singles Restoration*, Osprey Publishing, Great Britain 1991

C. Cathcart, *Ducati Exklusiv*, MBV, Germany 1992

M. Shafer, *Ducati, die Königswellen-Twins, Motorrader die Geschichte Machten*, MBV, Germany 1992

AA.VV., *Cycle World on Ducati 1982/91*, Brooklands Books, Great Britain 1993

M. Walker, *Ducati Twins Restoration*, Osprey Publishing, Great Britain 1993

C. Guislain, *Motoscopie no. 5: Ducati, les V-Twins à couples coniques*, Editions Gallett, France 1994

M. Walker, *Illustrated Ducati Buyer's Guide*, Motorbooks USA 1994

M. Clarke, *Ducati Scrambler Desmo e Mark 3*, Giorgio Nada Editore, Italy 1995

G. Conti, *Ducati Superbikes*, Giorgio Nada Editore, Italy 1995

B. De Prato, *Ducati Power*, FBA, Italy 1995

W. Tons, *Ducati*, Art Motor Verlag, Germany 1995

M. Walker, *Ducati Technothek*, Heel, Germany 1995

W. Zeyen, *Ducati Desmoquattro 748, 851, 888, 916*, MBV, Germany 1995

AA.VV., *Ducati Forza Italia 1946-93: l'histoire des grandes marques moto*, Freeway, France 1996

AA.VV., *Ducati Calender*, Art Motor Verlag, Germany 1996

AA.VV, *Ducati 1960-1973 Gold Portfolio*, Brooklands Books, Great Britain 1996

AA.VV, *Ducati 1974-1978 Gold Portfolio*, Brooklands Books, Great Britain 1996

I. Falloon, *The Ducati Story*, PSL, Great Britain 1996

AA.VV., *Ducati Paso 750, Paso 906*, in *Révue Moto Téchnique*, hors série n° 7, ETAI, France 1997

AA.VV., *Ducati 916*, FBA, Italy 1997

AA.VV, *600, 750 & 900 2 valve twins 1991-96*, Haynes, Great Britain 1997

L. Bianchi, M. Masetti, *Motociclismo racconta la storia della Ducati*, Edisport, Italy 1997

M. Clarke, *Ducati 1978-1982 Gold Portfolio*, Brooklands Books, Great Britain 1997

M. Walker, *Ducati Twins*, Osprey Publishing, Great Britain 1998

Ducati
The Official Racing History

Edited by

Eugenio Martera

Marco Montemaggi

Patrizia Pietrogrande

Texts by

Marco Masetti

To introduce this book is a source of great satisfaction for me. It gives me the opportunity to speak directly to all those who have appreciated our work and above all the great results that have been achieved. This book offers them a sort of "reminder", a "ledger" covering the fundamental stages and all the successes in the long and glorious history of Ducati. Another reason to be proud is the fact that so much has taken place in just a few months since the inauguration of the Ducati Museum, of which this volume can be considered the catalogue.

When I came to work at Ducati a few years ago, I realized that the strength and potential of this company stems from its past, from that magical blend of great passion and of the highest professionalism, from the human and technical resources that have allowed it to attain its most ambitious goals. These inevitably rub off on anyone who enters the orbit of the Ducati world, be they employees, suppliers, riders or supporters.

In order for new generations of *ducatisti* to understand and to experience the historic legacy of the company, it was necessary to give it tangible form. Thus was born the idea of the Ducati Museum which we decided to locate at the heart of the establishment at Borgo Panigale, in the very place where decisions are made and production is carried out, to bear witness to the strength of the link between the past, present and future of Ducati.

Set up in just a few months on a tide of enthusiasm, the Museum can be seen as the flower in the buttonhole of a company that is more vibrant than ever, a company that has doubled its turnover in the space of a few years. Rather than a point of arrival, however, it is intended to be a starting point, a stimulus to attain new and even more ambitious objectives and a solid base on which to build other exciting ventures.

Federico Minoli
President and Managing Director
Ducati Motor Holding

The idea of a Museum for Ducati arose out of the search for a new means of communication, a way of putting across a message that would be different from the now obsolete vehicle of the image. In a "hypermedia society" where more information is available at any instant than we are capable of taking in. Whence the need for the company to find a new way of presenting itself, a way that would truly allow it to "be there." And this could only happen on a lasting basis if it proved possible to stir people's interest, to get them involved: i.e. if a relationship were to be created between the two sides involved in the act of communication. So we decided that the best course to follow was to create a physical place (though it would not just be physical) in which a profound relationship could be established, a connection that would not be based on the kind of "frantic communication" to which we are constantly subjected and whose inevitable fate is to slide rapidly into oblivion.

It is my personal view that the principal concern of publicity today should no longer be that of persuading people to buy a certain product. The quantity of information with which we are flooded is so enormous as to make it unlikely that a conventional advertisement will "make an impact." Viewed from the "surface", one sales pitch is like another, one brand the same as another, one product as good as any other. And yet there is an essential difference: at a deeper level the product or make that is capable of rousing strong feelings, of imparting a sense of belonging to something, really does have a greater value. Our efforts need less and less to be directed toward conveying a "subtle, cunning or sly message", for the simple reason that industrial communications are increasingly founded on just these criteria. So a Museum can provide a new way for a company to present itself: a Museum that creates a world with which people can identify, a "red world" like Ducati's, capable of arousing the same kind of emotional reaction as you get from watching a Superbike race or riding a 996 around the track.

In ensuring the success of a brand – and here our task has been made easier by the history of the Ducati Mark – it is becoming increasingly necessary to shift the emphasis in communication from persuasion/fascination to genuine emotional involvement. All of us who have worked on the creation of this Museum have done so in an attempt to construct a "showcase of emotions", aimed at those who wish to follow and enjoy the heroic and enthralling story of one of the most glorious makes of motorcycle in the world.

I would like to conclude this brief introduction by thanking all the people who have worked with me on the design and construction of the Museum. Without them, and without numerous "boys" working at Ducati under direction of Massimo Bordi, the task could never have been accomplished. Among many others, I am particularly grateful to my family, to Giuliano Pedretti (most precious source of informations about Ducati history) and to Micaela Rambelli.

I would also like to mention two "special" friends, at least for me. The journalist Marco Masetti, with whom I spent many hours in pleasant conversation during the writing of this book, talking about camshafts and pistons, but also about Schnitzler or Pasolini, always with the same enthusiasm. The other is the first person at Ducati to have shown confidence in me and my capacities at the outset of this adventure, and that is Federico Minoli.

Marco Montemaggi
Curator of the Ducati Museum

Giovanni Marchi, Marco Montemaggi and Marco Masetti in the old Ducati plant.

Some time ago I met at Ducati a young man, Marco Montemaggi, and architects Patrizia Pietrogrande and Eugenio Martera (respectively Curator and planners of Ducati Museum). Surrounded by building materials and teams of bricklayers at work, they tried to explain to me what the Ducati Museum was going to be like. They succeeded in conveying all their enthusiasm and in involving me in the compilation of the fascinating history of men and motorbikes that is to be found in this volume.

I have been writing about motorbikes for almost twenty years, but the passion I have held ever since childhood has never left me, offering me thrilling moments as well as bitter disappointments.

I am a lucky man: as a child I got a close look at Agostini and Hailwood, as they shot past on motorbikes just a few steps from my house. Living inside a race track can leave an indelible mark on your life, and that is just what happened to me.

I have been fond of Ducatis ever since a "bigger" friend took me for a ride on the back of his Scrambler, but my real passion stems from the day when, on the banks of the Santerno, I watched Smart and Spaggiari win hands down. And it was confirmed when I got to exchange a few words, in dialect, with Fabio Taglioni and discovered that he was not a gruff engineer of the old school but a classical Romagnese, a race to which I myself belong and know very well. And it is to him that I would like to express my gratitude first of all, as well as to his wife, who always treats me with great courtesy whenever I ring up or drop by. Naturally, I would also like to thank Ducati, for having given me the opportunity to work on this book: thank you Minoli, thank you Bordi, I won't forget you in my prayers. But I also owe a great deal to Franco Farné (who showed incredible patience in answering my endless questions), to the "guys and girls" at the Museum, Micaela, Livio and Giordana, to the imperturbable Pedretti, to Mengoli, Domenicali and Terblanche. And to all the people working at Borgo Panigale who have given me their help.

I would also like to thank my colleagues Paolo Gozzi, Carlo Bartalini, Niccolò Minerbi and Giuseppe Gori, for their invaluable assistance in drawing up the texts in this book. Nor can I forget Marcello and Alberto Peruzzi, lifelong *ducatisti*, who together with their friend Massimo Clarke have helped to give depth to my passion. Thanks must go too to the Libreria dell'Automobile in Milan, which contributed to the compilation of the bibliography, and to Crispino Moretti, enthusiast and collector who never fails to goad me on with his "corrections". Then there has been the indispensable collaboration of Edisport and the editor of *Motociclismo*, Luigi Bianchi, who gave me access to archive material with the enthusiasm of a true *ducatista* (he has two of them in his garage). Finally, I must express my gratitude to all those who have given me a hand, to my wife, who had to put up with my frayed nerves while I was working on the book, and to my parents, always encouraging me, even if they have never been able to grasp why a man should be as hopelessly in love with motorbikes as I am.

It may seem strange, but working on something connected with Ducati means that you make a lot of friends. I would like to list them all, just as they do in the credits of American movies, but I don't want to take anything away from the true protagonists of this history, the historic motorbikes of Ducati.

Marco Masetti

The Ducati Museum

Curator:
Marco Montemaggi

Research and Technical Consultant:
Giuliano Pedretti

Motorcycle Restoration and Chief Mechanic:
Primo Forasassi

Assistants to Curator:
Micaela Rambelli, Livio Lodi and Giordana Ferraresi

Architectural design, preparation and graphics:
Patrizia Pietrogrande
Progetti Integrati Studio Associato (in the person of Eugenio Martera)
Michele Zacchiroli
with Barbara Lami
and the collaboration of Leone Pecchioli, PaolaTiradritti and Sven Hebeler

Acknowledgments

A large number of people (technicians, collectors, journalists and enthusiasts) have contributed to the creation of this book in various ways. It would be impossible to mention them all, but we would like to express our deep gratitude to them here.

Special thanks are due to the collectors who have generously placed their historic motorbikes at the disposal of the Ducati Museum, helping to make the display as comprehensive as possible.

In addition, we would like to thank "La Libreria dell'Automobile" in Milan, along with the publishers "Edisport", the magazine *Motociclismo*, Gianni Perrone, Massimo Clarke, Marcello Peruzzi and Ivo Tosi, for their invaluable assistance.

Finally, our sincere gratitude goes to Massimo Bordi, Gianluigi Mengoli, Claudio Domenicali, Franco Farné, Giuliano Pedretti and to all the people at Ducati who have shared their knowledge with us, making a decisive contribution to the historical depth and technical accuracy of this book.

Credits

The technical appendices on pp. 264-9 are taken from Ian Faloon's book *The Ducati Story* and reproduced by kind permission of the author.

Paolo Gozzi, Carlo Bartalini, Giuseppe Gori, Niccolò Minerbi, Barbara Premoli and Kristin Schelter have made important contributions to the texts.

The Roll of Honor has been drawn up by Benito Magazzini.

The bibliography has been compiled in collaboration with "La Libreria dell'Automobile" in Milan.

The photographs of the models on show in the Ducati Museum were taken expressly for the purpose of this book by Giovanni Marchi.

The photographs with views of the Ducati Museum are by Mario Ciampi.

The other photographs come from the Ducati Museum Archives.

We apologize to anyone whose name has inadvertently been omitted from the acknowledgments, owing to the short time available for production of this volume, and remain at the disposal of any copyright holders with whom we have been unable to get in touch.

Contents

The Ducati Museum

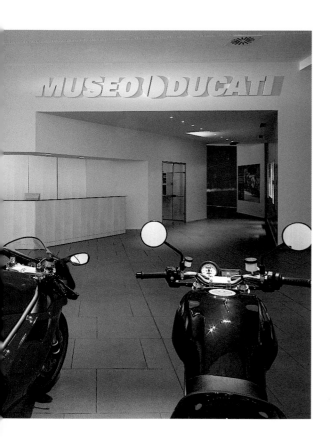

The entrance of the Ducati Museum.

Facing page: beginning of the route through the exhibition telling the story of Ducati Racing.

Building a World

by Marco Montemaggi

The Ducati Museum retraces the steps of Ducati race history – from the days of the Cucciolo to the glory of Superbike Racing today – and, in doing so, relives a legend. The object of this permanent exhibition is to tell the Racing history of the Bologna-based company by recreating, stage by stage, its most significant moments. A chronology of Ducati Racing has been divided into seven main sections. Each of these describes a distinct period in the company's technological and Racing development as well as the formidable human talent that have all made Ducati the leading light at Racing circuits the world over.

The story begins in 1946 with the Cucciolo, Ducati's first engine (up to this point, the company, which was founded in 1925 by the Cavalieri Ducati brothers, had mainly been concerned with electro-mechanical manufacturing).

Then the Fabio Taglioni era opens with the arrival of the legendary engineer at the company, a man who became famous for, among other things, the desmodromic valve system. From that moment to the present day, this system would distinguish Ducati bikes. Taglioni was also responsible for the very successful Marianna 100 and 125 Gran Sports, kings of the Motogiro d'Italia in the mid 1950s.

The third section describes a brief but intense period, that of the tri-camshaft Racing twins which mark the debut of a young rider named Mike Hailwood.

We then return to the singles which achieved some significant victories, despite limited means and their close relationship with production models.

The fifth section marks the unveiling of V-twins with bevel gears. This era is best represented by two unforgettable riders whose careers mark the beginning and the end of the period: Paul Smart, winner of the 1972 Imola 200, and Mike Hailwood, winner of the 1978 Tourist Trophy.

This is followed by the arrival of the famous Pantah twin cylinder (fitted with the new belt distribution engine). The Pantah was conceived at the end of the 1970s, with the very successful TT2 and 750 F1 as direct descendants.

The story continues in 1986 with the revolutionary and current four valve desmodromic engine; its designer is a man whose name has become synonymous with the modern Ducati marque: Massimo Bordi. These are the bikes – first the 851 (later to become the 888) and then the current 916 – that make modern-day Ducati the envy of the industry and a winner at the Superbike World Championships. Finally, a special mention is reserved for the 1993 Supermono, a much-coveted, single-cylinder race bike designed by Ducati's Pierre Terblanche that has enthusiasts demanding a street version.

The Ducati Museum (planned by architects Patrizia Pietrogrande and Eugenio Martera) has been designed to offer visitors two ways of following the Ducati story. The first approach places the bikes in chronological order along a circular route. The second is a set of thematically organized rooms which provide more detailed information on each of the Museum's seven sections. As well as containing display panels that describe the most representative models, each room tells a part of the Ducati story in greater detail with specially written essays by international motorcycle journalists.

This passionate interest in the marque shared by journalists, collectors, riders and enthusiasts – all *ducatisti* – has made the Museum project possible. It stands as a tribute to their expertise, efforts, dedication and love for Ducati – Campione del Mondo.

The Shape of Speed

by Eugenio Martera and Patrizia Pietrogrande

The Ducati Museum has been conceived as a dream "racetrack" housing fifty years of Ducati history and giving physical expression to the idea of speed - and the human longing to attain it.

In the rooms set aside for the "Racing Museum" at the company headquarters of Borgo Panigale, the creation of a complex viewing space was envisaged. In it were to be displayed the motorcycles and other important exhibits eloquently narrating the history of Ducati Motor S.p.A.

The functional and formal problems arising from the need to operate in a space that is not independent of the factory's management and production facilities was exacerbated by the configuration of the area available. The building, rectangular in shape, was located right next to the entrance to the administrative section of the establishment and consisted, after demolition of the partition walls, of a single free space of around 1000 square meters, or 11,000 square feet, but interrupted in the middle by the walls of a light well. This represented a serious problem for the layout of the space and has become the pivot around which the whole project turns.

Designed, therefore, to be located inside an architectural structure being used for industrial purposes, the Museum is intended to fit into it perfectly, fusing its own contents with those of the production process. It represents and idealizes, in visual terms, the very same speed that is the goal of the work being carried out just a few meters away.

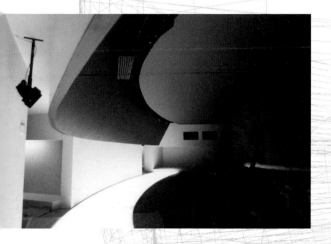

View of the Museum under construction.

Facing page: view of the Museum under construction.
Bottom: panorama of the finished Museum.

The Museum has a proper entrance through a "facade," which constitutes its "gateway" but does not separate the Museum from the reception and waiting area. In the same section, near the entrance to the Museum, a space was set aside for the bookshop.

The route leading into the Museum proper, shaped like a narrow and elongated funnel, recounts the early history of the great factory at Borgo Panigale, a history that was also rich in technology and innovation. The right-hand side is intended as a sort of "wall of memory". Framed by a large photograph of the factory and its 5000 workers taken in 1930, some of the articles manufactured by Ducati in those days – devices that were at the cutting edge of technology in their time – are on display: a radio, an electric razor, a miniature camera, so tiny that it was considered a nothing short of a miracle when it was brought out, and a projector for the first "shorts".

After this first section, you come to the heart of the exhibition. The Museum's undisputed protagonist is the motorcycle and its technological development, treated not so much as an object to be displayed, but as the concrete expression of an ideal of speed, of a legend and a cult, with constant reference to the positive values of competition.

The whole setting is characterized by soft volumes and sinuous lines, intended to underline the aerodynamic character of the forms and to suggest, like a vision in a dream, the same view that the rider has of the circuit during a race, a view distorted by wind and speed.

The idea of competition and speed is made concrete in the track, represented by a luminous circular band of about forty meters in length. This forms the route through the exhibition and is lined with the twenty-six motorbikes that, by winning the most prestigious races, have forged the Ducati legend. The track is enclosed by a circular wall on which all the victories achieved by Ducati bikes are recorded. They are engraved on a steel band and interspersed with figures listing the most significant years, when the largest number of races were won. Competition and speed are further suggested and underlined by the sloping band set above the circuit, as if trying to envelop it. Upon this are set images of bikes racing, to convey the idea of a fantastical contest between all the bikes that have propelled Ducati onto the podium between 1948 and the present day. In addition to the idea of speed, the bikes "racing" in the blown-up images suggest the uninterrupted flow of time and give a positive view of competition itself, as a way of improving the means at your disposal and surpassing your own limits.

The conceptual and geometric center of the hall is another enveloping creation of circular shape, and one very familiar to the motorcyclist: it is a colossal crash helmet in Ducati red - an object that has a powerful visual impact, an element "shaped by speed" forming the hub of the entire exhibition. It has also served the practical function of obscuring the light that enters through the roof. The giant helmet contains, on one side, a small auditorium for lectures and presentations and, on the other, a display of the latest Ducati models.

Pictures recording some of the phases in the construction of the "helmet."

Outside the track are located a series of thematic rooms, each focusing the visitor's attention on one of the "main families" and telling the story of the many Ducati victories. These cubicles of motorbike history are accessed through openings in the wall which, by drawing our gaze beyond the track of light, lead visitors away from the "race" and into a space where reality and imagination are brought together. Here, a display of documentary materials, now become cult objects, are presented in cabinets and on pedestals. They are an integral part of the great legend.

The contents of the thematic rooms are organized in a manner that is intended to escape the static character of traditional Museums and to avoid making the displayed objects seem detached or intimidating. In this case they are "artifacts" as well as works of art. Objects, photographs and drawings are on show, each giving a perspective from its own time within the framework of a story that is not just about races and motorcycles, but also about people in a social context all embarking on a thrilling adventure. To this end, the shape itself of the rooms has been treated as a material that can be molded to suit particular needs. By means of "extrusions" and "excavations", the walls and ceilings have been "shaped" around tales and anecdotes: pedestals, daises, partitions and niches have been placed, carefully illuminated, within tailored walls.

It has been a particularly demanding task to design and to prepare the Ducati Museum, in many ways an unusual structure which imposes a series of predetermined constraints. The various goals of the design have frequently come into conflict with one another, often appearing irreconcilable and unattainable – an enriching and stimulating experience.

Human beings, forever seduced by the idea of speed, continuously seek new, faster means of thought, invention and communication. In architecture, as in a race, it is the provocative confrontation between an objective and the challenge of realizing that objective which produces the most innovative and rewarding results.

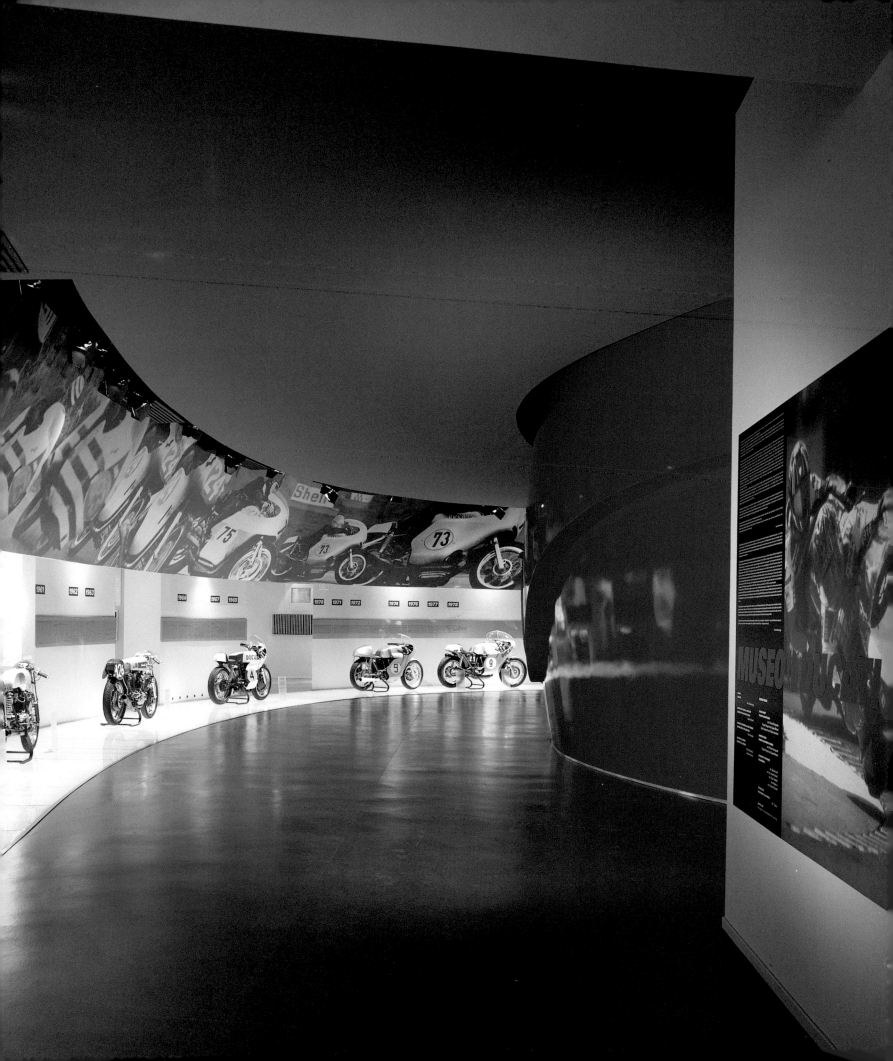

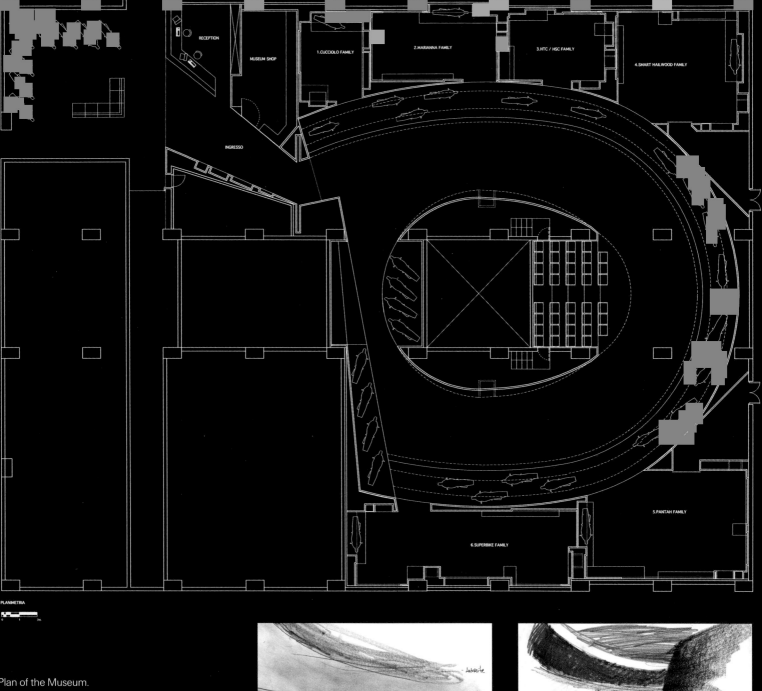

RECEPTION

MUSEUM SHOP

1.CUCCIOLO FAMILY

2.MARIANNA FAMILY

3.HTC / HSC FAMILY

4.SMART HAILWOOD FAMILY

INGRESSO

5.PANTAH FAMILY

6.SUPERBIKE FAMILY

PLANIMETRIA

Plan of the Museum.

Facing page: view of the central hall from the entrance.

Right: design sketches for the central hall.

Below: cross section of the Museum.

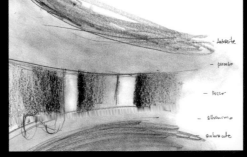

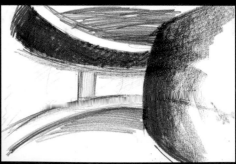

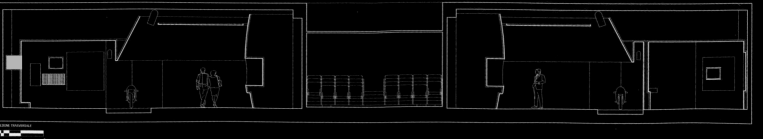

SEZIONE TRASVERSALE

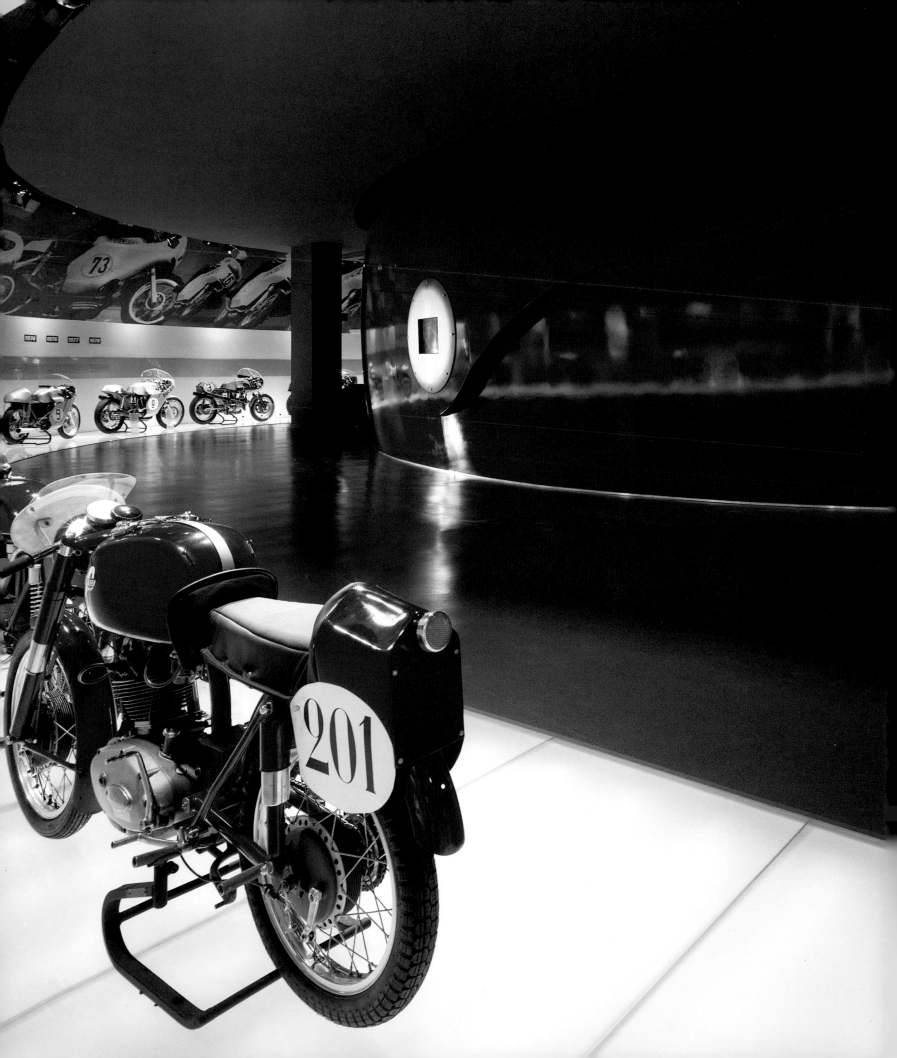

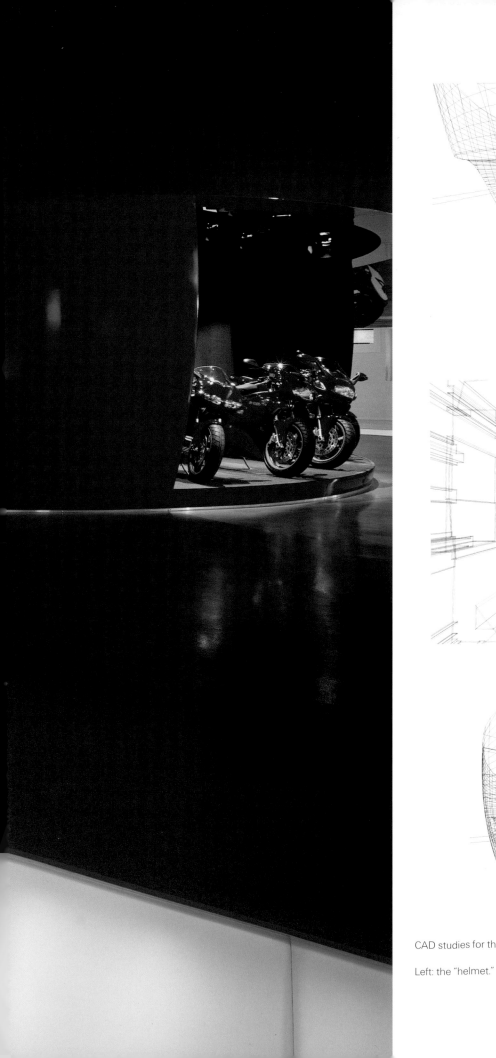

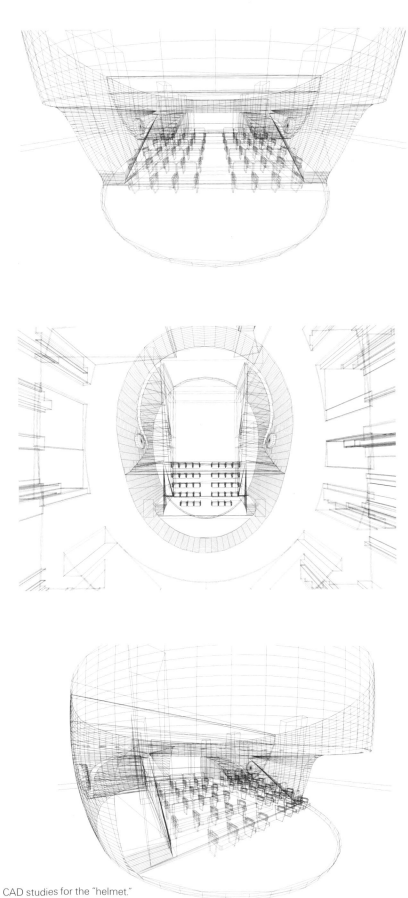

CAD studies for the "helmet."

Left: the "helmet."

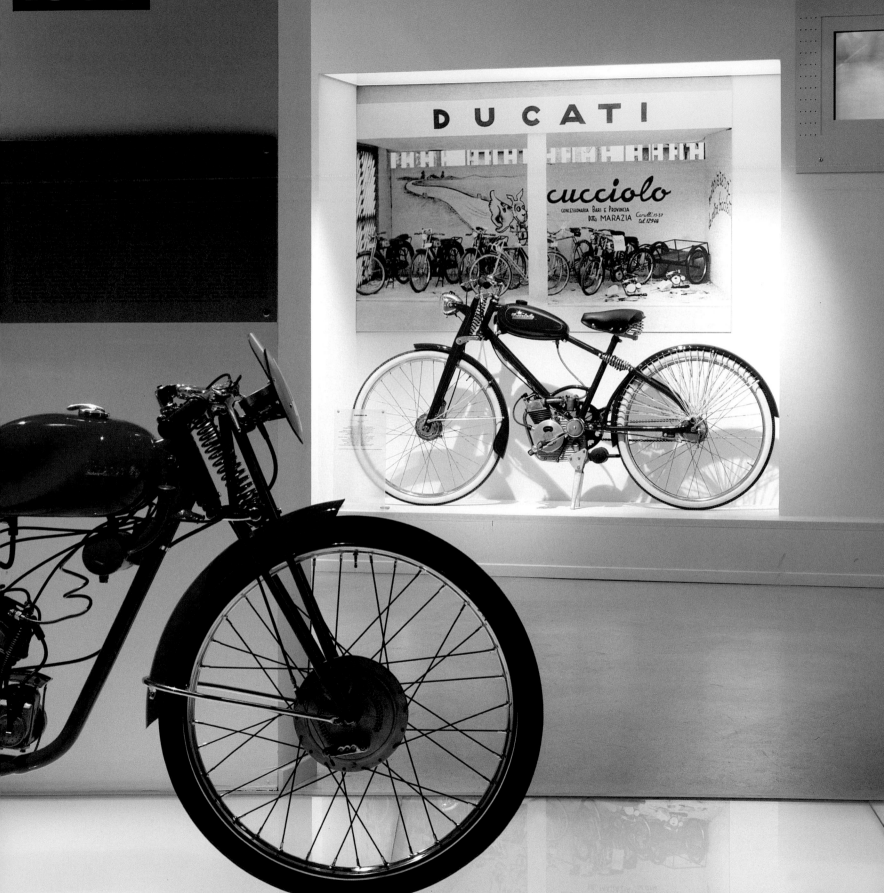

1953

1946: CUCCIOLO

DUCATI

cucciolo

Facing page: the first thematic room, devoted to the Cucciolo.

Right: the room devoted to Paul Smart and Mike Hailwood's twins.

The in-line twins room.

Other views of the thematic rooms.

Detail of the Marianna room, with the legendary "Siluro".

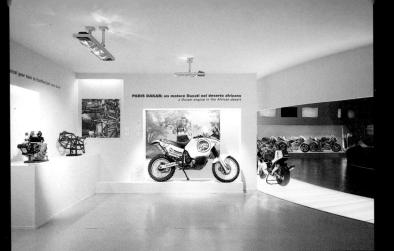

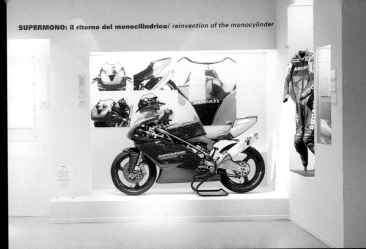

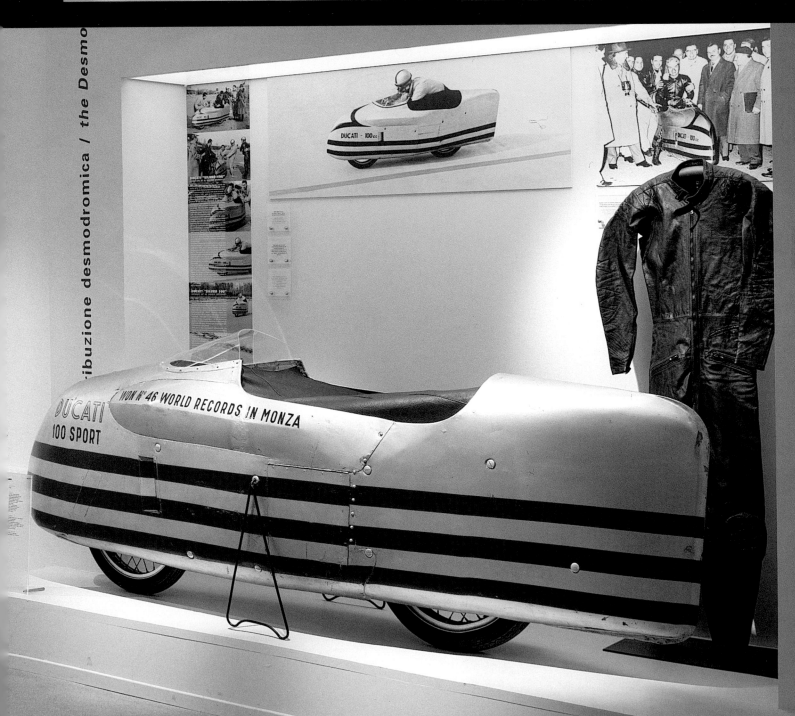

View of the "track" and the dais inside the "helmet."

Facing page: the first section of the "track."

On following double-spread: other views of the "track": from the Pantah to the Superbike.

Final tracking shot of the championship machines of the Superbike world.

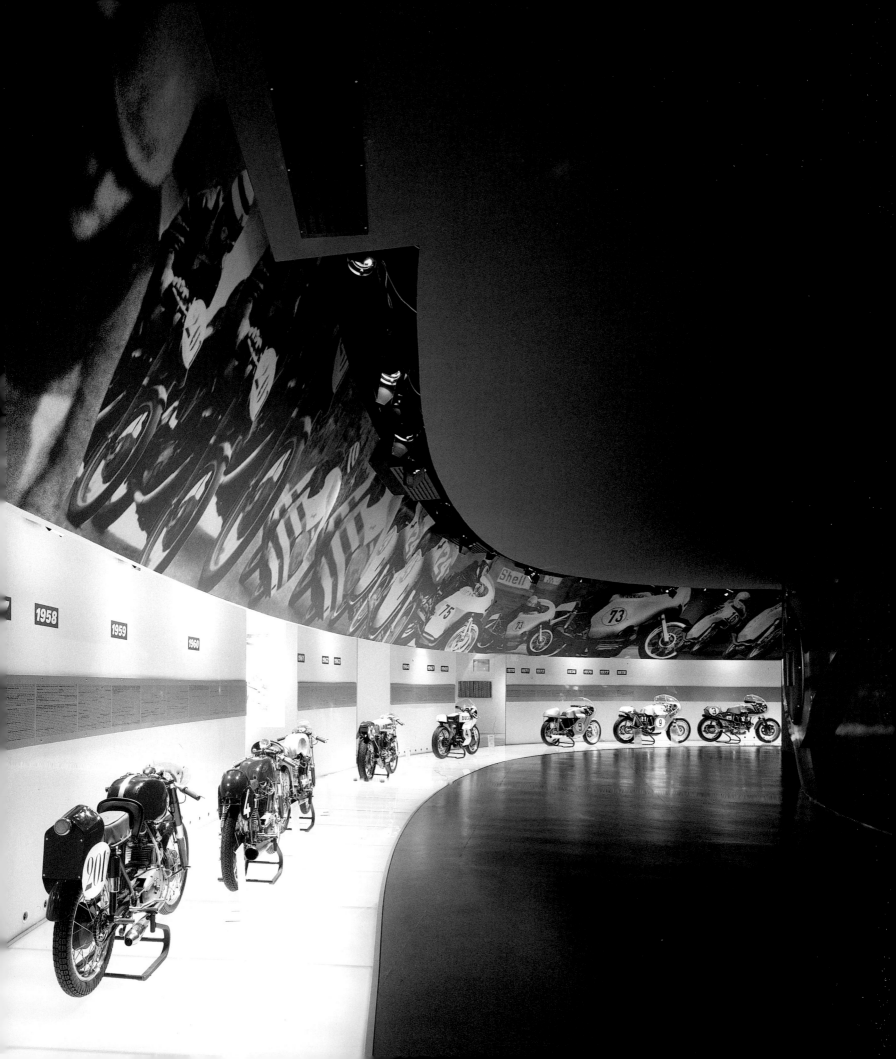

1989

PARIS DAKAR: un motore D... a Ducati engine in the...

1990 1991 1992 1993

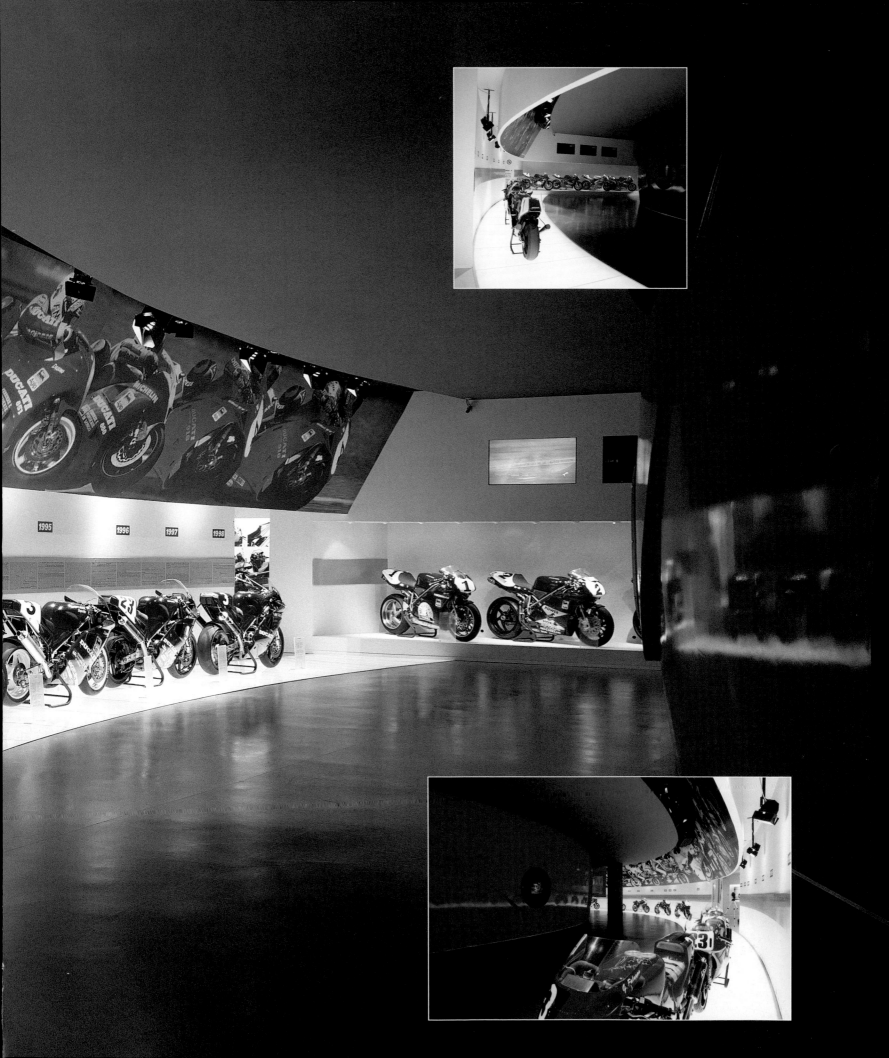

The staff of the Ducati Museum: from the left,
Giordana Ferraresi, Giuliano Pedretti, Micaela
Rambelli, Marco Montemaggi (curator), Primo
Forasassi and Livio Lodi.

Patrizia Pietrogrande and Eugenio Martera with the design team in Florence.

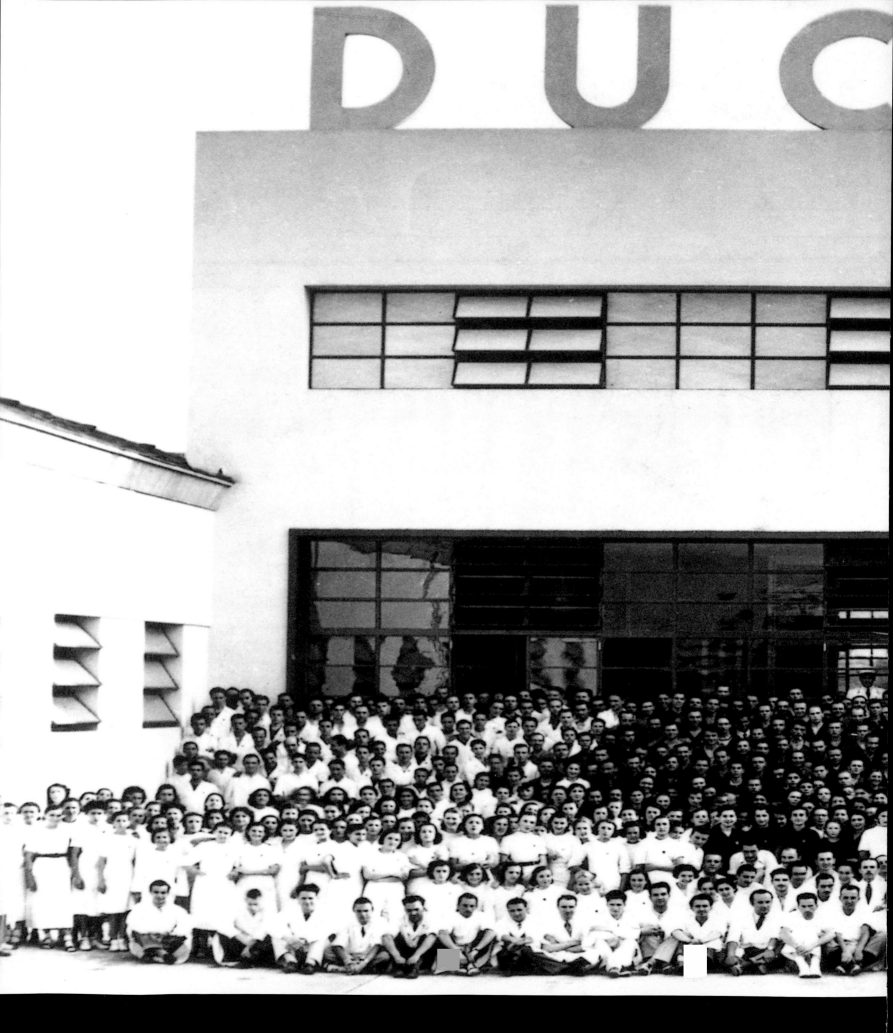

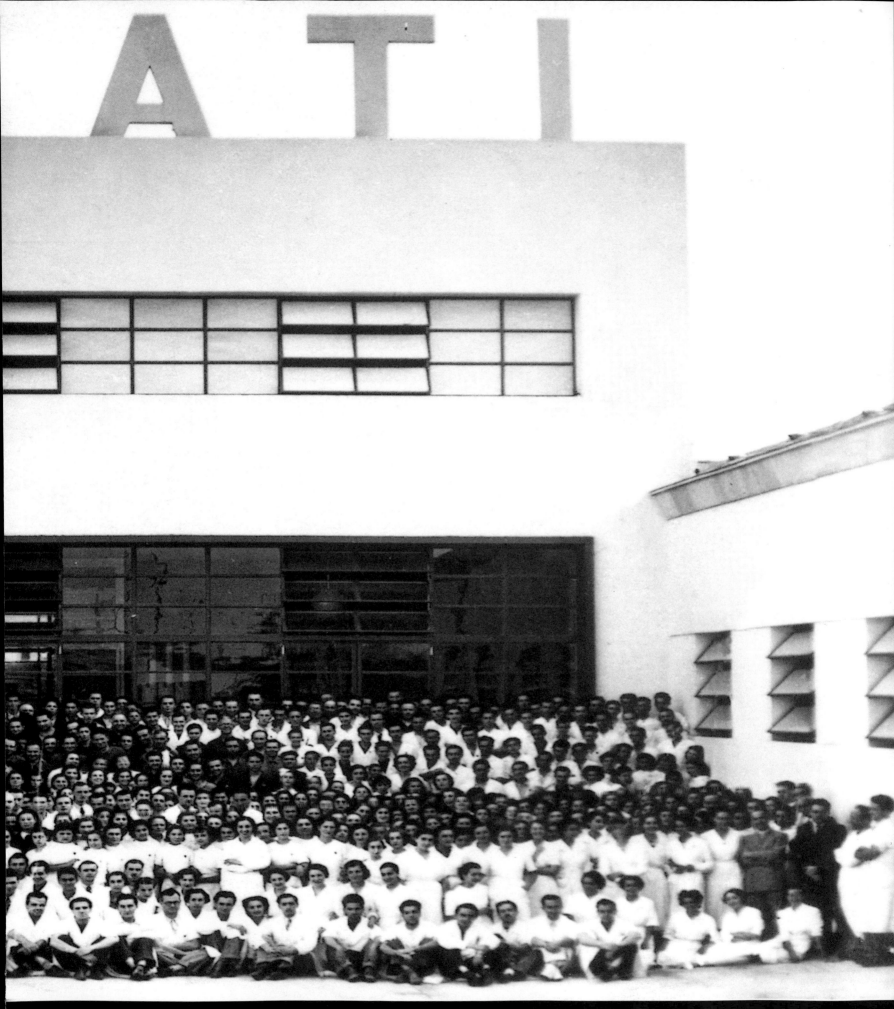

The Factory

The Beginnings

The inventor and industrialist Adriano Cavalieri, founder of Ducati, together with his brothers.

The plant at Borgo Panigale before the Second World War in a brochure of the period.

It would be difficult to tell the story of Ducati, a fascinating tale that spans much of the twentieth century, without first describing the geographical and historical context from which this great company emerged and developed up to the present day.

Bologna and its surrounding territory have been famous since the sixteenth century for their textile and grain mills. In the past, with its network of canals (such as the Navile canal which, despite being covered in part, is still visible today), Bologna was a city of water. These waterways were used to drive these complex mills thus creating, among the inhabitants of the region, a culture intimately familiar with machinery. By the end of the nineteenth century, the intensive cultivation of cereals on the vast plain that surrounds the city made Bologna an ideal place for the introduction of the earliest farming contraptions. Pioneering equipment, often in need of repair required the specialization of many workers who, even before the onset of the industrial revolution, were familiar with the rudiments of mechanics.

In addition to this "empirical" experience and tradition, Bologna boasts a number of other truly unique characteristics. Its university, for instance, founded almost a thousand years ago, went through a period of great excitement at the beginning of the twentieth century following discoveries in the electrical field by Augusto Righi, a distinguished professor who had donned the mantle worn long ago by the Bolognese physicist Luigi Galvani. Then there is the scientific – and historic –legend of another great product of Bologna University, Guglielmo Marconi, the inventor of wireless telegraphy, who made it possible to communicate at a hitherto inconceivable speed and, in the early twenties, was the most popular and acclaimed scientist in the world.

It was in this fertile climate that, in 1922, a nineteen-year-old student of physics, Adriano Cavalieri Ducati, began to study the science of radio communications and to take a pioneering interest in the practical applications of scientific discoveries. He started to make radio transmitters of limited power operating with short waves of 100 meters, instead of the usual high-power ones (2000-3000 kW) operating at long or very long wavelengths.

Ducati products shipped off to the markets of SouthAmerica (late thirties).

In 1924, Adriano Ducati succeeded in linking Italy to the United States by radio. A few years later, in collaboration with the Italian Navy, he was able to establish a connection between the Canaries and New Zealand, islands located at the furthest extremities of the globe. Following this breakthrough, Adriano Ducati experimented with much shorter wavelengths as well, creating the ancestor of the walkie-talkie and thereby rendering radio communication even more popular and accessible.

To understand fully the history of Ducati, however, it is necessary to take another step back in time and look at the origins of the Cavalieri Ducati family. Originally from Sardinia, but long since settled in Romagna, the family bore aristocratic titles. They were patricians of Ferrara, lords of Castelsaggio, nobles of Comacchio and were made counts by Rudolph I. Over the centuries, it produced men of law and science like the mathematician and optician Bonaventura Cavalieri, who developed the method of "indivisibles" (known as "calcolo sublime").

Having developed a taste for the study of engineering by his uncle Giovanni (a nineteenth-century engineer and patriot), Antonio Cavalieri Ducati arrived in Bologna in 1885 and commenced his career in a needle factory. He went on to work for Count Aria di Marzabotto, where he researched methods of cultivation. He designed aqueducts at Chieti and Trieste (then under Austrian rule), and later returned to Bologna where he lived with his wife Lydia and three sons Adriano, Bruno and Marcello until his death in 1927. The multi-talented Antonio Cavalieri Ducati designed and constructed aqueducts, railroads, land improvement schemes, artificial lakes and drainage systems.

In 1925 the Ducati brothers, along with Carlo Crespi, founded the Società Scientifica Radio, a small company set up to make Manens condensers, which were just starting to be recognized worldwide. The following year their father decided that young Adriano's talents deserved more and thus established, with a deed drawn up by notary Marani of Bologna, the Società Scientifica Radio Brevetti Ducati (S.p.A.) to exploit the patents taken out by his son.

The Ducati Workmen's Club at a sporting event held in the Municipal Stadium of Bologna in the forties.

Advertising material from the forties.

As early as the fall of 1926 the newly founded company received its first important order from Mario Argento, an Argentinean businessman. He first had them tested by his own technicians and then, persuaded of their fine quality, requested a large quantity of condensers from the company.

From that moment on Ducati experienced spectacular growth. Within the space of a few years, its success carried it from its first, small workshop in the basement of the family home on via Guidotti to the famous plant at Borgo Panigale, where the company is still based today.

"Before the hardworking and loyal people of the countryside and the workshops / the founders of the Società Scientifica Radio Brevetti Ducati / today laid the first stone of their new factory / May God always bless their activity. June 1, 1935." These words, written on a scroll of parchment sealed in a bronze tube, were laid along with the foundation stone of the establishment at Borgo Panigale on the western outskirts of Bologna, near the ancient Via Emilia.

A total of 120,000 square meters or nearly 1,300,000 square feet of land were bought for the factory, and the buildings that were quickly erected on it were truly advanced for their time. In addition to the production units, the planners included a vocational school (named after Antonio Cavalieri Ducati), kitchens, a canteen, social services and a clinic. There was even a dental surgery unit! A model establishment which received awards and attracted students, its various units, named after great Italian scientists (Cardano, Galilei, Marconi, Torricelli), were used to attract leading scientists and engineers, but above all, were intended to make a strong impression on the workers who, having received thorough training, felt like part of a huge family.

This was a time of exceptional growth for Ducati, which produced all kinds of electromechanical devices such as condensers, calculating machines, radios and precision instruments. Ducati (which had links with companies all over the world in those years) employed 11,000 people: it was the second largest company in Italy.

Ducati cameras with lenses and accessories.

Prototype of the Manens condenser, Ducati's first product.

But the specter of war was already upon Italy: in 1938 the factory was placed under the "Commissariat for War Manufacturing," a fate shared by all the electromechanical industries. As Ducati was fulfilling direct and indirect production orders for the Italian armed forces, its skilled workers were exempted from military service. When the war started, production was spread over a number of other locations (Bazzano and Crespellano in the Bolognese region, as well as Salsomaggiore and Valpolicella in the Parma and Verona regions, respectively), and this decision saved much of the machinery from the German requisition that stripped Italy of many of its industrial assets between 1943 and 1944.

A day after the publication of the armistice marking Italy's withdrawal from the war (September 8, 1943), twenty German tanks and a large group of soldiers arrived in Borgo Panigale and took over the Ducati factory.

The Ducati management decided in great secrecy on a policy of "no man and no machine goes to Germany". Equipment and production lines were spirited away at great risk and hidden at secret locations, constantly under the threat of German checks and Allied bombs.

This extremely daring operation saved much of the material but not the factory itself, which was practically razed to the ground by a massive bombing raid. On October 12, 1944, Flying Fortresses dropped about a hundred tons of high explosives on Borgo Panigale. Little was left standing.

Reconstruction

The consequences of the war were grave for Ducati: the factory at Borgo Panigale had been almost completely destroyed and the damage was assessed at around 500 million lire (something in the order of 1000 billion lire, or over 600 million dollars today), while its machinery was scattered all over Northern Italy. This meant starting virtually from scratch.

Furthermore, the Cavalieri Ducati brothers lived on a knife edge. In the feverish days that followed April 25, 1945, they even ran the risk of being shot by a group of partisans, until the legitimacy of their position was recognized by both the Allies and the CNLAI (Upper Italy Committee of National Liberation). However, the family's firm commitment and dedication to the company enabled

Effects of the Allied bombing raid in 1944: the factory suffered heavy damage.

them to regain control of the company and, just a year later, in 1946, the first Cucciolo mopeds - bicycles with auxiliary engines – came into production at Borgo Panigale. The first true motorcycle produced by the factory, it was the fruit of an agreement with SIATA of Turin, which ceded the license for its manufacture to Ducati.

The plant in Bologna also produced condensers, miniature cameras and projectors, while the factories in Milan, Cavalese, Piacenza, Longarone and Bazzano turned out radio equipment, ophthalmic lenses, wheel hubs for bicycles, dynamos and calipers. The workforce began to rise toward prewar levels: over 4500 employees in all. Calm seemed to be returning, and yet the real problems were about to begin....

The drought of 1947 and the consequent "cutting" of the power supply, subsequently halting production, combined with its heavy bank debts, forced the Cavalieri Ducati family first to make a capital increase and then to turn to the FIM (Fund for the Financing of Mechanical Engineering). The Fund agreed to the "rescue," on condition that the company went into receivership: the Ducati brothers were given little more than token positions. Adriano and Marcello were appointed "general consultants", while Bruno became General Manager, a post that had barely more than symbolic significance.

The Ducati office in Milan in an illustration by Riccardo Ricas for a brochure published in 1946 (the company's twentieth anniversary).

Right: new buildings under construction in the sixties.

In less than a year, due to mis-mananagement by the Fund and considerable internal unrest, and despite growth in the sector (the Cucciolo was proving increasingly popular), the company's filed for bankruptcy (the arrangement with creditors was settled at the Milan court in 1949). The family, now detached from the company, accepted the company's expropriation by the State and looked for new outlets for their energies. Adriano went to the United States to work on the application of electronics in the aerospace industry. He died in 1991. Marcello remained in the field of electromechanics until 1998, the year of his death, while Bruno continued his career as an engineer, devoting his attention to nuclear power, safety and research, carrying out studies and obtaining patents. He is still active today.

A stand at a Turkish trade fair in the fifties (photo Grollo).

Right: work on the engine casing in the seventies (photo Beghini).

Since 1949, Ducati has continued to develop without the contribution of the Cavalieri Ducati family. It was a fairly complicated corporate structure, on which we will have more to say later, but one which, unexpectedly, laid the foundations for the company's future. Of particular interest in our examination of the period from the end of the Second World War to the mid-fifties, is what we would call the "company vocation" today. In those years, Ducati was known for its electromechanical and optical equipment, its calculating machines and its razors, and only secondarily for its production of motorcycles. Moreover, it was fairly normal in Italy at that time, almost completely lacking in consumer goods and emerging from a disastrous war, to see manufacturers covering a whole range of fields (motorbikes, household appliances, mechanical engineering) without worrying too much about rationalizing production. The assets on which Ducati was still able to draw were, in addition to its tradition of precision engineering, those of a vast area that was slowly beginning to recover and, above all, a skilled workforce. On the other hand, management of the company was certainly not consistent, and they did not always take the right decisions. Not to put too fine a point on it, Ducati Meccanica risked closure on more than one occasion. Fortunately, through a mixture of courage and fate, it has survived to the present day. But how was this accomplished? The next two chapters are an attempt to answer this fascinating question.

The Adventure
of the Motorbike

Postcard commemorating the round-the-world tour made by Tartarini and Monetti in 1958

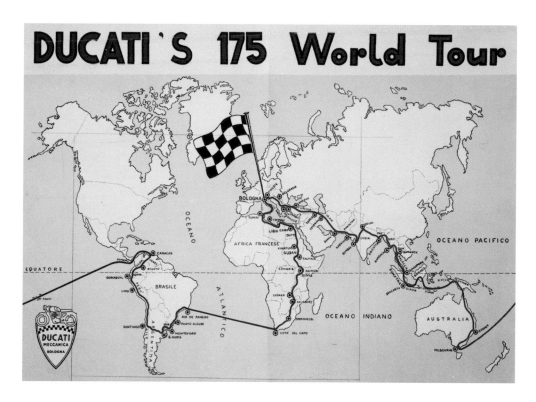

Ducati Notiziario has been for years the official Ducati house organ, with many great journalists as collaborators. In early fifties editor-in-chief was Enzo Biagi, one of the most famous names in Italian journalism.

In postwar Italy there were two watchwords: reconstruction and mobility. This entailed the rebuilding of houses, cities, hospitals and factories (at incredible cost) to permit the country's recovery. But getting around was far from easy. The road system had literally fallen to pieces and the pool of vehicles in circulation had been almost completely exhausted by requisitions and use under the harshest conditions imaginable. In addition, fuel was rationed and tires were in short supply. Economic resources were tight at all levels and even a bicycle was considered a valuable means of transport (as is apparent from Vittorio De Sica's movie *Bicycle Thieves*, a classic of Italian postwar cinema). Thus the moped proved to be a perfect choice. But the Cucciolo was not just a makeshift vehicle, typical of a period when dozens of manufacturers, often on a fairly large scale, were moving into this area of production. It was also Ducati's first venture into the sector of the motorcycle, which it was never to abandon again. The original design of the SIATA motor, by the Turinese lawyer and designer Aldo Farinelli, was almost immediately modified and rationalized (version T2) and later used as a base for the production of lightweight motorcycles (the 55, 60 and 65 cc bikes, for example) which marked Ducati's entry into the field of the manufacture of complete motorcycles. So, within a short time, Ducati passed from the role of a supplier of "detached" drive units to that of making parts for various kinds of cycle (from ordinary bicycles to small sports models inspired, for example, by the Racing Guzzi) and then to that of a manufacturer in its own right. In addition, even at the time of the Cucciolo, Ducati began to explore the world of motorbike Racing as a powerful vehicle for promotion and technical development.

The production of mopeds and lightweight motorcycles was soon supplemented by more complex projects, such as the series of "98s" with push rods and the ambitious Cruiser scooter which, as early as 1951, offered users a vehicle with faring, automatic gearbox and electric starter: practically the forerunner of today's extremely popular models. But it was in 1954 that Ducati made a

Races have always been an excellent way of promoting production bikes (in this case a T 98).

radical change in direction. With Giuseppe Montano at the head of the company, motorbikes became the absolute priority. This meant that a man with new ideas was needed, a great designer.

The right man turned out to be a young engineer called Fabio Taglioni. From neighboring Romagna, he had already gained experience at Mondial, as well as producing a fine 75 cc sports bike on his own. For a very long time Taglioni was the most important man in the history of Ducati and his contribution proved decisive. After an experimental 50 cc bike, Taglioni went on to design and produce the GS 100, better known as the Marianna and later powered up to 125 cc. The Gran Sport was a concentrate of rationality and performance and, from the time of its launch in 1955, became the bike to beat in long-distance races like the Milan-Taranto and Motogiro, as well as the ideal charger for over a generation of riders all over the world. But Taglioni was not just a great designer in love with Racing: he was very well aware of the practical necessity for his engines and bikes to have a commercial outlet. Indeed he derived from the Marianna, retaining the same basic approach, a series of road bikes that quickly proved a hit with the public. With engines ranging from 125 to 250 cc, and touring as well as sporting lines, Ducatis started to attract attention in the United States as well, where they were imported by the Berliner brothers. The American market inspired Ducati to bring out the Scrambler series (250, 350 and 450 cc), which was a great commercial success, as well as the incredible four-cylinder Apollo (which never got beyond the prototype stage): a brute of almost 1300 cc that was intended to compete with Harley-Davidson, it appeared in 1963 and was given a rating of 80 hp.

But Ducati's allure still stemmed from racing, for which Taglioni designed in rapid succession a 125 cc double-camshaft single-cylinder in 1956 and, the following year, the fabulous triple-

The Cucciolo engine (in the photo a T2) marked the beginning of Ducati's production of motorcycles. The first engines were built under license from SIATA of Turin.

Right: publicity at "full volume" for the Cucciolo.

Trying out the "four-valve" machines at the first World Superbike Championships; the entire staff of the Racing department is present. In the middle, with beard and tie, the engineer Massimo Bordi.

Publicity celebrating the victory in the 1972 200 Mile race at Imola.

camshaft desmo that came very close to winning the world title. Thus the Romagnese designer introduced desmodromic valves as early as the fifties. This innovation was later adopted for production motorcycles as well, helping to spread the legend of Ducati's sophisticated engineering. Even today the bikes produced at the desmodromic plant and winning races all over the world make use of this system. It should also be pointed out that the two refined Gran Prix 125s of the fifties were derived directly from the Marianna and were therefore very similar to the mass-produced bikes. This is still a distinct characteristic of Ducati, which makes it almost unique among the world's manufacturers and has made no small contribution to the brand's reputation. The fact that still today the same engines used on the bikes that compete for and win the world Superbike and Supersport titles as on those sold commercially is a testament to those inpired insights of half a century ago. This is further confirmed by the history of the sixties when, after Ducati's official withdrawal from the GP world championships, individual drivers raced all over the world with single-cylinder bikes derived from production models.

In 1957 Ducati commenced production in Spain by setting up Mototrans, which for many years had commercial success with four- and two-stroke single-cylinder bikes in the Spanish-speaking markets. The company also made its mark on the sports world, culminating in victories in local races and above all in endurance trials, such as the Montjuich 24 Horas.

The end of the sixties and the beginning of the seventies saw the last step in the evolution of single-cylinder engines which continued to be used with very few modifications either on the racetrack or on the road. Above all, however, this was the period that heralded the arrival of the L-head twin-cylinder, another historic design born out of Taglioni's fertile imagination.

The invasion of world markets by Japanese manufacturers and their powerful motorbikes in the early seventies completely changed the scene: the bike ceased to be an economic alternative for those who were unable to afford a car and became essentially a leisure and sports vehicle, offering high performance and aimed at enthusiastic and well-to-do consumers.

The longitudinal 90° V-type twin-cylinders were immediately covered in glory, taking the first two places in the 200 Miglia at Imola in 1972. It was from this time on that the Ducati range came

One of the most recent and interesting Ducati proposals of the new era: the Sport Touring ST4.

Top: the French rider Raymond Roche, first to win the World Superbike Championships with a Ducati in 1990; in 1991 the Frenchman had the number one on his 888.

to include high-powered V-type twin-cylinders, essentially sporty in their styling and performance. It is no accident that the victories of those years served to feed the company's passion for Racing bikes, in spite of a variety of different policies implemented by the management, which often attempted to suspend the production of motorcycles altogether (see the chapter on this). At the end of the seventies the Pantah series was brought out. Initially with a displacement of 500 cc, but later increased to 750, it had a new set of drive units (again designed by Taglioni) that boasted single camshaft gears, the desmodromic system (also used on the single- and twin-cylinders with bevel-gear), while the timing system was based on modern belt drives.

The early eighties were marked by stagnation: the big bevel-gear engines were still winning (including Mike Hailwood's sensational victory in the world TT races on the Isle of Man) and the Pantah series performed very well (victories in the TT2 races in Italy and Europe and four world titles with Tony Rutter), but the owners of Ducati (the State) had no faith in motorbikes. Fortunately, the company passed into the hands of the group led by the Castiglioni brothers in 1985: true enthusiasts, they immediately revived the production of motorcycles. Finally released from previous constraints, the Ducati designers (in addition to Fabio Taglioni, Massimo Bordi and Luigi Mengoli, generations of excellent engineers have passed through Ducati's Technical Department) were able to carry out new projects.

The four-valve, twin-camshaft, desmo, liquid-cooled twin-cylinder, (i.e. the engine that is still used on Ducati's top range), marked a substantial leap forward for the company, which finally had a drive unit at the cutting edge of technology. It is further worth pointing out that some ten years ago people thought that the four-cylinder engine was pre-requisite for high-performance bikes. But now, after Ducati's many successes in the Superbike competitions, even Japanese manufacturers have started to produce sports bikes with this kind of powering. There could be no more convincing demonstration of the validity of Ducati's approach to motorbike construction.

The brothers Marcello, Adriano and Bruno Cavalieri Ducati with Raymond Roche's bike.

The Owners

The Cavalieri Ducati brothers: from the left, Bruno, Marcello and Adriano.

Right: group photo taken in 1998.

From the left, engineer Fabio Taglioni with Calcagnile and Spairani, managers of the company under State ownership.

The history of Ducati commenced on July 4, 1926, with the foundation of the corporation "Società Scientifica Radio Brevetti Ducati." Within a short space of time, thanks to the soundness of the products that grew out of Adriano Cavalieri Ducati's scientific discoveries, the company experienced exponential growth. In less than ten years, this transported the company from the small premises set up in the family home (on via Guidotti, near the Municipal Stadium and the portico running from Porta Saragozza to the sanctuary of San Luca) to the opening of the plant at Borgo Panigale where it specialized in electromechanical and optical devices and in precision instruments. Towards the end of the Second World War, Ducati was occupied by the German armed forces and suffered heavy allied bombing, leaving only a few remains.

In 1948 Ducati came under the control of the FIM (part of the IRI, or Institute for Industrial Reconstruction) about which Bruno Cavalieri Ducati has raised some disturbing questions in his book *Storia della Ducati* – and bankruptcy ensued in 1949 and expulsion of the family from the company. In the same year it came under poor management by the receiver Mantelli, followed by the more diligent efforts of the attorney Stoppato, who split production (concentrated chiefly at the Borgo Panigale establishment) into three distinct sections: mechanics (motorbikes, scooters and mopeds), wireless electronics (radios and condensers) and optics (cameras, projectors, binoculars and lenses). The future, however, remained uncertain, in part because of difficulties – with labor unrest being commonplace and once the factory itself was occupied by staff. In 1953 the company was broken up further, with the creation of two separate corporations, Ducati Meccanica and Ducati Elettrotecnica. The latter was taken over by Breda, then the French company CFS and, in 1977, the

Dr. Montano (on the right wearing a dark jacket), for a long time in charge of Ducati.

Right: Pier Francesco Chili (on left), Abel Halpern (Managing Director Europe TPG), David Bonderman (Founding Partner TPG), Carl Fogarty and Federico Minoli (President and Managing Director of Ducati Motor Holding) during the 1998 WDW.

From the left, Claudio Castiglioni, His Excellency Romano Prodi and Gianfranco Castiglioni.

Zanussi group. Today there is a Ducati Elettronica located in Bologna (but with no links to Ducati Motor) and a Ducati Radiotelecomunicazioni, based near Milan.

The story of Ducati Meccanica, still located at the establishment in Borgo Panigale, continued, thanks to its President, Dr. Giuseppe Montano, a great supporter of the production of motorbikes. In addition to the creation of Mototrans, which built Ducati bikes in Spain, commercial ties were established with the United States through Berliner, its distributor in North America. The company also sold a large number of single-cylinder engines to the Swiss company Condor, which produced bikes for that country's army. In those years Ducati was the Italian distributor of Triumph cars, Leyland commercial vehicles and Penta outboard motors.

In 1970, facing persistent financial problems, Ducati came under the control of another State-owned group, the EFIM (Industrial Financing Board for the Metallurgical and Mechanical Industries), which maintained the commitment to motorcycles as well as establishing the company at Borgo Panigale in the VM group, specializing in the construction of electric generators and diesel engines for use at sea and on land. These too, from the corporate standpoint, were trying and uncertain years, in which the "partisans" of the motorbike within the company found it hard to keep the tradition alive.

In 1983 Ducati entered into an agreement with the Gruppo Cagiva (Castiglioni Giovanni Varese, headed by the brothers Gianfranco and Claudio Castiglioni). The two Lombard entrepreneurs started by producing Cagiva motorbikes fitted with Ducati Pantah engines (the Alazzurra, for example), and then went on to acquire the entire factory in 1986. The sale to the private group was authorized by the President of IRI, Romano Prodi, who later became the prime minister of Italy. The Gruppo Castiglioni (which was also the owner of another historic Bolognese manufacturer, Moto Morini) gave a great boost to Ducati, taking it back to the summit both in production and Racing.

Yet another change in company ownership came in 1996: the Castiglioni brothers sold 49% of Ducati to the Texas Pacific Group, a group of private investors. An additional 3% remained the property of another private investor. The situation changed again in July 1998: Texas Pacific Group and Deutsche Morgan Grenfell Development Capital Italy, along with other partners, acquired the remaining stock still in the hands of the Castiglioni brothers. Since the spring of 1999 the Ducati Motor Holding, with Federico Minoli as Chairman and Managing Director, has been a corporation listed on the New York and Milan stock exchanges.

The New Era

In the long history of Ducati we have encountered not only legendary bikes and champions both of which have left an indelible mark on the hearts of sports fans, but we have also seen a series of different owners and, as a consequence, different company philosophies. From the model factory of the years preceding the Second World War, in fact, there has been a shift, first to state ownership under various groupings, and then to the private holding companies of the recent past and present. In spite of this variety, Ducati has always maintained its essential character, in other words, it has always produced sports bikes, characterized by the use of advanced technology (even when it appeared rather old-fashioned, like the use of twin-cylinder engines on Racing bikes, later taken up by other constructors), and have won the hearts of enthusiasts all over the world. It was only natural that many things would change with the arrival of the latest owners. The company was in need of rationalization and, above all, needed a management team that would know how to deal with the current realities of globalization, and thus make use of the most advanced marketing techniques.

Many of the more "conservative" enthusiasts were apprehensive of bold changes that might undermine Ducati's historic charisma: the company's bikes are famous all over the world for their speed and responsiveness, their twin-cylinder desmo engines, their lattice frames and their striking Racing colors. Without going so far as to patent the sound of the exhaust, as one American manufacturer has done, any bike that comes out of Borgo Panigale is recognizable by its distinctive design...or by its unmistakable sound!

Carl Fogarty, world Superbike champion of 1998 with the official Ducati 996.

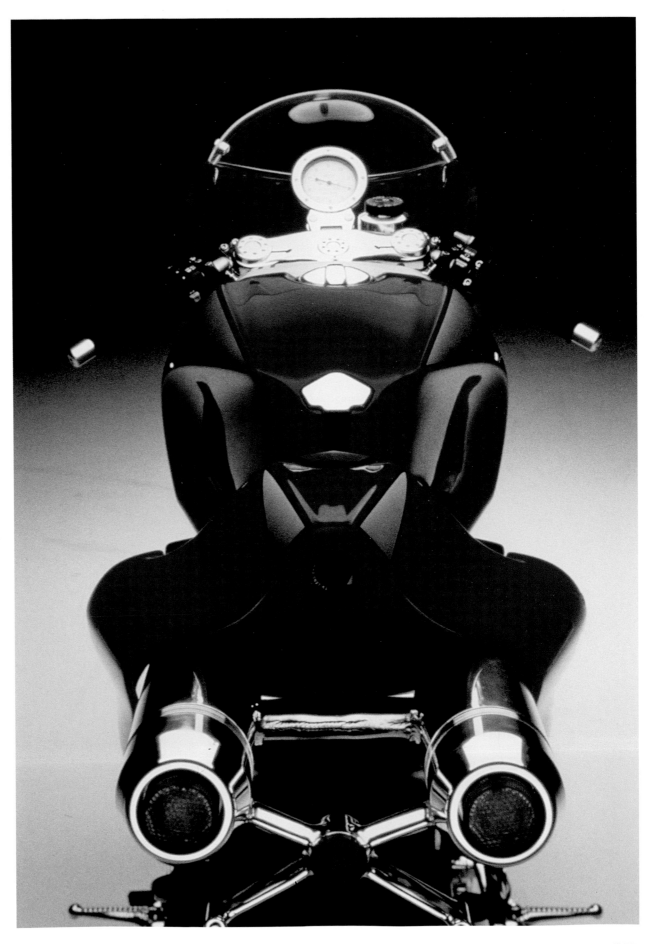

The futuristic MH
900e.

On double-page spread: the MH 900e dream bike with sketches produced at various stages of its design. Made by Ducati Design, it was presented at the Munich Show of 1998.

Pierre Terblanche, Director of Ducati Design.

Thus the new era which Ducati has entered does not mean that the legend has been forgotten (and the setting up of a Museum is the clearest proof of this) nor that the identity of the bikes has changed: they remain – of course – sporty, desmo twin-cylinders with tubular frames and bright colors!

It is obvious that the principal concerns of a motorcycle manufacturer lie in the areas of technology, styling and performance. From this point of view Ducati has done a great deal in terms of the improvement and rationalization of its product, and the commitment to the further development of the bikes that compete in and win world championships has certainly not lessened. From this perspective, the new management has shown a strong commitment to the future, underlined by the development of such a motorcycle as conceptually revolutionary as the ST4, which combines the mechanics and handling of a Racing machine with fittings designed for touring. This bike represents an attempt to follow in the footsteps of Italian Granturismo, with its fast and professionally equipped touring cars that are also perfectly suited to couples on a journey with baggage and all.

One of the principal innovations has been the Ducati Stores, specialized sales outlets that sell not just bikes but also the Ducati Gear lines of clothing and equipment for motorcyclists, expressly developed in collaboration with specialized firms. The first of these stores was opened in Manhattan in March 1998. Since then many have been set up all over the world including Vienna, London, Istanbul, Sydney, Johannesburg, Cape Town, Geneva, Bahrain and Tokyo just to mention a few – as well as 22 successfully opened in Italy. Sixty more are shortly to be opened. The Ducati Store is not just a sales outlet for the company, but a meeting point for bike lovers, who will find not only specialized products but also information supplied by clubs of Ducati owners located in many parts of the world and linked together on-line. Anyone who possesses a Ducati motorbike can ask for the Desmo Card, indicating his or her membership of the Ducati Desmo Owners Club, an association linking together all the supporters of the Italian constructor. The club organizes a series of initiatives: travel, transport to and from races, riding courses and much more besides.

For the more dedicated sports enthusiast there are also the Ducati Performance parts, which merit separate discussion. For sometime, kits and special components for customizing or improving the performance of almost all Ducati models have been produced all over the world. Many of these are worthy additions, but others are not. It has thus become necessary to produce an extensive catalogue of parts totally guaranteed by Ducati (whether of a purely aesthetic character, like wind deflectors and components made out of carbon fiber, or more specialized parts such as cylinders, axles, cams and exhausts). Thus the

Performance line offers every kind of special component for Ducati bikes, designed by the same people who build them and fully checked and tested before being put on sale. A bike fitted with Performance special parts will never be a "hodgepodge" – on the contrary, its resale value will actually increase.

While the Ducati Stores and the line of Ducati Gear (two great ideas that came directly from Federico Minoli and Carlo Simongini, Chairman-Managing Director and Sales and Marketing Manager respectively) constitute the most obvious innovations, we should not forget about two more new ventures that have only just got under way: Ducati Design and Ducati Corse.

Ducati Design is a team of designers, engineers and model makers who have been entrusted with the task of designing new bikes and accessories. It is led by the South African Pierre Terblanche, who has already designed the Supermono and the 900 SS. An in-house styling department is necessary if new products employing highly-advanced technology are to be brought out on a short time scale. This is a process in which the relationship between this "branch" and the other departments (technical, marketing and sales) is of vital importance. External suppliers are also able to work with

The Ducati Store in
Manhattan.

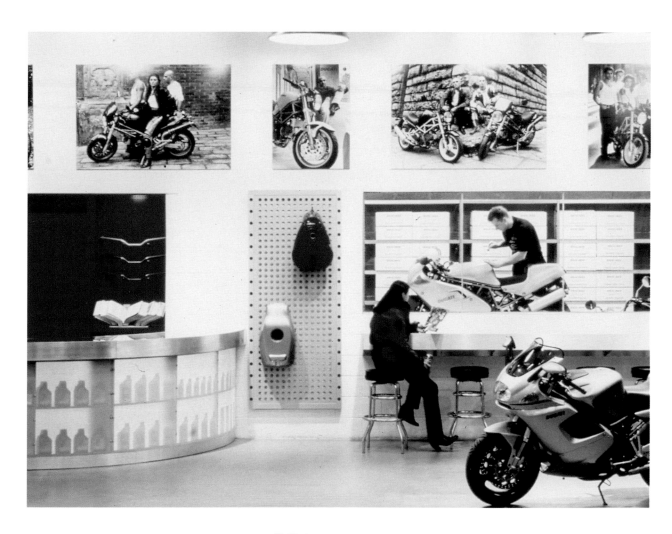

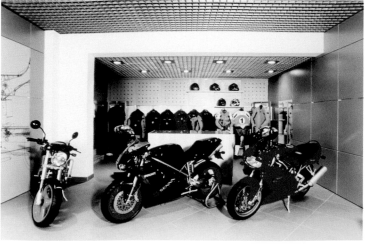

The Ducati Store in
Genoa.

The 1999 Ducati range.

Ducati Design, allowing them to produce parts for new models without any waste of time. Ducati Design is a classic example of a dynamic, modern structure which brings together creativity and rationality, the two fundamental ingredients in Ducati's unique recipe for exciting, new motorbikes.

The first fruit of the team's efforts was presented at the Munich Show in 1998: the MH 900e dream bike, a model that fuses the essential design of the classic Italian motorcycle (the Ducati Mike Hailwood Replica) while reaching out to the bike of the future, as is evident from the braking system derived from aeronautical engineering and the rearview video system. This is truly a neo-classical motorbike that harks back to projects from the past, filtering them through the technology of the present, but still easily identifiable as a true Ducati. For the moment this is just an experiment, a mobile test-bed for ideas and techniques, but there can be no doubt that it is on the right road.

Ducati Corse is the in-house structure (totally independent but controlled by Ducati Motor) that has the job of representing the manufacturer on the world's racetracks. Headed by the engineer Claudio Domenicali, a young and talented designer who has grown up at the heart Ducati, its cutting edge is the dream-team, unparalleled in depth and quality, made up of riders Carl Fogarty and Troy Corser, who are competing in the world Superbike championships (defending the first place achieved last year), and Paolo Casoli in the world Supersport championships. The Team Manager at the track-side is the former Ducati rider Davide Tardozzi. Ducati Corse also produces the bikes that are used by private competitors from all over the world.

Today the would-be owner of a Ducati can choose between the Monster series (ever more extensive and customizable), the hyper-sports 996 and 748 models, enriched by SPS (Sport Production Special) versions which are directly derived from the bikes used in the world championships and fitted with special parts, the Sport Touring range with the innovative ST2 and ST4 models and the SS 750s and 900s, motorbikes that evoke the aura and fascination of the classic Ducatis but with the lines and technology of today. A total of twenty-four models capable of meeting all the needs of the motorcyclist looking for an essential, technically-advanced bike with a marked personality that retains strong links with the world of Racing: in short, a Ducati.

The Plant
at Borgo Panigale

The Ducati plant is situated on the western outskirts of Bologna, in a town called Borgo Panigale. The entrance is on a street named Via Cavalieri Ducati in honour of the founder of the company. The factory, covering an area of roughly 100,000 square meters, produces motorbikes ranging from 600 to 996 cc, all with 90° V-type twin-cylinder engines and desmodromic distribution. There are four "families": Sport (SS series with two-valve engines), Superbike (748 and 996 cc with four-valve engines), Sport Touring (the ST2 and ST4 models with two- and four-valve engines) and Sport Naked (otherwise known as Monsters, from 600 to 900 cc). In 1999, there are about 850 staff at Ducati who produce approximately 35,000 bikes a year, 80% of them exported all over the world, with the remainder sold in Italy. The main units of the factory are the general warehouse, the aluminum and steel machining areas, the engine mounting section and bike assembly unit, as well as a paint shop. The Desmo twin-cylinder engines are designed and manufactured in their entirety at Borgo Panigale: engine know-how has always been Ducati's strongpoint. The central block of the plant houses various offices (including the administration and purchasing departments). The technical department is perhaps the least accessible part of the factory as it is there that research is carried out to ensure the continuation of the excellence of Ducati. The Ducati Museum embedded at the very heart of the establishment.

Aerial view of the plant at Borgo Panigale.

Facing page: several phases of production.

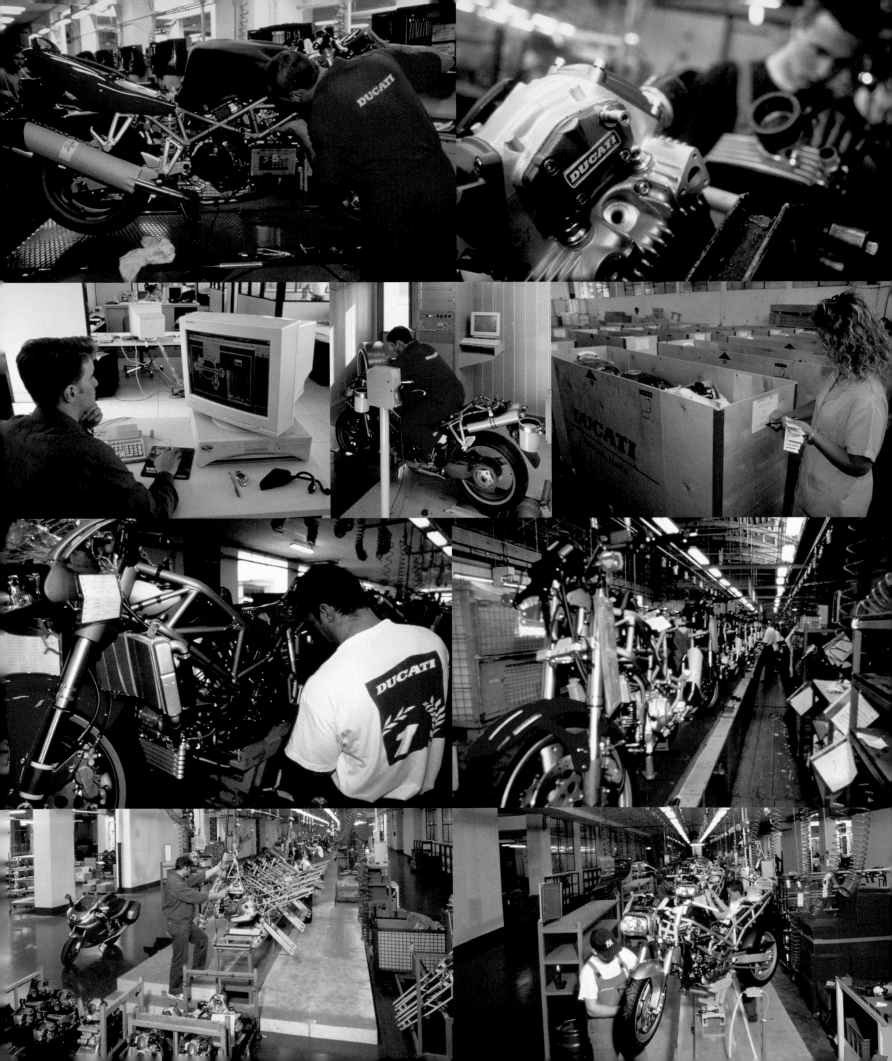

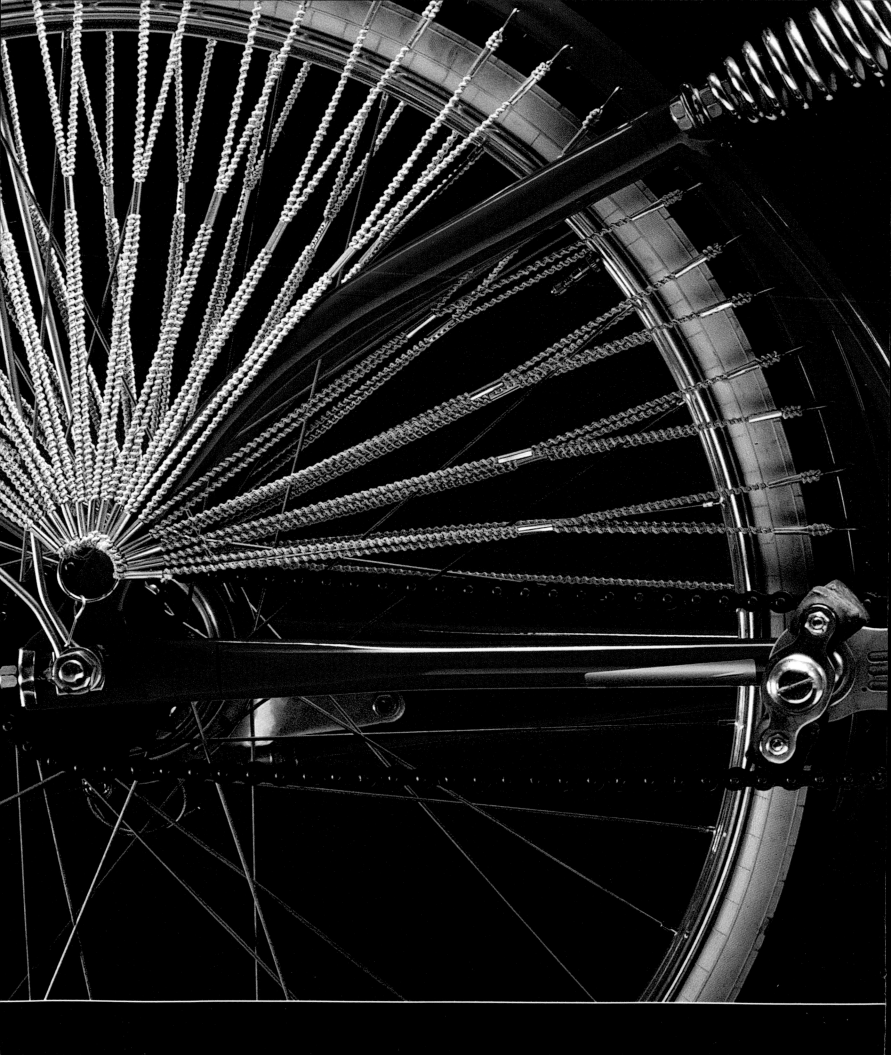

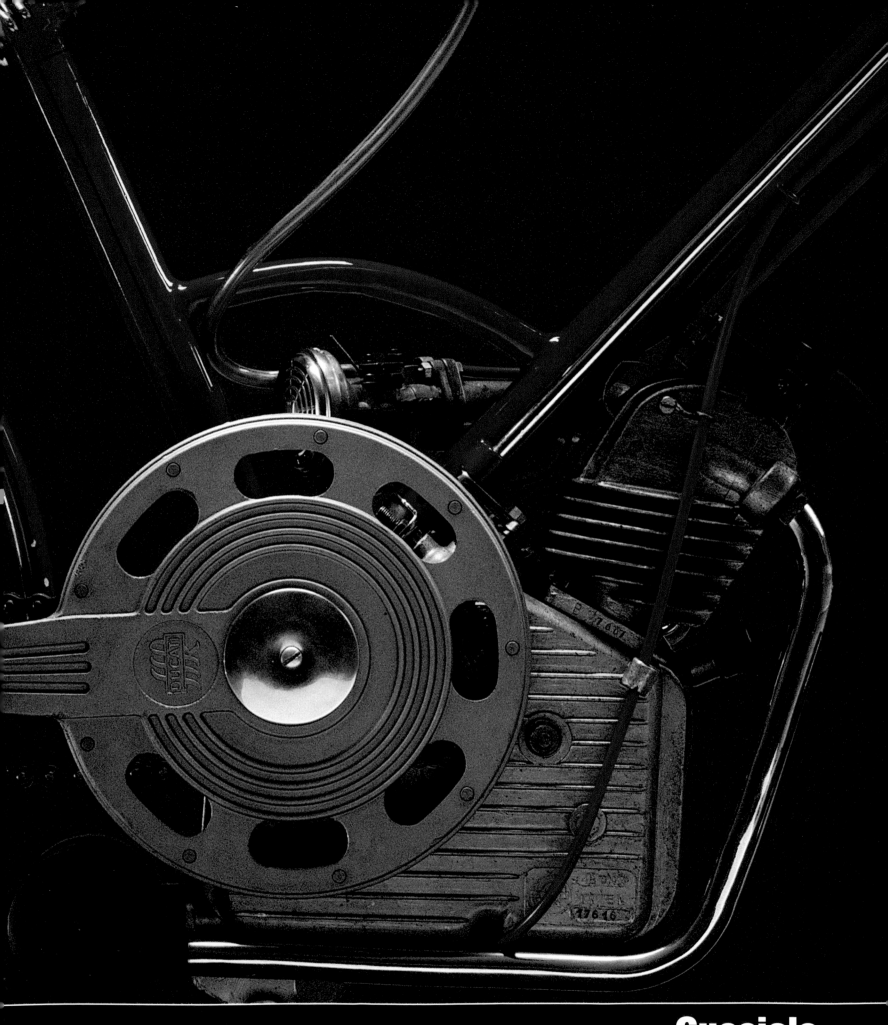

Cucciolo

Cucciolo

At a time when the war was still being waged, and in the northern part of the country occupied by the Germans, a Turinese lawyer and designer called Aldo Farinelli developed the prototype of an auxiliary motor to be mounted on a bicycle, then the most widely-used means of transport in Italy. Farinelli's design had undoubted advantages over most of the competition, beginning with its four-stroke cycle and two-speed gearing. This used the engine's power to its fullest potential, even when going uphill with a full load. In fact in those days it was not rare to see two people, with all their baggages, traveling long distances on a motorized bicycle!

Farinelli's design was adopted by SIATA (Società Italiana Applicazioni Tecniche Auto-Aviatorie, the "Italian Company for Auto-Aviation Technical Applications") of Turin, a firm that was already famous for its "overhead-valve" conversions of car and motorcycle engines and that would go on to sell kits for the conversion of two-stroke models to "four-stroke" ones. SIATA, which had had some success in racing circles before the war, used the same foundry in Lombardy as FIAT and sold a fair number of these engines, called Cucciolo or "Puppy", but the demand soon proved far in excess of what the Turinese company could handle. It needed a partner with superior production facilities and the one that fitted the bill was Ducati, still a major manufacturer in spite of the damage it had suffered during the war. Without fuss, a handbill was distributed in June, 1946 declaring that Ducati had entered the motorcycle sector. A "note" written in fairly small print at the bottom of the leaflet

Glauco Zitelli, winner of the Gran Premio Fiera di Milano with the Cucciolo in 1948.

Moped race at Milan in 1948; number 23 is riding a Cucciolo.

stated: "To meet the innumerable requests from the domestic and foreign markets, the Cucciolo is now being mass-produced by both the SIATA Works in Turin and the Bologna Plant of S.S.R. Ducati".

It should be noted that the name Ducati was still preceded by the initials S.S.R. (Società Scientifica Radiobrevetti, "Scientific Company for Radio-Patents") and that the partnership between Ducati and SIATA seems to be closely linked with the needs and economic situation of the time.

Thus by the end of 1946 it could be said that the Cucciolo had become exclusively Ducati. There were two notable features: the auxiliary motor (it was not yet time to talk about complete motorcycles) was actually made under license from the French company Rocher, while a small batch was produced in Italy by CANSA of Novara, another factory that had worked for the Italian armed forces during the war, producing equipment for airplanes. The first series of engines produced by Ducati were identical to the T1 model made by SIATA and can be recognized by the fins set parallel to the ground (and therefore not at the same angle as the cylinder). It should also be noted that the cylinder (with the rod now made of steel) formed a single unit along with the casing (made of light alloy, like the rest of the motor).

Nettunia handmade frame and running gear for a
Cucciolo T2 engine.

But the T1 had some other interesting features: for instance, the movement of the two valves (with a diameter of 12 mm) was regulated by a set of small rods driven directly by a cam set in the crankcase. The whole system was exposed to view. Then there was the "crude" system of splash lubrication. Consequently, the engine had no oil pump. Other peculiarities of the T1 Cucciolo: an ordinary bicycle chain was used for the transmission, while a pre-selector allowed the rider to use the pedals to shift gear. With the pedals vertical the gears went into neutral, while moving the left pedal forward put them into first and the right one into second. There was a lever on the left side of the handlebar to work the clutch: pulling it halfway gradually disengaged the clutch and, when pulled all the way out, it operated the gears, allowing them to be shifted with the pedals. On the other side of the handlebar, another lever was used to open the butterfly valve of the carburetor, in practice a hand-operated throttle control. When pulled upwards it functioned as a valve lifter, used to start or stop the engine. This may seem very complicated but in reality, given the extremely low level of traffic on the roads in the years following the Second World War, the bike was easy to handle. Another characteristic of this motor was the backward-facing exhaust pipe, terminating in a small muffler located in the rear part of the crankcase. The carburetor was a Weber with a 9-mm choke tube (although motors with Dell'Orto carburetors were also produced), while the ignition and power supply relied on a flywheel magneto with two coils (Ducati). Its capacity was around one horsepower at just under 4500 revs a minute.

In 1948 Ducati came up with its first "independent" design, the T2. This was a development on the T1, from which it took a great deal. The changes amounted to retouches intended to improve the engine's efficiency, robustness and, above all, the rationality of its construction. The cylinder, for example, was redesigned (with different fins) and made removable. Thus it was no longer built into the casing, which had been completely overhauled so that the drive mechanism was now easily accessible. The cylinder head had also been modified, with the exhaust facing forward instead of backward as in the T1. The rating was also raised, by just over a quarter of a horsepower. The com-

The first example of a Cucciolo engine, still with the SIATA brand.

pany also sold (though only to order) a Sports version of the T2 engine, capable of delivering 2 hp and reaching a top speed of 60 kilometers an hour when mounted on a Racing cycle frame. Among the various models of the Cucciolo, it is also worth mentioning the T0, practically identical to the T2 but with no gears or clutch and characterized by an even softer and more linear delivery, but of only limited power. Over the two-year period from the beginning of 1947 to the end of 1948, production was in the order of 240 pieces a day: pretty good going for the time!

In 1948, under the guidance of the engineer Giovanni Florio (then Technical Director at Ducati, which in the meantime had chosen to make motorbikes its main line of manufacture), the first engine designed in its entirety at Ducati, the T3, went into production. A natural derivation of the first Cucciolo, the T3 had a three-speed gear system, a grease-lubricated valve gear enclosed in a case (and therefore no longer exposed as on the SIATA engine and its early derivatives). The cylinder capacity was 60 cc, with a bore and stroke of 39 x 43·8 mm. In 1949, a special tubular frame with rear suspension (instead of a simple adapted bicycle frame) was developed for the T3 by Caproni of Rovereto, another company that had been building airplanes and seaplanes during the war and was now looking for new lines of production. A year later, the Sport version of the 60 was brought out, marking the company's move into the world of competition. It had a capacity of 65 cc and, while the first version still used the frame with triangular rear suspension, the second had a swing-arm fork and two pairs of telescopic shock absorbers.

With Caproni abandoning production of the frame (having decided to make its own motorbikes under the Capriolo mark), Ducati commissioned new ones. These became more and more closely related to those used for motorbikes, in part because subsequent development of the T3 led to improvements in performance. The Cucciolo T3 series of engines were produced in various capacities (50, 55, 60, 65) up until almost the end of the fifties and, as we shall see, were to bring the company its first successes in the world of sports.

Hand-Built Frames

The first Cucciolo engines were designed to be mounted on simple bicycles, and so were sold with gas tanks that were placed above the rear wheel: this allowed the cycle to be quickly converted into a motorized vehicle. But it was not long before small firms operating in the field started to offer interesting examples of complete bikes, ready to be fitted with the Ducati engine. In some cases partnerships were set up between Ducati and constructors of Racing bikes, while in others small batches were produced and sold directly by the constructor under its own brand name. The one reproduced here has a T2 engine (capacity 50 cc, bore and stroke 39 x 40 mm, compression ratio 6·25:1, Weber carburetor with 9 mm choke) is housed in an elegant tubular frame with elastic rear suspension. The rear axle swings and two horizontal springs absorb the shocks from the road surface. This solution, called cantilever suspension, would be rediscovered by builders of off-road bikes in the early eighties, though they were to use oleo-pneumatic shock absorbers. The girder fork was once again controlled by a spring. The pads and calipers used on bicycles were replaced by a more powerful braking system, as is evident from the two drum brakes. The two-speed gearbox was controlled by hand from a lever mounted on the right side of the vehicle alongside the gas tank. It should be noted that it was with these Cucciolos that Ducati commenced its Racing activities.

There is one more lasting memory of the Cucciolo - its extremely low fuel consumption. In its advertising brochures, the manufacturer claimed that it was possible to travel 90 kilometers on one liter, although in reality consumption was not far off an impressive 60 kilometers to the liter.

Advertisement for the Ducati Cucciolo aimed at the French market.

On double-spread and following page: hand-built frame with elastic rear suspension and girder fork (Ducati Museum; owner Massimo Pierobon; photo Giovanni Marchi).

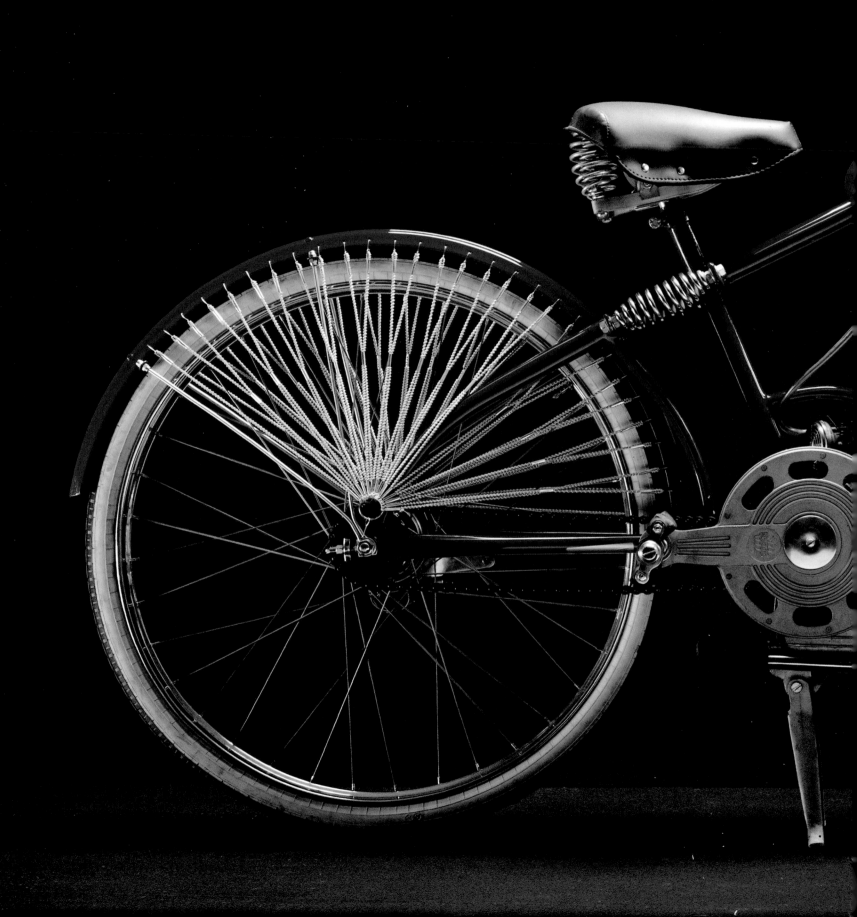

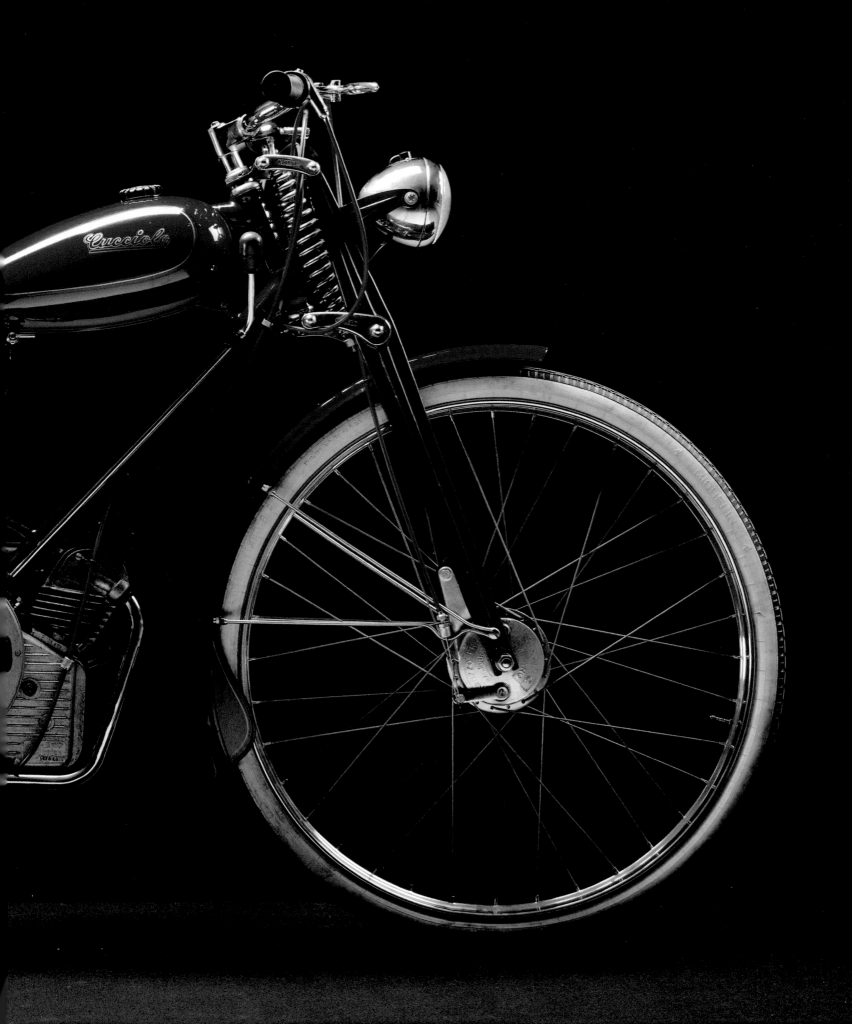

Budget
Competitions

At the beginning of the fifties, and above all with the arrival of the T3 engine, a sturdier and more powerful engine and equipped with a three-speed gearbox, Ducati stepped up its involvement in sports. Riders like Zitelli, one of the best to ever mount a Cucciolo, won race after race, while Ugo Tamarozzi (who became famous for the world records he set riding the Cucciolo) took part in the International Six Days Trial, the Olympics of motorbike Racing, winning the bronze medal. The ideal base for a Racing Cucciolo was a T3 engine with a capacity of 60 cc (bore and stroke 42 x 40 mm, compression ratio 8:1). The type of frame used by riders

with the closest links to the manufacturer was that of the first 60 model, i.e. with cantilever rear suspension, friction shock absorbers and telescopic fork. These models, which were also produced in small batches, were fitted with a long saddle that allowed the rider to lie almost flat on the bike. When output is low (around three horsepower at the most), it is necessary to keep wind resistance to a minimum. The engines once again had backward-facing exhausts like on the T, while Dell'Orto carburetors were introduced, like the MA 16 used on this Racing bike, which provided a steadier feed on a vehicle that was now capable of reaching 75 kph.

The model on show in the Museum is not the same type as was used by Tamarozzi and other drivers linked to Ducati (such as Zitelli): it is a beautiful and very special bike that echoes, on a small scale but with great elegance, the characteristics of the Racing bikes of those years. In practice a mixture of what would be found, at the competition level, on Guzzis and Benellis. It has a guided-wheel rear suspension, while the fork is the parallelogram type. There was a choice of three kinds of gear changer on this type of engine: pedal, handlebar grip or hand-operated lever. The most widely used were the grip, set on the left side of the handlebar, and the pedal.

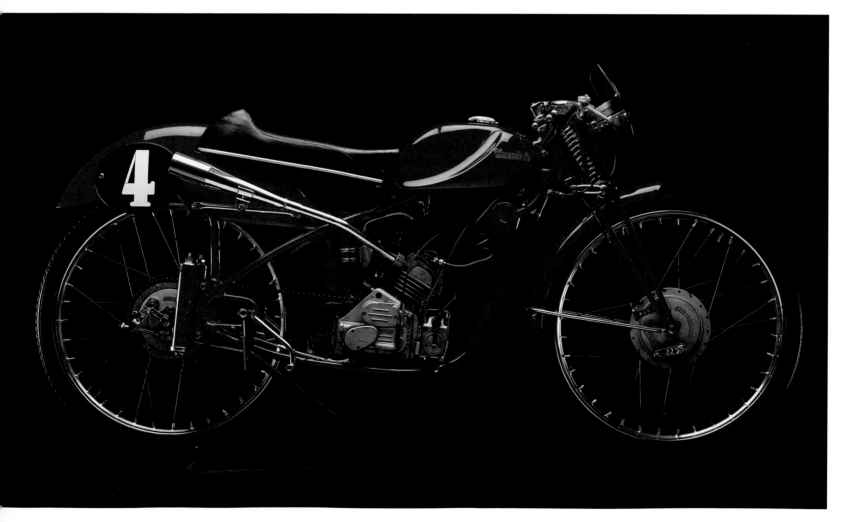

On double-spread and following page: another hand-built frame for a Racing Cucciolo (Ducati Museum; owner Ducati Motor S.p.A.; photo Giovanni Marchi). The model is that of the Grand Prix bike of those years. Note the guided-wheel rear suspension above and the supplementary tank for the oil on the right.

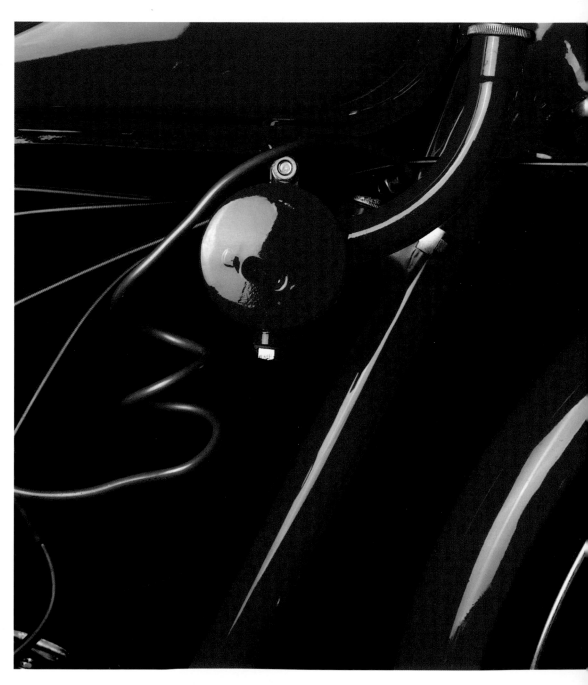

The Racing Cucciolo.

Right: the engine of the Racing Cucciolo,
constructed from various mass-produced parts.

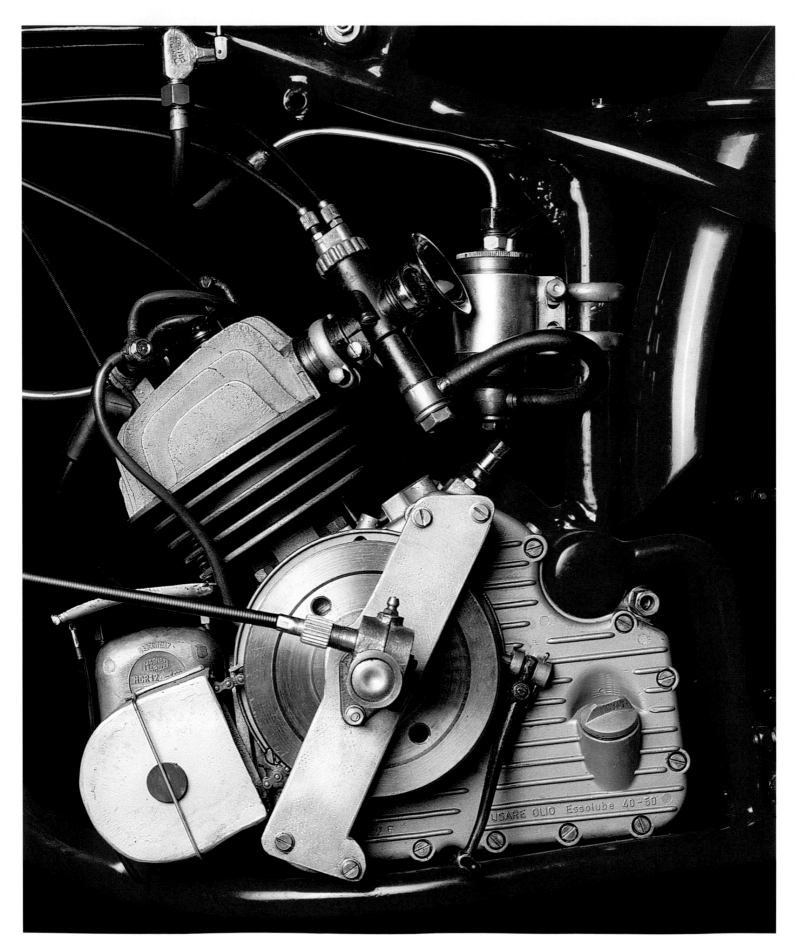

Ambitions
and Pragmatism

1952 was important one for Ducati. In that year it presented two interesting new models at the Salone di Milano, the most important motorcycle show in the country, both of them designed by Fiorio's staff: the 98 and the Cruiser scooter. Neither of these vehicles are recalled with particular affection by Ducati fans today, but they marked a significant turning point for the firm, which had now thrown caution to the winds and assumed the role of a motorcycle constructor.

The Cruiser was a decidedly ambitious project, way ahead of its time. A four-stroke 175 cc engine, automatic gear change with hy-draulic converter, electric starter and styling by the Turin car designer Ghia: these could all be features of one of today's top-of-the-line scooters, rather than a vehicle designed in 1950!

The 98 series, on the other hand, marked Ducati's entry into the world of the "real" motorbike. It was actually a very rational design with no frills that set out to offer customers a robust and versatile machine. The engine was a single-cylinder four-stroke with pushrod and rocker-arm valve gear, overhung in a pressed-steel frame. It was not a sporting bike but Ducati, whose Director at that time was the engineer Giuseppe Montano, put its faith in this motorcycle, which it saw as a springboard for the competitions. After a great deal of work on the reliable but low-performance engine, initially rated at only 4·5 hp at 6250 revs, the first successes were achieved as early as 1954: two silver medals at the Welsh Six Days and a third place for Gandossi at Moto-giro. Despite the appearance of new models, many versions of this Ducati pushrod and rocker-arm series remained in production up until the sixties (the Bronco and Aurea models) with 125 cc engines.

The development of Cucciolo engines continues: contemporary advertising leaflets for the 65 TS – already a sporty bike – and the cheaper 55 with an elastic frame.

DUCATI 65TS

lightweight motorcycle motolégère

specifications:	65 c.c. Four stroke — overhead valves Petrol consumption: at 35 m.p.h., 180 m.p.g. Maximum speed: 44 m.p.h.
caractéristiques du bloc:	65 cm³ — 4 temps — distribution à soupapes en tête Consomm. essence 1 lt. pour 65 Km. à la vitesse de 55 Km/h Vitesse maximum: 70 Km/h

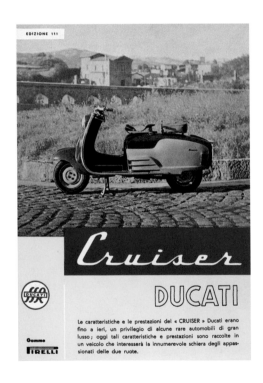

EDIZIONE 111

Cruiser

DUCATI

Gomma PIRELLI

Le caratteristiche e le prestazioni del « CRUISER » Ducati erano fino a ieri, un privilegio di alcune rare automobili di gran lusso; oggi tali caratteristiche e prestazioni sono raccolte in un veicolo che interesserà la innumerevole schiera degli appassionati delle due ruote.

The Cruiser scooter, an ambitious and futuristic initiative.

DUCATI 55/e

ciclomotore elastico

caratteristiche principali	48 cm³ — 4 tempi — distribuzione con valvole in testa Consumo benzina lt. 1 per 90 Km. Velocità massima 50 Km/h

Facing page: the 98 with pushrod and rocker-arm valve gear.

Cucciolo Spin-Offs

ENGINE – Derived from the Cucciolo, the T3 engine had the same technical scheme, characterized by the same pull-rods valve gear, i.e. controlled by a camshaft in the sump. The pushrods and rocker arms were covered by a casing and were therefore better protected and, above all, more lubricated than in the first version of the Cucciolo. The bore and stroke were raised from the original 39 x 40 mm to 42 x 43 mm with a capacity of 60 cc, producing a maximum power of 2·25 hp at 5000 rpm. The 65 version had a bore and stroke of 44 x 43 mm and a rating of 2·5 hp. The gearbox was three-speed with a wet, multi-plate clutch. The ignition used a magneto, while the exhaust emerged on the right side of the cylinder head.

FRAMES – Among the derivatives of the Cucciolo it is possible to distinguish those with a pressed-steel frame made by Caproni of Vizzola Ticino for the 55 series and available in "elastic" or "rigid" versions (depending on whether the rear axle was sprung or not), and the later ones produced by external manufacturers (like Verlicchi), but always with Ducati specifications and under the Ducati name. More interesting are the sports models like the 60 and TS 65, which show a constant evolution in their frames: from the first 60s, with a twin pair of shock absorbers, to the TS 65, with its telescopic front fork and rear suspension with a swing-arm fork and mechanical shock absorbers.

PERFORMANCE – In its progress toward the manufacture of motorcycles, Ducati passed from the role of a constructor of auxiliary motors under license to that of a constructor in its own right. While the T1 did not even attain 1·5 hp, the performance was almost doubled and the top speed raised from the 40 kph of the first "autocycles" to the 70 kph of the TS 65 version. Even the accessories went through the same evolution: from the pedals of the T1 that did everything to true foot-operated gearshifts and kick starters, while the handlebar, bristling with "multipurpose" levers on the T1, became more practical, as we know it today. It was a sign that the emergency was over and that the difficult postwar years were finally coming to an end.

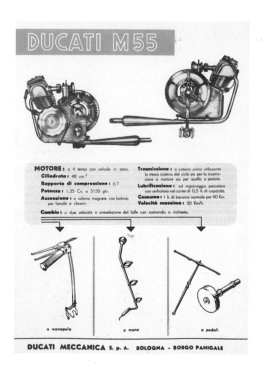

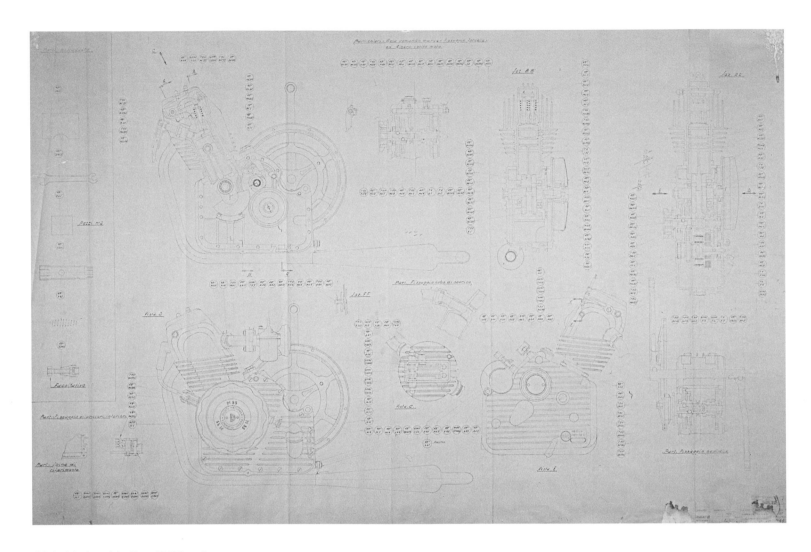

Original design of the Ducati M55 engine.

Races and Records

During Ducati's "pioneering" period, when the company was still making small motors, there emerged a hero in the shape of Ugo Tamarozzi. Having first competed in the Six Days Race, he went on, from 1950 onward and at the venerable age (for a rider) of forty-six, to set no less than thirty world records on his Cucciolo, prepared in a modest workshop with only limited means. From the "flying kilometer" achieved at an average of 77·753 kph, to the distance record over forty-eight hours completed at an average of 63·2 kph, no achievement was beyond him. In this last session, at the Monza racetrack, Tamarozzi was supported by other riders sent by the company to help him (Farné, Miani, Caroli, Sozzani and Pennati) and he proceeded to set a total of twenty-

seven world records in the 50 cc class. Of particular note among these was the twenty-four hour record, which held good for the 100 cc class as well. One of the secrets behind Tamarozzi's exploits was a special mixture of fuels developed by the rider himself, in which benzol and acetone were added to gasoline to increase compression.

The establishment of these records required an immense effort, and beyond the exploits themselves, such achievements were an extremely useful publicity vehicle for constructors and brought a great deal of prestige at the international level.

The races on both the road (the long-distance competitions known as Gran Fondo) and the track that were won by riders like Zitelli and Farné also show a great commitment to the sport, however

limited the vehicles may have been in terms of power and performance. There is something that defies belief in the very idea of competing in a Motogiro race today on a bike as Spartan as a Cucciolo or a 60 Sport, and yet the hunger for victory shown by these riders, who often went onto the track with improvised equipment, was truly voracious. The insatiable passion for Racing, of whatever kind, is clearly evident from photographs taken at the time, which show that the events, even those involving "autocycles", were always staged between long lines of spectators, ready to cheer on the riders in their valiant efforts: from Stradella to the Giardini Margherita track in Bologna, the enthusiasm shown by the public for the riders was perhaps the most effective spur of all.

Alberto Farné and his 65 at the finish of a race.

Facing page: an "official" Racing Cucciolo of 1948. The frame has a cantilever suspension with friction dampers; note the cushion on the gas tank to allow the rider to assume the most aerodynamic position possible.

Glauco Zitelli at the "Valli Bergamasche" with the 65.

The forty-nine-year-old Ugo Tamarozzi and the Cucciolo with which he set twelve world records in 1950.

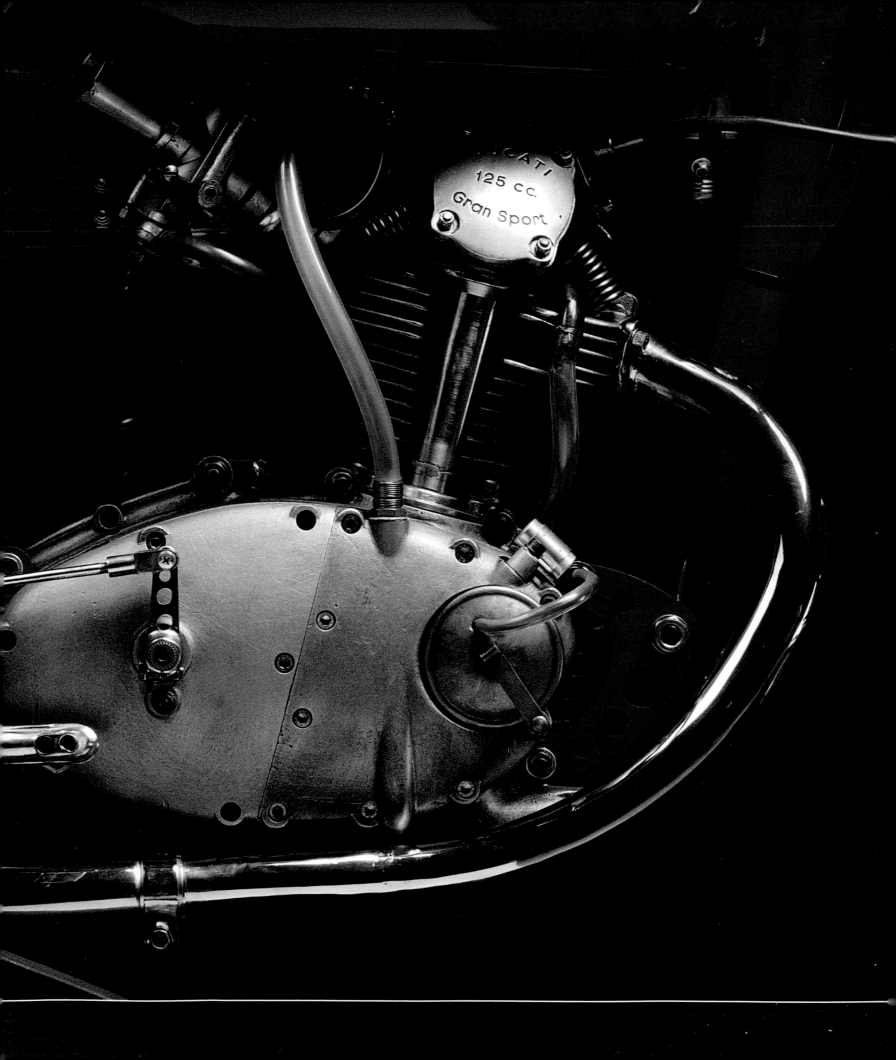

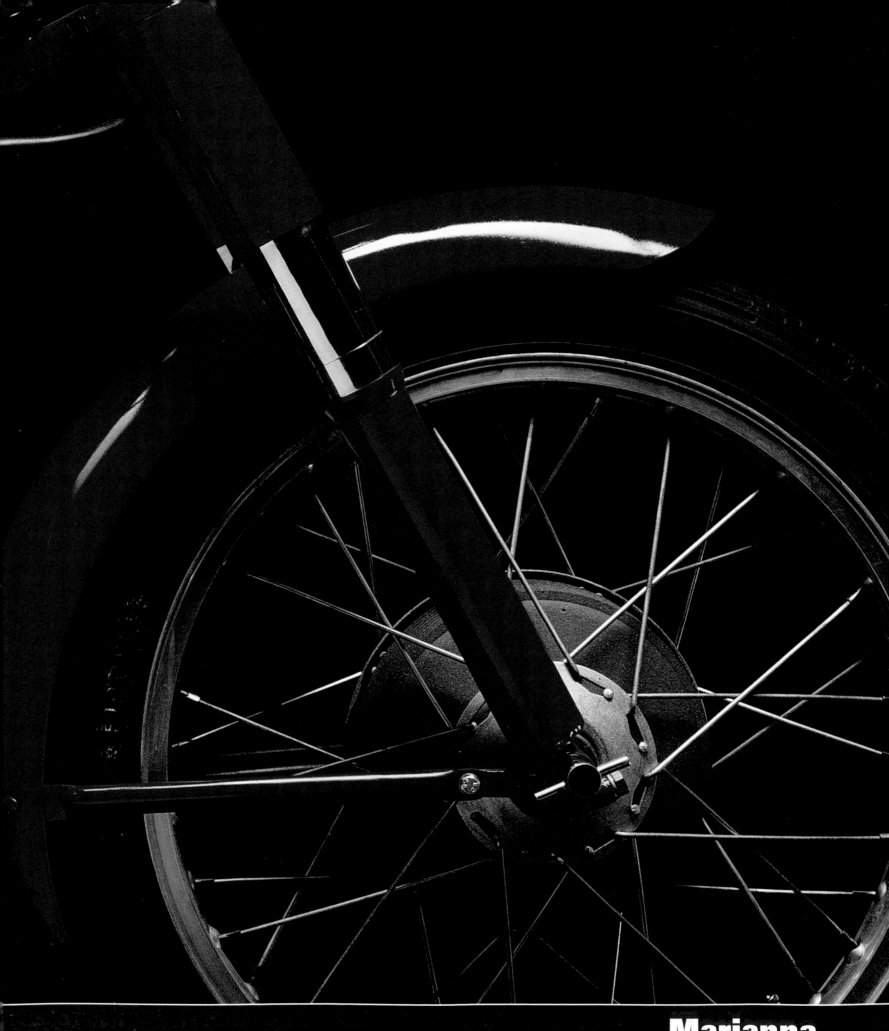

Marianna

Marianna

The true history of Ducati's sporting activity, of Sport with a capital "S", began in 1955. Everything that had taken place before, despite the indisputable commitment of those involved and the quality of the vehicles, can be considered no more than an appetizer. It should not be forgotten that ten years had now passed since the Bolognese manufacturer had started to make motorcycles and that, over that period, the Ducati name had become familiar all over the world. The leading products, those most popular with the public, were of course no longer small engines that hummed away happily on just a few drops of gasoline. In Italy, the passion was for speed. There were a great many races, most of them held in city streets (tracks were few and far between in Italy), but the ones which really drove the public wild were the long-distance competitions known as Gran Fondo, the Milano-Taranto and the Motogiro.

Vittorio Zito in action at the 1957 Motogiro (photo Cerreti and Pellegrini).

Giovanni Degli Antoni, shown here at the start of a track race, was one of the best of the Marianna riders (photo Minarini).

Right: Leopoldo Tartarini escorted by Dr. Montano (photo Breveglieri).

Winning these races was the best publicity a motorbike manufacturer could ask for. Television did not yet exist (or was restricted to just a few households), and news of a victory was communicated directly to enthusiasts through newspapers and movie newsreels (such as the popular *Settimana IN-COM*). Some of the bikes that took part bore famous names, but others were made by constructors who had only just come onto the scene, like Laverda, but who quickly built up a sound reputation. For Ducati, more and more committed to motorcycles, the prospect was tempting - but with the Cucciolo and the 98 victory remained no more than a pipe dream: Ducati simply didn't have the right bike.

What was needed was a motorcycle capable of winning, but which could also serve as the starting point for new ventures in construction, subsequently to be brought into mass production.

It seems that the President of Ducati, Dr. Montano, had a brainwave when, in 1954, (on the May-day holiday, according to legend) he hired a young engineer from Lugo in Romagna called Fabio Taglioni. He came to Ducati from Mondial, where he had been kept in the shade by other, more famous technicians who were naturally jealous of this young Romagnese man who had already built a fine Racing 75 with the help of his pupils at the technical college where he taught, and then sold the design to Ceccato. Taglioni was mad about Racing and good mechanics and, from his very first days

at Ducati, tried to give a new slant to production. He chose a bike with a capacity of 100 cc and single-camshaft, bevel-gear and therefore capable of running at high revs. This combination (to which Taglioni was to adhere for much of the rest of his career) was considered complex and costly to produce, unless you had exceptionally good machinery and highly skilled workers. Ducati gave him *carte blanche*, the result was the Gran Sport 100 - better known as the Marianna.

First the name: where did it come from? There are two possibilities. The first and most likely is that it was a reference to the fact that in 1995 the Catholic Church was celebrating "The Holy Year of Mary". There are also those who claim that the bike was named after Anna Maria, the saint on whose feast day it made its debut. Whatever the truth, it has to be said that the divine "patronage" of

Giovanni Degli Antoni first across the finishing line at the Third Motogiro (photo Breveglieri).

Right: Spaggiari and the Marianna at the Motogiro "between ancient walls" (photo Giornalfoto).

this motorcycle proved miraculous. For Ducati's rivals, on the other hand, it was something of a curse.

Taglioni designed the bike as a Racing machine: this is evident from the exposed valve springs, which could easily be replaced if they broke, as well as from the brilliance of the design, which immediately overshadowed everything else that had been built at Borgo Panigale. The running gear pre-empted what was to produced for many years to come: a bike with a single-tube, open cradle frame made of tubular steel, with the engine closing the frame at the bottom, telescopic forks and a swinging-arm rear suspension with twin shock absorbers. The Gran Sport was in a class of its own, and proved it by winning its first race hands down. It went on to dominate the Gran Fondo competitions of those years, in the 125 version as well, created by making just a few modifications to the 100. But the real importance of this bike was not immediately obvious: thanks to Taglioni's style, it proved possible to use the "Marianna" as a building block for mass-produced bikes with capacities of up to 350 cc and for sophisticated Racing machines like the twin-camshaft 125 and the triple-camshaft desmo, one of the finest single-cylinder motorcycles ever made. The Marianna also marked the beginning of the Ducati philosophy: to produce mass-produced bikes that win races.

The technical evolution of the Gran Sport also demonstrates the flexibility of the design: it is not easy to turn a sports bike into a mass-produced one and, at the same time, to study and build one of even higher-performance to run in the world championships. And yet this is just what was achieved.

In 1958, while the mass-produced Sport 100 and 125, naturally with single-camshaft and bevel-

gear, were being delivered to the concessionaries, the triple-camshaft desmo was making an attempt at the world championships. Hard to believe, but true: both were actually the "offspring" of the Marianna.

What is not surprising is that, by the time the Gran Fondo races of 1957 were over, the Marianna had excelled on the racetrack (with only the slightest of adjustments) and was successfully used by riders all over the world right up to the beginning of the sixties. According to sources in Ducati, around a hundred Mariannas were produced and at least forty Gran Sport 100s, many of which were converted into 125s. Yet others were converted into double camshafts for customers competing in the various championships. This is not to mention the extremely rare triple-camshaft desmos, developed expressly for Racing. Another spin-off from the Marianna was the F3 175, a beautiful "production-derived" bike

First version of the Gran Sport 100; note the pump for the tires in the triangle of the frame.

Right: Marcello Sestini and Gino Carena (photo Breveglieri).

that opened a new chapter in competition and strengthened even further the link between production and Racing, in addition to taking a leap upward in power, reaching new levels of engine capacity.

The Gran Sports won an incredible number of races. Particularly unforgettable among these were the two Milano-Tarantos and three Motogiris (along with the record of 103·172 kph set by Degli Antoni in the 1955 Milano-Taranto). The 125 won two Milano-Tarantos and two Motogiris (it was not entered for the '55 one, but only those of '56 and '57), the last of which produced a spectacular result: six Gran Sport bikes took the first six places. Nor should we forget the five consecutive Italian junior championships (from 1959 to 1964) and even a victory at the Coppa d'Oro Shell on the Imola racetrack in 1959, beating Grand Prix bikes from the 125 class. Franco Farné (at the time an excellent rider of these bikes who carried off many victories and later a Ducati technician) had no doubts as to the distinguishing merits of the Marianna: "they were simply fabulous." For a man like Farné, the adjective "fabulous" meant that the Marianna, as well as having a powerful engine (from the 9 hp of the first 100 version of 1955 to the 14 hp at 10,000 revs of the 125), was also well-balanced, light, compact and easy to handle.

The development of these bikes for use on the competitive circuit is equally interesting, especially after Ducati's decision to enter the Grand Prix world. After the provisional twin camshaft of 1956 (sporadically entrusted to the Romagnese veteran Alano Montanari and, later on, to private riders who used the double-camshaft head to update Gran Sport bikes) came the "triple-camshaft desmo," one of the most brilliant examples of the creative value of Taglioni's approach to Racing.

Three shafts might seem an unnecessary complication, but the way that they controlled the closing of the valves instead of entrusting the task to springs (which often used to break when the engine was running above a level of 10,000 revs) allowed the Ducati 125 Gran Premio to operate without problems at 12,500 rpm. The desmo won many races in Italy (Farné, for instance, took three out of three Junior 100 titles with it), but also gave great satisfaction in the 125 world championship, especially in the 1958 season. After winning the Italian title with consummate ease, the Ducatis of Gandossi and Spaggiari terrorized the MVs of Provini and Ubbiali on the tracks of the world championships, though a fall by Gandossi at Ulster cost the title.

Below: Leopoldo Tartarini (photo Telestampa).

Facing page, from left to right: Giovanni Degli Antoni, Mario Recchia, Bruno Spaggiari and Silvio Fabiani (photo Telestampa).

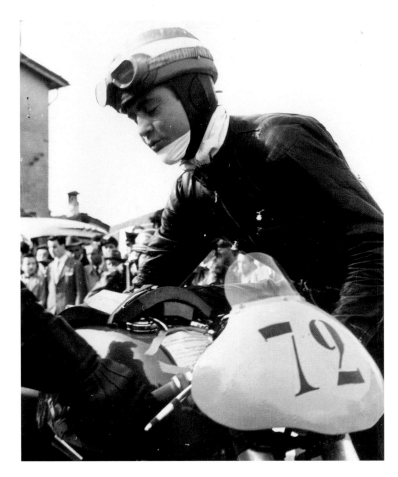
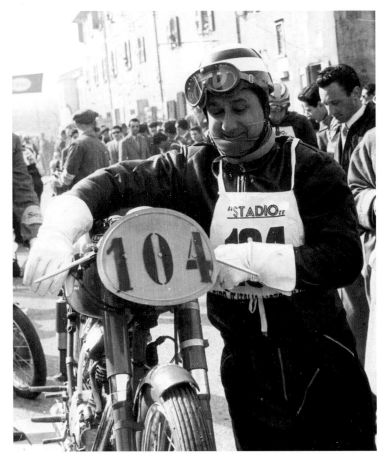
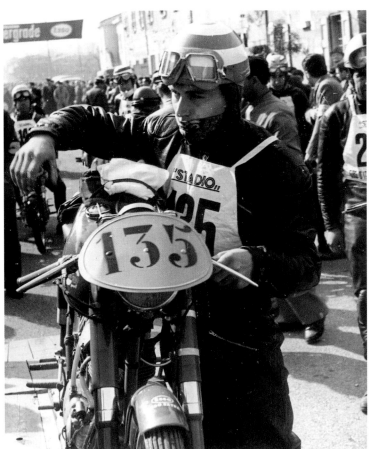
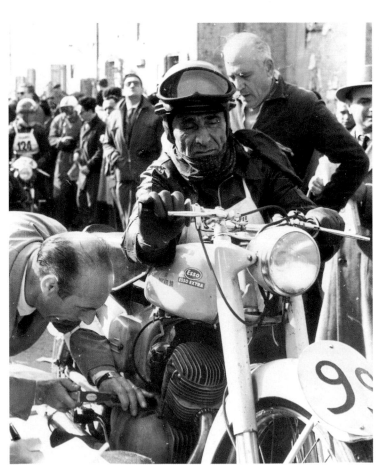

Gran Sport 100-125
The Unbeatable

Ever since its first appearance in the pages of the monthly *Motociclismo* at the beginning of 1955, the Ducati Gran Sport caught the imagination of enthusiasts. Still today the bike remains part of the collective imagination of the motorcycling world, evoking images that have the rare power to bring the same sparkle to the eye of a twenty-year-old from Helsinki as to that of a pensioner from Reggio Calabria. For everyone, the Marianna is one of those legendary bikes, though few have ever heard its hoarse and full-throated roar (which suggests so much more than its small capacity), nor have they seen it in action. The list of convincing victories makes it without doubt one of the most fascinating motorcycles of its time, but this is not enough to explain its fame. So let us attempt to cast some light on the awesome reputation of this Racing bike.

Appearance is a motorbike's visiting card. The Marianna could probably be described as the aesthetic manifesto of an inimitable Racing machine. To be quite clear about this, the Gran Sport's captivating appearance was not the result of a detailed examination of style. It stemmed more from the forms of its various components, all designed to produce the maximum performance in a race. In this case, the concept of form and function was truly pushed to its highest level.

The frame, for example, is disarmingly simple: in practice a circular tube that, tracing a beautiful curve, almost in freehand, joins the steering column to the area where the fork rests on its fulcrum. The structure is completed by more slender tubing and metal plates, as well, significantly, as by the engine itself, which

"closes" it at the bottom. Here "rationalization" reached one of its highest peaks, as the criterion that inspired this bike was simplicity.

The mid-fifties was a very fertile time for Italian motorcycles: Parilla, Benelli, Mondial, Guzzi, Morini, Laverda, Ceccato, Bianchi and MV Agusta all came out with vehicles of technical interest, designs that may not always have been rationalized but were nevertheless fascinating. Even the aesthetics of the bikes of those years is unrivaled: it was almost as if centuries of great Italian art had had a hand in the industrial design of that period, exercising an influence even on the panel beaters who made the gas tanks and fairings, or the technicians who designed towered valve gear that seemed to take their inspiration from the medieval towers of Italian cities.

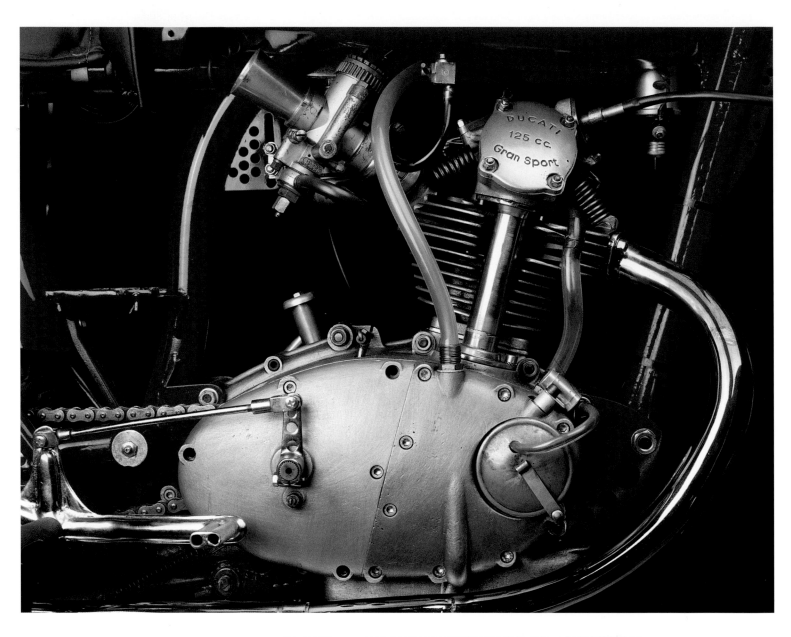

On double-spread and following page: the Gran
Sport 125 Marianna (Ducati Museum; owner Sergio
Radici; photo Giovanni Marchi). An example of style,
but also of extreme rationality aimed at winning
races, this bike was one of the finest works of
engineering of its time.

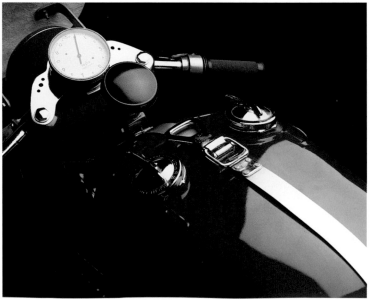

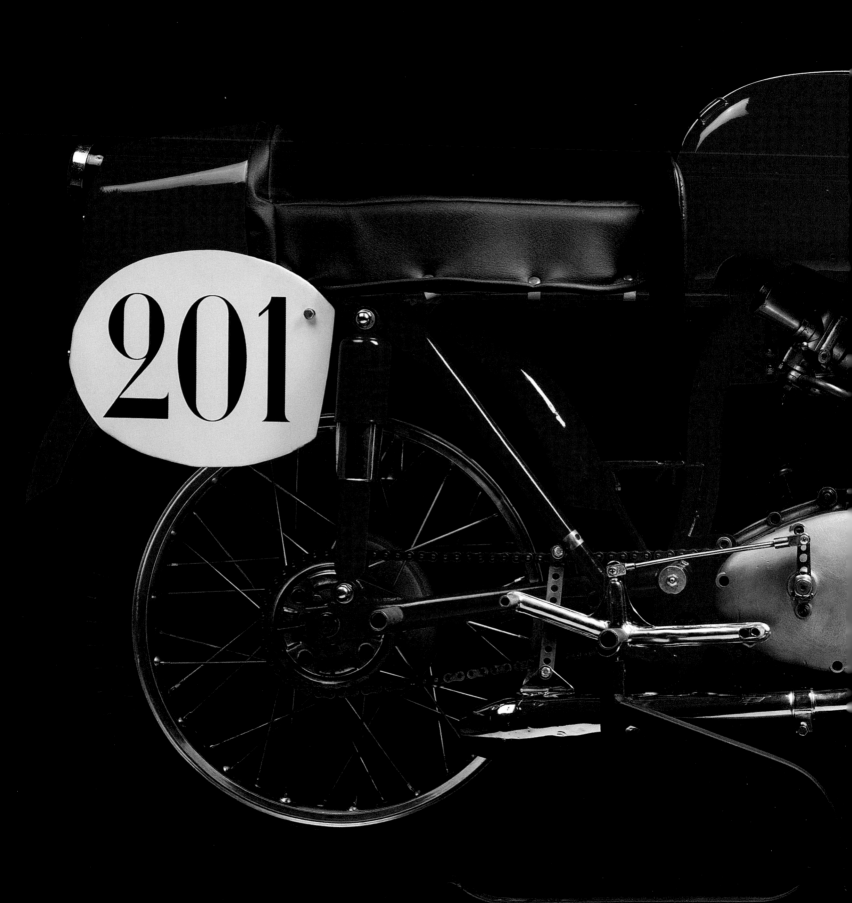

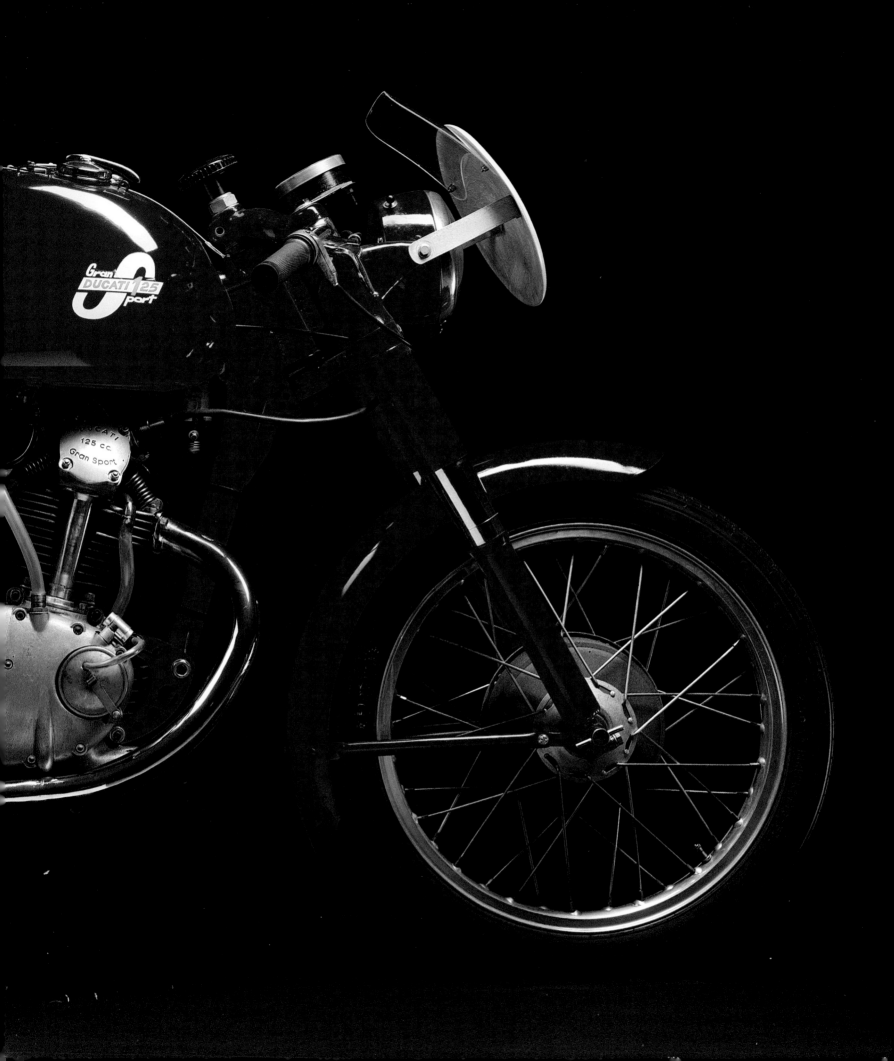

Ducati advertisement from 1956.

Below: The Ducati Racing Team van at the 1956 Motogiro (photo Breveglieri).

Facing page: Domenico Geminiani fêted at the finish of the Third Motogiro at Bologna.

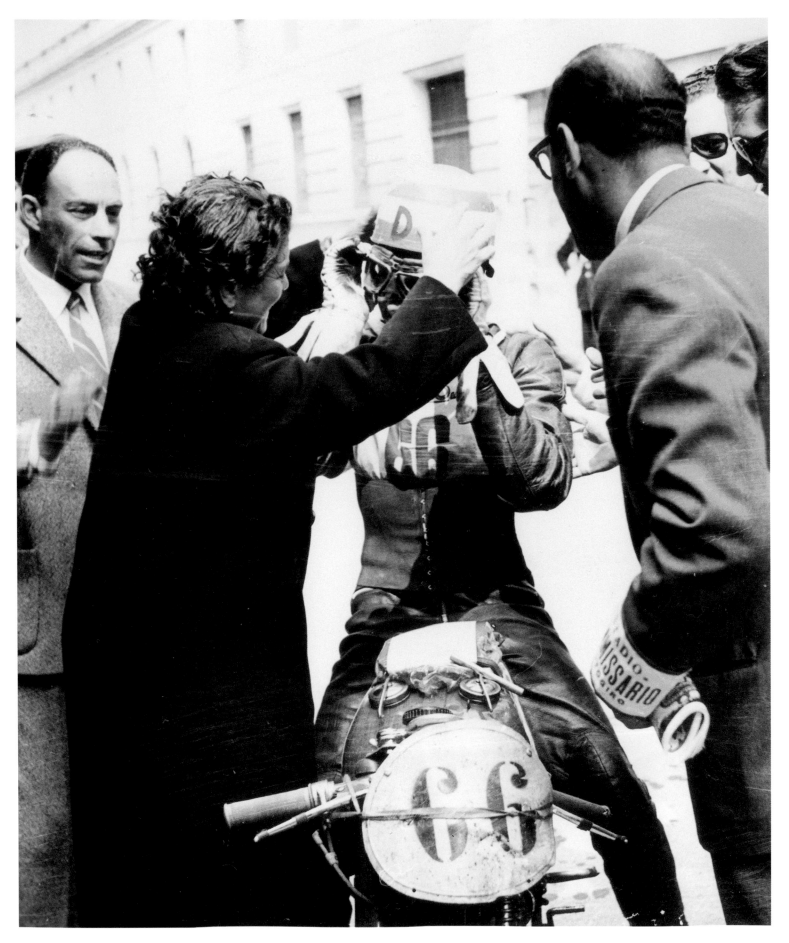

Bialbero 125
On the Trail of the Grand Prix

In 1956 the Racing career of the Marianna, in its two versions of 100 and 125 cc, was in full swing: the Gran Fondo competitions were the hunting ground for the single-cylinder single-camshaft Ducatis and results were starting to pour in thick and fast on the track as well. Yet the staff at the Italian manufacturer felt the need to explore new avenues. The world of the Grand Prix was growing ever more attractive, but to have a chance at the highest level something more than the Gran Sport was needed. The competition was using engines with twin-camshaft gear capable of delivering more power than the 14 hp of the Gran Sport 125: in this period the battle for the world title was between the Italian constructors Mondial and MV Agusta,

with Montesa, Gilera and DKW hot on their heels. A completely new motorcycle was called for and Taglioni was put to work on the project. The designer made a calculation: the 125 cc version of the single-camshaft Ducati was doing very well in competition. The Gran Fondo was its forte, and it wasn't going badly on the track (with more or less fanciful fairings to improve the streamlining). The bike was almost unbeatable (as would be demonstrated in 1957 when it won the Barcelona 24 Hours as well), and so something more could be attempted.

Thus the twin camshaft was born: to a Marianna engine with a capacity of 125 cc (bore and stroke 55·3 x 52 mm), Taglioni applied a cylinder head with double-camshaft (*bialbero*) valve

gear that brought the power up to around 16 hp at 11,500 revs, producing a top speed of 170 kph. Various types of fairing were tried out on the twin camshaft: from the full wrap-around one (permitted at the time) to the partial kind with one fairing fixed to the top of the forks and another small one on the rear part. The frame had the same tubular structure as the Marianna, but a variation with a double tube running down from the steering column instead of a single one was also tried out. The bike was not entered in the 1956 world championships, but did take part in national races with the constructor's official rider Degli Antoni and the veteran Alano Montanari, a rider who had earned great popularity with the public through his sportsmanship.

On double-page spread: the twin-camshaft Ducati 125 Grand Prix, prepared in 1956 from a Gran Sport 125 (Ducati Museum; owner Gianpietro Parmegiani; photo Giovanni Marchi). The magnesium-alloy Amadori brakes (right) had conspicuous air intakes for cooling. The engine (below) delivered around 16 hp.

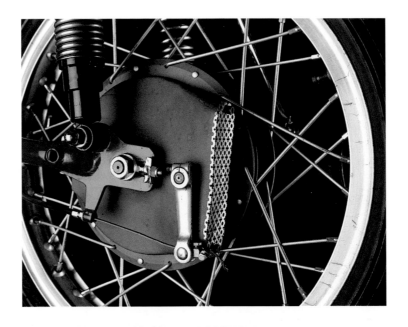

Degli Antoni was the first to try out the twin-camshaft Ducati and, before his death, raced the three-camshaft Desmos as well.

Left: Franco Farné in an Italian championship race at Riccione in 1958, riding a Desmo 125 (photo Terreni).

Bottom: a Bialbero on the Limon Circuit in Venezuela in 1958. Wraparound fairings were still permitted in South America (photo Fulvio).

Facing page: Raffaele and Franco Farné at Busto Arsizio in 1958.

Marianna

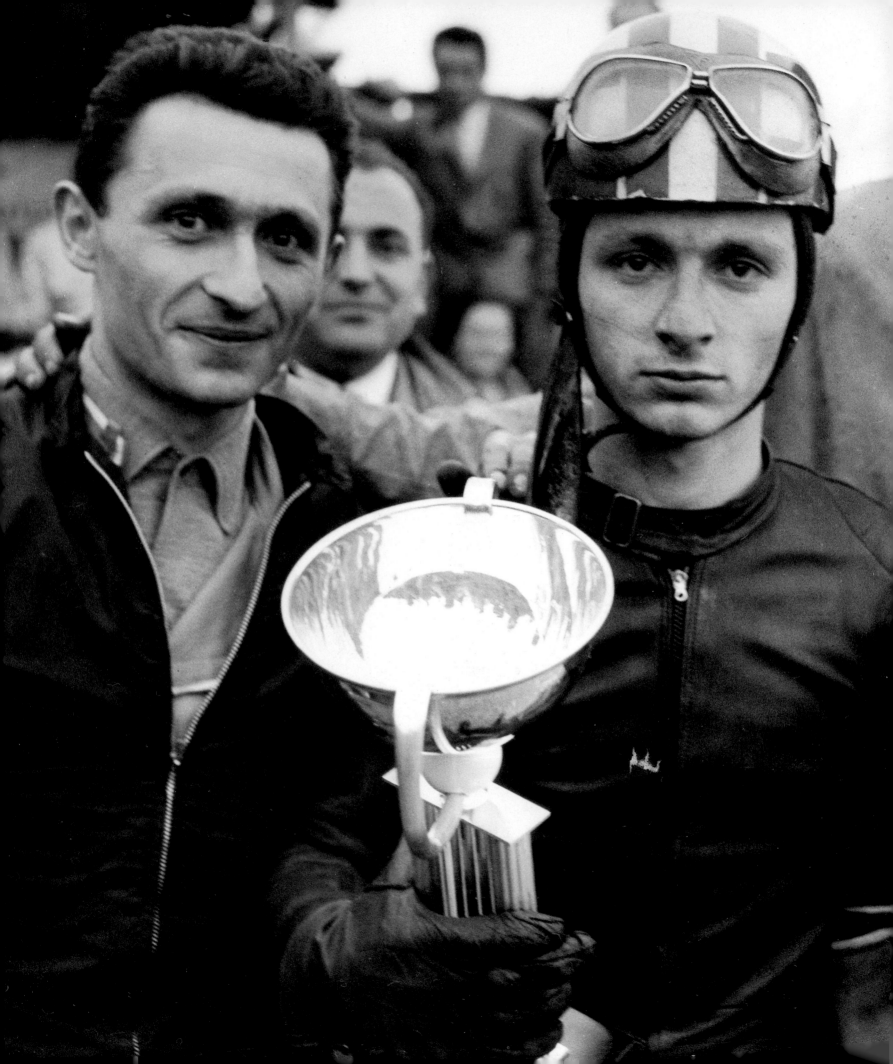

175 F3

Production-Derived Bikes

The second half of the fifties saw a new boom in Italy, that of the 175 class. It was a sign that the motorcycle market was no longer solely interested in strictly utilitarian vehicles, but was beginning to ask for something more in terms of both styling and performance.

The major manufacturers fought for control of the market by bringing out beautiful bikes, often with shrewdly-designed sporty characteristics, that usually had attractive four-stroke engines.

At the Salone di Milano of 1956 Ducati showed its new 175 Turismo, sober in appearance but with out-of-the-ordinary mechanics. Its single-cylinder four-stroke engine had a block derived fairly directly from that of the Marianna, while the head housed a single camshaft with bevel-gear shaft, absolutely identical to that of the Gran Sport. The difference lay in the valve springs, covered by a lid. The power was rated at 11 hp at 7500 revs (1957 version) and the maximum speed was over 100 kph.

It was from this bike that the Formula 3 was developed. Intended to compete among the "production-derived" vehicles that were highly popular at the time, the F3 was a beautiful machine because it took the technology and performance of the sports bike for the road to the peak of its time. On the triumphant day of the Nations Cup Grand Prix (Monza 1958, five bikes in the top five places of the

In 1958 the Indonesian M.A.T. Gumilar (above on the podium and below at the start with the number 54) raced and won with a 175 derived from a production bike.

125 class), this bike also won Ducati the race in its category, with Francesco Villa in the saddle. But it also triumphed in Spain (Barcelona) and the United States (Daytona 1959, with Franco Farné, shipped overseas to race the bikes built at Borgo Panigale and increase their popularity).

The official bikes (about forty of them were built) had an engine with a bore and stroke of 62 x 57·8 mm, a maximum output of 16 hp at 9000 rpm and a top speed of 160 kilometers an hour.

The motorcycle was very close to the production version, although there are those who insinuate that not one piece was interchangeable: a common failing among the production-derived bikes of those years. It is precisely the sophisticated equipment of these motorcycles that makes them prized collector's pieces today: for instance the F3 had the same magnesium alloy brakes as were used by the official desmos entered for the Grand Prix, as well as components and details that were prepared with painstaking care.

Above, and on following double-page spread: the recently restored Ducati F3 175 (Ducati Museum; owner Ducati Motor S.p.A.; photo Oliver).

Left: page in the September 1958 issue of the magazine *Motociclismo* devoted to Francesco Villa's victory on the Ducati 175 F3.

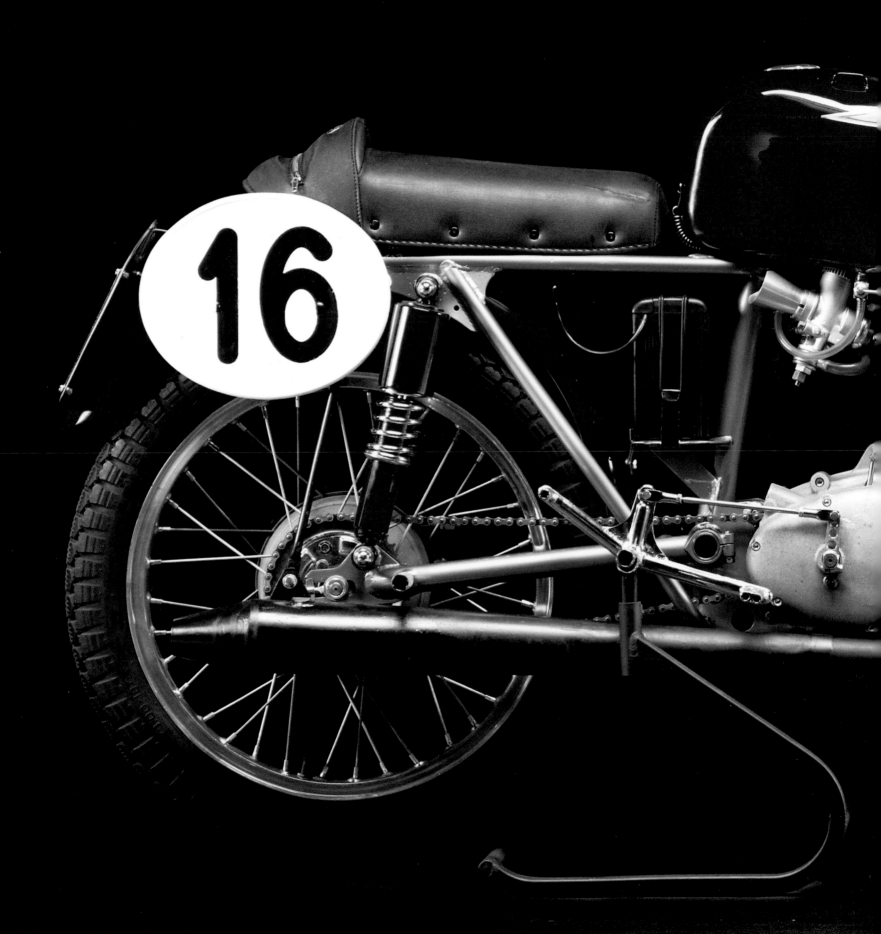

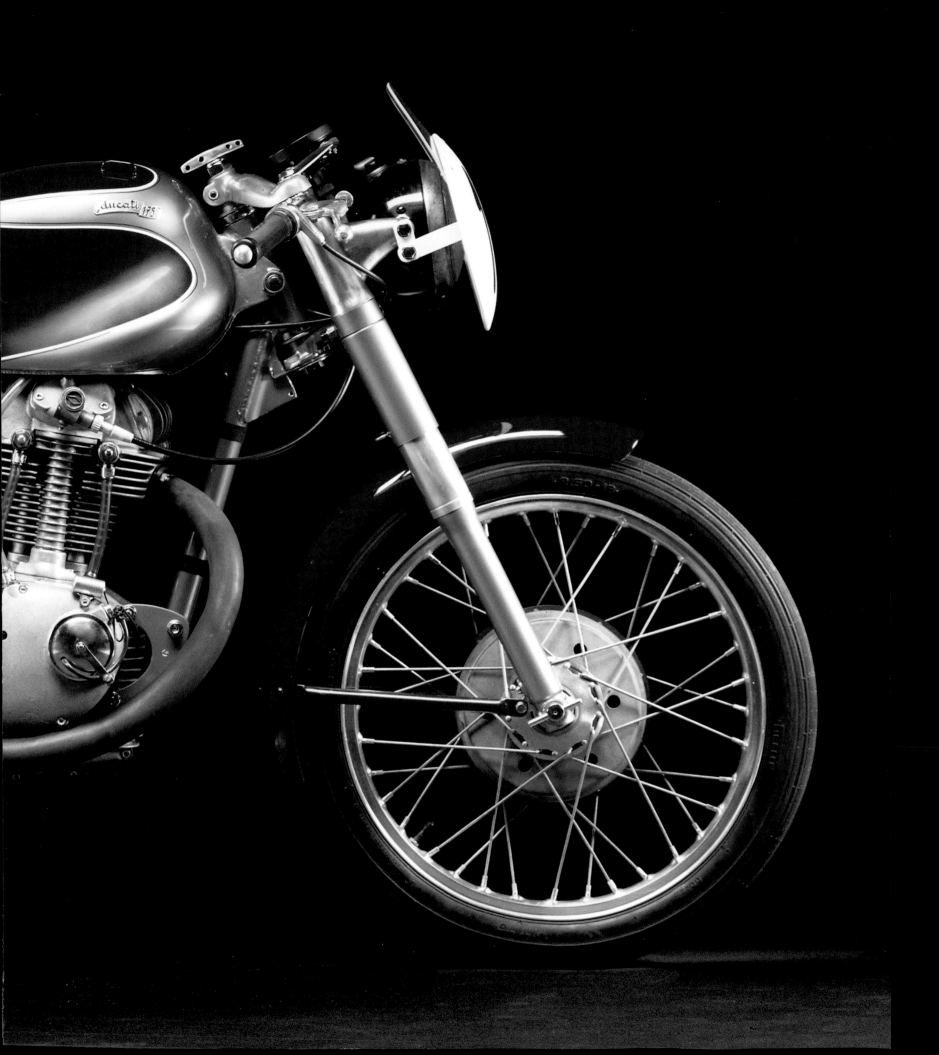

Trialbero Desmo 125
Unlucky King of the Road

"This system, which we call desmodromic," i.e. drive with controlled movement, "has demonstrated its greater efficiency for many years now, even if it is mechanically more complicated and more costly". This was the conclusion to a report by Fabio Taglioni on the desmodromic distribution system, a characteristic of Ducati's sports machines of yesterday and today, and a hallowed technical "plus" of the Bolognese bikes.

The desmo made its debut in 1956, when Taglioni used a sort of hybrid between the twin-camshaft system (which was retained to control the opening of the valves) and the single-camshaft one (used to close the valves) in his design of the new 125 for Grand Prix Racing. The engine, derived from the Gran Sport and fitted with this new cylinder head, was mounted on the frame of the Bialbero (practically the same as the Marianna's) and immediately proved competitive. It won the Swedish Grand Prix in 1957 (though the race did not count toward the world championship). But while waiting for an opportunity to take on its rivals in the race at Monza, an accident during trials killed Gianni Degli Antoni, the constructor's chief rider. A halt was called until the following season, by which time the "triple-camshaft" had dual ignition (two 10 mm spark plugs), carburetors ranging from the 29mm used on the fast circuits to the 23 mm for road races and a rating of 19 hp.

The riders were Luigi Taveri, Alberto Gandossi, Bruno Spaggiari, Romolo Ferri and Francesco Villa, along with the Englishmen Dave Chadwick and Sammy Miller. The bike, with the partial fairing that had been made obligatory that year, proved superior to the competition, partly as a consequence of continual technical developments. This meant that hardly one of the bikes was like another. For example, double- and single-cradle frames were tried out, along with a whole range of other solutions (exhausts, carburetors, ignition systems). Ducati lost the title by a hair's breadth (and a fall), but in the last race at Monza took the first five places. At the end of the season official sporting activity practically came to a stop. It is worth pointing out that the 125 desmo twin-cylinder, of which we shall have more to say soon, made its debut in that last race of 1958.

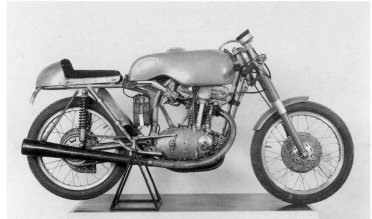

The first "nude" pictures of the triple-camshaft Ducati designed by the engineer from Lugo.

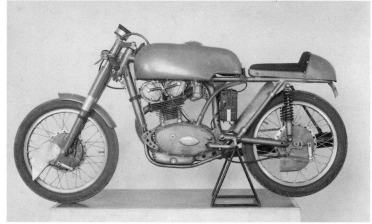

Alberto Gandossi on the triple-camshaft Desmo 125 was perhaps the most effective combination of the 1958 season (here, in Breveglieri's photo, we see him in action at Modena).

Facing page: Luigi Taveri (photo Motor Cycling).

The triple-camshaft Desmo 125 with the wraparound fairing used in the 1957 season. The rearing horse is a tribute by Fabio Taglioni to his illustrious fellow townsman, the flying ace Francesco Baracca.

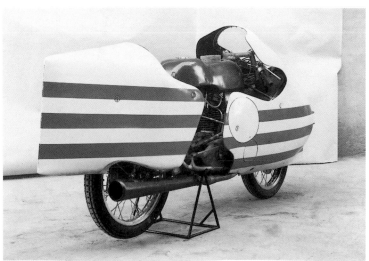

97

Gran Sport 100

FRAME, FORKS AND RUNNING GEAR –
Taglioni decided that the engine had to close
the frame at the bottom, making the whole
structure more rigid. So the frame was
simplified to the maximum: one thick tube
formed the main structure, while another tube
ran down from the steering column and
ended in two plates used to anchor the motor.
The GS 100 had 17 inch wheels (18 inch on
the 125) with aluminum rims and
magnesium-alloy brakes made by Amadori.
The rear suspension was of the type that
became common in just those years: a swing-
arm fork coupled with twin hydraulic shock
absorbers with external springs.

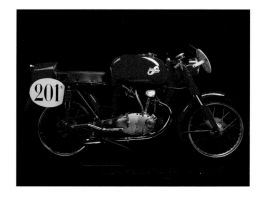

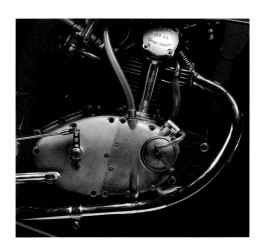

ENGINE – The first masterpiece Taglioni
designed for Ducati (the engine of the Gran
Sport 100 of 1955) was an air-cooled single-
cylinder (bore and stroke 49·4 x 52 mm,
capacity 98 cc), four stroke, with a 10°
forward angle configuration. It had a single-
camshaft distribution with twin valves.
Movement was transmitted through a vertical
shaft that drove the camshaft by helical
gearing. This was a difficult system that
required excellent equipment and highly-
skilled workers to function properly, but which
was soon introduced on mass-produced
motorcycles as well. The carburetor was a
Dell'Orto SS 20, while the ignition was a
battery-coil. The maximum power of the first
version was 9 hp at 9000 rpm but, with
continual technical improvements, was raised
to 12 hp a 10,500 revs.

THE BIKE – Small, compact and light (80 kg
dead weight), the Gran Sport 100 at once
proved its worth, as did the 125 cc version
produced with bore and stroke
measurements of 49·4 x55·3 mm and fed by
a carburetor with a diameter of 22 mm. The
GS 125 delivered 14 hp at 10,000 revs.
There was nothing superfluous on this bike:
every detail, even the most insignificant, had a
precise function. For example, the hooks on
the gas tank were used to attach padding so
that the rider could lie flat on the bike during
the long high-speed sections of Gran Fondo
races. The soundness of the design became
apparent when the triple-camshaft desmo
(which had a similar frame and running gear)
made its debut on the racetrack: in spite of the
greater power and higher speeds that could
be attained (almost 180 kph as opposed to
the 140 reached by the GS 100 in the
Motogiro), the bike always held a stable
course and was easy to handle.

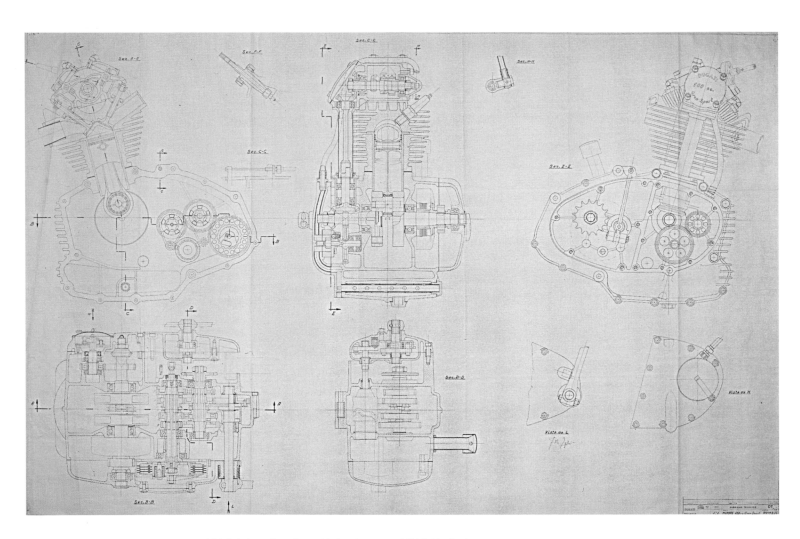

Original design of the Ducati Gran Sport 100 "Marianna" engine, with the signature of Fabio Taglioni.

The Gran Fondo Races

The pictures taken in those years tell the incredible story of the long-distance races known as Gran Fondo, which caught the imagination of the whole country in the fifties, better than a novelist ever could. The exhausted expressions of the competitors in the Milano-Taranto after spending almost a whole day riding their bikes the length of Italy, from north to south, are eloquent. Each of those riders had accumulated memories that would last him a lifetime: steep curves, moments of fatigue, discomfort and exaltation in an extraordinary, multi-faceted experience. The race used to set off in the early hours of a Sunday morning from Milan (Idroscalo), run down the Via Emilia in darkness between lines of spectators on each side of the road and then ascend and descend the Appennine passes, head past Rome and down toward Taranto, along the long straight stretches of the Tavoliere di Puglia. The winner was the one who did it in least time, and it was a tremendous race.

The Motogiro, on the other hand, was a race in stages across Italy. The public was equally enthusiastic about this competition, in which all the Italian constructors took part (it should not be forgotten that there were many of them at the time and over thirty in 1955). A rivalry between manufacturers played out under the eyes of their potential customers: this was part of the fascination of the long-distance races.

The arrival of Ducati (and Degli Antoni, a brilliant rider in all types of races) crushed the competition which, until the abolition of the races (1957), had to settle for no more than crumbs from the table in the 100 and 125 classes.

To convey a better idea of the performance of the Gran Sport Marianna in the Gran Fondo races, here are the results:
Milano-Taranto 1955. 100 class: 1st Degli Antoni, 2nd Villa, 3rd Scamandri (12 Ducati in the top

14 places). 125 class: 1st Maoggi, 3rd Falconi. Milano-Taranto 1956. 100 class: 1st Gandossi, 2nd Spaggiari, 3rd Sestini (all on Ducatis). 125 class: 1st Degli Antoni, 2nd Maoggi, 3rd Marenghi. Motogiro 1955. 100 class: 1st Degli Antoni, 2nd Villa, 3rd Fantuzzi, 4th Spaggiari, 5th Maoggi, 6th Scamandri (the fastest rider not on a Ducati was Innocenti, who came in 29th on a Ceccato). Motogiro 1956. 100 class: 1st Gandossi, 2nd Villa, 3rd Spaggiari, 4th Geminiani, 5th Scamandri, 6th Farné (the first non-Ducati was Lolli with a Ceccato). 125 class: 1st Maoggi, 2nd Maranghi, 3rd Artusi, 4th Montanari, 5th Falconi. Motogiro 1957. 100 class: 1st Mandolini, 2nd Artusi, 3rd Sestini, 4th Carena, 5th Zito, 6th Malaguti, 7th Anemoni. 125 class: 1st Graziano, 2nd Pionava, 3rd Mondaini, 4th Scamandri, 5th Brabetz, 6th Rosati, 7th Massa (fastest non-Ducati was D'Angelo on a Benelli).

Tartarini (156) and Fantuzzi (131) at the start of a stage in the 1955 Motogiro (photo Breveglieri).

Left: a celebrated image, Maoggi showing incredible determination at the start of the 1956 Motogiro (photo Breveglieri).

Members of the Ducati Racing Team ready at the fueling station (photo Perini).

Facing page: left, riders in the long-distance races known as Gran Fondo – in this case Sandro Artusi – often had to cope with bad weather; right, official riders studying the route and quenching their thirst with the beverage produced by a sponsor of the time (photo Breveglieri).

Mass Production

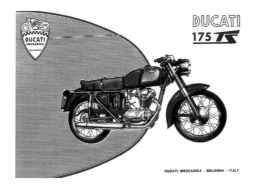

DUCATI
175 TS

DUCATI MECCANICA - BOLOGNA - ITALY

175 TS and 98 Bronco in a brochure of the period.

DUCATI
98 BRONCO

caratteristiche principali

98 cm³ - 4 tempi - distribuzione con valvole in testa a V
Consumo benzina lt. 2,3 per 100 Km.
Velocità massima circa 85 Km/h. - Cambio a 4 velocità.

The end of the fifties was not just a boom time for Ducati's sporting activities. The beneficial effects of competition showed up in the production bikes as well, with the arrival of new models and the technical improvement of earlier ones.

To present a clearer picture of the period, we shall take a look at two motorcycles of undoubted interest, the Sport 100-125 and the 175, including a part of the latter's wide range of fittings.

The former, available in two capacities and three versions (Turismo, Turismo Sport and Sport), was a direct descendant of the Marianna, indeed it was the model closest to it. Of course, the bike was designed to meet the needs of the "ordinary" market, and so the parts were sturdier and the power lower (around 6 hp), but the essence was the same. The distribution, to be precise, was still single-camshaft with bevel-gear, though the valve springs were covered. The running gear had changed little, and neither had the single-tube frame which was closed at the bottom by the engine. The

175, also available in T, TS, Sport and Super Sport versions, was another offspring of the Marianna and perhaps the most interesting motorcycle produced by Ducati in this period. In the first place, it was one of the few single-camshaft bikes available to ordinary customers and, in the most supercharged version (Super Sport), delivered a remarkable output of 14 hp, taking it to speeds of around 135 kph. Some models had twin exhausts on the right side: almost an anticipation of what you see on today's custom bikes. Speaking of American-style models, the 175 "Americano" represented Ducati's first attempt to penetrate the US market, with its cow-horn handlebars, split-level saddle, crash bars and a series of chromed accessories.

Between September 1957 and the same period of the following year, two 175s entrusted to the Bolognese riders Tartarini and Giorgio Monetti made an incredible journey of 60,000 kilometers or 37,000 miles around the world, passing through a total of forty-two countries!

The first Ducati 175, first shown at Milan in 1956.

Monetti and Tartarini at the start of their round-the-world tour in 1957, sprinkled with champagne by Dr. Montano.

125 TS "Liviana."

Record for the "Siluro"

In 1956 Ducati decided to make an attempt at a series of world records over various distances, from one kilometer to 1000 kilometers. Records were highly popular at the time and followed with interest by the public, and so Ducati prepared a record-breaking machine based on the Gran Sport 100. Apart from small retouches to make it as efficient as possible, the modifications were limited to the mechanics and running gear (the engine was prepared by the constructor and fitted with an SS 25 carburetor). On the other hand, great changes were made to the bodywork, which was designed by Ducati in collaboration with an aero-nautical engineer and the Tibaldi body builder, which specialized in the working of sheet aluminum. The result was a beautiful "flatfish" fairing that improved the streamlining of the bike. It was tested by the company's own staff, but then entrusted to two private riders. Mario Carini was an established Milanese rider who used a Vespa in trials and a Mondial 125 or 175 in circuit races. His companion was Santo Ciceri who had recently made a good showing in the Trofeo Cadetti on a Ducati 100.

The attempt was made on Friday, November 30, under the eagle eye of timekeepers from the FMI (Italian Motorcycling Federa-tion). Given the uncertain weather, an elastic sheet of waterproof material was used to cover the gap between the rider and the fairing, so as to stop the rain getting in and improve streamlining. The day ended in triumph: forty-four world records fell (thirteen in the 100 class, thirteen in the 125 class and the same number in the 175 class). The remaining five new records went to the Ducati bike in the 250 class, still with an engine that had a capacity of only 100 cc! The "Siluro" (torpedo) completed its fastest lap at an average of over 170 kph, while the average over 1000 kilometers verged on 160 kph!

Marianna

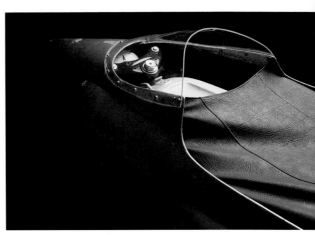

Ciceri gets ready at the start in front of the camera (photo Bonetti).

Facing page: Carini in full action on the Monza ring on November 30, 1956 (photo Bonetti).

Below and at bottom: the record-breaking Ducati 100 "Siluro" (Ducati Museum; owner Ducati Motor S.p.A.; photo Giovanni Marchi).

From the Family Album

The years of the Marianna, the period stretching from the debut in long-distance races in 1955 to the official participation in the 1958 world championships with the triple camshaft desmo, constituted only a short lapse of time, and yet a highly eventful one. Especially in Racing: thousands of kilometers flat out on the world's tracks or on the roads of Italy. Victories and defeats followed one another at an unheard-of rate, almost like a film being projected at two or three times the normal speed. There was nothing magic about this, Racing is like that: everything is decided in a few hours, and then all that is left are the sheets of paper listing the results. You turn the page and start thinking about the next race. Ducati's massive commitment in those years proved useful in many ways, above all in raising a generation of riders and bring-

ing technological improvements that were to serve the constructor for decades to come.

And then there was the finest hour of all, Ducati's triumph in the Nations Cup at Monza in 1958. The world title had slipped from its grasp, but Ducati did not miss the opportunity to remind the world that, without Gandossi's bad luck, it would have carried off the cup. And it did so very clearly, in a manner that brooked no argument, by wiping out the competition and taking the first five places. The triumph came late, but the fact is that Taglioni's triple-camshaft had been truly unbelievable that year: it did well not just on the track but also in the Motogiro (with Farné), showing that it could stand up to the rough conditions of long-distance Racing as well, and even won hands down in the Formula 2 and Formula 3 races in Italy.

Facing page: at top, a mechanic repairing the gas tank of a GS at the Motogiro (photo Publifoto); at bottom, on tour in the USA, Franco Farné is unable to resist the temptation to "ride" something really fast.

A famous image: at Monza, in the "Nations" Cup of 1958, the triple-camshaft bikes of Spaggiari (12) and Gandossi (8) ahead of the MVs of Provini (4) and Ubbiali (2). They are followed by two more Ducatis, ridden by Taveri (18) and Chadwick (20) (photo Publifoto).

Below left: Mario Carini (his goggles "sealed" to keep out the wind) with a friend on the record-breaking day at Monza (photo Bonetti).

Below right: the Mass celebrated by Cardinal Lercaro in the factory before the 1955 Motogiro (photo Breveglieri).

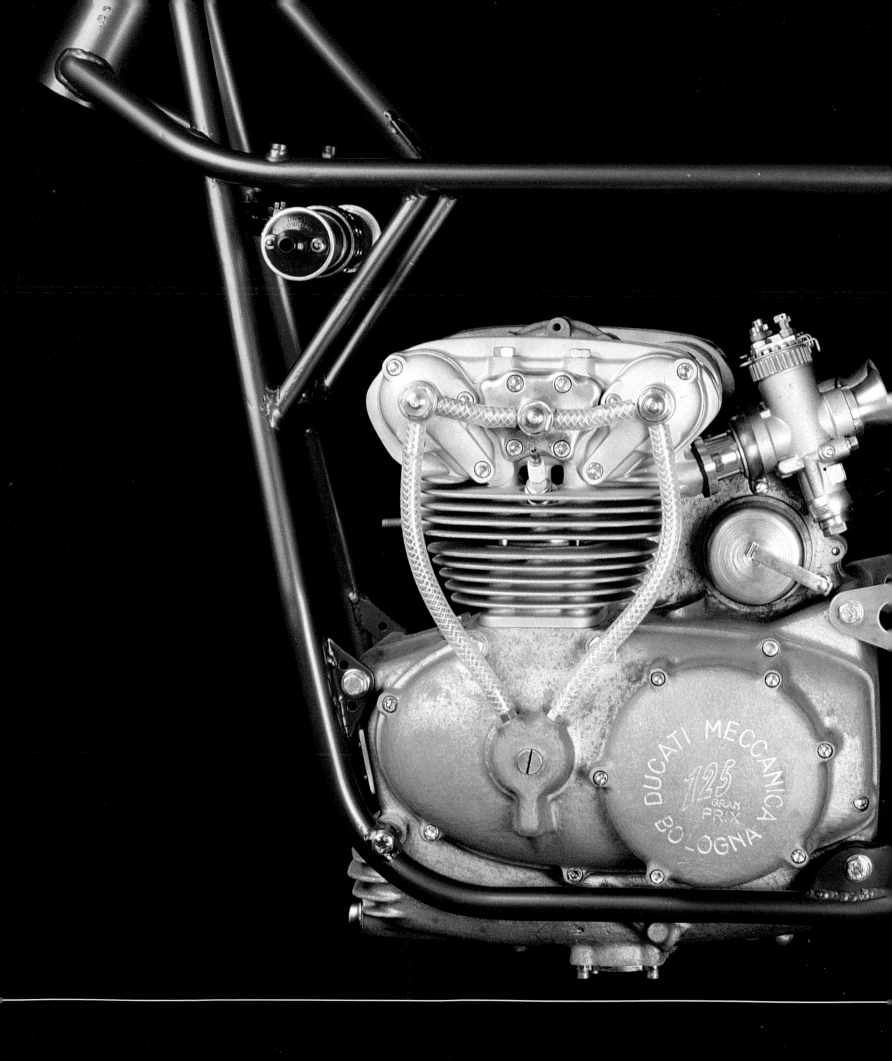

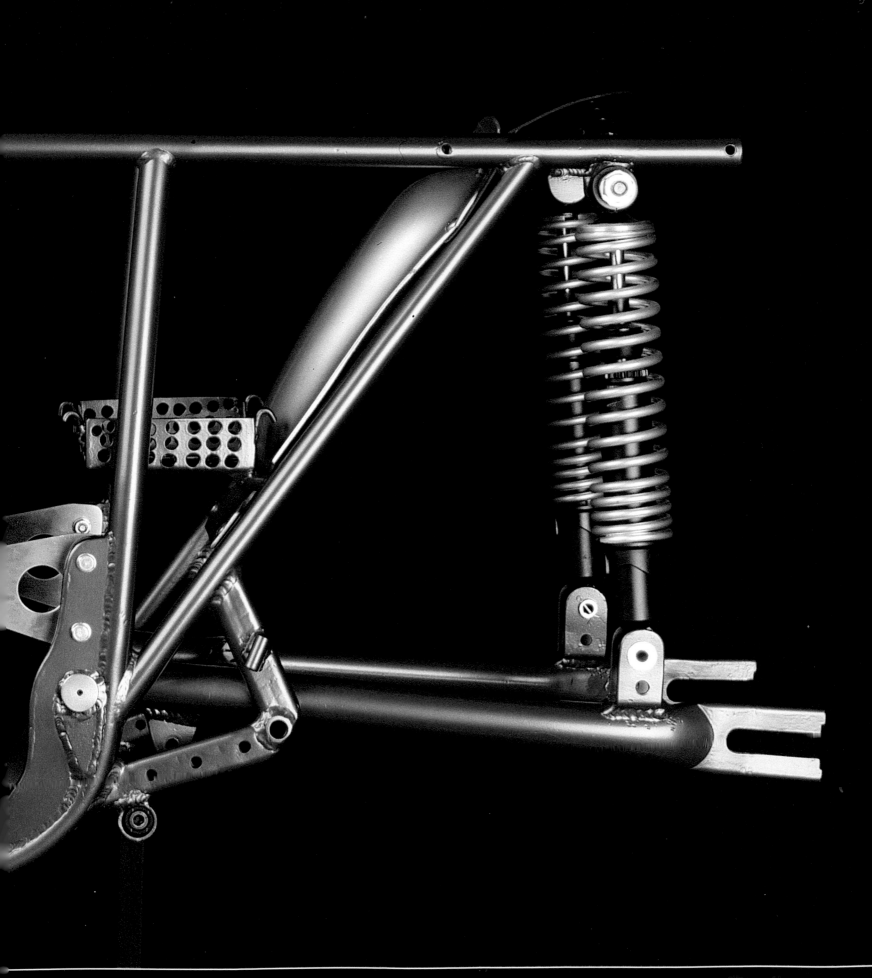

Triple-Camshaft In-Line Twins

Triple-Camshaft In-Line Twins

Mike Hailwood with a trophy won at home on the Ducati 250 twin.

A 125 Grand Prix that ended up in Northern Europe.

Right: a 175 Twin found by a collector, again in Northern Europe.

If you ask an enthusiast what are the typical configurations of a Ducati engine, the answer is bound to be: vertical single-cylinders and longitudinal 90° V twin-cylinders. There can be no doubt that these are the types of engine that have made the Italian company the great constructor that it is, but it should not be forgotten that, over the years, interesting machines with quite different configurations emerged from the Borgo Panigale plant. The picture has probably been distorted somewhat by the unflattering reputation of the in-line twin-cylinders produced during the seventies (350 and 500 cc), probably Ducati's biggest flop ever, but if we were to ignore this type of engine we would run the risk of overlooking some extremely interesting and rare bikes; bikes which help us to gain a better understanding of the company's history. Quite rightly, there is a whole room in the Museum devoted to in-line twin-cylinders, but the ones used on Racing bikes!

The first twin-cylinder designed by Taglioni was a 175 cc parallel vertical (bore and stroke 49 x 46·6 mm) with spring valve gear that was made in 1956 for the Formula Two races. The bike was shown at the Salone di Milano of that year and took part in the 1957 Motogiro. It was ridden by Leopoldo Tartarini (now a motorcycle manufacturer in his own right and President of Italjet) who could only reach the third stage before he was forced to retire. The bike had a maximum power of 22 hp at 11,000 rpm, and therefore a higher performance than the single-cylinder of the same capacity. However, it had an engine with a more restricted range and weighed considerably more, 112 kilograms to be exact. Recently a couple of photographs of a two-cylinder GP have turned up, much rebuilt by the person who salvaged it a long way from Bologna: the mysteries of the Racing bike, which often meets a truly strange fate and does not, unfortunately, always end up in the right hands or in a museum!

However, Taglioni continued to work on the concept of two cylinders, building a two-cylinder 125 for Grand Prix Racing in 1958 that was equipped with desmodromic valve gear (similar to that of the contemporary single-cylinder 125) driven by a gear train housed inside the engine. Only a few of these twin-cylinder 125s were made (no more than half a dozen according to Farné) and they were only rarely seen in competition. The most famous of them was the one that appeared in the historic "Nations Cup" of 1958, when, in the hands of Francesco Villa, it came third in the race that saw five Ducatis take the first five places. The twin-cylinder 125 had a bore and stroke of 42 x 45 mm and a maximum power of 22·5 hp at 14,000 revs, which took it to a top speed of 190 kph. The bike had a very restricted range of use and riders had trouble getting the best out of the engine, partly because it only had six gear ratios, which were probably insufficient to maintain the number

The ancestor of the Ducati GP Twins, a 175 ridden at the 1957 Motogiro by Leopoldo Tartarini. The valve gear was not desmodromic.

The 125 Grand Prix four-cylinder engine with twin-camshaft valve gear.

of revolutions at the right level. And while not much more powerful than the single-cylinder, it weighed considerably more. For this reason, and as a result of the constructor's decision to withdraw it from official competition, very few were ever raced. Its final appearances took place in 1966, when Bruno Spaggiari raced with it in Spain, under the colors of Mototrans.

Yet it was one of these bikes that attracted the interest of one of the most promising riders of the 1959 season, an Englishman called Mike Hailwood who was already displaying great skill (he came third with the Ducati in the 1959 125 championships). Unlike many of his penniless colleagues, Mike could count on the generous support of his father Stan, who was his real sponsor at the beginning of his career.

Taglioni prepared for Hailwood a fine twin-cylinder 250 with a bore and stroke of 55·25 x 55 mm, the same as the 125 with desmo valve gear. The distribution was driven by a central gear train. The bike delivered 37 hp at 11,600 revs and was equipped with a twin-tube cradle frame. Hailwood took the bike to England, along with the mechanic Oscar Folesani (from the Ducati Racing Department), and fitted it with such British running gear as a Roadholder fork, Girling shocks and a Smiths rev counter, though he kept the Oldani brakes. Hailwood's 250 won a few races at home but never really shone.

Mention should also be made of another design, perhaps the one of which Taglioni was least fond: the four-cylinder Grand Prix 125, probably the rarest and most "atypical" Ducati ever built. Taglioni designed this engine to overcome the limits of the single-cylinder (and even the twin-cylinder) in GP Racing. What came out was an air-cooled in-line four-cylinder with double overhead camshaft valve gear driven by a gear train in which, owing to the lack of space, it was not possibly to apply the desmodromic system. This meant it was "slack" and therefore not much to the liking of Taglioni, who had placed all his faith in the desmo. For this reason, and because of the closure of the Racing department, the four-cylinder vanished from the scene, at least until 1964, when the project was dusted off again at the request of Mototrans.

The engine – which had four valves per cylinder, a bore and stroke of 34·5 x 34 mm and an eight-speed gearbox, delivered 23 hp at 14,000 revs and was fed by four Dell'Orto carburetors with a 12 mm choke – was redeveloped and in 1965 Franco Farné tested the prototype mounted on a bike with a twin-tube cradle frame at Modena. Technical progress in the meantime, however, meant that some parts of the "four" were now fairly obsolete, while the power never exceeded the threshold of 24 hp, even though the number of revolutions had been raised to 14,000. One of the two engines that were built ended up in a technical Museum in the former Soviet Union, from where it was brought back to Italy a few years ago, together with the frame, which had found its way equally mysteriously to Yugoslavia. It is now in an Italian private collection.

Twin-Cylinder 125
Sophisticated Technology

It is inevitable that the objects on show in a museum lend themselves to different interpretations and that each visitor will assign a different value and importance to them. The ensemble (engine and frame) of the triple-camshaft twin-cylinder 125 constitutes a rare exhibit that perfectly sums up the historical moment from which its comes, i.e. the end of the fifties. From the technical viewpoint, this was one of the most fertile periods in the history of motorcycle Racing. In fact the international regulations, unlike those of today, gave a free hand to designers, who were able to try out every conceivable approach. Nowadays a Grand Prix 125, by regulation, can have only one cylinder and a maximum of six gear ratios. These strict limitations mean that in practice the bikes competing in the world championships closely resemble one another and, with very few exceptions, technical improvements are confined to the areas of electronics, tires and suspension. Lap times vary little from one bike to the next and this results in spectacular races, frequently decided by sprints on the final lap.

Now let us look at Ducati in 1958: just one year before its withdrawal from official participation in competition, the Bolognese constructor not only came out with its fantastic triple-camshaft single-cylinder desmo 125s, but also developed this twin-cylinder, which came third at Monza. At the same time, Taglioni was designing a double-camshaft four-cylinder! At bottom, during the fifties and sixties the greatest effort was put into the design and production of new engines (as has already been pointed out, Ducati went from the single-camshaft Marianna to double- and triple-camshaft engines in the same class in a very short space of time), while the frame and running gear remained more or less the same.

On show in the room of the Ducati Museum devoted to the In-line Twins, the drawing table of engineer Fabio Taglioni. On this table, later used by Gianluigi Mengoli, he designed the "four valve" engine.

Franco Farné riding another Grand Prix 125: the four-cylinder bike designed in 1958 and revamped in 1964.

Francesco Villa at the start of the 1958 "Nations Cup" with the 125 Twin; he came third.

113

Mike Hailwood's
Twins

There are pictures which encapsulate a moment in the history of motorcycling and one of these is the group portrait of Mike Hailwood, his father Stan, the mechanic Oscar Folesani and the Ducati 250, taken in 1960. On the bike is set a gigantic cup, with Mike's helmet hung over the top. It is held steady by a proud Hailwood Senior in a gray double-breasted suit. Mike (one of the greatest motorcycle riders of all time) is decked out in leathers while his trusty mechanic has his arm round his shoulders. The expression on Mike's face is that of a man who knows he has a great deal on his side (not least the financial support of his father which permitted him to order

bikes made to measure), but it is not hard to guess that this is a young man who was going to go a long way. Ducati, MV, Honda and then Racing cars (Formula One and Formula Two) and finally Ducati again, for his victory in the TT 1 world championships with the "bevel-gears" 900.

In the photograph we can also see the van in the background, with its sophisticated graphics and the logos of the bikes: a premonition of the slick professionalism of the present day. For Mike was a rider ahead of his time, as well as a man who was able to jump right back into the thick of things and win with a Ducati. It is no accident that all the men of the "old guard" at Ducati still re-

member Hailwood with a great deal of affection. A rider who drove Taglioni round the bend (the latter once said, as a joke, that his long feet, which stuck out sideways owing to the lack of space between the footrests and fairing on Ducatis, ruined the aesthetics of "his" bikes). But the bond between the two of them was very strong. Taglioni dealt with many champions, but the engineer's memories all revolve around Mike. There can be no doubt, Mike was a symbol for Ducati and the incredible fate that he met was a terrible loss. After a life of taking risks on the track, Mike was killed by a truck that crushed him in his car while he was waiting at a railroad grade crossing.

Triple-Camshaft In-Line Twins

The Hailwood father and son with Folesani, bike, trophy and van; a decidedly professional team for the time.

Facing page: Mike Hailwood on a in-line twin-cylinder 250 cc Ducati.

Folesani at work on Hailwood's 250; the technician accompanied "Mike the bike" during his racing season in Great Britain.

The limpid design of the 250-350 cc triple-camshaft twin-cylinder (photo Edisport).

Low-Powered Engines

Two-Strokes and Outboard Motors

The sixties saw Ducati engaged on the front of small-capacity engines and even scooters. In fact it continued to produce "pushrod and rocker arm" engines derived from the 98: curiously, they were developed by lowering the capacity to 85 cc. Then there was the inexpensive series of 125 cc bikes with parallel valves. Called Cadets, they were honest motorcycles that cost little more than a moped. But Ducati also produced two-stroke engines, used for the Piuma and Brisk mopeds, the Rolly and the Brio scooter, which was available in 48 and 100 cc versions. Then there was the off-road moped known as the Cacciatore (Falcon for the foreign market), which had forced air cooling and a double rear sprocket that allowed the gear ratio to be reduced when riding off the road. The company also sold sports mopeds, again with two-stroke engines, like the Setter and Sport (produced with a capacity of 80 cc as well for sale abroad) and the more powerful and even more sporty-looking SL. Around 1970, two new series of off-road bikes were brought out. Curiously, they were both given the same famous name: Scrambler. The first was a 125 single-camshaft four stroke, while the other had a two-stroke engine of either 50 or 100 cc.

The quest for new markets also led to a complete range of outboard motors for use on leisure and fishing craft.

Triple-Camshaft In-Line Twins

Two small Ducatis in 1964: the Brio scooter and the Piuma moped, both with two-stroke engines.

Facing page: in 1964 the Cacciatore 48 was produced for hunting and leisure use.

FUORIBORDO

DUCATI

Contemporary advertising leaflets: Ducati out-board engines and the Sport 80 with two-stroke engine and three-speed gearbox.

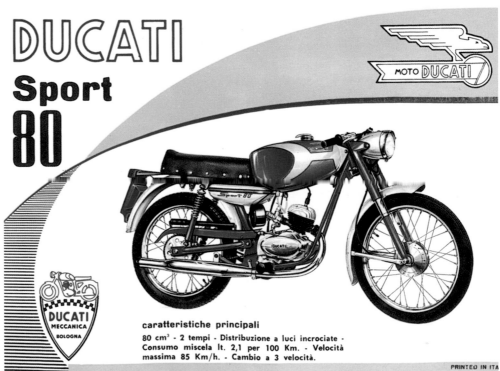

DUCATI
Sport
80

CUCCIOLO **5**

5 HP

caratteristiche principali

80 cm³ - 2 tempi - Distribuzione a luci incrociate - Consumo miscela lt. 2,1 per 100 Km. - Velocità massima 85 Km/h. - Cambio a 3 velocità.

Triple-Camshaft Twin-Cylinder 125

ENGINE – Derived from the "175 Formula 2" built at the end of 1956 and raced in the 1957 Motogiro, it was an air-cooled in-line vertical twin cylinder. It had a bore and stroke of 42·5 x 45 mm and on the bench produced a maximum power of 22·5 hp at around 14,000 revs. Thus the difference from the triple-camshaft single cylinder (rated at about 20 hp) was not so great. The distribution, with two valves per cylinder, was driven by a gear train housed in the middle of the engine, in other words between the cylinders. It had a six-speed gearbox, with primary reduction by gears, and a wet, multi-plate clutch.

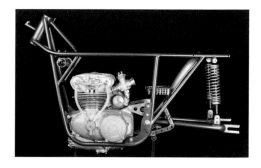

THE BIKE – According to Farné the twin-cylinder was a sturdy bike with no problems, which was pushed to really high rotation levels on the test bench (there is talk of 17,000 revs). Yet it is also said to have been less easy to handle than the single cylinder and it was undoubtedly heavier, with a dry weight of at least 92 kilograms, a couple more than the other bike. And this is no small matter in a 125. One is left with the suspicion that if a bit more attention had been devoted to its development, a lot could have been achieved.

Frame and engine of the 125 twin-cylinder restored by Rino Caracchi e Mario Recchia and exhibited in the Ducati Museum.

FRAME, FORKS AND RUNNING GEAR – The supporting structure of the twin-cylinder GP consisted of a twin closed cradle frame in steel tubing that encased the engine at the bottom. It had hydraulic front forks and a swinging-arm rear suspension with twin hydraulic shocks. The front and rear brakes were Amadori drums with conspicuous air intakes. It should be noted that this bike performed very well on the Monza track, one of the fastest in the world at the time. This offers further confirmation of the fact that it functioned well at high revolutions, an advantage on fast circuits. On more tortuous tracks, however, the low number of gear ratios and the restricted range of use put it at a disadvantage.

The 250-350 twin-cylinder engine (photo Edisport).

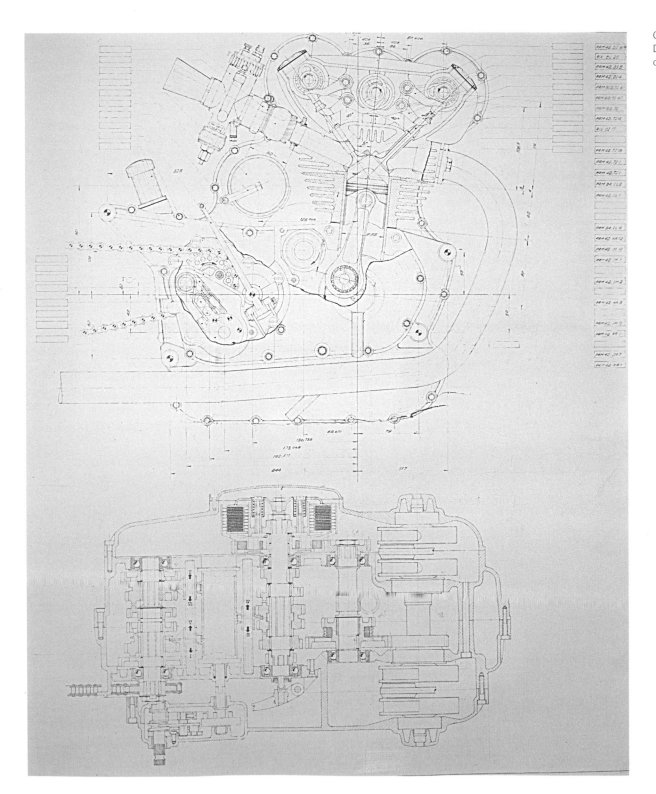

Original design of the
Ducati triple-camshaft twin-
cylinder engine.

Apollo. The American Colossus

In 1963 the Berliner brothers, who sold Ducati bikes on the affluent American market, entrusted Taglioni's technical staff with a really ambitious project: a rival to the Harley-Davidson, in other words the biggest and most powerful motorcycle ever built, at least by a European manufacturer since the Second World War. In all likelihood, this bike, which had from the outset technical specifications that were truly unusual for the time (and would still be so today), was intended to offer an alternative choice to the many different police departments in the United States: the idea of orders from them made the importers' mouths water. The Berliners' commitment to the project was wholehearted, as is evident from the fact that the bike (or rather the prototype that was actually constructed) bore the logo Db, i.e. Ducati Berliner, on its gas tank. The "monster" saw the light of day in 1964: a gigantic machine with a capacity of 1257 cc and a four-cylinder 90° V configuration (bore and stroke 84·5 x 56 mm), rocker-arm and pushrod overhead valve gear and four Dell'Orto TT 24 carburetors. It had a rating of 80 hp at 6000 rpm, but there were also plans to produce a Sport version with a rating of 100 hp, a truly fantastic power for the time. The beautiful thing about this colossus was that it was not just a design on the drawing-board or a "dream bike" to be presented at shows. It was subjected to lengthy road tests, and it was precisely during these that its main defect emerged: at the time there were no motorcycle tires capable of standing up to that kind of power and torque. Most of the tests were carried out by Librenti (who unfortunately died some time ago) but Farné also gave it a try; his opinion is unequivocal: "It was like driving a truck. I didn't like it." It is not hard to sympathize with the judgment of the technician, a lover of sporty and essential bikes.

In an attempt to make it roadworthy the power was reduced to around 65 hp and it was fitted with special Pirelli tires measuring 5 x 16, but the Apollo never got beyond the prototype stage and very few of them were built (only two in fact) along with some odd engines. Today only one survives. It is interesting to note that its electric starter motor was taken from an automobile, to be precise a Fiat 1100. It had a dry weight of 270 kilograms and a wheel base of 1537 millimeters.

The Apollo engine on display at the Ducati Museum.

Facing page and right: the prototype of the Apollo.

Mototrans. The Spanish Ducati

It was in 1957 that Ducati began to penetrate the Spanish market, through a company called Mototrans and based in Barcelona. This was not just an importer, for over the years Mototrans designed motorcycles of its own and went on producing "wide-casing" single-cylinder bikes up until 1982.

Mototrans was also involved in the world of sports, especially in the mid-sixties when, under its own colors and with the support of an experienced Racing division that included a number of Italian technicians like Armaroli, it took part in local competitions with Farné, Spaggiari and Villa. Nor should we forget the four-cylinder Grand Prix bike that it built in the same decade to the design of the Italian tech-

nician Savelli. Mototrans went in for long-distance Racing too: in addition to the races held on the punishing Spanish city circuits, true corridas run at Bilbao, Seville, La Coruña and Valladolid, great importance was given to the 24 Hours in Barcelona, an exhausting and highly popular endurance race. Famous riders were Angel Nieto, Ricardo Fargas, Juan Garriga, Benjamin Grau and Salvador Cañellas. Mototrans even sold bikes made in Spain on the Italian market, such as the Scrambler 250, as well as carrying out independent projects like the Strada and Vento series (single-cylinder road bikes), which had different frames from the Italian ones, or the 24 Horas and Electronic, which had different bores and strokes.

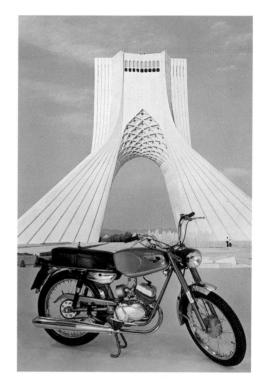

A very rare document attesting to the joint-venture between Ducati and Taheri of Teheran (Iran) for the manufacture of small-capacity bikes. Engine and components were all made in Italy. The project was abandoned after the revolution that deposed the Shah in 1979.

The Scrambler 250, built in Spain as well by Mototrans; note the Telesco fork.

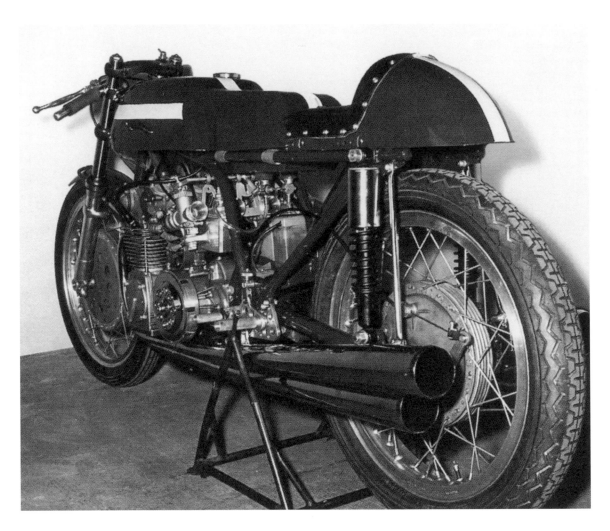

The four-cylinder 250-350 built in Spain (photo Edisport).

Four-valve twin carburetor head for the single-cylinder "bevel gears" engines, also built in Spain (photo Edisport).

The 50 TT moped, made by Mototrans of Barcelona.

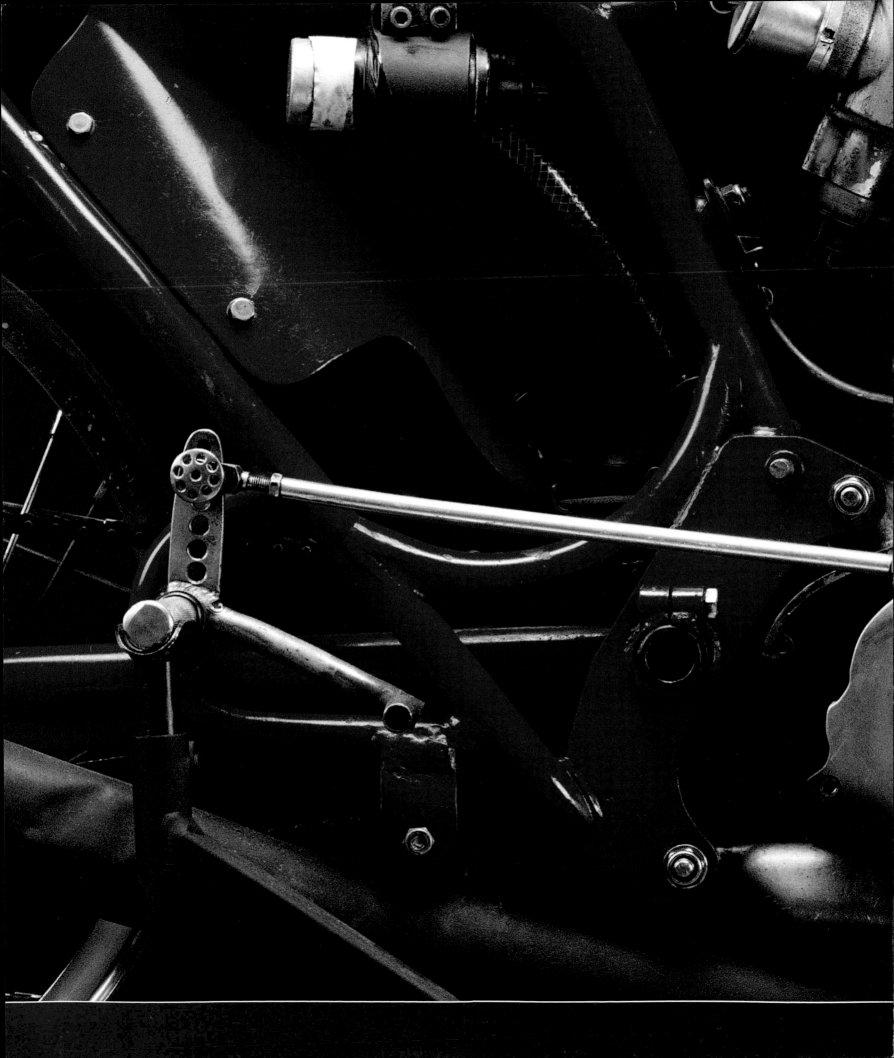

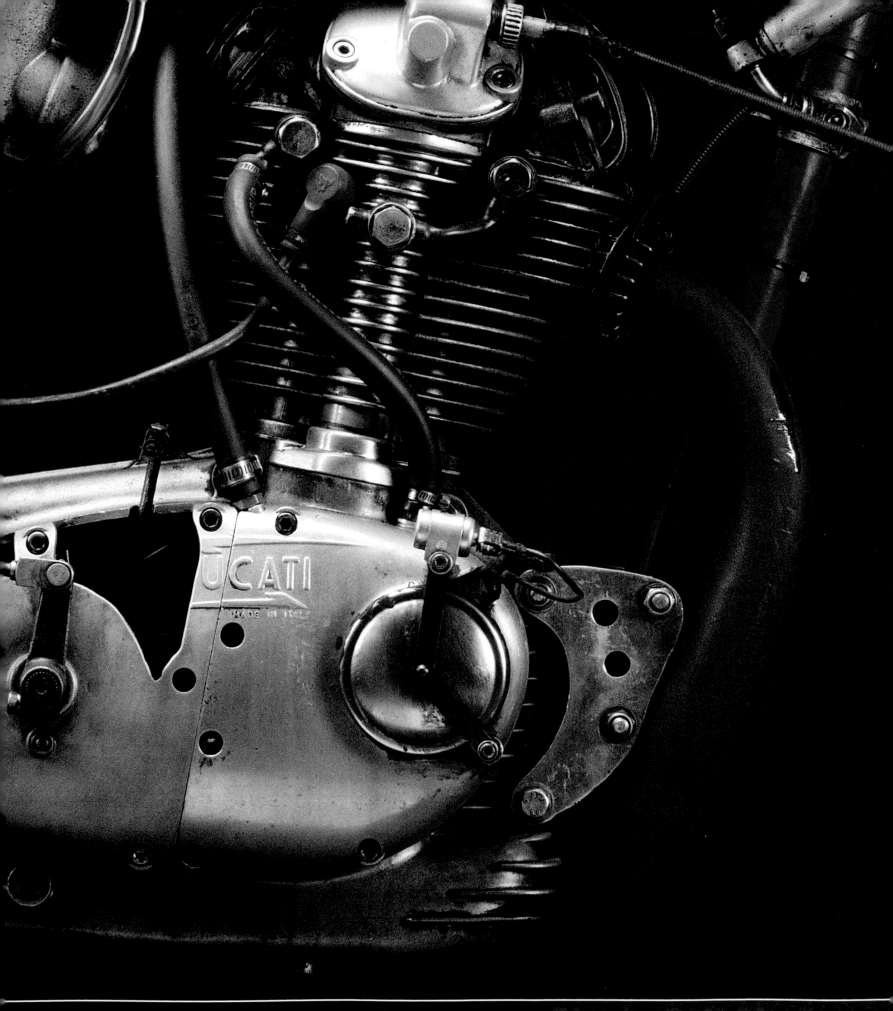

Single-Cylinders

Single-Cylinders

The Desmo 350 of 1973, the sporting single cylinder par excellence.

To understand Ducati production in the sixties and seventies (as well as the constructor's participation in racing, almost always on a semi-official basis), it is necessary to take a look at the evolution of single-camshaft single-cylinder engines and their division into "narrow casings" and "wide casings." Related to the Marianna, the Ducati single cylinders quickly grew in capacity from 100-125 cc to 175 cc and then, in the early sixties, to the 250 cc of the Diana model. This was already able to offer a great deal of satis-faction to the motorcyclists of the time, given that in ideal conditions (straight-through exhaust, choke wide-open and the rider in a head-down position), the bike could reach 140 kilometers an hour. This sports bike was followed, in 1965, by the even more combative Mach 1 250, an authentic classic of its time that took the concept of the sporty single-cylinder Italian-style bike to its logical conclusion.

The "narrow-casing" series left room for the Sebring model (intended chiefly for export to the US) to be taken to 350 cc, but it was clear that the design had to be brought up to date, especially in view of the need to make further inroads into the American market, always hungry for bikes with a greater capacity. In 1966 Ducati had begun to study engines and running gear better suited to an increase in power and performance. It was this that led to the new "wide casings." On the bench and the track, the new engines won the confidence of the designers (principal among them, of course, Taglioni, who found himself backing his concept of the single-camshaft single cylinder yet again). Thus the first bike equipped with this type of engine, the Mark 3, was brought out at the end of 1967.

The new engines were distinguished by two crankcase halves of die-cast aluminum that were much larger than before and joined together vertically. In addition, they had wider rear attachments to the frame (in order to make the structure at the back of the bike more robust, which was also the reason for the large triangular plates in the various Scramblers, Mark 3s and Desmos) and a more capacious sump that held two and a half liters of oil instead of the two in the narrow casings. The starting mechanism was made more sturdy as well. But these were not the only changes: in fact the two types of engine had little in common. With the advent of the "wide casings", Ducati production took a significant step forward,

An ancestor of the "wide casing" single cylinders: the Diana 250 Mark III in decidedly sporty guise.

From 1965 onward Ducati raced with the single-cylinder machines derived from road bikes: here we see Farné in the USA with a 250.

The splendid Mark 3 D 350 of 1969 with its headlight screen, tachometer and gas tank with two caps.

a fact borne out by the arrival of such popular models as the Scrambler (with capacities of 250, 350 and 450 cc), the Mark 3 (with spring or desmo valve gear, but again in the same three capacities), the T/TS (closer to touring bikes in conception), the specialized off-road RT and, finally, the Desmo, which remained in the Ducati catalogue until 1964, the last sports single cylinder to do so.

Ducati had abandoned international Racing in 1959, but the fire was still smoldering under the ashes: whatever the circumstances, there was always someone at the company with his mind on competition. Identifying a predecessor for the racing bikes of the sixties (though the single cylinders actually went on racing well after the end of the decade) is no easy task, but perhaps it can be identified in the Formula 3 175s and the 250 "specials" raced by Farné in the United States in 1965.

The single cylinders entrusted to Farné underwent considerable technical development, as can be seen from the existence of a fine bike built in 1966, with twin ignition, an engine with a rated maximum power of 32 hp at 10,500 revs and a weight of only 87 kilograms. But it was with the arrival of the "wide casings" that interesting proposals began to emerge for private individuals competing in the junior and senior races and hill climbs in the 250, 350 and 500 cc categories. From 1968 onward, the constructor no longer played an official part in the development of these bikes (which were almost always hand-built), but the indirect support of the Racing division and of people associated with Ducati (such as the skilled technicians Caracchi, Nepoti and Librenti) produced excellent results. Back in 1967 (and so well ahead of mass production) Farné tested a 350 with sand-cast casings that anticipated the new series of single-cylinders. At the start of the spring races (international, but which qualified for the Italian title) a 250 (35 hp) and a 350 (41 hp) were ready to be put through their paces by Roberto Gallina and Gilberto Parlotti. These bikes, which were followed a year later by a 450 (50 hp) intended for the 500 category, were equipped with twin ignition and a desmodromic cylinder head. In 1968 the leading rider Bruno Spaggiari took third place in the Italian 350 championships (he was beaten by Agostini and Pasolini, on an MV and a Benelli respectively). The next year, Spaggiari managed to do very well in races that were otherwise monopolized by the multicylinder bikes. The image of Bruno leading Phil Read and the Yamaha under the rain at Imola is one that cheers the sporting heart, so great was the difference in power between the two bikes. The adventure of the Ducati single cylinders continued in 1970 under the colors of the Speedy Gonzales stable, which had the support of Ducati and Spaggiari as leading rider. The 1970 bikes had production die-cast casings and 42 mm carburetors ("only because Dell'Orto didn't make them any bigger," says Farné, who collaborated on the project) and were prepared with maniacal care. The frame and rear suspension, for example, were heavily reinforced at critical points, while the fork was a Marzocchi (before a Ceriani GP had been used); the front brake was a 230-mm Fontana in magnesium alloy (though the 250 usually had a "small" Fontana or an Oldani). While the 450 of 1970 (and by this time the Japanese were already producing two strokes for sale to private individuals) had no chance of victory, it still managed good results. It is worth mentioning the fact that a four-valve cylinder head was also tried out for this bike. Ducati "wide casings" competed in the senior races up until the early seventies thanks to the commitment of the "crack" rider from Lugo, Sergio Baroncini, but it was in hill climbing that they produced their best results: riders like Marcello Peruzzi and Augusto Brettoni dominated the timed hill trials right up to the end of the decade.

Single-Cylinder 250

A Truly "Private" Bike

Although the fine 250 on show in the museum, preserved in exactly the condition in which it ceased its sporting career in 1978, never raced in official colors, it perfectly embodies the spirit of the single-cylinder racing bikes of those years. Bikes that competed at every level, on the track and in hill climbs, without showing much deference to their Japanese rivals, who were now offering high-performance models even to ordinary customers.

As has already been said, after the experiments carried out in the sixties and continued up until the end of the decade, the constructor no longer took a direct interest in its single cylinders, leaving the job to outsiders. Nevertheless, they did receive help in terms of know-how and the odd special part, slipped more or less secretly out of the Borgo Panigale plant. The decision is understandable: in 1970 Ducati had embarked on the adventure of the twin cylinders (first for Grand Prix Racing and then for the road) and thus had more important things to think about.

But the chronic "hunger" for competitive motorcycles led quite a few private racers to find a way round the obstacle. Look at how this 250 was created, for example. In 1970, starting from a Scrambler 250 (!) and, according to the owner, using frames from a small series produced by Verlicchi that were superior, this essential racing bike was prepared for the rider Claudio Bergami. The frame was strengthened at key points (steering head, plates and forks) and given Marzocchi shocks (others from Ceriani were used when funds were tight), a steering damper, two 18-inch alloy rims and two Fontana magnesium brakes with the same diameter of 210 mm. The bike was fitted with an elongated fiberglass gas tank and a saddle with a tailpiece. The finishing touches were two half handlebars, set-back pedal controls and a Veglia Racing tachometer. More work was probably done on the engine: it was an ordinary "spring" motor and therefore

not desmodromic (this was a fairly common choice among private competitors), prepared by "special recipes" passed from hand to hand in the manner of a secret club. In practice, the engine had twin ignition (with two coils), a special connecting rod (though the standard ones were perfectly good too), Dell'Orto SS 40 carburetor and a straight-through trumpet exhaust, camshafts with pronounced lifts, while painstaking attention was paid to every detail. The maximum power was over 35 hp, with a marked propensity for the engine to give its best at over 8000 and up to almost 12,000 revs.

The bike is owned by Marcello Peruzzi, who used it with success in timed Tuscan hill climbs like the Alberi-Montaione and Saline-Volterra up until 1978. In one race, the record he set in the 250 four-stroke class still stands.

With a similar bike, his son Alberto has been dominating the 250 category in Group 5 (races for vintage motorcycles) for a long time now.

In the races for vintage bikes held today the Ducati 250 dominates the field (photo Gori).

On double-spread and following page: the 250 on which rider Marcello Peruzzi raced (Ducati Museum; owner Marcello Peruzzi; photo Giovanni Marchi). The tachometer (left) is marked with a red line that the rider must not exceed to avoid damaging the engine.

Franco Farné in 1967 during testing of the single-cylinder 350 (photo Zagari).

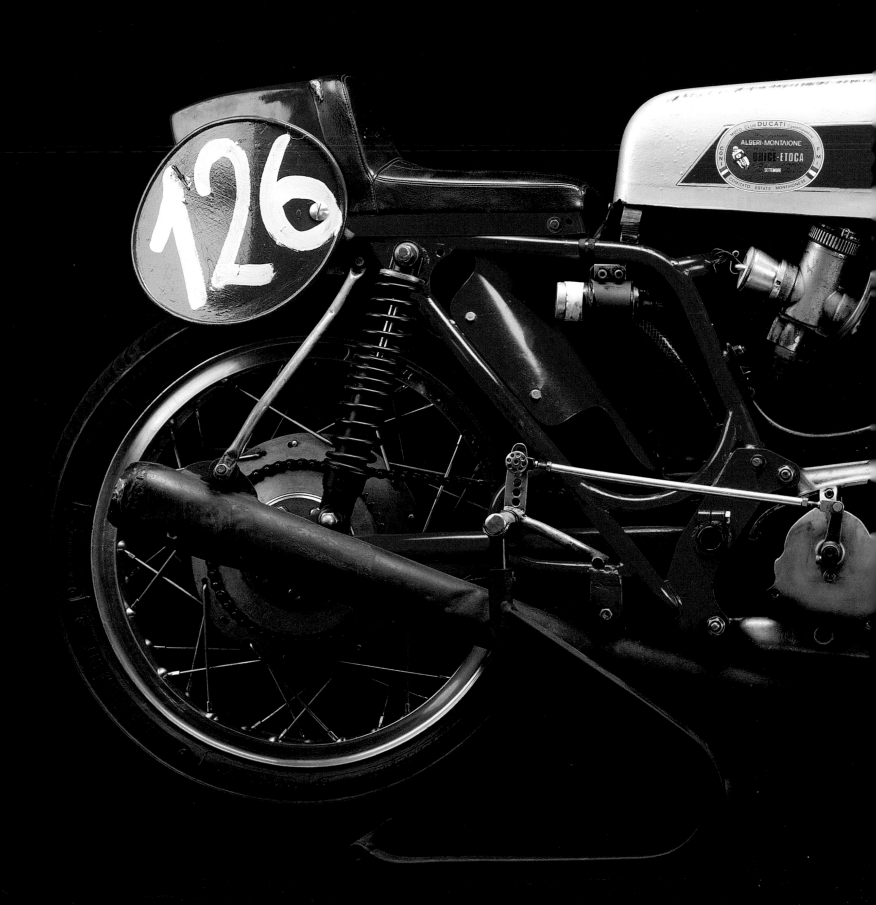

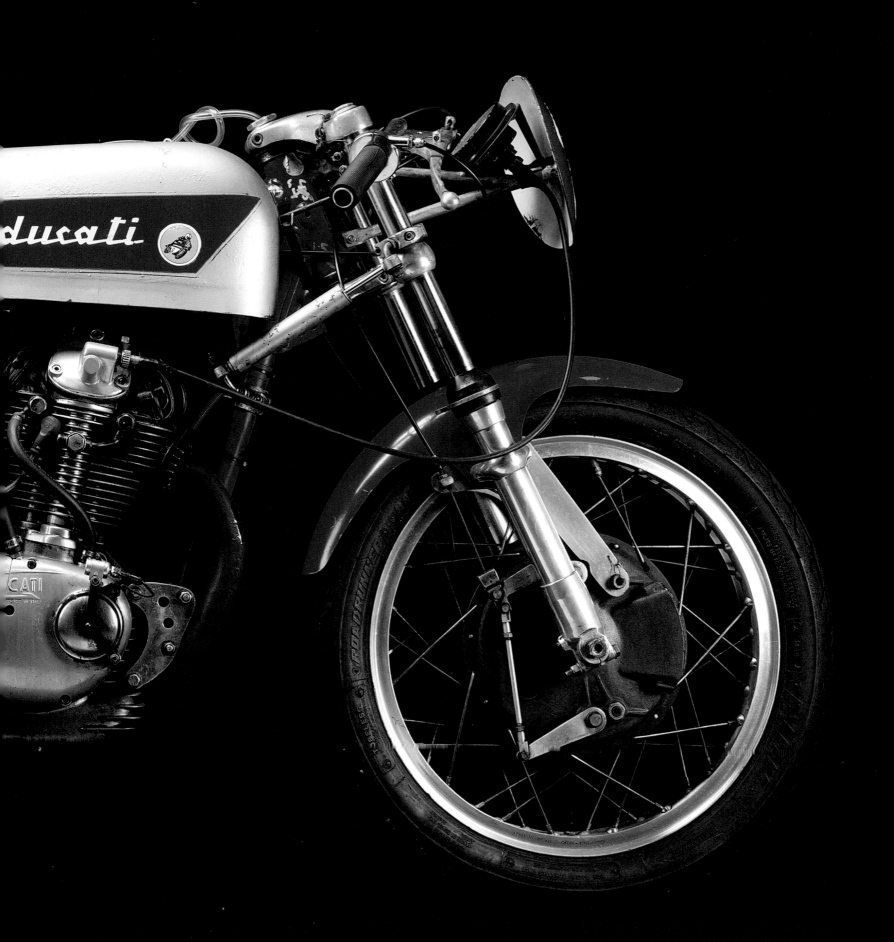

Mass Production

Using the new "wide-casing" engines, Ducati came out with new models from 1968 onward: three "families" in particular were to prove very important for the company's future, especially where exports were concerned, given their popularity in the United States and Northern Europe. The Mark 3s (250-350-450) were direct descendants of the sportier single-cylinders in the "narrow-casing" series. The earliest versions in particular, characterized by fuel tanks with twin caps and Racing-type instrumentation (some models just had a tachometer protected by a small alloy fairing), are beautiful examples of Italian design and still sought-after by collectors today. Very soon (1969) these bikes were made available in the D version as well, i.e. with a desmodromic cylinder head, making them even more attractive to those interested in sport. But Ducati had another ace up its sleeve, the Desmo model which, especially in the first version, dated 1971 and recognizable by its unmistakable metalized livery (with silvery specks embedded in the glass fiber of the superstructures), represents the highest level ever attained by a sports single-cylinder road bike.

The third family, to which we shall devote a well-deserved section of its own, was that of the Scramblers, bikes which anticipated the phenomenon of the enduros and sold well all over the world. The Scramblers also gave rise to the RT (road and track) models, which were used in American desert races and by the Italian national team in the 1971 International Six Day Trial on the Isle of Man.

Returning to the Desmos (again available in the three classic capacities), it is worth recalling the second version (1973-74) which had electronic ignition and a gas tank made of sheet metal instead of fiberglass. The last models to be produced had a Brembo 280-mm-diameter front disc brake. The final version of the Mark 3 was much more of a touring bike than the Desmo. The T and TS, which in Italy were sold chiefly to municipal police forces and other motorized corps, were even more steady and tranquil and had a far less elegant appearance than the extremely sporty Desmos. In 1974 a 239-cc version was produced for the French market, where the country's legislation placed this capacity in a lower tax band. Very few of them were ever seen in Italy...

DUCATI 250 350 Mark 3 d *DESMO

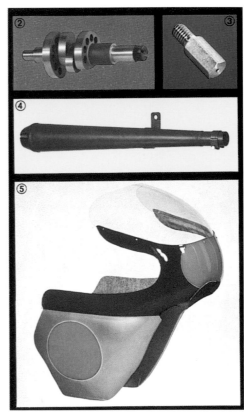

350 Mark 3 D
DESMO

250 Mark 3 D
DESMO

On double-page spread: illustrations from a brochure advertising the Mark 3D. On request, Ducati supplied a kit made up of camshafts, jets, exhaust and fairing to convert the single-cylinder Mark 3 into a sports bike.

Desmo 450
Roar of Thunder

To think about entering a Grand Prix in 1970 with a four-stroke single-cylinder (the scene was dominated by MV, while the best bike available to private competitors was the two-stroke three-cylinder Kawasaki) was something verging on madness. But, as we all know, passion drives people to do strange things... With the help of the constructor several special single-cylinder 450s were built in 1970 for the Emilian stable Speedy Gonzales and, above all, to suit the talents of a rider inextricably bound to Ducati, Bruno Spaggiari.

A number of technicians with links to the company worked on the bike, including Farné, Librenti, Caracchi and Nepoti, and it used the best material available on the market. Great care was taken over its presentation, but there were no "esoteric" parts made for the purpose. The casings, for instance, were taken from production bikes, while the heads were skillfully worked by specialists to get the best out of them, even if it was a question of fractions of a horsepower scraped together wherever possible. The 450 was fitted with a Dell'Orto SS 42 carburetor and had a long exhaust pipe. Later, shorter ones were tried out in an attempt to improve output at low revs, something useful in hill climbs, for instance. The outstanding features of the frame and running gear were the reinforcements to the frame (extended to the rear suspension as well), the Marzocchi forks and the 210-mm Fontana brake. On the bike on show at the Ducati Museum the front brake is a massive Fontana 230, the most powerful available at the time for large-capacity bikes.

With Spaggiari driving, the bike took fifth place at Milano Marittima and a fourth at Cesenatico in the international races held at the beginning of the season: frankly no more could be expected of it. The 450s were a great stimulus to the Ducati technicians, who built replicas of Spaggiari's bikes. The one raced by Speedy Gonzales was passed on to the Romagnese rider Baroncini the following year, and, with it, he achieved very good results.

On this page and the following double-spread: the Desmo 450 used by the rider Nencioni (Ducati Museum; owner Carlo Saltarelli; photo Giovanni Marchi). These "specials" were derived from the bike built for Spaggiari in 1970. The powerful front brake (right) is made by Fontana and has a diameter of 230 millimeters.

Facing page: from 1971 onward Baroncini raced with what used to be Spaggiari's bikes. Here we see him in action at Modena.

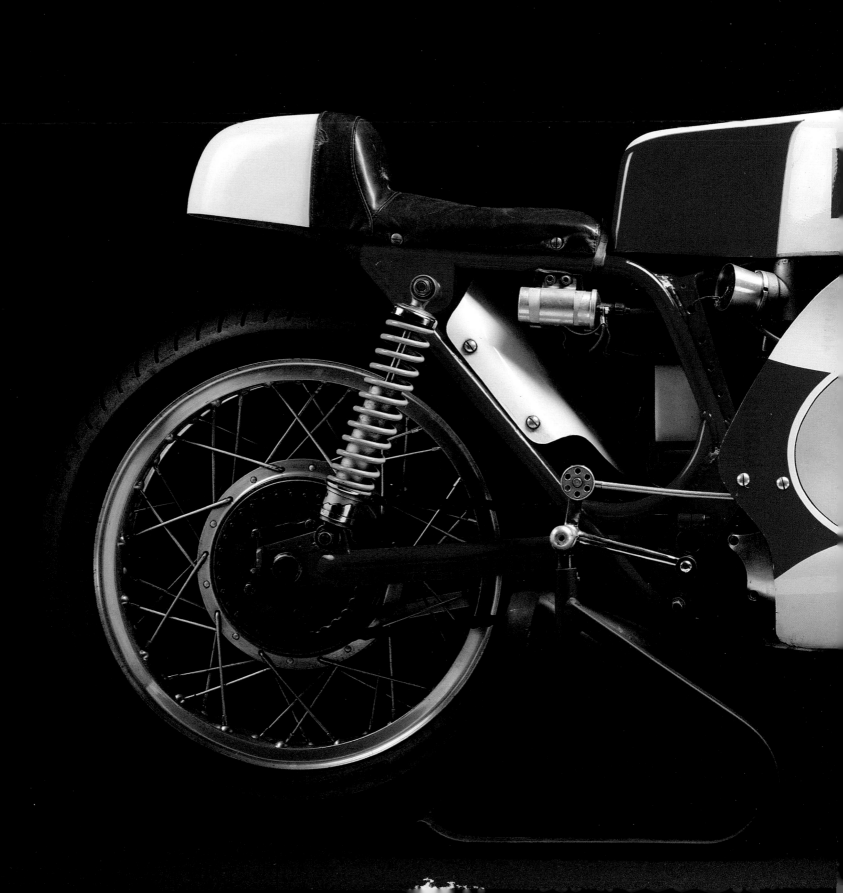

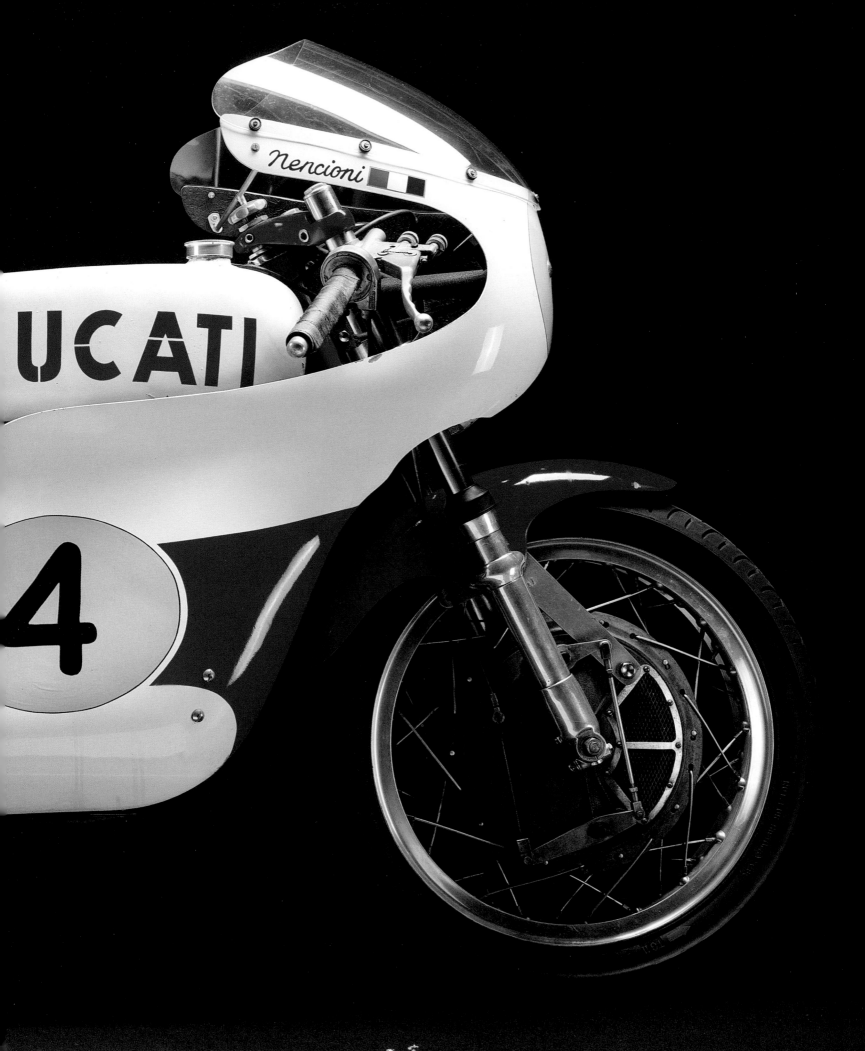

Desmo Corsa

ENGINE – Air-cooled vertical four-stroke single cylinder, with 10° forward angle configuration. Head and block made of light alloy (with cast-iron liner). Bore and stroke 74 x 57·8 mm (250), 76 x 75 mm (350), 86 x 75 mm (450); capacities: 249, 340, 436 cc. Compression ratio 10:1. Desmodromic single overhead camshaft with bevel-gear and two valves. Dell'Orto SS 40 carburetor (for the 250 and 350), and 42 for the 450. Contact-breaker ignition with points and two sparkplugs (one 10 mm and one 14 mm). Wet sump forced lubrication. Multi-plate clutch. Five-speed gearbox.

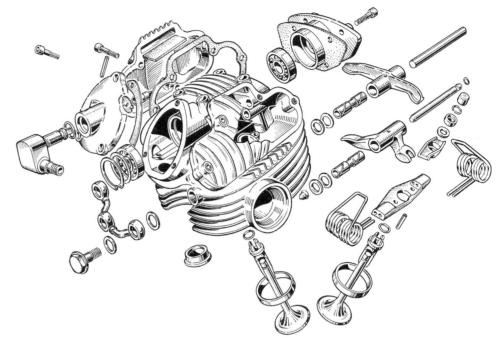

FRAME, FORKS AND RUNNING GEAR – Simplex open-cradle tubular-steel frame. Telescopic hydraulic front forks, swinging-arm rear suspension with two shocks. Brakes: 210-mm (or 230, in some cases) drum at the front; drum at the back. 18-inch light-alloy rims. In these frames the engine closed the structure at the bottom and was anchored to plates that were an integral part of the frame.

DIMENSIONS, WEIGHT AND PERFORMANCE – Length 2000 mm, wheelbase 1360 mm, dry weight around 110 kg. Maximum power: 35 hp at 11,500 revs for the 250, 41 at 10,500 for the 350 and 50 at 9000 for the 450. Top speed: dependent on ratios. Fiberglass body, fuel tank, saddle and fenders. Light-alloy Menani controls on the handlebar. Veglia Racing mechanical tachometer.

Fabio Taglioni, the engineer who made Ducati's fortune.

Original design of the Ducati single-cylinder engine.

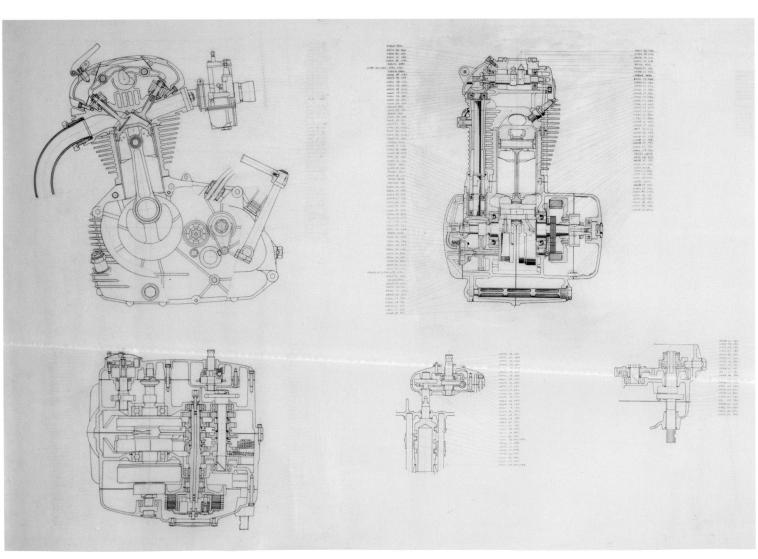

The Time Trials

In the sixties the "pre-championship" phase of the contest for the world motorcycle title did not consist of trials staged all over the world as it does today. Traveling such distances was unthinkable at the time, the costs being far too high for a sport as strapped for cash as motorcycling. Yet there was a splendid opportunity to get some practice: the Spring Time Trials ("Temporada di Primavera"), a series of races that counted toward the Italian championships and commenced at Modena (on the old airdrome-cum-race track) on the feast day of St. Christopher and then continued on the urban circuits of the Adriatic coast (Milano Marittima, Cesenatico, Riccione, Rimini). Courses laid out in the streets and avenues of seaside resorts, offering them the chance to get the tourist season off to an early start and permitting an enthusiastic public to watch the world's best riders in action and get a close look at the new bikes. All the Italians were there to contest the national title, while foreign riders were happy to come to Romagna, drawn by the truly warm welcome they received and the excellent opportunities for making some money. Anyone who lived through that period will have found that everything afterwards seemed a little flat. The script was always the same: the rival of the moment (Pasolini, Bergamonti, Hailwood) challenged Giacomo Agostini and his MV, but there was more... For instance the Honda and Yamaha teams, the Suzuki 125s and their eighteen-speed gearboxes and, above all, a large number of private riders hoping to make a breakthrough.

Ducatis filled up the starting grids in the senior and especially the junior races and, every so often, even managed to trouble the big names and their multicylinder bikes. As Spaggiari did at Imola in 1968 when, under the rain, he managed to fend off Phil Read and his powerful two-stroke Yamaha, literally sending wild the spectators, who naturally supported the Italian rider – thrilling years, undiluted passions. Right-angle bends, rotaries that would be packed with tourists just a few weeks later, became a theater for fierce duels. The riders had to contend with two special hazards on these improvised circuits: the wind-borne sand that made curves treacherous and the roots of pine trees, which made bumps in the asphalt and caused the bikes to buck like broncos.

Spectacular flight by Spaggiari at Cesenatico in 1968, with both wheels of his 350 off the ground (photo Bernagozzi).

Facing page: again at Cesenatico, but in 1969, Spaggiari ahead of Bergamonti and Milani's Aermacchi (photo Edisport).

Right: Spaggiari, in the rain at Imola in 1968, fends off the Yamaha 250 of Phil Read (photo Edisport).

Below: Gilberto Parlotti, another rider with close ties to the Italian constructor.

Scrambler

The ancestor of the Scrambler was the Motocross 200 produced for the US market at the beginning of the sixties, which was soon followed by the Scrambler 250 with a narrow-casing engine (1962). These bikes, aimed chiefly at the American market, underwent constant development (spurred on by the importer Berliner) until 1968, the year when the true Scramblers with "wide-casing" engines were brought out, first in the 250 and 350 versions and then, in 1969, the 450. The Scrambler series included a few bikes with desmo cylinder heads and was subjected to

continual technical tinkering (Dell'Orto VHB carburetors instead of SSIs, the lighting system, electronic ignition, the front brake) right up until 1974, the year in which production was halted. It should be noted that many 250s were made in Spain and sold in Italy as well. They were recognizable by their Telesco forks and Amal carburetors.

There were plenty of good reasons for the Scrambler's commercial success: to start with it had an excellent frame (which was even used for racing on the track, something that is probably unique in world production) and an

engine that was really perfect for a bike of this kind. It was certainly not the fastest of its day (there were already production bikes around that could do 200 kph and more), but its "all-round" performance (acceleration, ease of handling, steering), combined with a perfectly-centered riding position, made it one of the most delightful mechanical toys you could lay your hands on. In addition, it had really good looks: rounded lines, at one and the same time classic and modern, and bright colors (orange, yellow) contrasting with the black of the running gear and the chrome of the gas tank.

Cross-country test for the RT 450.

Facing page: the Scrambler 450.

Illustrations from a contemporary advertising brochure for the Scrambler series.

DUCATI

SPORTS M

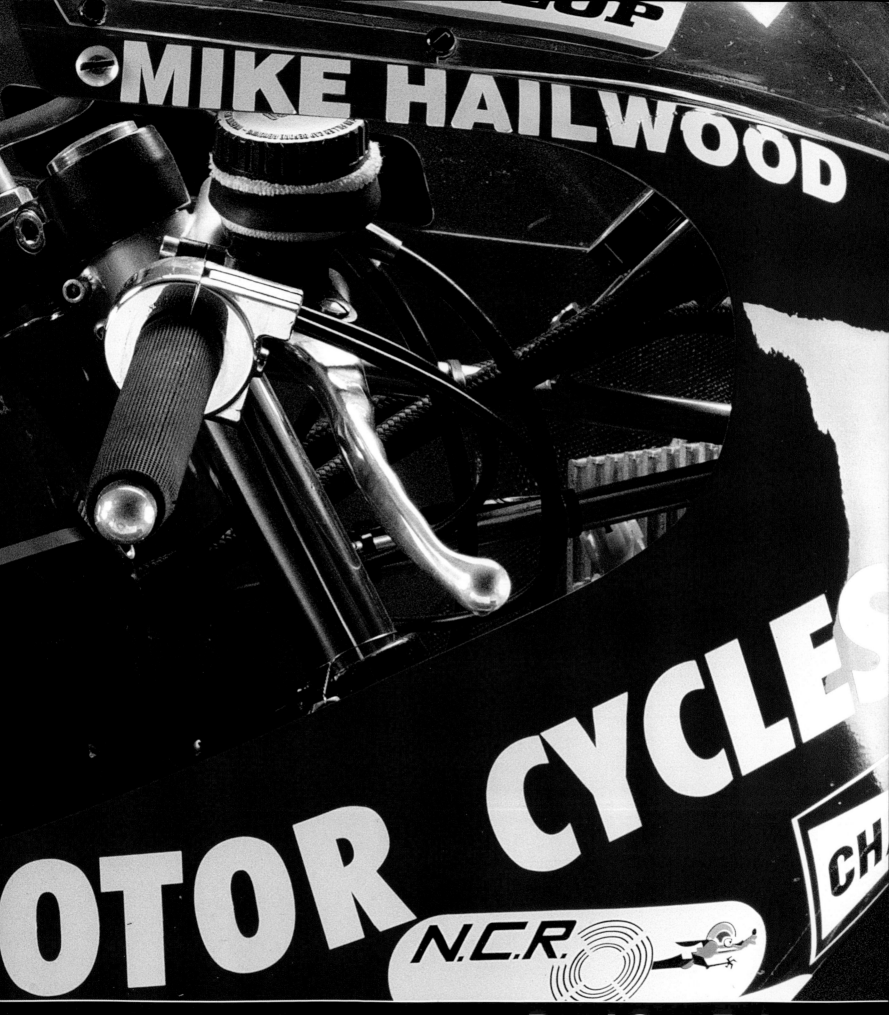

Bevel-Gear Twins

Bevel-Gear
Twins

First races with the Ducati 750 for a great champion, Franco Uncini.

Facing page: at the Pesaro Circuit in 1971, Bruno Spaggiari with the 500 GP leads Giacomo Agostini and his MV Agusta.

Origins are often cloaked in mystery: this is true of great cities, illustrious families and even famous motorbikes. On the other hand, the bevel-gear twin-cylinders with a 90° V configuration, long known as an"L-twin" configuration because of the position they assumed in the frame, have a precise date of birth: March 20, 1970. For those who believe in astrology, therefore, they were born under the sign of Pisces. According to the British historian Ian Falloon, Fabio Taglioni drew the first sketch of perhaps his most famous and best-loved engine, which over the years was to acquire the affectionate name of the *pompone*, or "big pump," on the very last day of winter in 1970. This is confirmed by the Italian journalist (and Ducati afficionado) Bruno de Prato, who says in his book *Ducati Power* that he saw the first design for the twin cylinder at just that time. Taglioni himself, in an interview given to the writer of this book, reaffirms these claims.

What is more difficult to determine, however, is the precise moment when the engineer was given the go-ahead for his project. Most likely, it was the boom in large-capacity bikes (not just from Japan, but from elsewhere in Europe too) that persuaded the directors of Ducati to speed things up, so that Bologna could offer world markets a rival to the Honda CB 750, Kawasaki three-cylinder 500 and 750 and four-cylinder 900, Laverda SF and Guzzi V7. It is likely that Taglioni already had the basic idea in

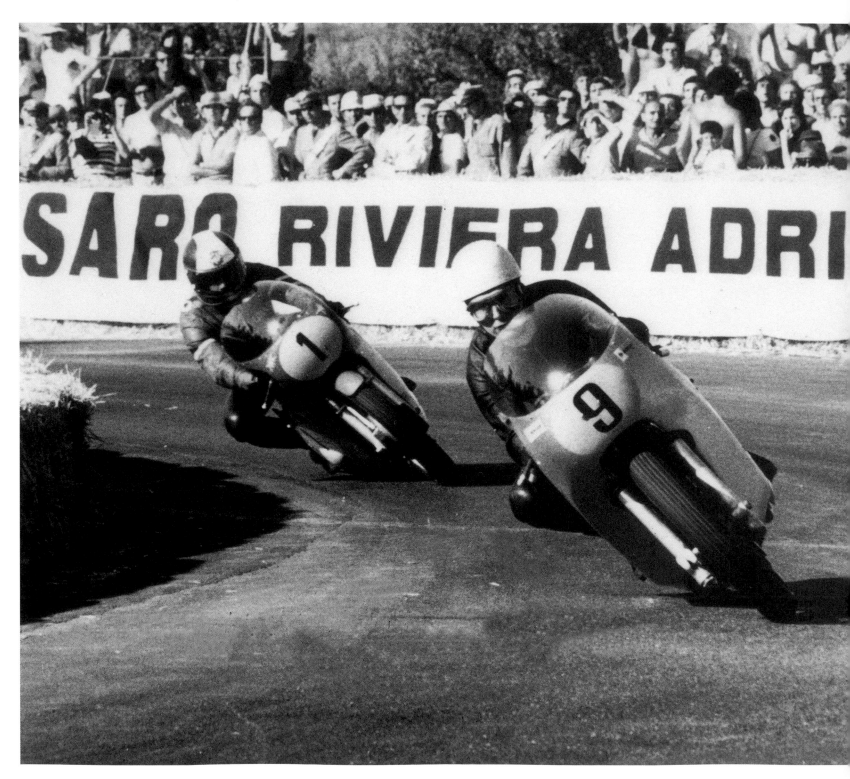

Perhaps the most representative and fascinating bike with a "bevel-gears" engine: the Super Sport 750. It would be followed by the similar 900.

Below: Mike Hailwood.

his head and it was not long before the prototype was on the bench. It was a twin-cylinder (the ideal structure for a motorcycle engine, much more lively and pulsating in its performance) arranged longitudinally (and therefore with a front section more or less the same as that of a single-cylinder) and in a 90° V configuration. This was also the best choice from the viewpoint of balance. The positioning of the cylinders in the Ducati twin (with the one at the front set almost parallel to the ground and the one at the back vertical) had an illustrious precedent in the prewar Guzzi 500, which was still winning at the 1947 TT with Tenni – but the twin from Mandello had its cylinders at an angle of 120°.

Taglioni's approach was clear, exemplary and efficient. The distribution used the same single overhead camshaft driven by bevel-gear as the single-cylinders, while the capacity of 750 cc was obtained with a bore and stroke of 76 x 75 mm, the same as the excellent 350 single, from which it also took the cylinder. The prototype was built in a great hurry: the result was a very personal sort of motorbike, in which the engine played a dominant role even in its aesthetics. For Taglioni it had to be a sports machine, and this is evident from the fact that it only had a kick start, while almost all its rivals already had electric starters. Equipped with Dell'Orto SS 35 carburetors and a front brake with four shoes (first Fontana and then Grimeca), it convinced its tester, Farné, who recalls that it delivered around 65 hp and was capable of putting on a remarkable burst of power, even though the heads were not yet desmodromic.

The definitive bike closely resembled the prototype. Called the GT750, it appeared in June 1971. The frame, however, was more proportionate, though still an open cradle, while the carburetors were 30-mm Amal Concentrics. At the front it was fitted with a Lockheed disc brake derived from the ones used on the Morris Mini and Marzocchi forks with a raked pin. The name, Gran Turismo, declared from the start that it was no sports bike, but the potential of this twin was immediately apparent to enthusiasts. It was to one of them, Claudio Bergami, that fell the honor of making its Racing debut, when he rode what was practically a production bike at Modena.

However, since the end of sixties Ducati was working on a 500 Grand Prix: Taglioni was convinced of the great sporting possibilities offered by his twin and, to persuade everyone of the value of his idea on the Racing circuit too, prepared a Grand Prix bike to compete in the 500 class: this was really a lot to ask from a design conceived for the road, but it is well-known that the "grand old man" of Ducati always had competition in the back of his mind.

First of all a series of sand-cast crankcases (lighter and more compact than the production ones) were prepared to house the cylinders of the Desmo 250 (bore 74 mm, stroke 57 mm). The principal aim of the bike was to convince riders of the validity of the bold Ducati project (at a time when

In 1971 the 750 GT reached the market.

The peak of development of the "bevel-gears" road bikes: the Mike Hailwood Replica 1000, last "cry" of a great family of engines.

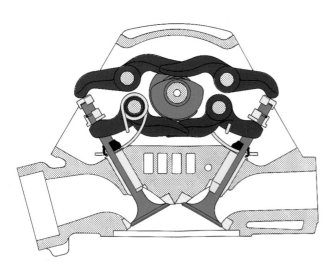

Layout of the desmodromic valve gear.

Cook Neilson racing
(photo Lustig).

Right: Carlo Perugini,
a fine rider with the
official 900.

The beautiful twin-cylinder desmo engine.

Left: Oscar La Ferla in action.

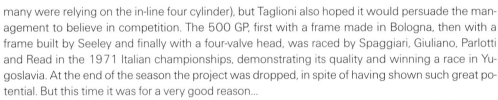

many were relying on the in-line four cylinder), but Taglioni also hoped it would persuade the management to believe in competition. The 500 GP, first with a frame made in Bologna, then with a frame built by Seeley and finally with a four-valve head, was raced by Spaggiari, Giuliano, Parlotti and Read in the 1971 Italian championships, demonstrating its quality and winning a race in Yugoslavia. At the end of the season the project was dropped, in spite of having shown such great potential. But this time it was for a very good reason...

The event that literally changed the destiny of the Bolognese twins took place in 1972: at Imola, in the course of a memorable 200 Mile race, in which the best large-cylinder bikes in production contended for supremacy (on the basis of the AMA regulations imported into Italy by Checco Costa, a great organizer of races and the father of Claudio Costa, the doctor who invented the Mobile Clinic). To give an idea of the level of competition, MV entered a very special four-cylinder 750, ridden by Giacomo Agostini. Ducati lined up at the start with a team of four riders on bikes derived straight from production versions, as was evident from the fact that they still had lugs for a central stand!. Ducati took the first two places, with Paul Smart coming in just in front of the old lion Bruno Spaggiari, and the world finally understood that the twin-cylinder (at last with desmodromic distribution) was a thoroughbred Racing bike.

In the production series, the GT was followed by the Sport (still with a spring head) and above all the beautiful SS 750, one of the motorbikes that best embodies the spirit of the Café Racers, with its essential lines, exposed mechanical parts and the allure that came straight from the track. Rude and muscular but elegant too, it remains one of the finest examples of motorcycle design. And, let's be clear about this, it was not just for looking at. Its steering and handling convinced many racers that, while power may be important, a well-designed frame and an engine with high torque are much more gratifying.

Other bikes were to follow, always with "bevel-gear" engines of ever-increasing capacity: the 860, the 900 Super Sport and the less successful Darmah, SD and S2. The 900 was to give rise to the last "bevel-gear" twin, the Mille or 1000 cc, (in the Sport and Mike Hailwood Replica versions), which brought one of the most thrilling and significant chapters in the history of Ducati to a close in 1985.

It was during this period (we have now reached the end of the seventies) that the Ducati legend received one of its most phenomenal boosts: in 1978 Mike Hailwood won the Bolognese manufacturer the world title that had always eluded it hitherto, taking the TT1 championship on the extremely perilous Isle of Man course. Mike's return to the saddle of a Ducati, his continued close relationship with people like Taglioni and Farné and his victory over some far more powerful bikes made it a story that is told even today.

The 900 NCR fitted out for the endurance races with the colors of the French Val d'Oise team. Ducati often placed its trust in private but well organized teams.

500 GP
Tested at the Races

Ducati had taken no official part in the world speed trials since 1958, and so the appearance of the 500 Grand Prix in 1971 sent the constructor's supporters into ecstasies. At last they were able to see their favorite make coming back in grand style.

The bike was developed in just six months: Taglioni used the "prototype" sand-cast crankcase (more compact in size than the production ones and lighter into the bargain) which he had come up with for his first experiments on the 750. To this he applied two cylinders from the 250 single

(with spring and not desmo heads). To get the best out of the motor a sixth speed was added to the gearbox, though, originally, this was not provided for. Problems with the gearbox and the electrical equipment were the main brake on the success of this bike which, with a rated output of 72 hp at 12,000 revs (though with two valves per cylinder and single-camshaft valve gear), could be considered competitive with the other 500s in the world championship, with the exception of the MV which was decidedly ahead of the field.

The race at Modena (the traditional opening of the Italian championships) was chosen for its debut. The two riders (Spaggiari and the young test rider Ermanno Giuliano) and their Ducatis immediately showed what they were capable of, although teething troubles forced them to retire before the end of the race. In the next race at Imola, Spaggiari had to retire again, but Giuliani came in behind Agostini and his unassailable MV three-cylinder. At Cesenatico, another second place for Giuliano and another withdrawal for Spaggiari.

The bike had proved competitive from the outset, and so Ducati looked for a rider capable of battling it out at a high level. First to come to mind was Hailwood, but the Englishman had other commitments. Racing automobiles with John Surtees (he went on to win the Formula 2 title). In the end they found the highly-motivated Phil Read, who came second after Ospedaletti (with Parlotti third and Giuliano fourth). Read also raced in the world championship competition at Imola (which saw Smart make another bid after his success in the 200 Miles), where he stayed in second place for a longtime before finishing fourth, slowed down by gearbox trouble. For GilbertoParlotti, another great rider who was to meet a premature death like Ermanno Giuliano, there came the honor of the only victory achieved on these bikes in an international race, at Skophia Loka (Yugoslavia).

The Ducati 500 GP introduced some almost unprecedented elements into the world championships, such as disc brakes (first single and then double) and the fork with a raked pin. Originally the bike had a Verlicchi open-cradle frame, but this was then replaced by one made by Colin Seeley in England, on the advice of the British importer, which gave excellent results.

Mechanics of the Racing Department in the early seventies. From the left: Ugolini, Farné, Cavatti, Caracchi, Massimo Nepoti, Recchia and Giorgio Nepoti.

Facing page: Ermanno Giuliano, Ducati rider and test driver, at Ospedaletti with the 500.

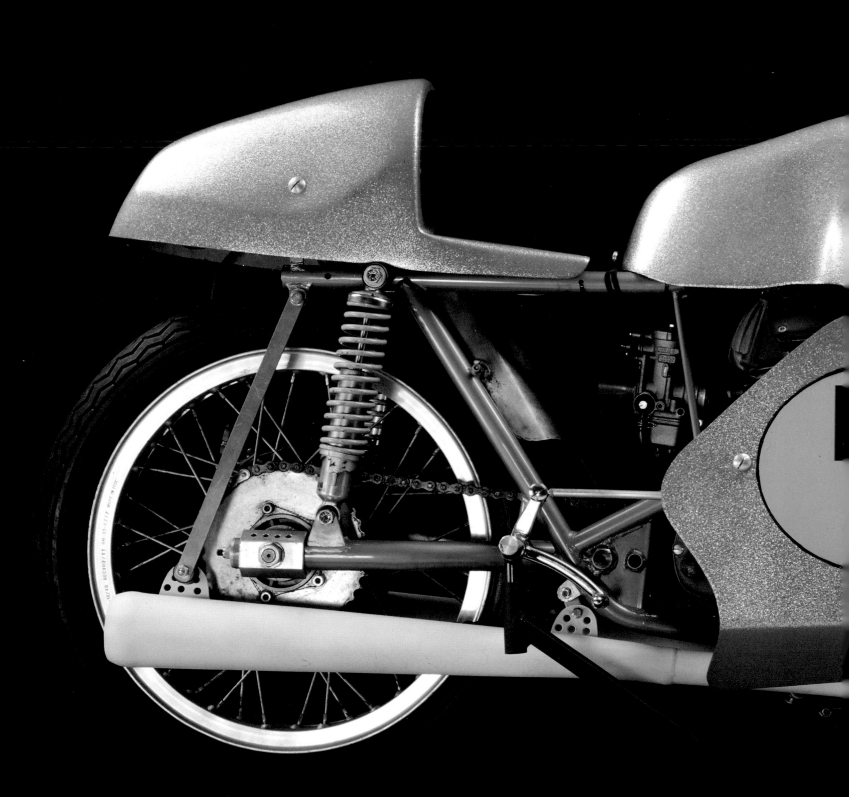

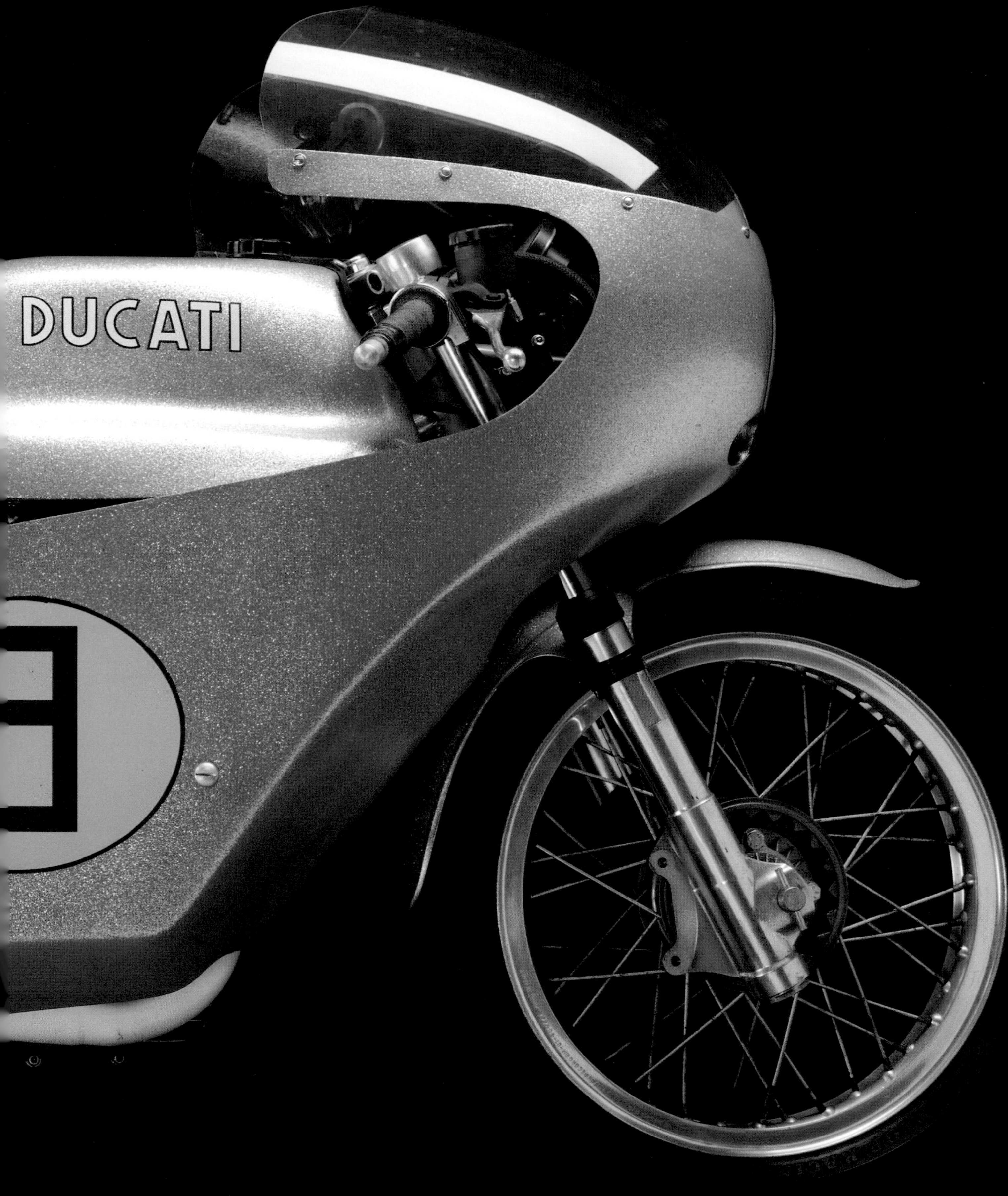
DUCATI

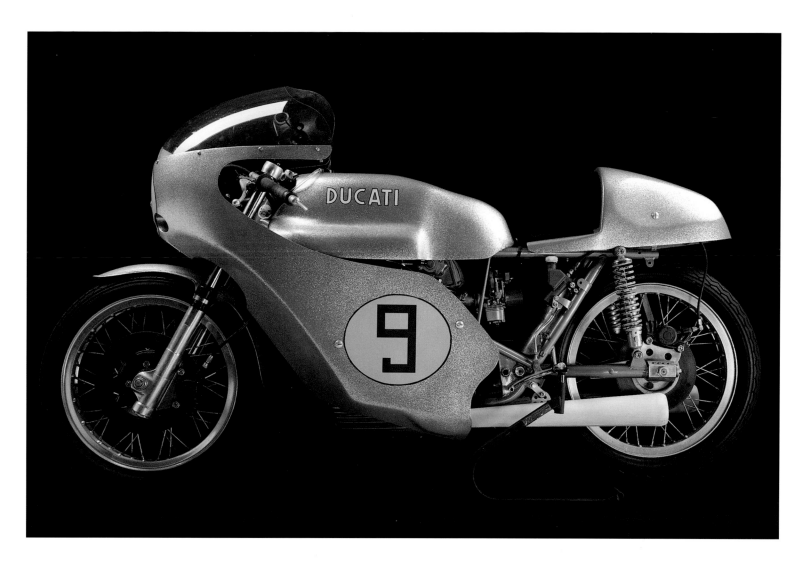

On this page and the preceding double-spread: the 500 GP of 1971 (Ducati Museum; owner Marcello Peruzzi; photo Giovanni Marchi).

Right: 1971, working on Spaggiari's 500 at the Imola track.

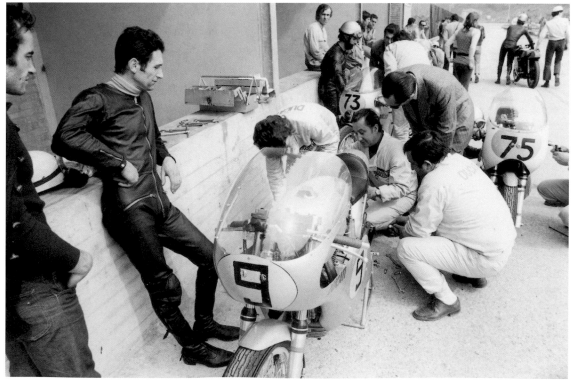

Bevel-Gear Twins

The British specialist Colin Seeley with the prototype of the frame that would be used for the 500 GP (photo Edisport).

Phil Read with the Ducati 500 GP; the British ace fell in love with the twin, which he rode in Italian races and the world championships.

200 Miles
Triumph at Imola

The victory in the 200 Mile race at Imola in 1972 was one of the most enthralling in Ducati's history. Much has been written about the fantastic charge led by Paul Smart and Bruno Spaggiari, side by side almost all the way to the finishing line (and the two riders have not always given the same version of what happened, especially when it comes to the question of how much gas was left in the tank...), but little has been said about how this race changed the destiny of the Italian constructor, with effects that are still discernible today. That win alone defined the approach that Ducati would take to Racing from then on, with the manufacturer focussing its attention almost exclusively on competitions reserved for production-derived machines. However, before talking about Smart, Imola and the fabulous number sixteen we need to take a step backward in time.

In 1972 the brilliant Checco Costa brought the 200 Mile formula to Italy and Ducati prepared an array of eight bikes to be ridden by Smart (who signed up at once, thanks to his wife Maggie, though already committed to race in the USA), Bruno Spaggiari, Ermanno Giuliano and Alan Dunscombe (another Englishman recommended by the importer Vic Camp). The bikes had production frames and engines (they were taken off the assembly line), but were prepared as usual in a very short time (Farné simply says "working at night") and with great enthusiasm. Special connecting rods were fitted, along with new camshafts and desmodromic cylinder heads prepared with great care. The greater part of all this work, however, would probably pass unobserved, as it was concerned with the most insignificant details: each bike was filed down and lightened, with extreme pains taken over every stage in the process. In addition, new Dell'Orto PHM carburetors with 40-millimeter choke tubes and accelerator pumps arrived just in time, providing a perfect supply of fuel for the big twin-cylinder, which delivered 80 hp of power at the wheel at 8500 rpm.

Facing page: the unmistakable Racing style of Paul Smart, first at Imola in 1972.

Right: for Spaggiari the disappointment of a lost opportunity; he reached the finishing line with his gas tank almost empty and could not take victory away from Smart.

On this page and the following double-spread: one of the most famous bikes in the world, the 750 "Imola Desmo" (Ducati Museum; owner Paul Smart; photo Giovanni Marchi). Note (below) the transparent strips on the tank showing the level of fuel and the steering damper knob.

Smart on the podium at Imola, celebrating with champagne while Spaggiari looks on; on the right, Walter Villa, who came third.

159

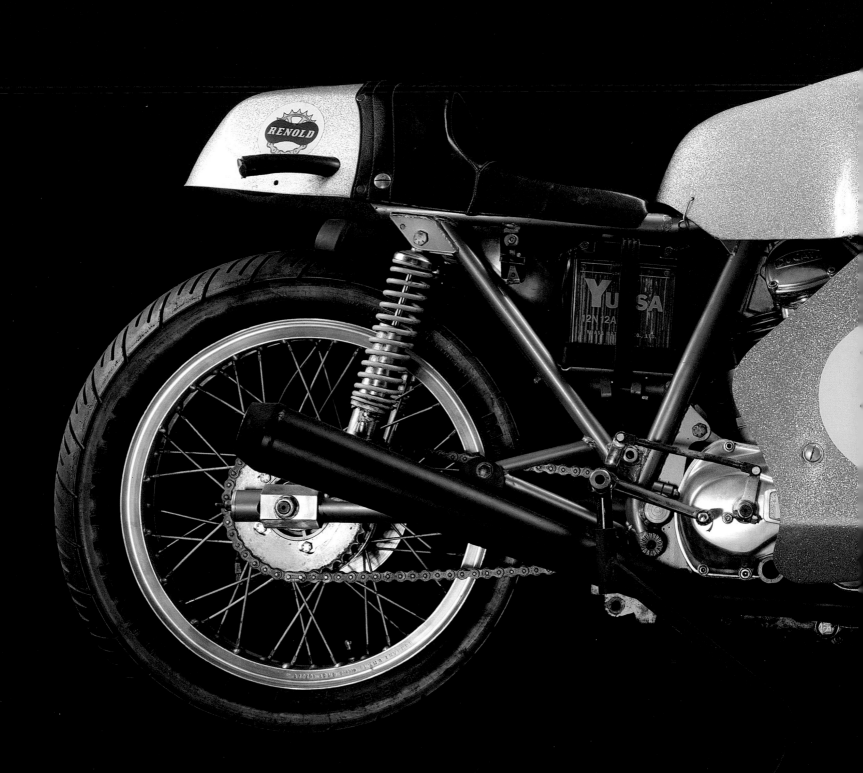

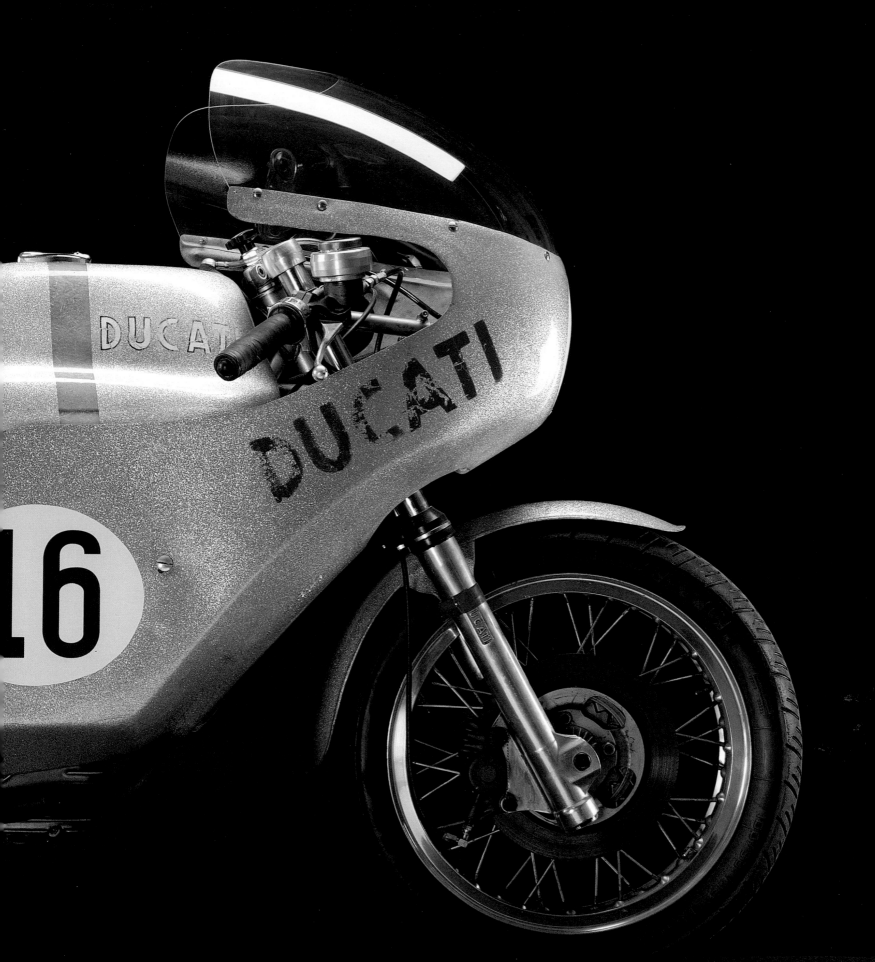

Between Production and Sport

After the fantastic victory at Imola in 1972, Ducati began to concentrate most of its energies on developing the "twins," which had now become the main pillar of production. The GT 750 (the first mass-produced twin-cylinder) was followed by the provisional Sport 750 of 1973 (in practice, a sportier version of the previous model, but still without desmodromic heads), and then by the fabulous Super Sport 750 of 1974. This was perhaps the finest Italian motorbike of its time, in part because it perfectly embodied the concept of an essential sports machine. A direct descendant of Smart's bike, it finally had the desmo gear drive, single-piece connecting rods, PHM 40 carburetors, a Marzocchi fork with axle

pin and a Brembo 280-mm-diameter twin-disc front brake, with Lockheed calipers. Fast, stable and flawless when holding its course (something that could not be said of its Japanese rivals), it immediately became a legend among members of the sporting world, to whom Ducati also offered a special tuning kit for production races. Bruno Spaggiari, who had now come to the end of his Racing career, became the Team Manager and, with even more "special" SSs, gave a number of great new riders a chance to win, including Franco Uncini, world 500 GP champion in 1982.

The "bevel-gear" bikes continued to do well in competition. In 1973 Taglioni prepared a new bike for the 200 Miles at Imola, the "short-

stroke" 750, a true Racing bike. With a bore and stroke of 86 x 64 mm, the same as the Cosworth 3000 F1 engine, and with new heads, the bike produced 93 hp at 10,500 revs and even the frame and running gear proved more competitive. It came second at Imola in 1973 with Spaggiari (behind Saarinen on the Yamaha 350), but the other rider, the Swiss Bruno Kneubüler, might have won the race had he not had a fall.

With the 860 that was derived from the "short stroke" 750, the Spanish riders Salvador Cañellas and Benjamin Grau won the 24 Horas of Montjuich at Barcelona in 1973, clearing the way for Ducati to take on the endurance races.

The 860 designed by Giugiaro, father of the Volkswagen Rabbit, or Golf as it is known in Europe.

Facing page: the 750 SS of the Scuderia Spaggiari, raced by Franco Uncini as well (Ducati Museum; owner Ducati Motor Spa; photo Giovanni Marchi).

Below left: the Darmah 900 with its characteristic square casings, needed to house the starting motor.

Below right: the more successful Super Sport version, and not just from the aesthetic viewpoint.

Mike Hailwood's Motorbike

The veneration shown by enthusiasts for some bikes and certain riders is yet another demonstration of the fact that motorcycling is not all logic and rationality. The story, almost a legend, of the world title won by Mike Hailwood on the Isle of Man in 1978 with the Ducati 900 SS is one that is really worth looking at closely. In 1977 the British rider, with nine world motorcycle titles and a Formula Two automobile Racing championship under his belt, had practically brought his career to a close after a terrible accident in Germany in 1974 at the wheel of a McLaren. Mike was living in New Zealand and at the most took part in the odd minor bike race, just to keep in touch with his old passion. At Silverstone in 1977, however, he met Steve Wynne, concessionaire, former rider and owner of Sport Motor Cycles Ltd. in Manchester.

On that occasion Wynne let Hailwood try out a Ducati he had prepared, but just by sitting on it: the old champion was favorably impressed by the "old-style" riding position. Almost as a joke he offered to race it in the TT of the following year. They came to an agreement – Mike even wanted to race under a pseudonym, so sceptical was he of his chances – and a contract was quickly drawn up: 1000 pounds for the event and a Ducati all for himself.

Wynne bought three bikes from Ducati out of a small batch of twenty 900s prepared to compete in endurance races. The bikes had a chrome molybdenum frame made by Daspa and a sand-cast crankcase, narrower at the back and fitted with reinforcements, twenty of which were made by Ducati itself (though Farné speaks of forty engines produced for

clients...). They also had lighter Borgo pistons, one-piece connecting rods, Dell'Orto-Malossi carburetors with a 42-mm choke tube and a beautiful dry clutch with metal discs. These bikes, created at Ducati and as always worked on by its most trusted technicians in their spare time, were then assembled by NCR.

The bike reached 87 hp, which was perhaps not much if it was going to beat Read's official four-cylinder Honda, built expressly for the purpose of winning the TT1 world championships. But in the saddle, and ready to exploit all the potential of the Italian 900, was Hailwood: after an absolutely sensational contest, he won both race and title, repeating the feat a week later at Mallory Park (a circuit in theory not suited to the Italian bike) and once again beating the Japanese competition.

The splendid 900 Replica, launched on the market to the joy of real enthusiasts.

The great "Mike the bike" in action on the Isle of Man.

Hailwood jumping with the 900 at Ballaugh Bridge,
in the less successful 1979 TT races.

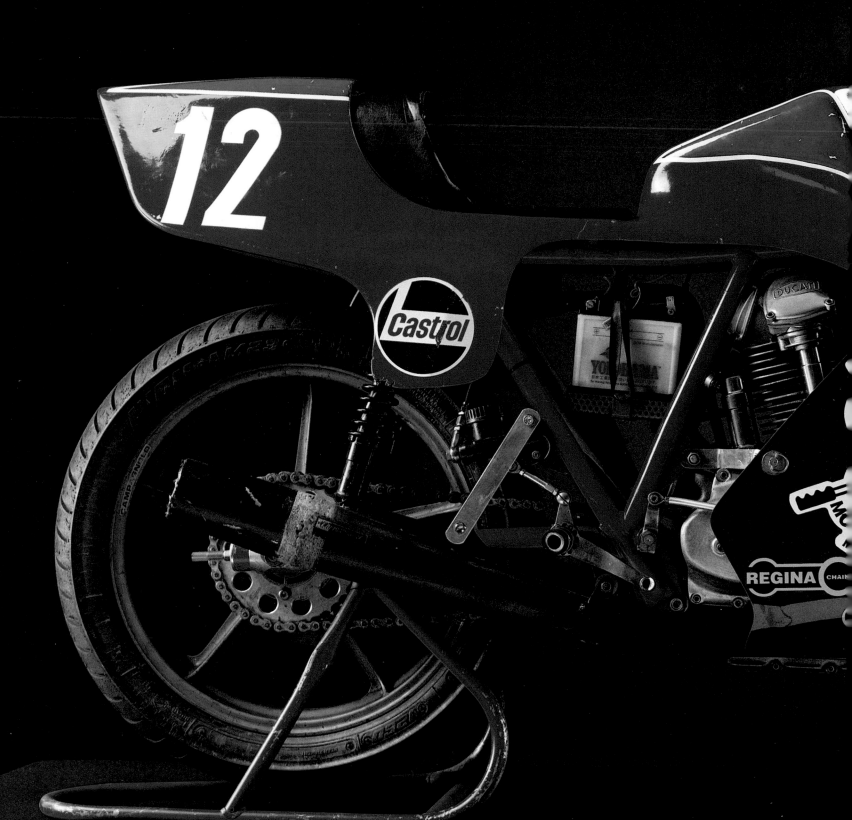

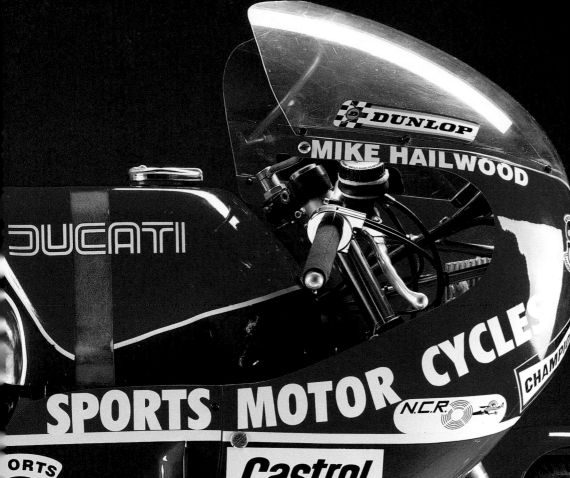

Hailwood hard on the heels of Read with the four-cylinder Honda; he is about to overtake.

On double-spread and preceding page: the motorbike that collectors dream of, the 900 ridden by Hailwood, TT F1 world champion in 1981 (Ducati Museum; owner Larry Auriana; photo Giovanni Marchi). Built by Ducati, with the collaboration of NCR, it was then prepared by the Englishman Wynne with the help of technicians sent out by the constructor: true teamwork!

The front of Hailwood's bike, with the holes that allowed air to pass through to the radiator of the lubrication system.

The opening to let air through to the clutch: technician Pedretti made it before the start, with a simple hacksaw.

750 Imola

ENGINE – Air-cooled four-stroke longitudinal 90° V twin-cylinder configuration. Longitudinally-cut crankcase, heads and blocks in light alloy; cast-iron liner. Bore and stroke 80 x 74·4 mm; capacity 747·95 cc. Compression ratio):1. Desmodromic single overhead mshaft driven by bevel-gear. Twin-plug contact-breaker ignition. Two Dell'Orto PHF 40 carburetors with accelerator pump. Wet sump lubrication with 5 liters of Castrol R40 oil. Primary reduction by gears, final by chain. Wet multi-plate clutch, five-speed gearbox.

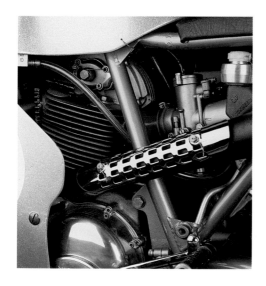

FRAME, FORKS AND RUNNING GEAR – Duplex open-cradle tubular-steel frame. Marzocchi telescopic hydraulic front forks with raked pins; swinging-arm rear suspension with two Ceriani 310-mm shocks adjustable to five different positions. Brakes: front twin 280-mm discs with Lockheed calipers; rear 229-mm disc with Lockheed caliper. Borrani light-alloy rims, Dunlop KR tires, 3·25 x 18 at the front and 3·50 x 18 at the back. Fiberglass fuel tank with a capacity of 24 liters and transparent panels in the sides to check the level.

DIMENSIONS, WEIGHT AND PERFORMANCE – Length 2018 mm, wheel base 1530 mm, rake 60 mm, inclination of steering column 30°, height of handlebar 920 mm, height of footrests above ground 370 mm, height of seat above ground 790 mm. Weight: 163 kg declared at the time, with oil but no fuel (though Taglioni, in an interview, has spoken of a much higher weight, around 178 kg). Maximum power at the wheel, 82 hp at 9000 revs, top speed about 250 kph. It should be noted that the throttle of Smart's bike was covered with a layer of rubber cut from an inner tube to compensate for a problem he had with his right wrist, injured in an accident.

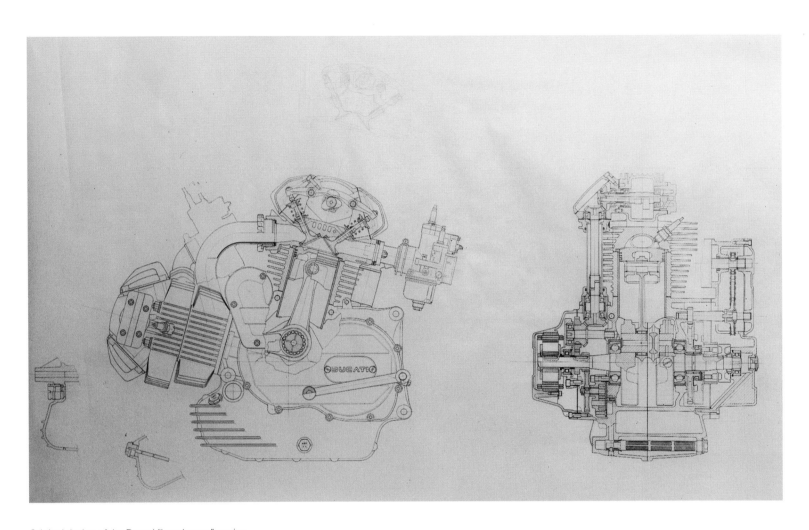

Original design of the Ducati "bevel-gears" engine.

The NCR Stable

Via Signorini, on the western outskirts of Bologna: a small but well-equipped workshop where for years Racing bikes were built. A magician's cave in which every detail, even the most insignificant, was studied, weighed, pared down, bored out, polished... It was here that Rino Caracchi and Giorgio Nepoti worked from 1967 to 1995: two true wizards of mechanics who, with the support of Farné, Pedretti, Recchia, Cavazzi and Taglioni himself, created fabulous bikes, intended, of course, for Racing. The NCR stable (Nepoti, Caracchi and Rizzi, though since the third partner left, the R has stood for Racing) was for many years a Racing department independent of Ducati. Out of it came bikes like the 900 NCR, designed for endurance races but used by Mike Hailwood to win the TT1 title as well as by a series of excellent Italian riders like Vanes Francini, Mauro Ricci and Carlo Perugini. In later years, the bikes of Rutter and Polen were to owe a great deal to NCR.

But what was NCR? A workshop that prepared Racing bikes or a real Racing department? The question is a complicated one, and we prefer not to answer it directly. NCR was a great school, but something more: it was the material expression of a philosophy of motorcycling in which everything could be improved, everything could be made lighter. For one horsepower is made of many fractions of a horsepower and a kilo of a thousand grams – even the most trivial of screws can work better and be unscrewed more quickly, perhaps at a crucial moment in a race, if its function has been rationalized. The people at NCR worked without computers (there weren't any around at the time), but each of them carried an real database in his head. Even today, if you ask them about a bike or something that went on behind the scenes, they can remember everything, down to the last stroke of a file.

Bike being prepared at the NCR stable in Bologna.

Facing page: the 900 NCR prepared by the Racing stable of the same name (Ducati Museum; owner Ducati Motor S.p.A.; photo Giovanni Marchi).

Below left: the maniacal work of lightening the clutch case.

Below right: the plates of the Marzocchi fork and the Veglia Racing tachometer.

Gallery

Old photographs, some of them never published before, emerge from the archives of the Ducati Museum. For those of us with a passion for this sort of archeology, the photos always stir strong emotions, and the gamut of feelings runs from the nostalgia that springs up when we come across a friend who is no longer with us (the rider Mauro Ricci, killed in an accident) or to the excitement caused by the picture of a prototype you have never seen before, perhaps in a configuration that led nowhere, but which has left its mark on the faded photographic paper.

The period of the bevel-gear twin-cylinders was the most exciting and engrossing in the history of Ducati. It marked the end of an era and of a corporate structure. For enthusiasts these were the finest bikes designed by Taglioni: suitable for mass-production, but with an incorrigible bent for sport, in all its facets. What cannot be described, though, is the full and fantastic roar of these motors, fruit of the mechanical genius of a man who was somehow able to impart his own unruffled and Romagnese charisma to the metal itself. It was an era in which motorcycling was still a hard-up sport: blue, oil-stained overalls and sandwiches instead of the luxurious hospitality to be found at today's Grand Prix. It feels like a thousand years ago, and yet we are talking about things that happened just two decades ago. But in a world that moves as fast as that of Racing, twenty years is an eternity.

Escorted by Spairani and Taglioni, Smart and Spaggiari head for the podium after the 200 Mile race at Imola.

Below: a friend who is no longer with us: Mauro Ricci, one of the best Italian maxi bike riders tragically killed in an accident.

George Fogarty, father of Superbike champion Carl, in action with a 900 at a British race.

Facing page: a 900 starts again with a push from the mechanics in an endurance race.

Right: Franco Uncini in action with the 750 SS of the Scuderia Spaggiari.

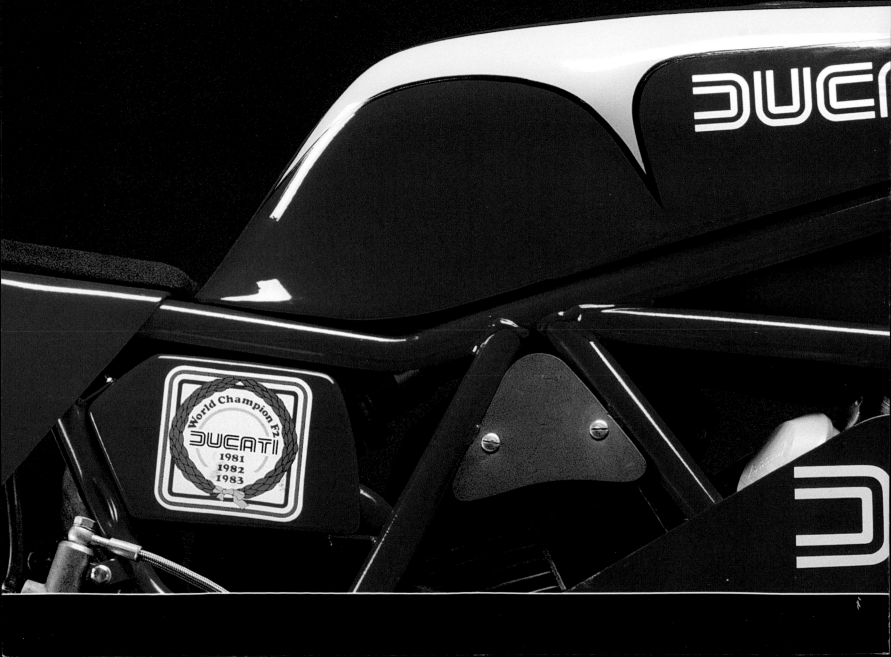

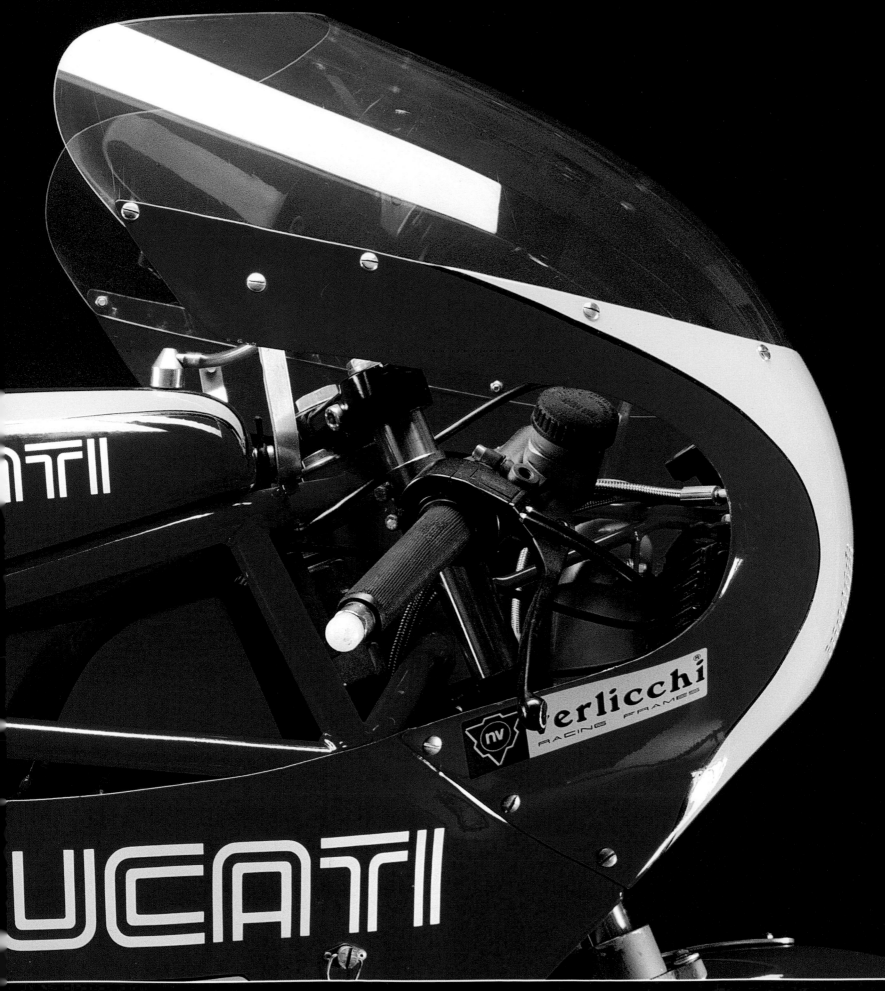

Pantah

Pantah

The Pantah 500 SL, probable the best sports bike of its generation.

Massimo Broccoli in action with the TT2.

The story of one of the most celebrated and popular of all Ducati bikes, still in production in a modified version today, opened with a failure. The in-line twin-cylinder engines that the manufacturer had developed to extend its range downward, i.e. to include bikes of 350-500 cc, never caught on, partly because of their configuration (of which Taglioni was not very fond, even though the Romagnese engineer, who was not responsible for this design, had built a prototype 500 cc in the sixties along these lines) and partly because of their far from flawless functioning and excessive vibration.

The managers of Ducati asked the technical staff to come up with an engine that would be cheaper to produce, less complicated and quieter than the bevel-gear twin-cylinder, but that could serve as the basis for a new line of motorbikes. The prototypes of this new series started to appear in 1977: housed in the frame of an "in-line" Sport 500, the engine had the classic 90° V configuration, with the front cylinder almost horizontal (so that the press and public called it an "L configuration"), single camshaft valve gear and two valves.

At first sight there is little novelty here, but on closer examination we find that the valve gear was controlled by toothed belts of reinforced rubber (a system derived from automobile engineeering but already tried out on motorbikes, such as the Ducati 500 GP developed by the technician Armaroli). For this 500 Taglioni had dusted off the bore and stroke measurements of the 500 GP dating from the early seventies (74 x 58 mm), but he had also carried out a sophisticated thermodynamic analysis of the cylinder heads. As well as making the engine highly efficient, this meant that the fuel consumption of the Pantah was moderate even in the Racing versions. In addition, the cylinders no longer had cast-iron liners but were coated with Gilnisil nickel-silicon carbide. The valve gear was desmodromic and the engine (with filters and silencers) already performed well at high revs (over 9000), developing around fifty horsepower.

The public (and the specialist press) greeted the Pantah 500 with enthusiasm in 1979, as the best half-liter "sport touring bike" (as it would be called today) of its generation. Due to the shortcomings of external suppliers, the bike was imperfect in its details and had a troublesome clutch, but on the road it went like a bomb: 200 kph were within reach and it handled magnificently. Two

The finest Racing version of the Pantah series, the TT1 F1 750, here without a fairing (Ducati Museum; owner Ducati Motor S.p.A.; photo Giovanni Marchi).

projects that were developed in parallel stemmed from this bike: the 600 and 350. Two good motorbikes, but the larger of the two was the better one, with the capacity of the original design. The 600 also gave rise to a 650, which was chiefly marketed in the Cagiva range.

In 1980 production-derived Pantahs began to win races more or less everywhere. Private riders used a kit sold in the Ducati catalogue. There were also, however, bikes officially prepared by the constructor, which had a capacity of 582·7 cc (bore and stroke 80 x 58 mm), Marzocchi front forks with magnesium-alloy legs, Marzocchi gas shocks, a two-in-one exhaust and steep-angle camshafts. The Pantah Racing (it had no official name) had glass fiber bodywork, a full fairing derived from those used in endurance races and reached 70 hp at 9800 revs. It won races for production-derived bikes in America and Europe; in Italy Guido Del Piano and Vanes Francini were the first to ride it to victory.

But the most interesting new development came in 1981, when Ducati (which had officially started to race again), in collaboration with NCR and using Verlicchi frames, Campagnolo wheels, and Marzocchi and Paioli suspensions, produced a small series of competition bikes (around thirty in all), which were known simply as TT2s. The TT2 class of that time allowed for the participation of production-derived bikes (in practice the forerunners of today's Supersport machines), although with more flexible rules about the modifications that could be made to them. So a splendid tubular-steel space frame was prepared and fitted with real GP running gear (the wheelbase was less than 1400 mm and the dry weight 125 kilograms), while the engine had many parts made of magnesium (though not, of course, structural ones). The main changes were made to the cylinder heads (a 41-mm inlet manifold instead of the 35-mm one mounted on the production bikes) and camshafts with a very steep angle.

The era of the Pantah saw some welcome returns, such as that of the four-time world champion Walter Villa (the brother of Francesco, a Ducati rider since the fifties) who placed his vast experience at the service of the Ducati twins, especially on the arrival of the second series of sports bikes, the magnificent F1 750. This was a bike that won fewer races than the TT2, from which it was derived, but one which has also left an indelible mark on the history of the Italian make.

At the time the Pantah series came out Ducati entered a new chapter that was going to have a profound effect on its future, a change of ownership. In 1983 Cagiva, a company that had only recently entered the world of motorcycling by taking over what was left of the once glorious Aermacchi, had already

In 1977 a prototype of the Pantah 500 was shown at Bologna, equipped with Campagnolo "hydroconical" brakes.

Right: Anthony "Tony" Rutter.

won a fair share of the Italian market with its two-stroke 125s (such as the Aletta) and was on the lookout for new bikes in order to extend its range to higher capacities. Initially it came to an agreement with Ducati, which took the role of a supplier of engines. The ones that interested Cagiva most were the Pantahs, which the company used to bring out touring bikes with a capacity of 350 and a 650, called Alazzurra. But the ties between the two groups grew ever closer and in the mid-eighties Cagiva acquired a majority shareholding in Ducati from the State holding company Finmeccanica, led by Romano Prodi.

It was the beginning of a new era, in which the owners of Cagiva, the Castiglioni brothers, immediately gave a new impetus to the production of motorcycles in all their forms. Industrial motors, diesel marine engines and other lines of production from the years of State ownership vanished: from that moment on only motorbikes were to come out of Borgo Panigale.

While the four-valve twin camshaft (forerunner of today's liquid-cooled Ducati engines) was beginning to take shape in a secret corner of the factory, it was the Pantah series that flew the flag. But it was also what kept things going. In Racing (the brothers from Varese were crazy about sport) and in mass production, the Pantahs were taking the lion's share. New bikes appeared: the extremely sporty F1, inspired by the constructor's official Racing bikes, but also the custom Indiana (for years the most sporty American-style bikes ever produced, a sign that the Ducati temperament could not even be overshadowed by the myth of *Easy Rider*), the small 350- and 400-cc F3s, the high-performance Super Sport 750 and the Cagiva Elefant enduros. So out of the Pantah design came splendid bikes that gave the constructor a new lease of life prior to the arrival of the four valves and the Superbikes also helping to reinforce Ducati's image. The success of Ducati today is a tribute to the technical insight of a group of men who always believed in the value of a

Postcard with the original autograph of Tony Rutter, four times F2 champion with the Ducati TT2.

The first Pantah 600 Racing, from which the TT2 was derived, here in the official 1980 version.

Right: Del Piano, another Italian rider on the TT2.

good idea: bikes should have an open-space frame, a desmo twin-cylinder engine and lots of personality. They needed to offer a thrilling ride and be easily identifiable: in other words they had to have a touch of that passion for sport which had been in the air at Borgo Panigale ever since the day the first Marianna was produced. These were years filled with victories and defeats, flops and triumphs, years that have made a lasting impression on the memories of motorcyclists all over the world. For them the handcrafted details of an F1 are genuine works of art, as are the space frames of the TT2 and the desmodromic valve gear. These were rare cases where the requirements of mechanical efficiency and aesthetic objectives fully coincided.

From 1986 onward the "two-valve" twins split into two families: the first, derived from the original Pantah design, had capacities of 600 and 750 cc (Monster and Supersport 750 and 600 series); the second, developed in parallel and with a greater capacity (900 cc), were the "wide-casing" twin-cylinders. These derived from a design which had emerged along with the one for the "four valves". The lower part of the 900s (engine casing) was related to that of the twin camshafts, with the same external dimensions and attachments to the frame.

TT2 600 New Frontier

In 1981 the Ducati Racing Department took the production Pantah – which had already proved itself competitive by winning several races – and used it to prepare a fantastic Racing twin known simply as the TT2. The frame, designed by Taglioni in collaboration with Verlicchi (a specialist manufacturer in Bologna) was an extremely light space frame (7 kg) made of steel tubes with a very narrow section (25 mm in diameter), anticipating those of the later 851 and 888 models. The constructor concentrated on the entirety of the running gear: the fork was a Marzocchi with magne-sium-alloy sheaths (the same as the one used in the world motorcycling championships), while the single-shock cantilever (i.e. not pro-gressive) rear suspension used a single Paioli unit (later replaced by Marzocchi gas shocks). Then there were Campagnolo ultralight-alloy wheels with a diameter of 18 inches; later the bike was fitted with a 16-inch front wheel. It had a Brembo braking system, with a twin 280-mm disc at the front. The engine was tak-en to the limit permitted by the regulations (597 cc) by increasing the bore to 81 millime-ters. The bike, very light and so compact that it was not suited to tall riders (wheel base 1395 mm, dry weight 122 kg), was fitted with a swept-back fairing and a fuel tank lodged be-tween the tubes of the frame.

The TT2 was put through its paces by An-gel Nieto and Salvador Cañellas and on March 29, 1981, won its first race in Italy, a stage in the Italian TT F2 championships held at Mis-ano, with Sauro Pazzaglia. In the meantime a British rider, Anthony Rutter, known to every-one as Tony, won the Tourist Trophy race with a Pantah 500 SL, modified by Steve Wynne and Pat Slinn. Seeing that the Englishman,

though now almost forty years old, had a chance of taking the title, Ducati gave him a TT2 to race at Ulster. Tony came second, winning the world championship for the category. At the end of the season Massimo Broccoli took the Italian title on a TT2 and, with a bike "reduced" to 500 cc, came seventh in the race reserved for Gran Prix 500s at Mugello, competing against two-stroke four-cylinder Suzukis and Yamahas!

In 1982 the TT2 won the Italian title with Walter Cussigh, dominating all the races, while Rutter took the world title again. It is worth noting that the bikes used 41-mm carburetors (output of 78 hp at 10,500 revs) in Italy, but the different regulations that applied in the world championships obliged Rutter to race with 36-mm ones. In addition, the Englishman, a rider of the old school, went on using an 18-inch front wheel rather than the 16-inch one. At the Tourist Trophy Rutter's TT2 clocked a top speed of 232 kph. Over the course of the 1982 season the first replicas for private riders appeared.

In 1983 Rutter was champion of the world again. Among other things, the TT2 managed a one-two on the Isle of Man, with Tony first and Graeme McGregor second. Walter Cussigh took the Italian title again. In 1984 Rutter won the championship yet again. In Italy the title went to Fabio Barchitta with the Ducati 600, while the brand-new TT1 entrusted to Walter Villa won straight off. To distinguish an official TT2 from a "customer" one you just have to look at the joints of the frame: if they are rounded, the bike was built for private use, whereas the official ones have "sharp" edges.

Facing page: Massimo Broccoli in action at Misano in 1982: note the 16-inch front wheel.

Right and in the two following double-spreads: the Ducati TT2 600 (Ducati Museum; owner Daniele Casolari; photo Giovanni Marchi). At the front note the Marzocchi fork with magnesium sheaths and the Brembo brake with its many holes.

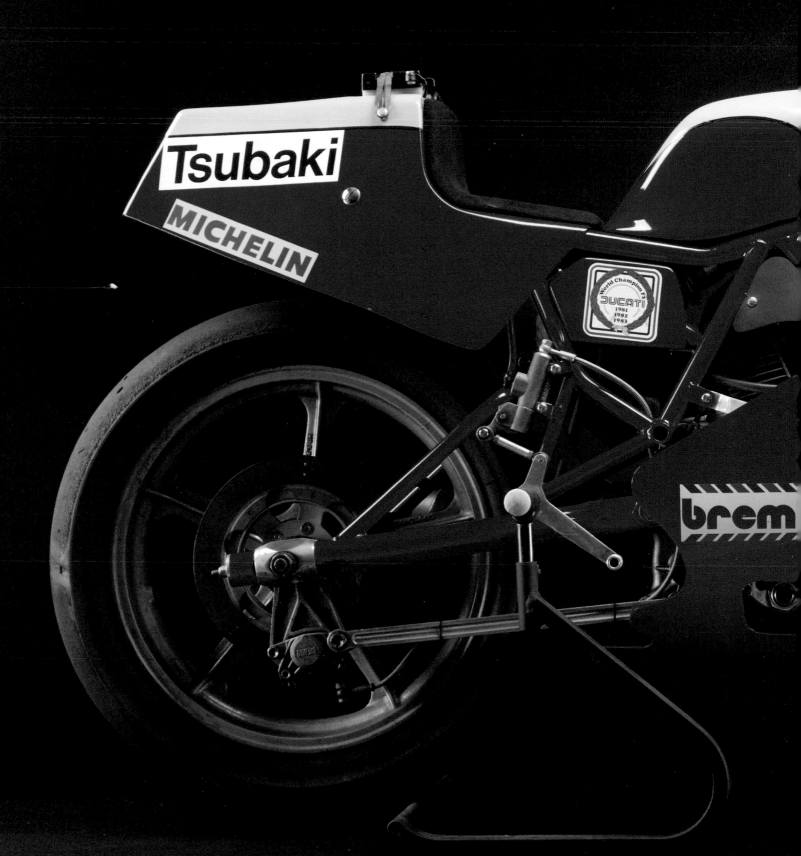

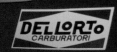

Sauro Pazzaglia, another rider who achieved success with the TT2.

Right: Anthony "Tony" Rutter and his TT2; an unbeatable combination, even though the rider had already passed his fortieth birthday.

Pantah

The yellow-and-red coloring was a mark of the TT2, which was only available in this livery.

Left: detail of the tubes of the reduced-section frame; it weighed only seven kilograms, or fifteen and a half pounds.

Fantastic "Twin"

In the mid-eighties, under pressure from the Japanese manufacturers who wanted to promote their sports models, the regulations of the TT1 and endurance Racing tended to favor 750-cc bikes. Ducati attempted the big leap: the continual victories at Montjuich and the experiment made by Jim Adamo at the Daytona 200-mile race in 1982 with a TT2, raised to 750 cc by Rino Leoni, made the prospects look good. Taking the stroke to 61·5 mm, tested out on the Pantah 650 SL, and the bore to 88 mm, the capacity was almost "full" (748 cc, a figure that we will come back to later) and the power developed by the bikes was rated in the company's own tests, car-

ried out by Franco Farné, as 80 hp at the wheel with wide margins for improvement. The TT1, from which the F1 street bikes would also derived, differed from the 600 in no more than a few details (at least at the outset): the rear suspension had a reinforcing truss, while the wheels were fitted with a quick-release system for use in endurance races. On the subject of these long-duration trials, the TT1 raced at Le Mans in 1984 and came fourth with the Frenchmen Guichon, Vuillemin and Granie, fourth at the 1000 Km in Austria, third at the 24 Hours in Liège and fourth at the Six Hours in Mugello. Walter Villa, often paired with Cussigh, competed with an official

Below and the following double-spread: the TT1 F1 with which Marco Lucchinelli won the Battle of the Twins at Daytona, a race reserved for two-cylinder machines (Ducati Museum; owner Ducati Motor S.p.A.; photo Giovanni Marchi).

Facing page: Marco Lucchinelli, world 500 cc champion in 1981, in action at Daytona in the "BoT."

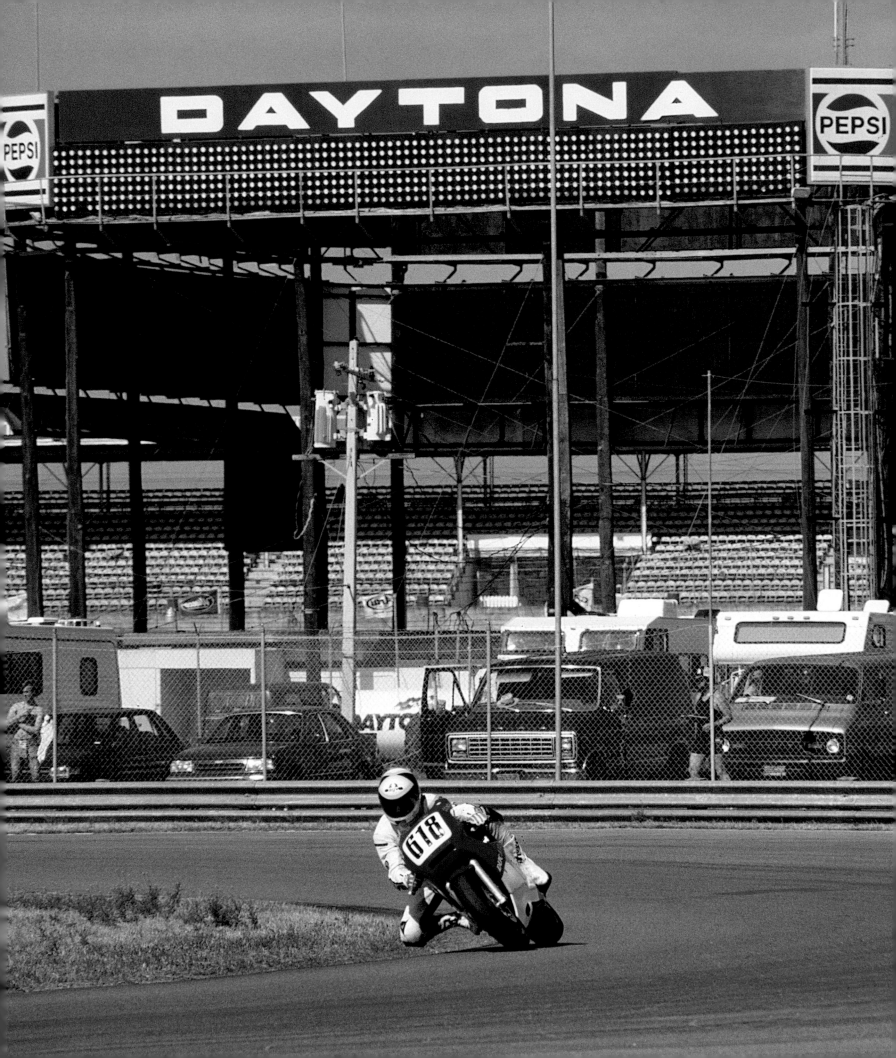

Virginio Ferrari, a GP ace at his ease with the Ducati 750 as well.

Right: Walter Cussigh, who grew up with the TT2, also raced with the Ducati 750.

The form of the windshield on the TT1 F1 derived from an advanced study of aerodynamics.

bike equipped with GP-derived parts, such as a Kayaba fork (though Marzocchi were used as well), new Brembo 300-mm discs and Marvic three-spoke wheels of various sizes (16, 17 and 18 inches), confirming the constant attention that was paid to technical improvement. Even the engines were fitted with new Carillo connecting rods, 44-mm-diameter valves, Dell'Orto 41-mm carburetors and special pistons. The power reached 94 hp at 10,000 revs (but was reduced to 90 for endurance races). In 1985 the results were not spectacular: only a fifth and a sixth place for La Ferla-Cussigh and Lucchinelli-Ferrari (what a pairing!) at Monza; Dieter Rechtenbach managed a few good placings in the Formula One championship while Lucchinelli came sixth at Daytona. In Italy, however, Ducatis dominated the TT1 with Ferrari and Lucchinelli monopolizing the championship. The 750s raced in 1986 as well: Lucchinelli won the Battle of the Twins at Daytona with a bike taken to 851cc (92 x 64 mm bore and stroke measurements) and the opening race of the TT Formula 1 championship at Misano. Garriga, Cardus and Grau won the Montjuich 24 Hours, a traditional Ducati fief, with another two-valve 851.

The bike had now reached the end of its development (and the four valve was knocking on the door...), but new solutions were still being tried out, such as the White Power fork prepared by Gazzaniga, in which the mechanical part was separated from the hydraulic one. In addition, a special frame was built by the Spaniard Cobas: this made a good impression on Kenny Roberts, who tried it out at Misano, though it was actually raced by Garriga.

The TT1 F1 750 on show in the Museum was built in 1987and has an experimental fork with a central spring.

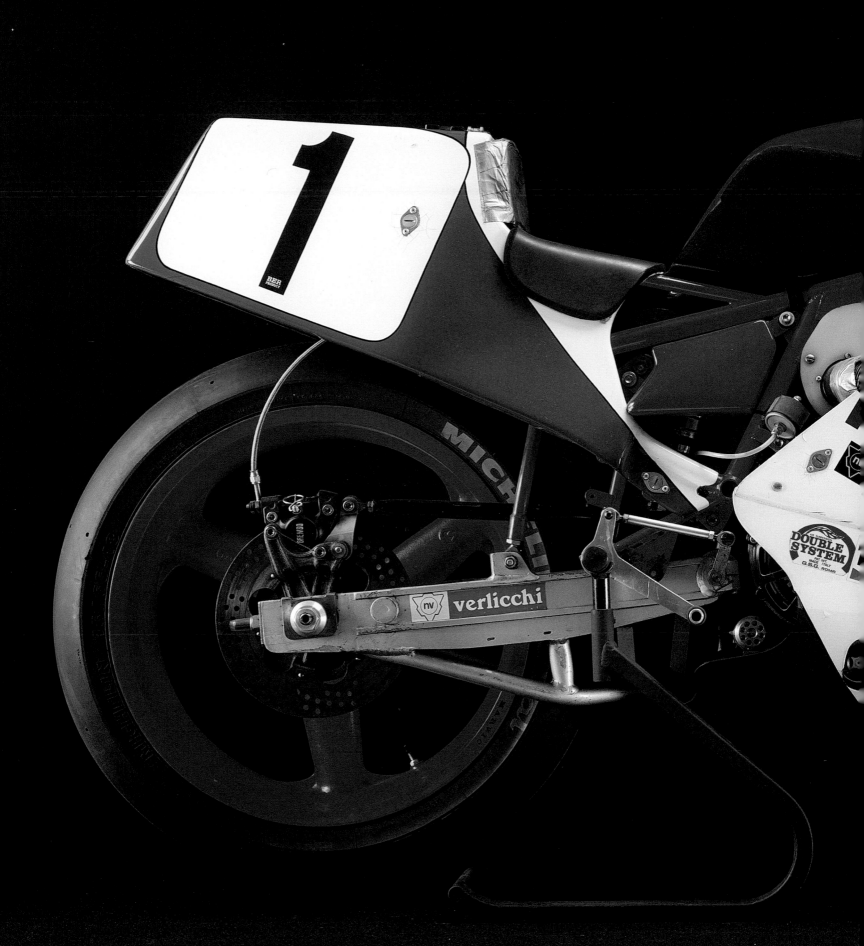

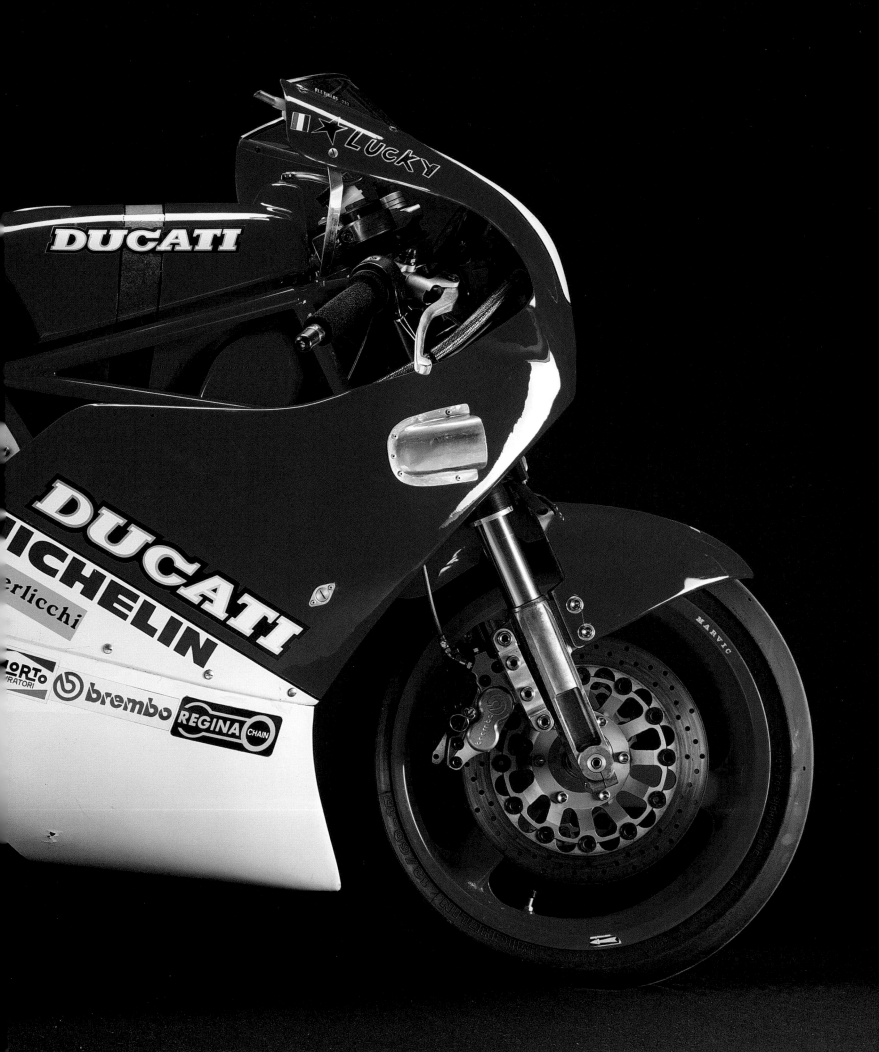

Jim Adamo (photo Scagliarini).

Right: Vanes Francini.

Facing page: Tich Porter.

Pantah

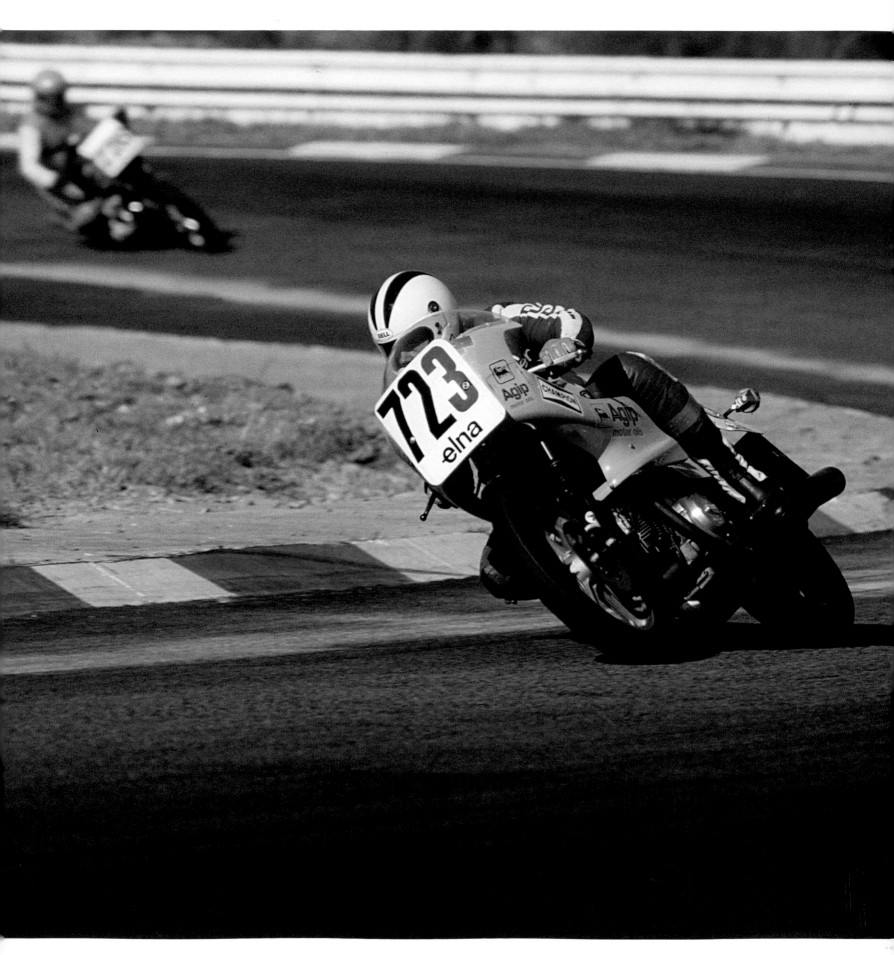

TT1 F1 750

FRAME, FORKS AND RUNNING GEAR –
Tubular-steel Cr-Mo space frame with the
engine bearing part of the load and the rear
suspension pivoting on the casings. Marzocchi
Racing forks with 35-mm stanchions (later
increased to 40), Marzocchi single-shock rear
suspension. Brakes: Brembo 300-mm twin-
disc at front, Brembo 230-mm disc at back.
Marvic alloy wheels in various sizes: 16, 17
and 18 inches, Michelin slick tires, usually
120/60 at the front 160/70 at the back.

ENGINE – Four-stroke twin-cylinder,
longitudinal 90° V configuration. Air-cooled,
with aluminum heads and cylinders. Bore and
stroke 88 x 61·5 mm, capacity 748·1 cc.
Compression ratio 10:1. Belt-driven
desmodromic single overhead camshaft valve
gear with two valves per cylinder. Two
Dell'Orto-Malossi PHF 41/42-mm
carburetors. Wet-sump forced lubrication.
Bosch electronic ignition. Primary reduction
by gears, final by chain. Multi-plate dry clutch.
Five-speed gearbox.

DIMENSIONS, WEIGHT AND PERFORMANCE –
Length 2000 mm, wheelbase 1400 mm,
seat height 785 mm, dry weight 155 kg.
Maximum power about 90 hp at 10,000
revs. Top speed over 260 kph. Fuel tank
capacity 22 liters. The bike in the photograph
is one of the last to have been built. The
Ducati management of the time decided to
use the colors of the Italian flag for the
production bike as well (known as the F1), to
emphasize the Italian image. It should be
noted that many champions raced with this
bike, including Tony Rutter, Marco Lucchinelli,
Virginio Ferrari and Walter Villa, each of whom
brought his own experience to its
development. Thus the data refer to an ideal
"average" model.

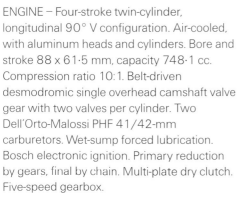

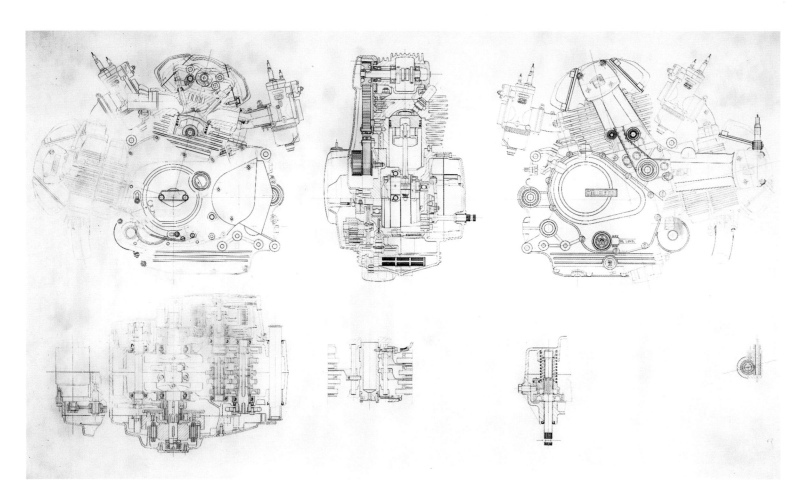

Original design of the Pantah engine

The Evolution

of the Pantah Series

After the Pantah 500 of 1979 came the 350- and 600-cc road models. Innumerable versions of these were produced, including the eccentric XL 350 and TL 600, not very successful attempts to bring out touring bikes with a stylish look.

With the arrival of the Castiglioni brothers, however, the passion for sports bikes was revived, and the F1 range, starting with the initial model of 1985 (the tricolor one inspired by the works bikes), won fans all over the world. Even the special series of the F1 were in great demand: these were the Montjuich, Seca and Santamonica bikes, so-called to celebrate the victories in these races by riders like Grau and Lucchinelli and fitted with special parts like aluminum swinging-arm

suspensions, Brembo "Gold Seal" brakes, sectional wheels and, above all, engines capable of developing 73 hp at 9250 revs. A separate line of development was followed by the F3, similar to the F1 but with the capacity first reduced to 350 cc and later increased again to 400. This was aimed chiefly at the Japanese market, traditionally hungry for Ducatis but, owing to the legal limits placed on high-capacity bikes, obliged to stick to the medium and low range.

In 1986 the Paso arrived, a bike of revolutionary appearance and fitted with highly-advanced running gear. The engine was a development of the Pantah with a capacity of 750 cc, but the rear cylinder was rotated through 180°. It had a twin-

choke carburetor borrowed from the automobile sector and housed in the middle of the V formed by the cylinders. This was followed, in 1989, by the 750 SS, which had similar mechanics but a frame and running gear based on those of the F1: it was proposed as an "entry-level" model in the Ducati range of sports bikes. This family does not include the 900 SS of 1990, for the "bottom" part of its engine was related to that of the 851. The 350 Supersport Junior of 1992 was part of the family, however, as it was a development of the old Pantah, updated with Mikuni 38 carburetors. This engine (maximum power 37 hp at 10,500 revs) was also produced with a capacity of 400 cc, again for the Japanese market.

The Pantah 600 TL, a highly stylized but not very convincing bike.

Facing page: the F1 750, a tricolor dream.

The 750 Santamonica, a special series of the F1.

The fantastic line of the Paso 750, designed by Massimo Tamburini.

The Pantah 500 SL.

Endurance
The Long Race

Endurance races became extremely popular in the eighties. They were no new invention, though, as long-duration competitions have been staged since the dawn of motorcycling. Each race is a struggle against your rivals, but also, and above all, a battle with the snares and pit falls of a trial of exhausting length that puts every component to the test, and in which even the most insignificant part can betray the most meticulous technicians. Twenty-four hours are no joke, especially if you are going flat-out all the time. Not only are the bikes exposed to tremendous strain, but the riders have to be able to grit their teeth and keep going even when the light fades, visibility is reduced and the cold of the dawn works its way into your clothing

– to persevere even when there does not seem to be a ounce of energy left. For the men in the pit, too, there is not a moment's respite: getting ready for refueling stops and executing them in the shortest time possible, unforeseen technical glitches and, of course, the nightmare: a fall! Then we see the rider trying to make his way back to the pit, pushing the battered bike. The damaged parts have to be replaced, everything checked and the bike has to get going again with the minimum of delay. No other race is as severe as one which lasts 24 Hours. Anything can happen, there is always something unexpected: a mistake, or just fatigue, can change the outcome of a race, despite the most thorough preparation.

On double-page spread: the Trial version of the TT1 F1 (Ducati Museum; owner Ducati Motor S.p.A.; photo Giovanni Marchi). Note (on the left) the gas tank with a transparent insert showing the level of the fuel and (below) the twin headlight needed for riding at night.

Right: the Catalan rider Enrique "Quique" de Juan on the 750 F1 Endurance at the Montjuich 24 Hours in 1986.

Below right: the Ducati pit working at night during the 1984 Bol d'Or; the riders are Villa and Cussigh.

Burning Sands

Despite its avowed passion for Racing and sports machines for use on asphalt, Ducati has produced some fine examples of off-road bikes. From 175s for motocross (though never raced officially) to the RT 450s of the Six Days in 1971 and the two-stroke 125 Reliability Trials and Six Days, there has always been some room left over for cross-country bikes. But it was under the Castiglioni management that the real boom in off-road bikes came. Elefants fitted with Ducati engines competed in the Paris-Dakar Rally, the Rally de l'Atlas in Morocco and the Pharaohs' Rally in Egypt. The bikes bore the Cagiva logo, but the engines were prepared with extreme care by Farné and his colleagues, who thus discovered a whole new way of Racing.

The first Ducati to take part in an African race was a special bike, hand-built around a "bevel-gear" base in France at the beginning of the eighties. Ridden by Cheylan, it reached Dakar in eighteenth place in 1980. The official debut of a Cagiva-Ducati came in a race in Morocco, in 1984, where it was ridden by the late lamented Giampaolo Marinoni. The 650-cc bike proved competitive and just a year later Cagiva took on the great Hubert Auriol in the hope of winning the race that was so closely followed by the media and by so much of the public at that time. Bad luck halted the Frenchman when victory was almost within his grasp.

The Cagivas raced in Africa with varying degrees of success, in the hands of such excellent riders as De Petri, Arcarons, Laporte, Picard and Terruzzi. Victory finally came in the Paris-Dakar in 1990, thanks to one of the greatest off-road specialists, the Italian Edi Orioli. His bike was a 900 built in Varese by the special department of Azzalin, but it was powered by a Ducati twin-cylinder prepared in the Racing Department at Borgo Panigale and equipped with specially-made pistons, a reinforced clutch, carefully-worked and polished connecting rods and drive shaft and many details in magnesium.The bike had a capacity of 904 cc (bore and stroke 92 x 68 mm) and two Mikuni 38 carburetors. Its maximum power was 52 hp at 9050 revs and it could exceed 200 kph. In the long desert stretches this was no small advantage. The Elefant had a long wheelbase of 1560 mm and a dry weight of 180 kilograms. Cagiva-Ducati went on to win the Paris-Dakar a second time in 1994, again with Orioli.

On double-page spread: the Cagiva-Ducati 900, winner of the 1990 Paris-Dakar race with the rider Edi Orioli (Ducati Museum; owner Roberto Azzalin; photo Giovanni Marchi). Note (above) the twin headlight at the front, the extended fairing and the hand guards on the handlebars; (at top right) the gas tank split into two independent parts and the instrumentation needed to find your way in the desert (GPS, trip-master and road book).

Edi Orioli during the 1990 Paris-Dakar.

Pantah Ice Trophy

This was undoubtedly one of the most unconventional Ducatis ever produced: a 500 built in 1980 to compete in an experimental European trophy for speedway Racing on ice. A spectacular discipline of distinctly northern character, this type of Racing pits machines and riders against one another in short heats on an oval ice-covered track. Unlike traditional speedway, in which the bike skids on its rear wheel, the studded tires used on ice prevent the wheel from slipping. So the riders (the best in this field all come from northern regions, including Russia) lean with their bikes at really steep angles.

The bikes used in these specialist trials are usually derived from speedway machines, and are therefore single-cylinders with rigid frames designed expressly for this purpose and utilizing special fuels (alcohol for example) that permit very high compression ratios. However, this special Pantah (produced in a small series that made its debut in Italian races) was based on a road bike, something that would theoretically have made for easier access to this sport. The idea never took off in Italy, and so this bike remains a curiosity and a quite unexpected development of the Pantah line, which had already proved to be one of the most versatile in Ducati production, competing in speed trials, endurance tests, African rallies and even races on ice. Its en-gine developed 52 hp at 9000 revs and the bike could touch 200 kph!

Both wheels were 18 inches wide and fitted with special tires that were studded by specialized craftsmen who usually worked in the world of automobile rallies. Unlike the bikes usually raced in this specialty, the Pantah hung onto its braking system, made up of two 260-mm discs. Even the suspension (Marzocchi fork and swinging-arm rear suspension with two shocks) was based on that of the road bike.

Below and facing page: spins on the frozen track with the Pantah Ice Trophy.

The Pantah Ice Trophy, the Ducati created for ice Racing (Ducati Museum; owner Ducati Motor S.p.A.; photo Giovanni Marchi). Note (at bottom) the engine, a production 500 cc, and the spiked tire.

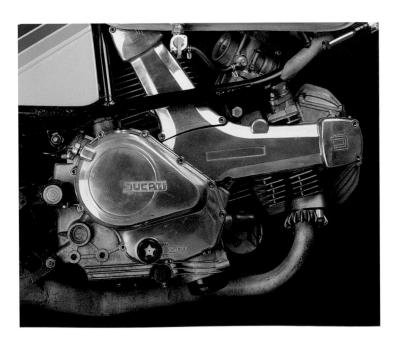

The Mark of the Champion

In the room in the Ducati Museum devoted to the Pantah series we find a number of interesting historical relics and intriguing details. Let us start with the Racing suit worn by Virginio Ferrari, one of the great riders who made history in the eighties. Coming from the Grand Prix (though in the past he had raced with production-derived bikes, mostly Ducatis), Ferrari was one of the best riders of his generation. In this connection it is worth recalling his fight to the finish with Kenny Roberts in 1979. Ferrari also raced with Cagiva in the Grand Prix before moving to Ducati. Here he used the TT1 F1 and went on to become Manager of the works team in the Superbike competition.

The marvelous mechanical structure made of narrow steel tubes belongs to the fabulous TT1. Note that the lattice framework anticipates that of other famous Ducatis still in production today. This simple and rational structure is still competitive and capable of winning races (for instance the world Superbike championship in 1998), in spite of all the fuss made over the superior qualities of duplex frames in light aluminum alloy in recent years.

But the Ducati legend spills over into other "specialized" areas, such as the sophisticated preparation of production motors: the motor of the Cagiva 900, for example, is twice the winner of the Paris-Dakar with Edi Orioli. The whole engine was subjected to careful testing and modification aimed not only at making it more powerful, but also more reliable over the 10,000 or so kilometers of the African marathon. The outer casings and covers are made of magnesium, a choice dictated by the need to keep the weight down. But there were also modifications made on the basis of experience on the track, such as the supplementary air intakes of a late-version TT1 F1, the one with the White Power fork with a central spring. The small but vital adjustments and details are what is needed to give a motorbike a winning edge – and they are born of the insight of a technician or from the hunches of an expert rider.

Marco Lucchinelli celebrating the victory at Daytona with engineer Fabio Taglioni and Giuliano Pedretti.

The twin-cylinder 900 engine prepared for the Paris-Dakar, in which extensive use was made of magnesium parts to reduce the weight (photo Giovanni Marchi).

Bottom left: the frame of the TT1, a "masterpiece" of contemporary Italian art.

The suit worn by Virginio Ferrari.

Bottom right: the supplementary air intake for the TT1 F1.

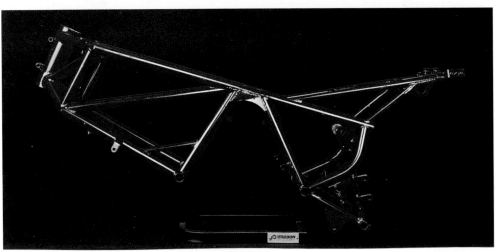

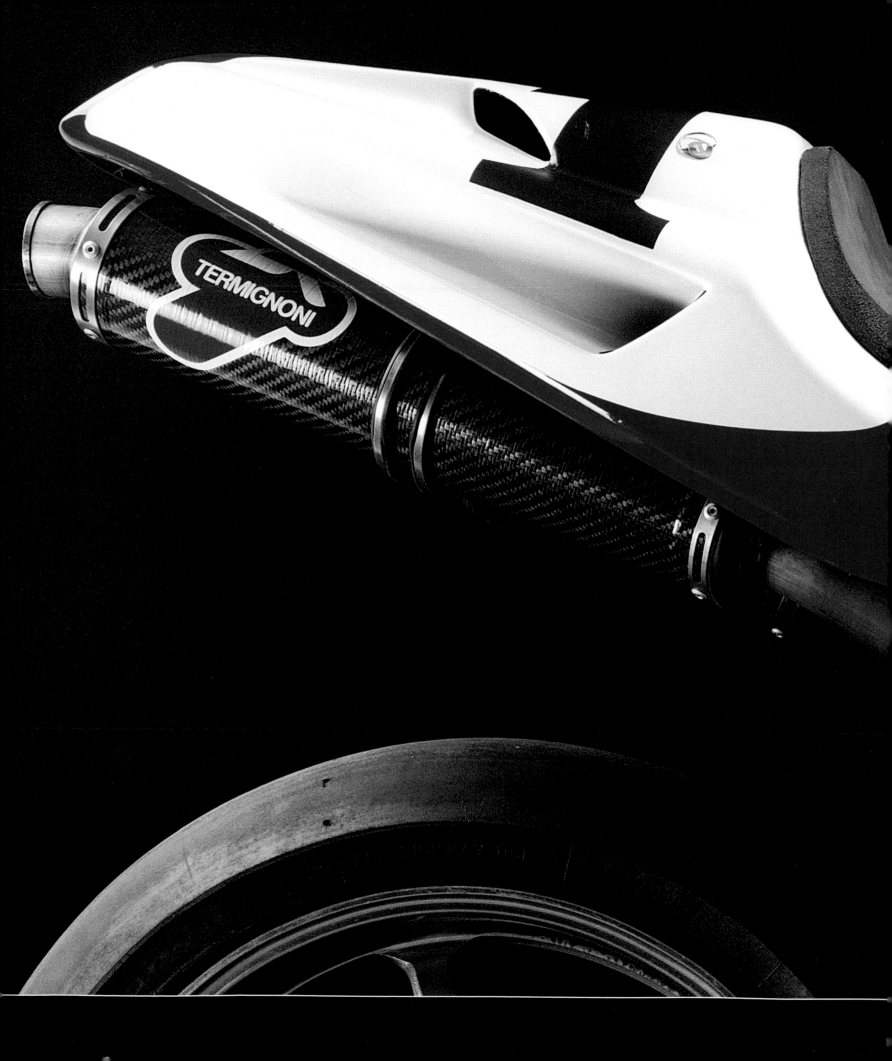

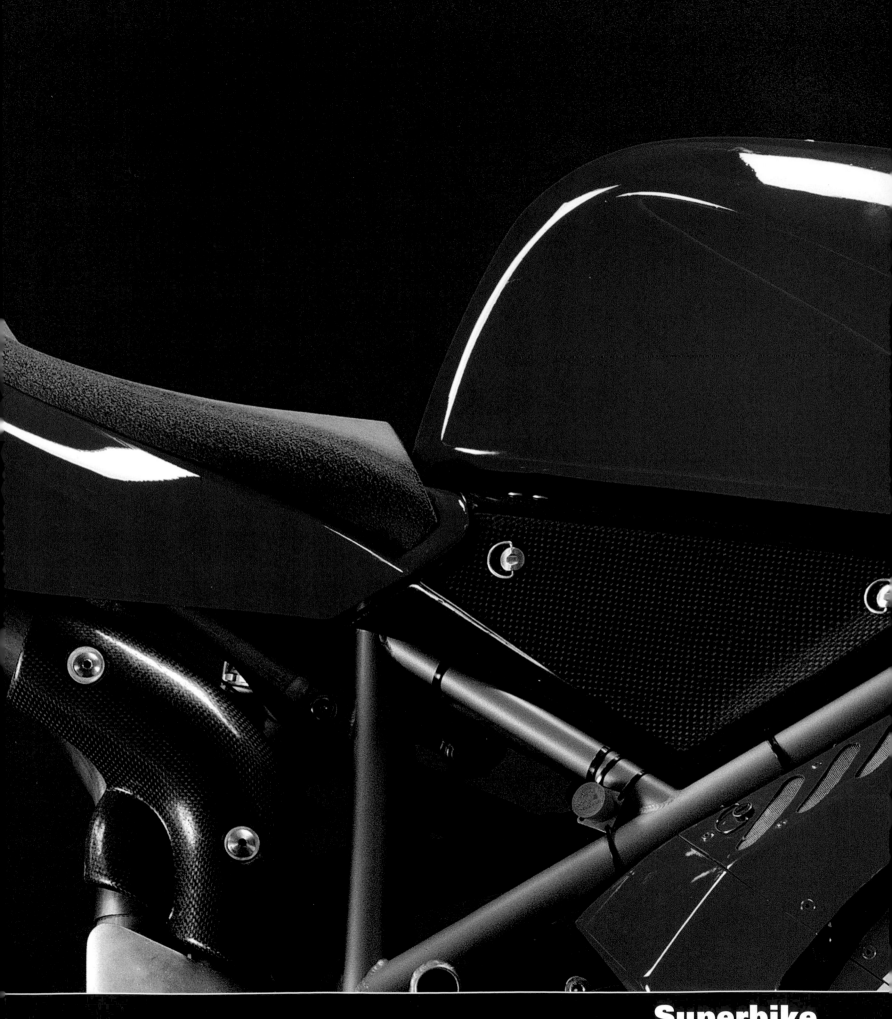

Superbike

Superbike

Lucchinelli makes his debut in the world SBK championships, winning at Donington Park (photo Gozzi).

Below: Baldassarre Monti (photo Gozzi).

851 – At the beginning that was it. A number just like any other. The adventure did not commence with fanfares and drum rolls, but in the misty silence of the outskirts of Bologna. They loaded it on a small OM van painted red. It must have taken quite a while to reach the Channel, board the ferry and drive the last 300 kilometers on the wrong side of the road to Donington. No one could have imagined that that drab little van was carrying a terrible weapon. A twin-cylinder motorbike, the Ducati 851 to be precise, the first ever made with the serial number ZDM 0001, ready for the first, great battle. April 4, 1988, the date of the first World Superbike Championship.

In the paddock at Donington were mustered the world's best Racing bikes – all derived from production models.

Ducati was not counting on numbers, but on quality. It had only one bike on the track, and the man who had been put in its saddle had no room for error. Everyone's hopes were riding on his shoulders. Marco Lucchinelli was used to "all-or-nothing" challenges: back in 1981, seven years earlier, he had staked all against Kenny Roberts. He was the first to realize that he wouldn't have another chance. To define a career, and a whole life, he had to win that race. You all know how it went.

Eight five one, just a number before the qualifying rounds. But only a few laps were needed to show the Japanese that the Ducati could prove a serious threat. Lucky made the fourth fastest time. A good start, but in front of him were Polen's Suzuki, Burnett's Honda and the Bimota ridden by a young man with excellent prospects, Davide Tardozzi.

The flag went down, and the adventure had begun. One, two, three, his rivals fell like skittles. Marco was going hard, and the "Big Pump" sang like a bird along the ups and downs of the track at the edge of Sherwood Forest. The pack was left behind and all that remained in front was the red-and-white silhouette of Tardozzi's Bimota. The young upstart won, the old champion lost. *Plus ça change...*

Lucchinelli had three hours to get his ideas straight and to decide that all was not yet lost. He went back onto the track with all the anger of a wounded but raging lion. He glued himself to his enemy's wheel and shadowed him for many laps, breathing menacingly down his neck. The reckoning came on the last lap: a few drops of rain fell, like a sign from heaven. Marco turned the accelerator right up, knowing that he could not be touched. And saw his adversary skid into the grass, vanishing from his field of view. Ahead of him absolutely nothing, a totally clear horizon that smelled of victory and glory.

Eight five one, a race, a victory. Three record figures. In that year of 1988 Lucchinelli won twice. England and Austria lay at his feet, but the best joke on the Japanese came in their own country's GP races, when Marco produced the fastest time in the heats.

888 - Three numbers that were used in 1990 to identify a guided missile. Guided by a Frenchman of diminutive size, but with a giant temperament, called Raymond Roche. He had arrived at the Ducati court at the end of 1988, making waves right from the start. The following season he was

Top: Juan Garriga.

Below left: Giancarlo Falappa, one of the most combative and unlucky riders in the history of Ducati.

Below right: Doug Polen, the champion from the USA, shown here at a race in 1991.

In the pit with the team at work (photo Morisetti).

Working on Lucchiari's bike at Zeltweg in 1993 (photo Gozzi).

ready to sell his soul to bring the world title to Italy, but his time of triumph was yet to come. In 1989 the former kid from the slums of Marseilles won five times, more than anyone else, but on a few occasions the bike was beset with technical problems and Honda took full advantage. Ducati was not yet ready to taste the greatest victory of all.

But mistakes are a great teacher and bad luck spurs men of valor onto new heights. Thus in 1990 Roche and Ducati returned to the track with a vengeance. Raymond climbed the highest step of the podium a total of eight times and for the first time ever the Italian constructor had the enormous satisfaction of winning in Japan, on the home ground of its principal rivals.

The championship turned into a triumphal march and was over even before the end: the 888 took the world title on a bright Australian afternoon, at a time when the sun had not yet risen back in Italy, on November 11, 1990. It was an historic date for the Italian motorcycle industry and for the entire sport.

Those three numbers, 888, were now a legend.

It is when the *tour de force* becomes the norm that you realize that you are dealing with one of those great upheavals that, every so often, run through the world of sport. The Ducati 888 was definitely one of these. The admiration and incredulity roused by Ducati's first conquest of the world title with Roche in 1990, soon gave way to quite different feelings following the quite incredible series of successes achieved by Doug Polen in 1991 and 1992. For twenty-four long months Ducati's rivals were faced with a bike and a rider that were in a different league.

The lad from Texas, at the beginning, had looked like he had a brilliant career ahead of him. But then a really serious accident put his future in Racing in grave doubt. Suzuki left him to his fate, so that Polen was forced to emigrate to Japan in order to keep racing. Even there, in an unfamiliar environment that made few concessions to foreigners, he was not slow in making an impact. But the real turning point came when he met Eraldo Ferracci, who at that time was Ducati's right-hand man in America, as well as the proprietor of the principal Racing team in the country. The former Benelli mechanic, who had emigrated to the USA in search of fame and fortune at the end of the sixties, had total faith in Doug's potential. A young man from the South with a frank and straightforward character, he was also endowed with great class.

In 1991 Polen should only have raced at home, trying to win that US superbike championship that Ducati had never managed to lay its hands on. But Eraldo Ferracci had set his sights higher, as had the rider himself. His manager persuaded the constructor to let him take part in the first race at Donington, with the excuse that he needed practice before starting on the American series. But the real aim was different.

In qualifying, Polen got his wheels in front of the world champion's, pushing Roche into second position on the grid. The Ducati number 53 was in front of number 1, and it didn't take much to grasp that things were changing. The Frenchman's reign was coming to an end. In fact the Texan came in an easy first and it was not hard for Eraldo Ferracci to convince the people in charge at Ducati: "If you want to win the world championship hands down, you know who to back."

And in fact that was just how it went. In 1991 Polen won seventeen times, a record number of victories that is likely to stand for a long time to come. Ducati celebrated its second world title at the end of September, three trials in advance. Perhaps they foresaw that the Polen tornado was not going to peter out any time soon. And they were right. The 1992 championship went more or less the same way as the one before. Doug and the Ducati 888 led the dance, while all the others fought over the crumbs. It was a very frugal meal that they shared: Polen won nine times, bringing the number 1 back to Borgo Panigale for the third time in a row.

The year before, Ducati had discovered a young man with a shy and unassuming appearance, unruly hair and an earring dangling permanently from the lobe of his right ear. Carl Fogarty, for several seasons the pride and joy of the TT, had fallen from grace. The withdrawal of the Honda works

Parade of Ducatis at Brands Hatch in 1997
(photo Morisetti).

team from the world superbike championship had left him out of a job. To earn himself a living he went to Malaysia, to race with the Kawasaki importer team in the local series. The pay was good and Carl could survive, but it was certainly not what he aspired to.

Ducati offered him a unique chance. The team fielded by the Ducati importer in the UK – the same one as had brought Mike Hailwood back to the track at the 1978 TT – took a Ducati 888 road bike out of the storefront and got Franco Farné to mount the odd "good" piece on it, just to see if the lad had it in him. And he certainly did: in the first race at Donington he flew off the track, but in the second he left them all behind.

Yet Fogarty did not take the title in 1993. Carl went very fast, but he made too many mistakes. That year he won often, eleven times in all, but even that great crop of victories was not enough to defeat the extremely astute Scott Russell, an outstanding rider launched by Kawasaki, who at crucial moments stayed cooler than his rival and in the end got the better of a trial of strength that lasted the whole season.

916 – The following winter the 888 was put contentedly out to grass. The 916 grew up more rapidly than expected. The Japanese did not even have the time to weigh up the threat properly. The new Ducati launched itself at its rivals with a fury. The engineers from the land of the rising sun couldn't believe their eyes when, in April 1994, they saw the 916 make its debut in England and

215

Group photo of the Ducati Racing Team: both 1998 teams are present, Ducati Performance and ADVF (photo Morisetti).

win straight off. Fogarty had found a new and magnificent traveling companion. The British acrobat, anxious for redemption, did not show a moment's hesitation: he lay flat on the gas tank, his head below the windshield, his wrist turned all the way in the right direction. Ducati had won another challenge that seemed impossible: building a bike that would make people forget all about the old and much-titled 888, and capable of winning right from the start.

That year "Foggy", with the powerful backing of the 916, created a legend of his own. Putting behind him all the uncertainties and tensions that had cost him the title the previous season, Carl mustered all his inner resources and made an extraordinary improvement in his approach. He was able to blend his incredible courage with a different vision of the race, understanding that world championships were not won just by putting your head down. The result was a complete champion, a rider in a class of his own, at last a worthy heir to the British school that had had the world at its feet until just two decades before. Russell found himself facing an unbeatable combination. In the dramatic duel at Phillip Island, Fogarty, whose chances were not fancied in this particular race, put up the best performance so far and gave the Kawasaki no quarter. The 916, a rookie of the highest class, was the new world champion.

In 1995 the world champion was not such a cliffhanger. Fogarty had it within his grasp right from the start and celebrated his second title long before the end. It was a wonderful season, marked by unforgettable moments. Like the one at Misano, when five 916s swept the field, allow-

Victory and champagne for Carl Fogarty.

Right: Stephane Mertens (photo Gozzi).

Raymond Roche, world champion in 1990 (photo Porrozzi).

ing Lucchiari, Fogarty, Corser, Chili and Pirovano to cross the finishing line in Indian file, ahead of everyone else. What a blow to the Japanese...

Ducati's "American Uncle", Eraldo Ferracci, had another ace up his sleeve after Doug Polen: Corser won the American championship in 1994, succeeding the Texan, and two years later carried off the world title as well. In doing so he beat both his friend and rival John Kocinski and above all Fogarty who, for one season, had decided to desert Ducati for Honda. The gamble did not pay off: Ducati had found a new hero.

The year 1997 has gone down in the annals as one of defeat. After three years of triumphs the 916 yielded to the Honda, but with the honors of war: the championship remained in the balance right to the end and Fogarty, back in the arms of his old flame, was betrayed by a couple of misfortunes. Not even the unbeatable can win every time. And when a defeat hits the headlines, as in this case, it means that it was less expected than a victory.

The most recent chapter in the Ducati saga is imbued with the pale colors of the Japanese fall. October 4, 1998, is a date that will be inscribed in gold in the book of records, as well as in the memories of *ducatisti* all over the world. The championship was decided in the last round, on Honda's home territory. Fogarty had a lead of half a point over his rival Slight, a margin that meant nothing. No calculations or tactics were involved. It was not a day for strategists, for weighers of risk, but for bold knights. It was "King Carl's" day.

The Englishman's daring was incredible. It seemed as if invisible wires held the 916 upright, in defiance of the laws of physics. Fogarty flew and annihilated the enemy. Honda didn't stand a chance. The rider carried off the most desperate exploit of his career. He was weeping as he crossed the line and then let out a cry of release in the arms of Ducati's mechanics and staff. Once again it was all over.

From Thesis to Track

It all started with a graduate thesis in engineering: *Four-Valve Cylinder Head with Desmodromic Control*. It was written by a young technician, Massimo Bordi, who already had the free run of Ducati. Bordi, who arrived at Borgo Panigale in 1978 (with the far from easy job of replacing Taglioni), had faith in his ground-breaking design: no more air-cooling, room for four valves, all-clear for innovations derived from Formula One motor Racing, and an opening for more electronics.

The project got off to a somewhat muted start in 1986: Bordi's theories were translated into concrete form by Luigi Mengoli, feverishly engaged in a painstaking task that made no allowances for breaks or weekends. By the summer the engine

was already being tested on the bench: it developed 93 hp. In the meantime the Experimental Department came up with a space frame with perimetrical design to house the new engine, which had an integrated system of injection and ignition set in the middle of the V formed by the cylinders. With very little fuss the bike, known as the 748 I.E. ("electronic injection") made its debut in the 1986 Bol d'Or with Garriga, Ferrari and Lucchinelli as riders. It was in seventh place before being forced to withdraw by the failure of a bolt in the piston rod. The 748 I.E was a one-off piece (only one engine exists), but it had to rival the latest version of the two-valve Pantah (the 95-hp 860, the last fling of Taglioni's school). Doubts were raised about Bor-

The engine of the 748 I.E., first of the new generation of four-valve Ducatis.

Gianluigi Mengoli in the pit with the 748 I.E., out for the first time at the 1986 Bol d'Or.

Left: Massimo Bordi and Carl Fogarty in the pit during a 1998 Superbike championships race.

di's new engine, which ran the risk of being dropped altogether. By raising the bore and stroke measurements from 88 x 61·5 mm to 92 x 64 mm (with new crankcases), however, the power was upped to 115 hp. The die was cast: this was going to be the new Ducati engine!

The technical staff worked unceasingly on the project, which was also met with the approval of the new owners. The following year the new 851 raced at Daytona, where Marco Lucchinelli won the Battle of the Twins. The bike was now capable of developing 120 hp: a few people showed interest in the bike, but it was pointed out that it would have difficulty beating the Japanese four cylinders with their multi-fractionated engines and aluminum duplex frames. The bike also had a few teething troubles, but development was continual. Bordi makes no bones about having studied the best that the four-stroke technology of the time could offer. At the end of 1987, the first series of 200 motorbikes was sold to sportsmen and collectors, and obtained recognition for the 1988 superbike championship, the first in the series: these

first 851s to be made and sold (known as "Kit", very rare and much sought-after) were followed by another batch of 300 bikes. Marked with the name "Strada", these bikes, had 16" wheels, while the "Kit" series had 17" wheels with slick tires.

Lucchinelli won on the bike's debut in Great Britain and Austria. Ducati did not take part in the final races of the competition and concentrated instead on getting ready for the next year. In the meantime the capacity was raised to 888 cc by increasing the bore to 94 mm.

The EPROM was also reprogrammed, the rear suspension made longer and the fork replaced by one with reversed stanchions.

In 1989 Lucchinelli became Team Manager and Roche arrived from the 500 cc championships. He ended the season in third place. In fact he had won a record number of victories, but suffered too many defeats – as well as having a few problems with the electronics. The 851 weighed 158 kilograms and had a maximum power of 128 hp. In Japan, signs of nervousness were starting to emerge over this two-cylinders.

Franco Farné lays his expert hands on the new engine.

Facing and following page: the Ducati 851 of 1987 (Ducati Museum; owner Ducati Motor S.p.A.; photo Giovanni Marchi).

The most attractive novelty of 1987, the twin-cylinder Ducati 851 with its unmistakable front profile (right) and gas tank with transparent sides for checking the fuel level (above).

Lucchinelli and the 851 escorted from the TT1 F1 by Stefano Caracchi.

Marco Lucchinelli in the victorious Battle of the Twins at Daytona, 1987 (photo Scagliarini).

888 First Triumphs

In the lion's den: Lucchinelli on the Sugo track in Japan in 1988 (photo Gozzi).

Raymond Roche, 1990 world champion (photo Porrozzi).

In 1990 Ducati reaped what it had sown in the previous seasons, with Raymond Roche, excellent rider and later team manager. The 888 underwent constant development, raising its power to over 130 hp at 11,000 revs, as well as a significant reduction in weight, which had fallen to 147 kg by the end of the season. This was made possible in part by the use of carbon-fiber parts. The fork was made by Ohlins (which had built up solid experience in the world championships), while the articulation of the rear suspension was revised. The most favorable feature of this bike was the high power it could develop at "medium" rates of revolution, around 110 hp at 8000 rpm. This was part of the reason for its success.

In 1991 the boy wonder arrived from the United States: Doug Polen. He was taken in hand by the two "wizards" of the twin-cylinder, who proved to have a golden touch with the new series as well: the Caracchi-Nepoti duo, otherwise known as NCR. Polen's bike developed 133 hp at 11,500 and had a capacity of 888 cc. Also using the 888, Roche took second place while Davide Tardozzi became the European SBK champion. There was no country in the world where the bike did not win races and in many cases the national title.

And the bike was prepared mainly with the scales in mind: they managed to get the weight down to 143 kg (only just over the minimum of 140 required by the regulations) by making more and more use of carbon fiber, even for the exhausts which were built by the specialist Termignoni.

As for the production bikes, a whole range of sports models (from the Strada version to the SP3) was brought out. All of them were closely related to the Racing bikes, even in their components.

On this page and the following double-spread:
the renovated 851, deployed by Ducati at the start of
the first season of Superbike races (Ducati Museum;
owner Ducati Motor S.p.A.; photo Giovanni Marchi).
The powerful braking system (right) is made by
Brembo. The exhausts (below) are raised so that
they do not touch the ground on curves.

Doug Polen triumphed again in 1992, winning the AMA title as well... in his spare time. Falappa was his partner in the team, which was managed by Franco Uncini (another return to the Ducati fold!). Roche had a team of his own, and then there were the bikes prepared directly by the constructor and entrusted to Amatriain, Mertens and Tardozzi. The 1992 version of the 888 did not differ greatly from that of the previous year: the power had been raised to 135 hp, the weight lowered to 142 kg. The fork was a new Ohlins with a diameter of 42 mm, while carbon-fiber discs were used for the first time on Polen's bike. The top-of-the-range production bike was the SP4, which had a lot of features in common with the Racing bike.

The 1993 season, the last one contested by the "old" superbike, concluded with a total of nineteen victories out of twenty-six races for Fogarty, Falappa and Meklau, and yet the title still went to Kawasaki. Polen won the North American championship again. The 1993 bike had a capacity of 926 cc (96-mm bore) and developed 143 hp at 11,500 revs.

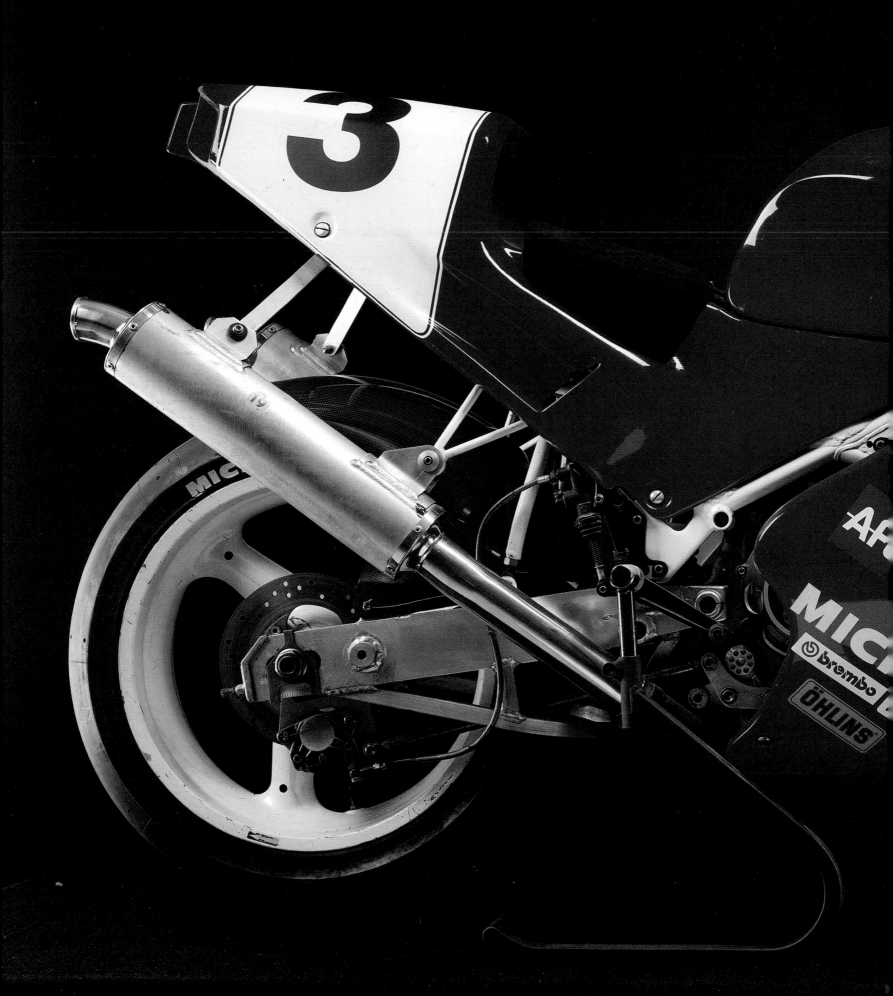

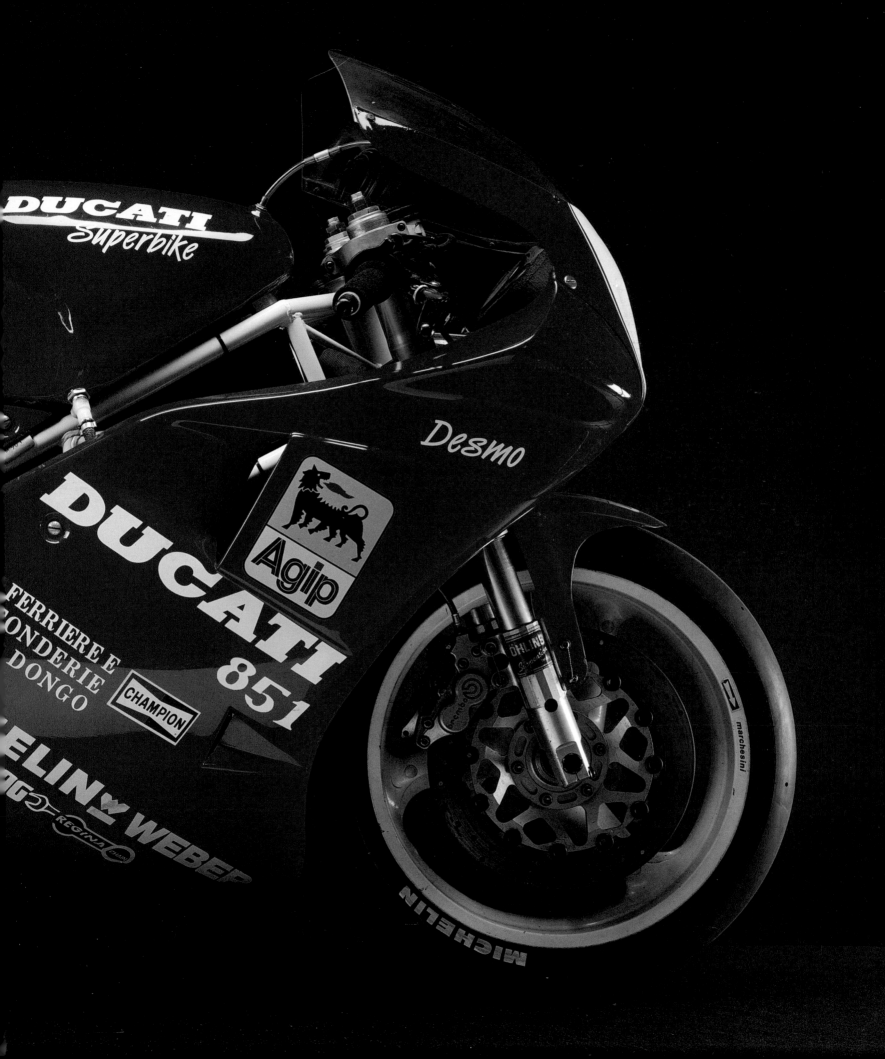

The 888 Superbike of 1992

The desmo four-valve distribution.

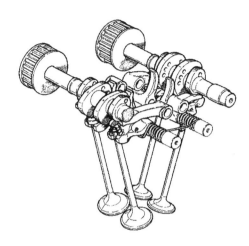

FRAME, FORKS AND RUNNING GEAR – Tubular-steel chromium-molybdenum space frame with engine part under stress. Ohlins front fork with 42 mm reversed stanchions, Ohlins adjustable rising-rate single-shock rear suspension. Brakes: Brembo 320-mm twin-disc with 4-piston caliper at front, 210-mm disc at rear. Dunlop (for Polen) or slick Michelin tires: front 120/60-17", rear 180/50-17".

DIMENSIONS, WEIGHT AND PERFORMANCE – Length 2030 mm, wheelbase 1430 mm, seat height 760 mm. The fuel tank is made out of carbon fiber and Kevlar and holds 20 liters. The rake is 94 mm and the angle of the steering head 24° 5'. Maximum power 140 hp at the shaft (133 at the wheel) at 11,000 rpm. Thanks to the extensive use of carbon-fiber parts, the dry weight is only 142 kg. Estimated top speed 290 kph.

ENGINE – Liquid-cooled four-stroke twin-cylinder, longitudinal 90° V configuration. Bore and stroke 94 x 64 mm. Capacity 888 cc. Compression ratio 11·6:1. Desmodromic twin overhead camshaft valve gear with four valves per cylinder, driven by a toothed rubber belt. Weber-Marelli alpha/numerical electronic fuel injection with four injectors per cylinder. Marelli IAW inductive discharge electronic ignition. Primary reduction by gears, final by chain. Multi-plate dry clutch. Six-speed gearbox. Wet-sump forced lubrication with 4 liters of oil.

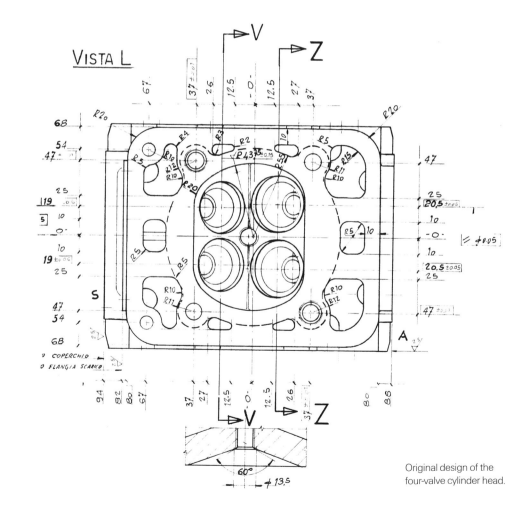

Original design of the four-valve cylinder head.

The 888 Superbike of 1992 (Ducati Museum;
owner Ducati Motor S.p.A.; photo Giovanni Marchi).

916
Touchstone

The end of 1993, at the fall shows where new models are customarily unveiled to the public, brought the 916, probably one of the most beautiful motorbikes ever made. It is not necessary to be a connoisseur of good design or a passionate Ducati fan to recognize this fact, but the incredible thing is that the 916 (and the bikes derived from it that are still racing today and constitute Ducati's top range) will also go down in history as a truly effective machine...

Behind the 916 lies the genius of Massimo Tamburini, a "Renaissance man" whose gifts of creative inspiration, technical skill and love of beauty are a combination that it is unusual to find in any one person. Tamburini had already designed such splendid bikes as the Ducati Paso and Cagiva Mito 125 and, before becoming the head of his own company in San Marino, had created the Bimota. It was from Ducati, in late eighties, that he got the assignment: to design a bike with a tubular frame and twin-camshaft, twin-cylinder engine. Tamburini did not confine himself to a mere exercise in styling, (something that was just not in his character), and he created a true work of art around that engine. The running gear grew up around a lattice of 28-mm-diameter steel tubes, with a single-arm cast-aluminum rear suspension. But Tamburini did more: he realized, for example, that an engine like the Ducati needed a particularly large air box, and so he exploited all the space available, using the bottom of the gas tank as a cover and molding channels into the bodywork. The result was the most handsome body seen on a sports bike in the last ten years.

The 916 embarked on its Racing career straight off. It was not easy to take the place of a bike as proven and successful as the 888. In addition, Honda entered the field with its new

RC 45 and the Federation introduced a modification to the rules that reduced the weight advantage of the twin-cylinders over the four-cylinders to a mere fifteen kilograms.

The bikes that were lined up on the starting grid of the 1994 SBK championships, in the capable hands of Fogarty and Falappa (Ferrari Team) and Pirovano (Tardozzi Team), developed about 150 hp at 11,000 revs and had a capacity of 955 cc, achieved by increasing the bore by two millimeters. The bike underwent constant development: an Ohlins fork with 46-mm reversed stanchions and a new air box. At the end of the season the title went to Fogarty, who was now Ducati's star rider. A bad accident brought Falappa's career to an end and his place was taken by Mauro Lucchiari.

In 1995 a bore measurement of 98 mm was tried out on the bike (taking its capacity to 996 cc), but the tune didn't change. On the contrary, the dominance of the bikes ridden by Fogarty (world champion), Lucchiari, Corser, Pirovano, and Meklau, as well as Chili (racing for a private team), was crushing.

Mauro Lucchiari racing.

The American John Kocinski, a rider of great class on the 916.

The SPS (Sport Production Special) series represents the peak of Ducati sports performance made available for use on the road: true Racing bikes with license plates.

229

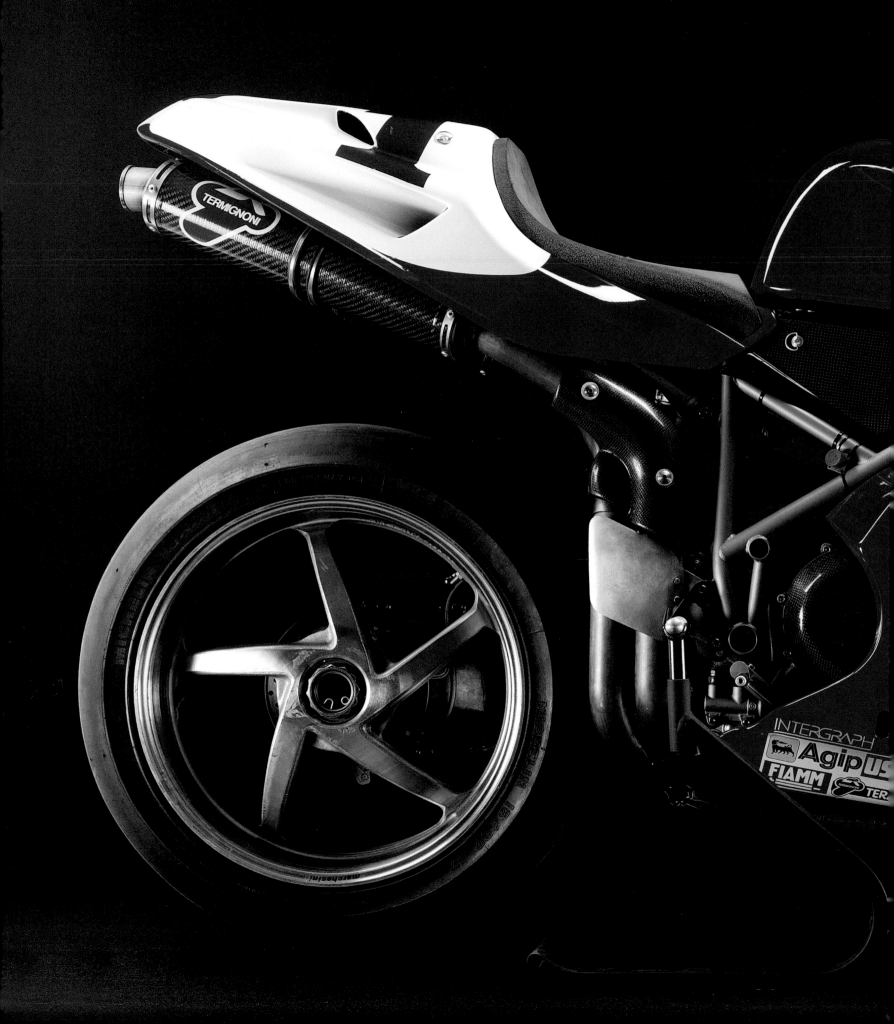

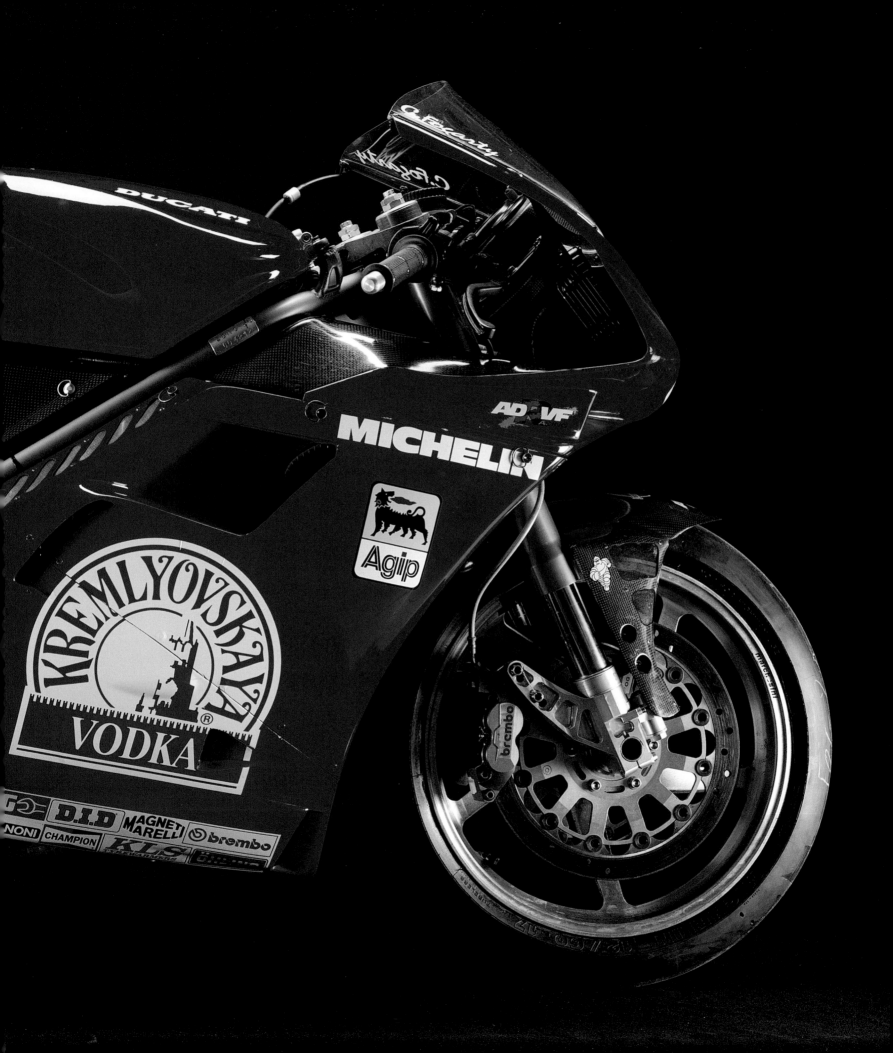

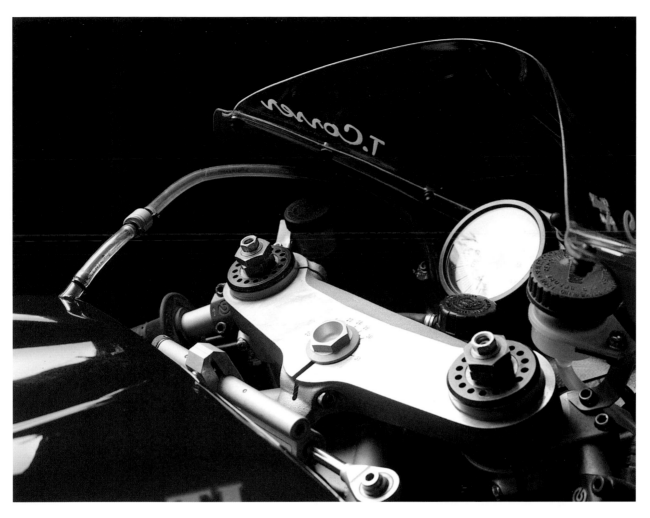

The upper plate of the fork, tachometer and horizontal steering damper of the Ducati 916.

Right: the fork with reversed stanchions and the twin disc.

The sculptural gas tank.

Suggestive back lighting under the rain for Fogarty in 1994.

Giancarlo Falappa (photo Gozzi).

Fabrizio Pirovano (photo Gozzi).

748
Super Sport Allure

Over the last few years a new category has emerged in international Racing: Super Sport. The formula is similar to that of the Superbike competitions and is open to four-cylinder bikes of 600 cc and twin-cylinder ones up to 750. This formula, in which the machines are even closer to production models, is extremely popular with the public.

Ducati had its weapon ready for the Super Sport World Series (the official name of the championship) in the 1995 season: it was called 748, another magic number. Identical in its technology and aesthetics to the 916, the 748 had the same measurements of bore and stroke (88 x 61·5 mm) as the first 4V that raced in the Bol d'Or in 1986 and developed over 100 hp (SP version). The development of the 748 followed the same course as had already been laid down by the other Ducatis of the Superbike series: a small production run was reserved for competitors (the SP series), while the Biposto ("Two-Seater", the name given to the less "hot" but still very sporty models in the range) was made in larger numbers.

The 748 proved an immediate success on the track and, although the World Series (decided in a single race between the two heats of the Superbike championships) did not yet have official status, won the competition three times in a row. In 1995 it was the Frenchman Paquay who rode it over the line and the year after that, the Italian Pirovano, while in 1997 it was the turn of Paolo Casoli, an excellent rider who shifted to this category from the world championships and left his rivals standing. For the world champion bike of 1997, the manufacturer declared a maximum power of 120 hp at 12,000 revs and a top speed of 270 kph.

Paolo Casoli in action with the world champion 748.

Facing page: the Ducati 748, champion of the world Series Supersport 1997, with Paolo Casoli (Ducati Museum; owner Daniele Casolari; photo Giovanni Marchi). The kinship with the 916 is really close. The production fork (right) is made by the specialist Andreani.

The boards for the riders in the Ducati pit: on the left "Gasolio" (Diesel) for Casoli, and on the right "Foggy," Fogarty's nickname.

The Legend Continues

The 1996 season got under way amidst a great deal of uncertainty: the Ducati team had lost Fogarty, who had passed over to Honda, and had engaged a champion with a touchy and unsociable character but a great deal of class, John Kocinski. Everyone was expecting the American to take the title but, at the end of a grueling season, the number one went to an Australian rider discovered by Ferracci and bursting with grit and determination, Troy Corser. Although the '96 bike weighed two kilos more owing to another modification of the rules, Ducati still managed to come up with a real winner that took Corser to the title. The bike's capacity was raised to 996 cc and its power was rated at around 155 hp.

In 1997 Ducati's preeminence missed a beat: the title went to Honda, despite six victories by Carl Fogarty and three by Pierfrancesco Chili. Many came to the conclusion that the fairytale was coming to an end.

And so we come to the 1998 season, with Fogarty, Chili and Corser pitted against Haga's Yamaha and the Hondas of Slight and Edwards. The bike had undergone no substantial changes and the championship proved a tough battle. Fogarty made some worrying "slips," culminating in the disastrous German GP where he was relegated to the back of the pack. It looked like it was all over, but the Englishman refused to give up and began accumulating points with all the grit of a British center-half (Carl is a great fan of the Manchester United soccer team and will appreciate the simile). In Japan, exploiting the opportunity provided by a fall that Corser took in the warm up, Fogarty found the chink he needed and triumphed.

The Ducati world champion bike was the fruit of a new approach. It was created by a team headed by the engineer Claudio Domenicali, which made the scientific analysis of every detail the secret of its success. A group of young engineers "brought up on milk and gasoline" (as Domenicali put it in an interview), who collected data and compared results. On the test bench the engine easily exceeded 160 hp at 11,800 revs, but what the team was looking for was manageability. And then innovations for use on production bikes come from Racing: that is the Ducati philosophy.

The main new development in 1998 was the modification of a "humble" crosspiece of the frame, which made it possible to increase the volume of the air box. This innovation led to a smoother output and the riders immediately took advantage of this. In fact Ducati's strong point in the 1998 season was just this increase in the range and linear output of the engine, free of "peaks" and instabilities. Also worth noting is the MF3 electronics derived from F1 motor Racing. One of the most marked differences from the production bike was the two-centimeter increase in the length of the rear suspension. When racing, depending on the track and the preferences of the rider, it was fitted with two 16·5-inch tires or with a 17-inch one at the rear and brake discs with a diameter ranging from 320 to 290 mm. The rear disc was very small, but that posed no problem for Fogarty: he never used it. The bike often didn't make the lower limit of 162 kg permitted by the regulations, and so had to carry a weight handicap.

Troy Corser, 1996 world champion (photo Morisetti).

Foggy in action.

A "sectioned" 4V engine.

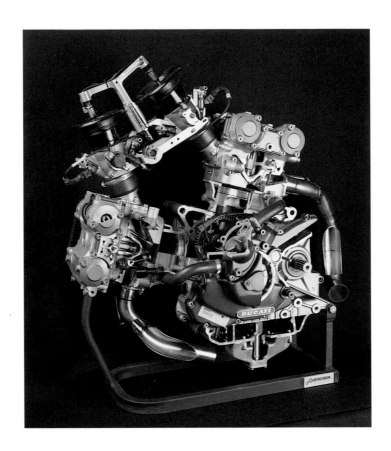

The Ducati 996, 1998 world champion (Ducati Museum; owner Ducati Motor S.p.A.; photo Giovanni Marchi).

Not an Impressionist painting, but a suggestive photograph of Gigi Soldano, with the steering damper "frozen" while everything else seems to be moving.

Carl Fogarty in the pit with his wife (photo Morisetti).

The sensor that signals the beginning and end of each lap to the data acquisition unit, recording the times and displaying them on the digital dashboard.

Carl Fogarty pulling
one of his famous
faces (photo Morisetti).

Right: Fogarty and
Davide Tardozzi,
formerly a Ducati rider
and now Sports Director
of Ducati Racing
(photo Morisetti).

Below: Fogarty
celebrates victory by
waving the Union Jack
(photo Morisetti).

Corser (11) and Fogarty (2) racing in the 1998
Superbike championships at Misano (photo Morisetti).

Right: Claudio Domenicali and Davide Tardozzi in the
pit during a race of the 1998 Superbike
championships (photo Morisetti).

Facing page: Fogarty competing in the 1998
Superbike championships at Laguna (photo Morisetti).

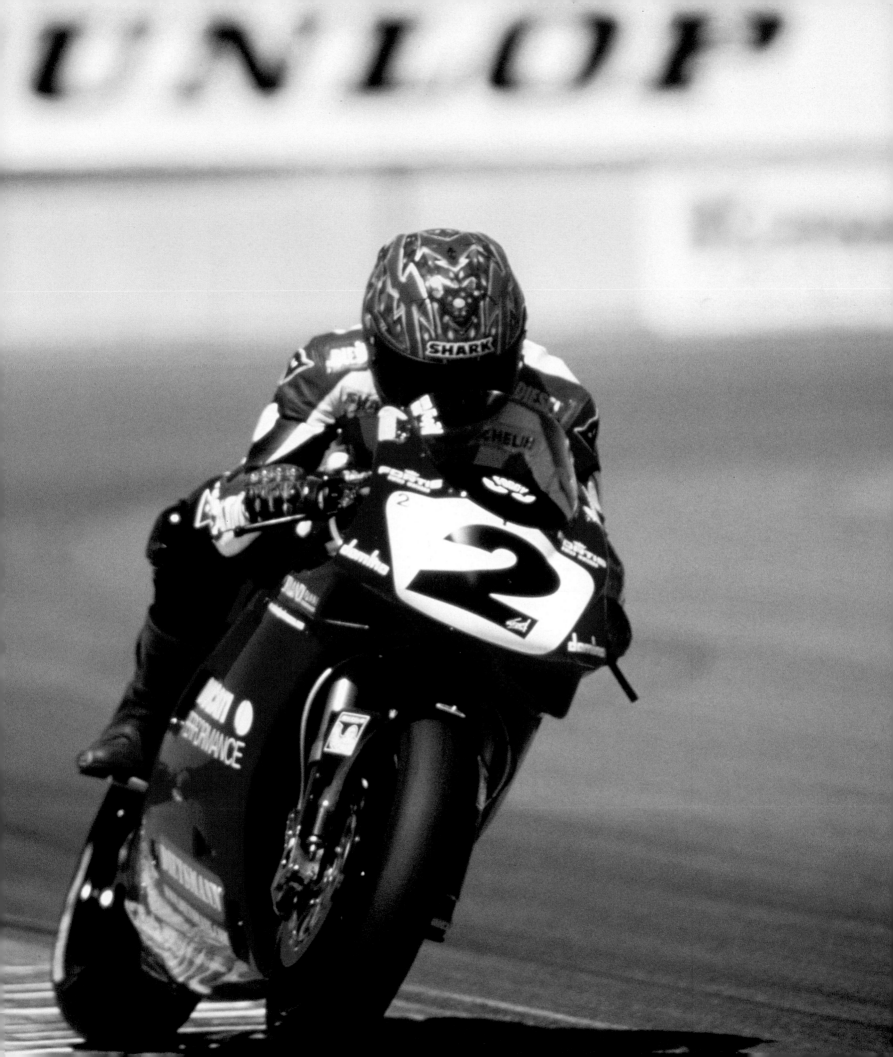

Fogarty (above) and
Casoli (left) in action
with their Ducatis
(photo Morisetti).

Fierce duel between Fogarty (2) and Slight
(photo Morisetti).

243

Fogarty celebrating victory in the Assen leg of the
1998 superbike championships.

Fogarty in the last and decisive race of the 1998 superbike championships at Sugo.

Below: Fogarty, world superbike champion 1998.

Fogarty's wife, Minoli, Tardozzi and the Racing team celebrating victory in the 1998 Superbike championships at Sugo.

The Superbike 996 of 1998

ENGINE – Liquid-cooled four-stroke twin-cylinder, longitudinal 90° V configuration. Bore and stroke 98 x 66 mm. Capacity 996 cc. Compression ratio 12:1. Desmodromic twin overhead camshaft valve gear with four valves per cylinder, driven by toothed rubber belt. Weber-Marelli electronic fuel injection with three injectors per cylinder. Marelli MF3 electronic ignition. Primary reduction by gears, final by chain. Multi-plate dry clutch. Six-speed gearbox. Wet-sump forced lubrication with 4 liters of oil.

FRAME, FORKS AND RUNNING GEAR – Chromium-molybdenum space frame made from steel tubes with a circular section and with engine part under stress. Ohlins front fork with 46-mm reversed stanchions and magnesium pins, Ohlins adjustable rising-rate single-shock rear suspension, with magnesium swinging arm. Brakes: Brembo 320-mm twin-disc with 4-piston caliper at front (replaced by 290-mm discs on slow tracks), 200-mm disc at rear. Slick Michelin tires: front 120/60-17", rear 180/67-17".

DIMENSIONS, WEIGHT AND PERFORMANCE – Length 2030 mm, width 685 mm, wheelbase 1430 mm. The fuel tank is made out of carbon fiber and holds 21·5 liters. Maximum power 158 hp at 12,000 revs per minute. Dry weight 162 kg. Estimated top speed 290 kph. Depending on the track, the bike has also been raced with 16 1/2-inch tires and rims of three different sizes: 3 1/4, 3 1/2 and 3 3/4.

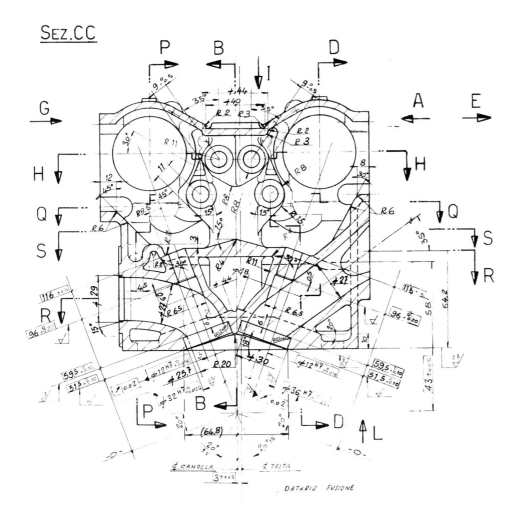

Original design of the 748 cylinder head.

The Ducati 996, 1998 world champion (Ducati Museum; owner Ducati Motor S.p.A.; photo Giovanni Marchi).

Right: the tubular steel frame.

Sound of Singles

The formula known as Sound of Singles (or *Supermono* in Italian) is a very stimulating one for designers, as the only limitation placed on them is the number of cylinders: one. Where everything else is concerned, total freedom! This class attracts not just enthusiasts who rebuild production bikes by hand and with great ingenuity, but also designers like Massimo Bordi, who allowed himself to be tempted by the challenge of the single cylinder. Legend has it that the idea came to him while stuck in a traffic jam in a car with no air conditioning on a hot summer's day. Bordi outlined the design, including a highly-advanced technical feature: a desmo twin overhead camshaft head with four valves (in practice the same as on the 888, with electronic injection from two injectors), along with liquid cooling and an ingenious system for canceling out vibrations with an auxiliary connecting rod.

Development of the idea was entrusted to the engineer Claudio Domenicali, placed in charge of the project, and his staff, who took care of its execution, including the definition of the running gear, while the designer Pierre Terblanche was responsible for the fairing and overall look. The outcome was one of the finest "pure" sports bikes ever produced, in the authentic Ducati style (tubular space frame) but of very small dimensions, as is evident from the length of only 1960 mm, the wheelbase of 1390 mm and the dry weight of 118 kg. There are details over which you could lose a whole day, such as the splendid aluminum rear suspension with a broad upper truss, or the bike's lines, absolutely unmistakable in their Racing style.

The engine had sand-cast casings (the bike was produced in a small run for competition only) and developed a maximum power of 75 hp at 10,000 revs. The capacity of 550 cc derived from a bore of 100 mm coupled with a stroke of 70 mm; the second series has a capacity of 570 cc (102 x 70 mm). The Supermono could reach 220 kph.

Entrusted to a variety of riders, from the British journalist Alan Cathcart to Lucchiari, it has always proved to be one of the best and most competitive singles ever made, despite having a lower capacity than its rivals.

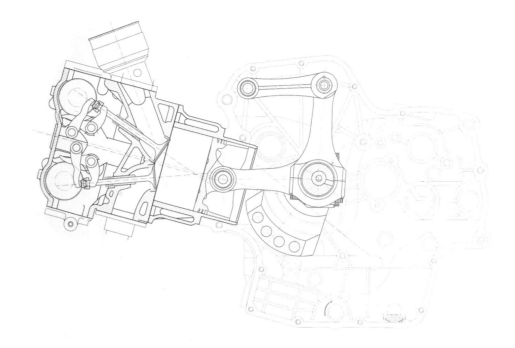

Right: the original design of the single-cylinder engine.

On double-page spread: the Supermono, one of the most extraordinary chapters in the history of motorcycle design (Ducati Museum; owner Ducati Motor S.p.A.; photo Giovanni Marchi). Note (below) the sharp front profile "modeled" by Pierre Terblanche, now at the head of Ducati Design.

The engine of the Supermono in section, with the supplementary vibration-damping link rod.

AMA, Planet USA

Cook Neilson before the start at Daytona in 1977 (photo Lustig).

Left: the starting line of the Battle of the Twins; with number 26, Jim Adamo's F1, and with number 618, Marco Lucchinelli on the same bike (photo Scagliarini).

There are even people have raced with a Paso at Daytona (photo Scagliarini).

Below: in curve with a "bevel gear" machine, one of the best US riders, Rich Schlachter.

As far as Racing goes, the United States is a world apart: a champion of the "European" world is unlikely to be considered number one on the other side of the Atlantic. In America there is the AMA, or American Motorcycle Association, which has its own rules, with classes, titles and races that set their own standards. Ever since the sixties Ducati, largely thanks to the efforts of the importer Berliner, has competed on US tracks. Farné and other Italian riders went over there in the middle of the decade to race with the 250 singles. Later people like Eraldo Ferracci started to race with the twins as well. In addition there is a very good technical school in America too, with mechanics especially skilled in the preparation of production bikes. In fact the AMA regulations have always paid particular attention to races for production-derived motorbikes. For example the "bevel-gear" Ducati 884 used by Cook Neilson (journalist and the winner of a Daytona 100) drew on the fluid dynamics studies of Jerry Branch, a Californian technician who had a knack for getting more out of an engine than anyone thought was possible. It is worth mentioning that the first engine for Hailwood's

bike at the 1978 TT was prepared on the basis of a formula from the USA. Then the works engine from Bologna arrived...

Joey Mills III, winner of the Pro Twins in 1983, Pete Johnson, champion of the 1987 Modified series, Dave Quarterley, first in the Pro Twins of 1988, and Jamie James (1990 Pro Twins champion) are all names that do not mean a great deal to the European enthusiast. But Doug Polen, AMA SBK champion in 1993, and Troy Corser, who won the same title a year later, do. As do the victories of Lucchinelli at Daytona and Freddie Spencer on the four-valve desmo and the growing importance of the Ducati USA teams in recent years: America is not so faraway any longer.

There remains the fascination of a world where, not just the bikes, but even the riders wear the colors of their team in competition, where the award ceremonies are show-biz events and where great importance is attached to image, with numbers artistically painted on fairings by specialists in fine arts. Everywhere else they are just daubed on, with the greatest concession to aesthetics being the use of a bit of masking tape.

The triumph of
Doug Polen,
AMA champion
with the Ducati
888 (photo Euro
Tech).

Gallery

The bike, especially if it's a Ducati, is important. But the rider needs more if he is going give his best on the track. For instance, perfectly designed accessories and made-to-measure clothing. From the helmet, fundamental to safety, to the suit, the gloves and the boots.

The helmet is made of composite fibers (fiberglass, carbon fiber, Kevlar), which make up the bubble, in other words the outer shell, which has to resist impact. Inside there is a layer of polystyrene, shaped to fit the head, which has the task of distributing the impact over the whole of the surface, damping and dispersing it. Then there is a hypoallergenic and comfortable lining. The visor is made out of a sheet of Lexan, treated to ensure the maximum of visibility. The suit is a genuine work of art, in which cowhide (still the best material because of its resistance to abrasion on asphalt, as well as for its properties of permeability and insulation) is combined with inserts of elasticized Kevlar, internal multi-ply padding and the famous knee sliders (or *saponette*, "soap cakes," as they are called in Italian), which allow the rider to put his knee down in curves without injury. These are attached with Velcro and thus easily replaced. The gloves and boots, also made of leather, have outer layers of carbon fiber to resist impacts and inserts of Kevlar fabric and felt to absorb them. Motorcycling today is a safer sport than it used to be, thanks to the great advances made by the manufacturers of equipment for riders.

A limited edition of the 916 series has been devoted to the memory of a great motor-racing driver, Ayrton Senna, killed in a tragic accident at Imola. It is a "production special" based on the specifications wanted by the Brazilian driver, a great fan of Ducati. The most recent version of the Senna uses the mechanics of the 916, while the running gear consists of all the most tried-and-tested components which, developed to meet the demands of Superbike competition, eventually make their way to the "ordinary" customer. The Senna Foundation and Ducati continue their collaboration over these "specials," which are produced in limited series and inevitably end up in the hands of collectors all over the world.

Facing page: Ayrton Senna at Montecarlo (dressed in a tuxedo) in the saddle of an M900 and (at bottom) the Ducati 916 Senna, brought out in 1998

The Dainese suit worn by Fogarty.

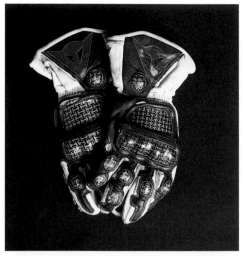

From top to bottom: the Dainese gloves with carbon-fiber inserts and Dainese boots with carbon-fiber and plastic padding used by Carl Fogarty.

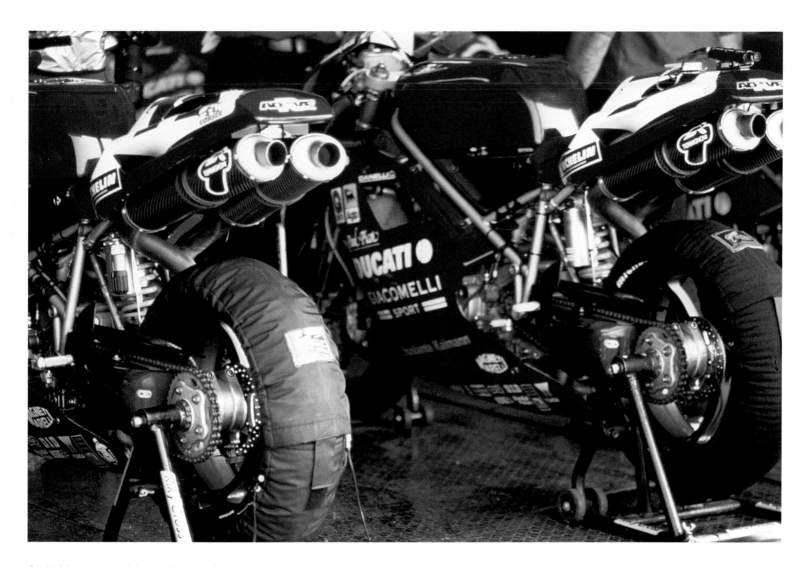

On double-page spread: images from the Ducati pit.

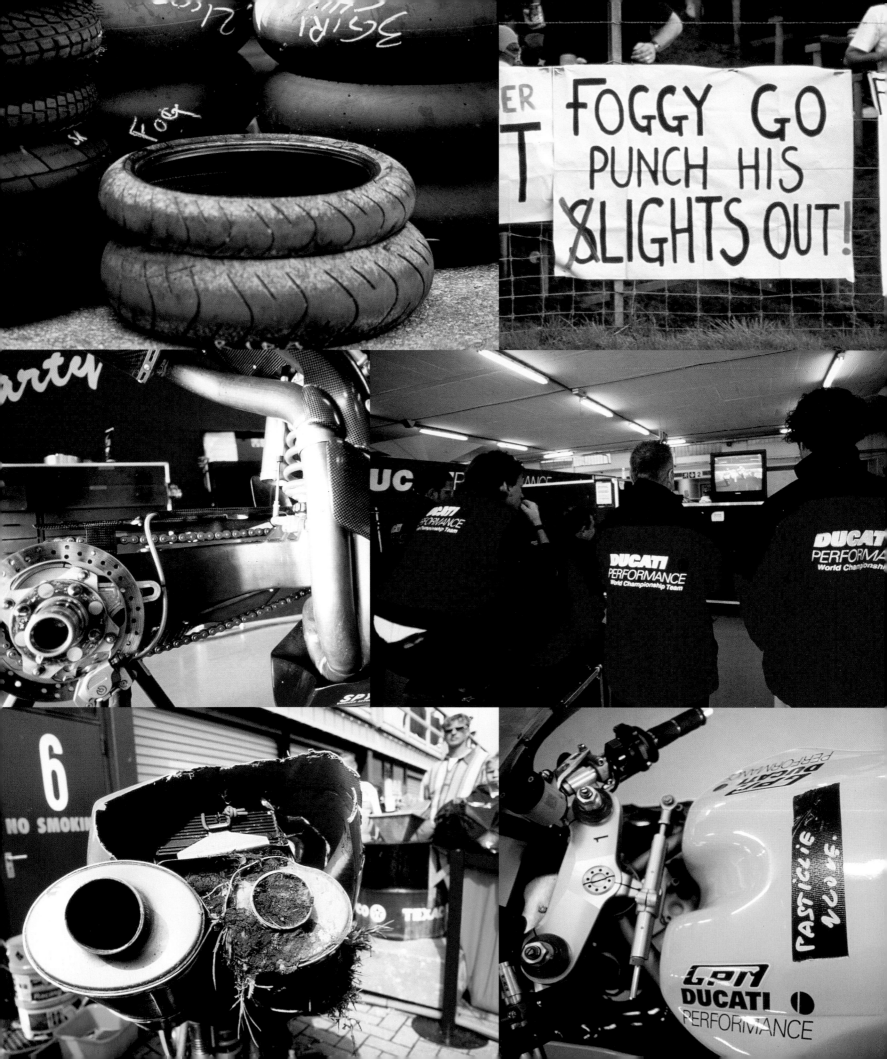

History and Technology

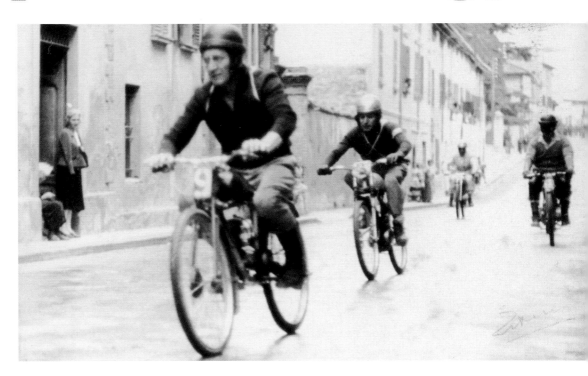

Prototypes
and Designs That Were Never Developed

The history of any motorcycle manufacturer is littered with experiments that never made it to the production line or the racetrack. Such experiments were usually conducted under conditions of strict secrecy and so there are very few people who can claim to have got a close look at them. In addition, there are prototypes built for motor shows (but which never reached the assembly line) and even projects where the process of design was contracted out. Recently Ducati, out of great respect for their historical value, has decided to make public a considerable number of these "one-off pieces" that hardly anyone knew about. They range from the in-line twin-cylinders of the sixties to the mighty four-cylinder "Bipantah" and from the "new series" singles to the three cylinder Grand Prix made in Great Britain by Ricardo.

The question that immediately springs to the enthusiast's mind runs something like this: would history have been changed by the arrival of this engine? For instance, if the Apollo had turned out to be a great success, might Ducati have gone onto specialize in high-capacity bikes in the American style? Or if the "Bipantah" had strangled the four-valve twin-cylinder at birth...? Leaving imponderables aside, let us just take pleasure in these projects that never got off the drawing board or past the first stages of testing.

We owe a particular debt of gratitude to the specialist journals *Motociclismo* and *Motociclismo d'Epoca*, which have urged the management of Ducati not to lose this material, but to make it available to the public instead. Their publisher, in addition, has kindly consented to reproduction of the pictures by Giuseppe Gori, which first appeared in a series of interesting articles.

In-Line Twins

In the history of Ducati, the chapter entitled "in-line twins" has never been a particularly happy one. Many enthusiasts prefer not to remember the mediocre 500s and 350s that were brought out in the seventies, but these engines (never popular owing to their vibration as well their configuration, which is certainly not in the Ducati style) have an interesting story to tell. The "in-lines" derived from a project dating from the early sixties, when Ducati's American importer asked the manufacturer to build a 500-cc in-line twin-cylinder with pushrod and rocker-arm valve gear. This was presented at the Daytona Show of 1965. The air-cooled engine was rated at a maximum power of 36 hp, but the bike was far from light, weighing around 180 kilograms. It was updated in 1968 by mounting the motor on the frame of a Mark 3. A "military" version of the bike was also developed in a bid to attract orders from the Italian army (including the Carabinieri), but this never went into mass production.

The first prototype was fitted with Dell'Orto SS 27-mm carburetors, though later on different types were used (the carburetors on Ducati's current bikes are the most recent kind with a "central float chamber"). The project, carried out under the supervision of the engineer Tumidei, was dusted off in the seventies for the GTL series, which also made use of the body design produced by the Giugiaro studio for the GT 860. Later the in-line twins were given a sporty restyling by Leopoldo Tartarini and renamed the Desmo Sport, but these "middle-sized" bikes were later dropped to make room for the Pantah series.

There is another in-line twin in Ducati's past, the fine twin-camshaft 700 of 1967. Designed by Taglioni, it had distribution driven by a gear train and was mounted on a complete bike equipped with an electric starter (like the other in-lines), as well as a maximum power of over 70 hp at 7500 revs. The engine had some problems with vibration, but above all came up against a lack of conviction on the part of the company, which preferred to direct its resources elsewhere and put this prototype aside.

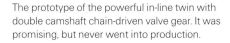

The prototype of the powerful in-line twin with double camshaft chain-driven valve gear. It was promising, but never went into production.

Top: the engine of the in-line twin-cylinder built in the sixties, mounted on a Mark 3 frame. It never went into production (photo Edisport-Gori).

Left: the "military" version of the in-line twin-cylinder that was developed for the Italian armed forces.

Facing page: a motor show in the Netherlands in the seventies. Before deciding whether to introduce a new model into the range, the constructor often needed to consult the public.

Study of a four-valve cylinder head tried out by engineer Fabio Taglioni (photo Edisport-Gori).

Top: a prototype of a single-cylinder engine with single camshaft "bevel gears" (photo Edisport-Gori).

Right: Mototrans's Forza 350 was an attempt to extend the life of the single-cylinder "wide casings" into the eighties.

Below: the Utah, presented here at a show in France, was appreciated by the public but never got beyond the prototype stage. It was to have replaced the Scrambler (photo Favero).

Singles

When it became apparent that the "wide-casing" single-cylinder was coming to the end of its glorious career, Ducati began to think about creating a new engine that would be able to take advantage of recent technical developments.

Mototrans had already tried this with the 350 Forza, which was an attempt to prolong the life of the great single by giving it colors and parts more in tune with the fashion of the eighties. But greater things were expected from Ducati itself... A number of interesting prototype 350s were produced, using a new engine with valve gear (single camshaft with two valves) driven by a toothed rubber belt (the same system as the Pantah) and mounted on the tried-and-tested frame of the Scrambler. Two prototypes were presented at the Milan Show of 1977: highly original in their styling, they were fitted with this motor and given the names Utah and Rollah. For frankly incomprehensible reasons (the Utah in particular was extremely interesting) it was decided not to bring these new machines into production. The boom in single-cylinder enduros was just around the corner (the Yamaha XT 500 dates from this period), but the Italian constructor gave up on singles, perhaps missing out on a lucrative market. It should not be forgotten that at this time the company was part of a State-owned group that had decided Ducati should go in for other areas of production as well. Luckily history took another turn.

An experiment with four valves was also carried out on a single-cylinder engine by the designer who was perhaps least fond of this approach. Using a "slice" of the engine from a Darmah, Fabio Taglioni tried out a head with four valves and single-camshaft bevel-gear. The engine was never put into operation owing to a lack of time. The Ducati Museum is left with this rare specimen, showing how the Romagnese designer had also ventured down a road that was not much to his liking.

Bottom left: the massive V four-cylinder engine built by Mengoli and Taglioni using thermic parts of the Pantah and a new casing (photo Edisport-Gori).

Below: prototypes built by the Giugiaro Studio during the development of the 860.

Bipantah

Let us start by saying that the name we have given to this 90° V four cylinder is not an official one. In fact the impression that this engine is the result of combining two Pantah engines is only a superficial one. In reality all they have in common are the cylinders. Its design was a collaboration between Mengoli and Taglioni (with the former producing a layout on four meters of tracing paper in just forty hours!) and was really advanced for its time. It included a large number of new features (oil cooling, removable gearbox, tunnel crankcase with a flange for the drive shaft), some of them influenced by the studies carried out by VM (leader of the EFIM industrial group), a manufacturer of diesel engines. At the end of this process (i.e. in the mid eighties) the engine was able to develop around 130 hp. This motor became a serious rival to the four-valve twin-cylinder designed by Bordi, at the very moment when the new chief executive was taking over from the now elderly Romagnese engineer. Taglioni had the latest development of his two-valve twins (Pantah series) going for him as well, but the new engine, after the disappointing first phase of its life (debut at the Paul Ricard and the lack of power that it showed during the first tests on the bench), soon began to eclipse its rivals.

In addition, the Japanese constructors, and Honda in particular, had already come up with advanced designs for V fours and the "Bipantah," which had stuck to two valves, was clearly lagging behind the competition.

Three-Cylinder Ricardo

The three-cylinder 350 cc engine built by Ricardo in Great Britain with the aim of challenging MV in the 1973 season. Dismantled, it reveals the belt-driven valve gear and the housing for a mechanical injection system (photo Edisport-Gori).

Right: Mengoli, Farné, Montemaggi and Forasassi showing the engine "just" returned from England (photo Edisport-Gori).

After gathering dust in the stores of the British firm Ricardo Engineering for a quarter of a century, this three-cylinder engine has recently come back to Ducati, which had commissioned its design in 1971. The motor, which was to have been used for a bike capable of challenging the MV in the 1973 world motorcycle championships, was designed by the British engineer Gammans, who brought together the most advanced solutions imaginable at the time, some which would still be viable today. It was a four-stroke in-line frontal three-cylinder with a capacity of 349·3 cc, obtained with a bore of 60 mm and stroke of 41·2 mm. The twin-camshaft valve gear was driven by a toothed belt and had four valves per cylinder. The compression ratio was 12:1.

Other noteworthy features of the Ricardo were the cylinder head cast in one piece with the block, cast-iron linings, separate exhausts (i.e. with two outlets from each cylinder) and, above all, mechanical injection. The motor also had a removable seven-speed gearbox and dry clutch. According to the constructor, the three cylinders developed 80 hp at 15,000 revs.

The reality was different: the engine had "structural" defects that proved hard to get round (for example, the cavities for the circulation of water and the supports of the drive shaft), while the "state of the art" for the suppliers of fundamental components, such as the timing valve gear and injection system, did not seem to be up to the demands of the designer. The engine was tested on the bench under emergency conditions (with the carburetors mounted by hand and parts reworked to deal with casting defects), and proved disappointing to say the least. So many problems were raised at a meeting between the representatives of Ducati and Ricardo in August 1972 that it was decided to call a halt to the project. Thus the attempt to unite the Bolognese technical school with the British one had little success. In any case, Taglioni's twin-cylinders had won the 200 Miles just a few months earlier...

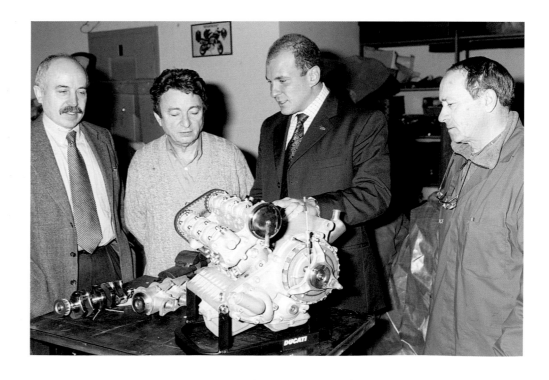

Technical Specifications
Ricardo-Ducati 350

Four-strike engine, three cylinders in line,
dry crankcase.
Capacity 349·3 cc
Bore and stroke 60 x 41·2 mm.
Compression ratio 12:1. Single-piece
crankshaft on four bench blocks
(with anti-friction bearings).
Twin-camshaft valve gear with four valves
per cylinder, driven by toothed belt.
Diameter of valves 23 mm (intake),
21 mm (exhaust).
Head cast in one piece with cylinder block,
cast-iron linings.
Separate exhaust manifolds.
Mechanical injection system.
Forced lubrication with dual pump
for delivery and collection.
Removable seven-speed gearbox.
Dry clutch.

Technical Specifications

Model	Years	Engine	Bore (mm)	Stroke (mm)	Displ. (cc)	Compress. Ratio	Cooling System	Fuel System	Gear (Speeds)	Front Susp.	Rear Susp.	Front Tire	Rear Tire	Wheel Base (m)	Weight (kg)
65 N, T, S, TL, TS	1952-57	1 Cyl. OHV	44	43	65	8:1	Air	Weber carburetor	3	Hydraulic fork	Twin shock swing-arm				55
98 N, T, TS, TL, Sport, Bronco	1952-62	1 Cyl. OHV	49	52	98	7:1	Air	Dell'Orto carburetor 16 mm	4	Hydraulic fork	Twin shock swing-arm	2·50x17	2·75x17	1·245	87
55 R/E	1954-56	1 Cyl. OHV	39	40	48	6·7:1	Air	Weber carburetor	2	Leading link	Twin shock swing-arm	2·00x18	2·00x18	1·092	45
125 TV, TS, Aurea	1956-66	1 Cyl. OHV	55·2	52	124	6·8:1	Air	Dell'Orto carburetor 18 mm	4	Hydraulic fork	Twin shock swing-arm	2·50x17	2·75x17	1·285	90
Bronco 85T, S	1957-61	1 Cyl. OHV	45·5	52	85	9:1	Air	Dell'Orto carburetor 16 mm	4	Hydraulic fork	Twin shock swing-arm	2·50x17	2·75x17	1·245	79
175 T	1957	1 Cyl. SOHC	62	57·8	175	7:1	Air	Dell'Orto carburetor 22 mm	4	Hydraulic fork	Twin shock swing-arm	3·00x17	3·00x17	1·320	103
175 Sport	1957-60	1 Cyl. SOHC	62	57·8	175	8:1	Air	Dell'Orto carburetor 22·5 mm	4	Hydraulic fork	Twin shock swing-arm	2·50x18	2·75x18	1·320	106
48 Sport	1958-65	1 Cyl. 2 stroke	38	42	48	9·5:1	Air	Dell'Orto carburetor 15 mm	3	Hydraulic fork	Twin shock swing-arm	2·25x18	2·25x18	1·180	54
100 S	1958	1 Cyl. SOHC	49	52	98	9:1	Air	Dell'Orto carburetor 18 mm	4	Hydraulic fork	Twin shock swing-arm	2·50x17	2·75x17	1·320	89
125 S T, TS	1958-65	1 Cyl. SOHC	55·2	52	124	8:1	Air	Dell'Orto carburetor 20 mm	4	Hydraulic fork	Twin shock swing-arm	2·50x17	2·75x17	1·320	100
175 TS Americano	1958-60	1 Cyl. SOHC	62	57·8	175	7:1	Air	Dell'Orto carburetor 22 mm	4	Hydraulic fork	Twin shock swing-arm	2·50x18	2·75x18	1·320	108 (118)
200 Elite Americano TS	1959-65	1 Cyl. SOHC	67	57·8	204	8·5:1	Air	Dell'Orto carburetor 24 mm	4	Hydraulic fork	Twin shock swing-arm	2·75x18	3·00x18	1·320	111
200 Motocross	1959-60	1 Cyl. SOHC	67	57·8	204	8·5:1	Air	Dell'Orto carburetor 27 mm	4	Hydraulic fork	Twin shock swing-arm	2·75x21	3·00x19	1·380	124
250 Monza	1961-68	1 Cyl. SOHC	74	57·8	249	8:1	Air	Dell'Orto carburetor 24 mm	4/5	Hydraulic fork	Twin shock swing-arm	2·75x18	3·00x18	1·320	125
250 Diana Daytona	1961-64	1 Cyl. SOHC	74	57·8	249	8:1	Air	Dell'Orto carburetor 24 mm	4	Hydraulic fork	Twin shock swing-arm	2·75x18	3·00x18	1·320	120
250 Scrambler	1961-67	1 Cyl. SOHC	74	57·8	249	9·2:1	Air	Dell'Orto carburetor 27 mm	4/5	Hydraulic fork	Twin shock swing-arm	3·00x19	3·50x19 (4·00x18)	1·350	109 (120)
48 Brisk Piuma	1962-67	1 Cyl. 2 stroke	38	42	48	6·3:1	Air	Dell'Orto carburetor 12 mm	1/3	Hydraulic fork	Twin shock swing-arm	2·00x18 (2·00x19)	2·00x18 (2·00x19)	1·160 (1·170)	45 (52)
80 Setter	1962-64	1 Cyl. 2 stroke	47	46	80	7·1:1	Air	Dell'Orto carburetor 15 mm	3	Hydraulic fork	Twin shock swing-arm	2·25x18	2·50x17		62
48, 50 Piuma, Sport	1962-66	1 Cyl. 2 stroke	38	42	48	6·3:1	Air/fan	Dell'Orto carburetor 15 mm	3	Hydraulic fork	Twin shock swing-arm	2·25x18	2·25x18	1·160	49

Model	Years	Engine	Bore (mm)	Stroke (mm)	Displ. (cc)	Compress. Ratio	Cooling System	Fuel System	Gear (Speeds)	Front Susp.	Rear Susp.	Front Tire	Rear Tire	Wheel Base (m)	Weight (kg)
250 Mark 3	1963-67	1 Cyl. SOHC	74	57·8	249	10:1	Air	Dell'Orto carburetor 27/29 mm	4/5	Hydraulic fork	Twin shock swing-arm	2·50x18	2·75x18	1·320 (1·350)	110 (112)
48/100 Brio	1964-68	1 Cyl. 2 stroke	38/51	42/46	48/94	7/10:1	Air/fan	Dell'Orto carburetor 12/16 mm	3	Leading link fork	Twin shock swing-arm	2·75x9 (3·50x8)	2·75x9 (3·50x8)		63·5 (80)
48/50 SL1/2	1964-69	1 Cyl. 2 stroke	38 (38·8)	42	48/50	7/11:1	Air/fan	Dell'Orto carburetor 15/18 mm	3/4	Hydraulic fork	Twin shock swing-arm	2·25x19	2·25x19	1·150	58 (61)
100 Cadet Falcon	1964-68	1 Cyl. 2 stroke	51/52	46	94/98	10:1	Air/fan	Dell'Orto carburetor 18/24 mm	3/4	Hydraulic fork	Twin shock swing-arm	2·25x18	2·50x18	1·160	66
100 Mountaineer	1964-68	1 Cyl. 2 stroke	51/52	46	94/98	10:1	Air/fan	Dell'Orto carburetor 18/24 mm	3/4	Hydraulic fork	Twin shock swing-arm	2·50x16	3·50x16	1·170	68
250 GT	1964-66	1 Cyl. SOHC	74	57·8	249	8:1	Air	Dell'Orto carburetor 24 mm	5	Hydraulic fork	Twin shock swing-arm	2·75x18	3·00x18	1·320	125
250 Mach 1	1964-66	1 Cyl. SOHC	74	57·8	249	10:1	Air	Dell'Orto carburetor 29 mm	5	Hydraulic fork	Twin shock swing-arm	2·50x18	2·75x18	1·350	116
160 Monza Junior	1964-67	1 Cyl. SOHC	61	52	156	8·2:1	Air	Dell'Orto carburetor 22 mm	4	Hydraulic fork	Twin shock swing-arm	2·75x16	3·25x16	1·330	106 (108)
350 Sebring	1965-67	1 Cyl. SOHC	76	75	340	8·5:1	Air	Dell'Orto carburetor 24 mm	5	Hydraulic fork	Twin shock swing-arm	2·75x18	3·00x18	1·330	123
125 Cadet, 4 Lusso, Scrambler	1967	1 Cyl. OHV	53	55	121	8·4:1	Air	Dell'Orto carburetor 18 mm	4	Hydraulic fork	Twin shock swing-arm	2·50x18 (2·75x16)	2·75x18 (3·25x16)	1·160	72 (75)
50 Rolly	1968	1 Cyl. 2 stroke	38	42	48	7:1	Air	Dell'Orto carburetor 12 mm	mono	Hydraulic fork	Solid	2·00x18	2·00x18		42
250 Scrambler (wide case)	1968-74	1 Cyl. SOHC	74	57·8	249	9:1	Air	Dell'Orto carburetor 27/26 mm	5	Hydraulic fork	Twin shock swing-arm	3·50 x19	4·00x18	1·380	132
250 Mark 3, (wide case)	1968-74	1 Cyl. Desmo	74	57·8	249	10:1	Air	Dell'Orto carburetor 29 mm	5	Hydraulic fork	Twin shock swing-arm	2·75x18 (2·75 x19)	3·00x18 (3·50x18)	1·360	127
250 Mark 3D, Desmo	1968-74	1 Cyl. Desmo SOHC	74	57·8	249	10:1 (9·7:1)	Air	Dell'Orto carburetor 29 mm	5	Hydraulic fork	Twin shock swing-arm	2·75x18 (3·25x18)	3·00x18 (3·50x18)	1·360	127
350 Scrambler	1968-74	1 Cyl. SOHC	76	75	340	9·5:1	Air	Dell'Orto carburetor 29 mm	5	Hydraulic fork	Twin shock swing-arm	3·50x19	4·00x18	1·380	133
350 Mark 3	1968-74	1 Cyl. SOHC	76	75	340	10:1	Air	Dell'Orto carburetor 29 mm	5	Hydraulic fork	Twin shock swing-arm	2·75x18 (2·75 x19)	3·00x18 (3·50x18)	1·360	128 (127)
350 Mark 3D Desmo	1968-74	1 Cyl. Desmo SOHC	76	75	340	10:1	Air	Dell'Orto carburetor 29 mm	5	Hydraulic fork	Twin shock swing-arm	2·75 x18 (3·25x18)	3·00x18 (3·50x18)	1·360	127
50/100 Scrambler	1969-74	1 Cyl. 2 stroke	38·78 52	42/46	50/98	10·5/11·2:1	Air	Dell'Orto carburetor 18/24 mm	4	Hydraulic fork	Twin shock swing-arm	2·75x18 (2·50x18)	3·50x16 (2·50x17)	1·150 1·180	59 (67)
450 Scrambler	1969-74	1 Cyl. SOHC	86	75	436	9·3:1	Air	Dell'Orto carburetor 29 mm	5	Hydraulic fork	Twin shock swing-arm	3·50x19	4·00x18	1·380	133
450 Mark 3	1969-74	1 Cyl. SOHC	86	75	436	9·3:1	Air	Dell'Orto carburetor 29 mm	5	Hydraulic fork	Twin shock swing-arm	2·75x18 (2·75 x19)	3·00x18 (3·50x18)	1·360	130 (127)
450 Mark 3D Desmo	1969-74	1 Cyl. Desmo SOHC	86	75	436	9·3:1	Air	Dell'Orto carburetor 20 mm	5	Hydraulic fork	Twin shock swing-arm	2·75x18 (3·25x18)	3·50x18	1·360	130 127
125 Scrambler	1971	1 Cyl. SOHC	55·2	52	124	8·5:1	Air	Amal carburetor 20 mm	5	Hydraulic fork	Twin shock swing-arm	2·50x19	3·50x18	1·340	105

Model	Years	Engine	Bore (mm)	Stroke (mm)	Displ. (cc)	Compress. Ratio	Cooling System	Fuel System	Gear (Speeds)	Front Susp.	Rear Susp.	Front Tire	Rear Tire	Wheel Base (m)	Weight (kg)
450 R/T	1971-73	1 Cyl. Desmo SOHC	86	75	436	9·3:1	Air	Dell'Orto carburetor 29 mm	5	Marzocchi fork 35 mm	Twin shock swing-arm	3·00x21	4·00x18	1·450	128
750 GT	1971-74	2 Cyl. SOHC	80	4·4	748	8·5:1	Air	2 carburetors 30 mm	5	Hydraulic fork 38 mm	Twin shock swing-arm	3·25x19	3·50x18	1·530	185
750 Sport	1972-74	2 Cyl. SOHC	80	74·4	748	9·3:1	Air	2 Dell'Orto carburetors 32 mm	5	Hydraulic fork 38 mm	Twin shock swing-arm	3·25x19	3·50x18	1·530	185
750 Super Sport	1974-79	2 Cyl. Desmo SOHC	80	74·4	748	9·65:1	Air	2 Dell'Orto carburetors 40 mm	5	Marzocchi fork 38 mm	Twin shock swing-arm	3·50x18	3·50x18 (120/90) (1·500)	1·530	180 (189)
860 GT GTE	1974-76	2 Cyl. SOHC	86	74·4	864	9:1	Air	2 Dell'Orto carburetors 32 mm	5	Ceriani fork 38 mm	Twin shock swing-arm	3·50x18	4·00x18	1·520	206 217
125 Six Days	1975-77	1 Cyl. 2 stroke	54	54	124	10·5:1 14·5:1	Air	Carburetor 30/32 mm	6	Hydraulic fork 35 mm	Twin shock swing-arm	3·00x21	3·75x18 (4·00x18)	1·420 (1·430)	108 (97)
900 Super Sport	1975-85	2 Cyl. Desmo SOHC	86	74·4	864	9·3:1	Air	2 Dell'Orto carburetors 40/32 mm	5	Marzocchi fork 38 mm	Twin shock swing-arm	100/90 3·50 x18	110/18 3·50 x18	1·500	205 (190)
860/900 GTS	1976-79	2 Cyl. SOHC	86	74·4	864	9·8:1	Air	2 Dell'Orto carburetors 32 mm	5	Hydraulic fork 38 mm	Twin shock swing-arm	3·50x18	120/90 x18	1·520	217
350 GTL	1976-78	2 Cyl. SOHC	71·8	43·2	350	9·6:1	Air	2 Dell'Orto carburetors 26 mm	5	Marzocchi fork 35 mm	Twin shock swing-arm	3·25x19	3·50x18	1·400	170
500 GTL	1976-78	2 Cyl. SOHC	78	52	497	9·6:1	Air	2 Dell'Orto carburetors 30 mm	5	Marzocchi fork 35 mm	Twin shock swing-arm	3·25x18	3·50x18	1·400	170
350 Sport Desmo	1977-80	2 Cyl. Desmo SOHC	71·8	43·2	350	9·6:1	Air	2 Dell'Orto carburetors 26 mm	5	Paioli fork 35 mm	Twin shock swing-arm	3·25x18	3·50x18	1·400	181
500 Sport Desmo	1977-80	2 Cyl. Desmo SOHC	8	52	497	9·6:1	Air	2 Dell'Orto carburetors 30 mm	5	Paioli fork 35 mm	Twin shock swing-arm	3·25x18	3·50x18	1·400	185
350 GTV	1978-80	2 Cyl. SOHC	71·8	43·2	350	9·6:1	Air	2 Dell'Orto carburetors 26 mm	5	Paioli fork 35 mm	Twin shock swing-arm	3·25x18	3·50x18	1·400	183
500 GTV	1978-80	2 Cyl. SOHC	78	52	497	9·6:1	Air	2 Dell'Orto carburetors 30 mm	5	Paioli fork 35 mm	Twin shock swing-arm	3·25x18	3·50x18	1·400	181
900 Darmah	1978-84	2 Cyl. Desmo SOHC	86	74·4	864	9·3:1	Air	2 Dell'Orto carburetors 32 mm	5	Hydraulic fork 38 mm	Twin shock swing-arm	3·50x18	120/90 x18	1·550	216
900 Mike Hailwood Replica	1979-84	2 Cyl. Desmo	86	4·4	864	9·3:1	Air	2 Dell'Orto carburetors 40 mm	5	Marzocchi fork 38 mm	Twin shock swing-arm	100/90 x18	110/90 x18	1·500	210·5
900 SS Darmah	1979-80	2 Cyl. Desmo SOHC	86	74·4	864	9·5:1	Air	2 Dell'Orto carburetors 32 mm	5	Marzocchi fork 38 mm	Twin shock swing-arm	3·50x18	120/90 x18	1·550	216
500 SL	1980-84	2 Cyl. Desmo SOHC	74	58	499	9·5:1	Air	2 Dell'Orto carburetors 36 mm	5	Hydraulic fork 35 mm	Twin shock swing-arm	3·25x18	3·50x18	1·450	180
600 SL	1982-84	2 Cyl. Desmo SOHC	80	58	583	10·4:1	Air	2 Dell'Orto carburetors 36 mm	5	I lydraulic fork 35 mm	Twin shock swing-arm	3·25x18	4·00x18	1·450	187
350 XL	1982-84	2 Cyl. Desmo SOHC	66	51	349	10·3:1	Air	2 Dell'Orto carburetors 30 mm	5	Hydraulic fork 35 mm	Twin shock swing-arm	3·00x18	3·50x18	1·450	177
600 TL	1982-84	2 Cyl. Desmo SOHC	80	58	583	10·4:1	Air	2 Dell'Orto carburetors 36 mm	5	Hydraulic fork 35 mm	Twin shock swing-arm	100/90 x18	110/90 x18	1·450	177
900 S2	1982-84	2 Cyl. Desmo SOHC	86	74·4	864	9·5:1	Air	2 Dell'Orto carburetors 40 mm	5	Marzocchi fork 38 mm	Twin shock swing-arm	100/90 x18	110/90 x18	1·500	190

Model	Years	Engine	Bore (mm)	Stroke (mm)	Displ. (cc)	Compress. Ratio	Cooling System	Fuel System	Gear (Speeds)	Front Susp.	Rear Susp.	Front Tire	Rear Tire	Wheel Base (m)	Weight (kg)
650 SL	1984-86	2 Cyl. Desmo SOHC	82	61·5	650	10:1	Air	2 Dell'Orto carburetors 36 mm	5	Marzocchi fork 35 mm	Twin shock swing-arm	100/90 x18	110/90 x18	1·450	187
Mille MHR, S2	1984-85	2 Cyl. Desmo SOHC	88	80	973	9·3:1	Air	2 Dell'Orto carburetors 40 mm	5	Marzocchi fork 38 mm	Twin shock swing-arm	100/90 x18	130/80 x18	1·500	198 (193)
750 F1	1985-88	2 Cyl. Desmo SOHC	88	61·5	748 10:1	9·3:1	Air and oil	2 Dell'Orto carburetors 36 mm	5	Hydraulic fork 38/40 mm	Adjustable single shock	120/80 x16	130/80 x18	1·400	175
350 F3	1986-88	2 Cyl. Desmo SOHC	66	51	349	10:1	Air	2 Dell'Orto carburetors 30 mm	5	Marzocchi fork 35 mm	Adjustable single shock	100/90 x16	120/80 x18	1·400	165
400 F3	1986-89	2 Cyl. Desmo SOHC	70·5	51	398	10·4:1	Air	2 Dell'Orto carburetors 30 mm	6	Marzocchi fork 35 mm	Adjustable single shock	100/90 x16	120/80 x18	1·400	165
Montjuic Lag. Seca S. Monica	1986-88	2 Cyl. Desmo SOHC	88	61·5	748	10:1	Air and oil	2 Dell'Orto carburetors 40 mm	5	Italia fork 40 mm	Adjustable single shock	120/60 x16	180/67 x16	1·400	155
750 Paso	1986-90	2 Cyl. Desmo SOHC	88	61·5	748	10:1	Air and oil	Weber twin shock carburetor	5	Marzocchi fork M1R 42 mm	Single shock rising rate	130/60 x16	160/60 x16	1·450	195
Indiana 750/650 350	1986-90	2 Cyl. Desmo SOHC	88 (82) (66)	61·5 (51)	748 (650) (349)	10:1	Air	2 Dell'Orto carburetors 36/30 mm	5	Hydraulic fork 40 mm	Twin shock swing-arm	110/90 x18	140/90 x15	1·530	180
750 Sport	1988-90	2 Cyl. Desmo SOHC	88	61·5	748	9·5:1	Air and oil	Weber twin shock carburetor	5	Marzocchi fork 40 mm	Adjustable single shock	130/60 x16	160/60 x16	1·450	180
851 Strada	1988	2 Cyl. Desmo DOHC	92	64	851	10·4:1	Liquid	Marelli electronic fuel injection	6	Marzocchi fork M1R 42 mm	Single shock rising rate	130/60 x16	160/60 x16	1·460	185
851 Strada	1989-90	2 Cyl. Desmo DOHC	92	64	851	11:1	Liquid	Marelli electronic fuel injection	6	Marzocchi fork M1R 42 mm	Single shock rising rate	120/70 x17	180/55 x17	1·430 192	190
888 Racing	1989-93	2 Cyl. Desmo DOHC	94	64	888	12:1	Liquid	Marelli electronic fuel injection	6	Upside down fork 42 mm	Single shock rising rate	S1016	S1423	1·430	155 (150) (145)
900 Super Sport	1989-90	2 Cyl. Desmo SOHC	92	68	904	9·2:1	Air and oil	Weber twin shock carburetor	6	Marzocchi fork 40 mm	Adjustable single shock	130/60 x17	170/60 x17	1·450	180
906	1989-90	2 Cyl. Desmo SOHC	92	68	904	9·2:1	Liquid	Weber twin shock carburetor	6	Marzocchi fork M1R 42 mm	Single shock rising rate	130/60 x16	160/60 x16	1·450	205
851 (888) Sport Production	1990-93	2 Cyl. Desmo DOHC	94	64	888	11:1	Liquid	Marelli electronic fuel injection	6	Upside down fork 42 mm	Single shock rising rate	120/70 x17	180/55 x17	1·430	188
350 Super Sport	1991-93	2 Cyl. Desmo SOHC	66	51	341	10·7:1	Air	2 Mikuni carburetors 38 mm	5	Upside down fork 41 mm	Adjustable single shock	120/60 x17	160/60 x17	1·410	173
400 Super Sport	1991-97	2 Cyl. Desmo SOHC	70·5	51	398	10:1	Air	2 Mikuni carburetors 38 mm	5	Upside down fork 41 mm	Adjustable single rising rate	120/60 x17	160/60 x17	1·410	172
750 Super Sport	1991-97	2 Cyl. Desmo SOHC	88	61·5	748	9:1	Air and oil	2 Mikuni carburetors 38 mm	5	Upside down fork 41 mm	Adjustable single rising rate	120/60 x17	160/60 x17	1·410	173 (176)
851 Strada	1991-92	2 Cyl. Desmo DOHC	92	64	851	10·5:1	Liquid	Marelli electronic fuel injection	6	Upside down fork 41 mm	Single shock rising rate	120/70 x17	180/55 x17	1·430 202	199

Model	Years	Engine	Bore (mm)	Stroke (mm)	Displ. (cc)	Compress. Ratio	Cooling System	Fuel System	Gear (Speeds)	Front Susp.	Rear Susp.	Front Tire	Rear Tire	Wheel Base (m)	Weight (kg)
900 Super Sport	1991-97	2 Cyl. Desmo SOHC	92	68	904	9·2:1	Air and oil	2 Mikuni carburetors 38 mm	6	Upside down fork 41 mm	Adjustable single shock	120/70 x17	170/60 x17	1·410	183 (186)
907 IE	1991-92	2 Cyl. Desmo SOHC	92	68	904	9·2:1	Liquid	Marelli electronic fuel injection	6	Marzocchi fork M1R 42 mm	Single shock rising rate	120/70 x17	170/60 x17	1·490	215
900 Superlight FE	1992-98	2 Cyl. Desmo SOHC	92	68	904	9·2:1	Air and oil	2 Mikuni carburetors 38 mm	6	Upside down fork 41 mm	Adjustable single shock	120/70 x17	170/60 x17	1·415	176 (179) (182)
Supermono	1993-95	1 Cyl. Desmo DOHC	100 (102)	70	550 (572)	11·8:1	Liquid	Marelli electronic fuel injection	6	Upside down fork 42 mm	Adjustable single shock	310/480 R17	155/60 R17	1·360	122
888 Strada	1993-94	2 Cyl. Desmo DOHC	94	64	888	11:1	Liquid	Marelli electronic fuel injection	6	Upside down fork 41 mm	Single shock rising rate	120/70 x17	80/55 x17	1·430	202
900 M Monster	1993	2 Cyl. Desmo SOHC	92	68	904	9·2:1	Air and oil	2 Mikuni carburetors 38 mm	6	Upside down fork 41 mm	Single shock rising rate	120/60 x17	170/60 x17	1·430	185
600 M Monster	1994	2 Cyl. Desmo SOHC	80	58	583	10·7:1	Air	2 Mikuni carburetors 38 mm	5	Upside down fork 41 mm	Single shock rising rate	120/60 x17	160/60 x17	1·430	174
600 Super Sport	1994-97	2 Cyl. Desmo SOHC	80	58	583	10·7:1	Air	2 Mikuni carburetors 38 mm	5	Upside down fork 41 mm	Adjustable single shock	120/60 x17	160/60 x17	1·410	172
888 Racing	1994	2 Cyl. Desmo DOHC	96	64	926	12:1	Liquid	Marelli electronic fuel injection	6	Upside down fork 42 mm	Single shock rising rate	120/60 x17	180/67 x17	1·430	145
916 Strada	1994	2 Cyl. Desmo DOHC	94	66	916	11:1	Liquid	Marelli electronic fuel injection	6	Upside down fork 43 mm	Single arm rising rate	120/70 x17	190/50 x17	1·410	195
916 SPS	1994-96	2 Cyl. Desmo DOHC	94	66	916	1·2:1	Liquid	Marelli electronic fuel injection	6	Upside down fork 43 mm	Single arm. rising rate.	20/70 x17	190/55 x17	1·410	195
748 Biposto	1995	2 Cyl. Desmo DOHC	88	61·5	748	11·5:1	Liquid	Marelli electronic fuel injection	6	Upside down fork 43 mm	Single arm rising rate	120/70 x17	180/55 x17	1·410	202
748 SP/ SPS	1995	2 Cyl. Desmo DOHC	88	61·5	748	11·6:1	Liquid	Marelli electronic fuel injection	6	Upside down fork 43 mm	Single arm rising rate	120/70 x17	180/55 x17	1·410	200
916 Biposto	1995	2 Cyl. Desmo DOHC	94	66	916	11:1	Liquid	Marelli electronic fuel injection	6	Upside down fork 43 mm	Single arm rising rate	120/70 x17	190/50 x17	1·410	204
916 Senna	1995-98	2 Cyl. Desmo DOHC	94	66	916	11:1	Liquid	Marelli electronic fuel injection	6	Upside down fork 43 mm	Single arm rising rate	120/70 x17	190/50 x17	1·410	201
916 Racing	1995-96	2 Cyl. Desmo DOHC	96	66	955	12:1	Liquid	Marelli electronic fuel injection	6	Upside down fork 46 mm	Single arm rising rate	120/60 17SC	180/76 17SC	1·420	154
750 M Monster	1996	2 Cyl. Desmo SOHC	88	61·5	748	9:1	Air and oil	2 Mikuni carburetors 38 mm	5	Upside down fork 41 mm	Single shock rising rate	120/60 x17	160/60 x17	1·430	178

Model	Years	Engine	Bore (mm)	Stroke (mm)	Displ. (cc)	Compress. Ratio	Cooling System	Fuel System	Gear (Speeds)	Front Susp.	Rear Susp.	Front Tire	Rear Tire	Wheel Base (m)	Weight (kg)
916 Racing	1997	2 Cyl. Desmo DOHC	98	66	996	12:1	Liquid	Marelli electronic fuel injection	6	Upside down fork 46 mm	Single arm rising rate	120/60 17SC	180/60 17SC	1·430	162
916 SPS	1997	2 Cyl. Desmo DOHC	98	66	996	12:1	Liquid	Marelli electronic fuel injection	6	Upside down fork 43 mm	Single arm rising rate	120/70 x17	190/50 x17	1·410	190
ST2	1997	2 Cyl. Desmo SOHC	94	68	944	10·2:1	Liquid	Marelli electronic fuel injection	6	Upside down fork 43 mm	Single shock rising rate	120/70 x17	170/60 x17	1·430	212
900 Super Sport	1998	2 Cyl. Desmo SOHC	92	68	904	9·2:1	Air and oil	Marelli electronic fuel injection	6	Upside down fork 43 mm	Single shock	120/70 x17	170/60 x17	1·410	188
400 M Monster	1998	2 Cyl. Desmo SOHC	70·5	51	398	10:1	Air and oil	2 Mikuni carburetors 38 mm	5	Upside down fork 40 mm	Single shock rising rate	120/60 x17	160/60 x17	1·430	174
900 M Monster S, Cromo, California	1998	2 Cyl. Desmo SOHC	92	68	904	9·2:1	Air and oil	2 Mikuni carburetors 38 mm	6	Upside down fork 41 mm	Single shock. rising rate	120/70 xZR17	170/60 xZR17	1·430	183 (185)
Sport Touring 2	1998	2 Cyl. Desmo DOHC	94	68	944	10·2:1	Liquid	Marelli electronic fuel injection	6	Upside down fork 43 mm	Single shock rising rate	120/70 xZR17	170/60 xZR17	1·430	209
900 M Monster, City, Dark City Dark	1999	2 Cyl. Desmo SOHC	92	68	904	9·2:1	Air and oil	2 Mikuni carburetors 38 mm	6	Upside down fork 41 mm	Single shock rising rate	120/70 xZR17	170/60 xZR17	1·430	185 (187)
750 M Monster, City, Dark, City Dark	1999	2 Cyl. Desmo SOHC	88	61·5	748	9:1	Air and oil	2 Mikuni carburetors 38 mm	5	Upside down fork 40 mm	Single shock rising rate	120/60 xVR17	160/60 xVR17	1·430	178 (180)
600 M Monster City, Dark, City Dark	1999	2 Cyl. Desmo SOHC	80	58	583	10·7:1	Air	2 Mikuni carburetors 38 mm	5	Upside down fork 40 mm	Single shock rising rate	120/60 xVR17	160/60 xVR17	1·430	174 (176)
900 Super Sport	1999	2 Cyl. Desmo SOHC	92	68	904	9·2:1	Air and oil	Marelli electronic fuel injection	6	Upside down fork 43 mm	Single shock rising rate	120/70 xZR17	170/60 xZR17	1·395	188
750 Super Sport	1999	2 Cyl. Desmo SOHC	88	61·5	748	9:1	Air and oil	Marelli electronic fuel injection	5	Upside down fork 43 mm	Single shock rising rate	120/70 xZR17	160/60 xZR17	1·405	183
Sport Touring 4	1999	2 Cyl. Desmo DOHC	94	66	916	11:1	Liquid	Marelli electronic fuel injection	6	Upside down fork 43 mm	Single shock rising rate	120/70 xZR17	170/60 xZR17	1·430	215
Hyper Sport 996 SPS	1999	2 Cyl. Desmo DOHC	98	66	996	11·5:1	Liquid	Marelli electronic fuel injection	6	Upside down fork 43 mm	Single shock rising rate	120/70 xZR17	190/50 xZR17	1·410	190
Hyper Sport 996	1999	2 Cyl. Desmo DOHC	98	66	996	11·5:1	Liquid	Marelli electronic fuel injection	6	Upside down fork 43 mm	Single shock rising rate	120/70 xZR17	190/50 xZR17	1·410	198
Hyper Sport 748 SPS	1999	2 Cyl. Desmo DOHC	88	61·5	748	11·6:1	Liquid	Marelli electronic fuel injection	6	Upside down fork 43 mm	Single shock rising rate	120/60 xZR17	180/55 xZR17	1·410	194
Hyper Sport 748	1999	2 Cyl. Desmo DOHC	88	61·5	748	11·5:1	Liquid	Marelli electronic fuel injection	6	Upside down fork 43 mm	Single shock rising rate	120/60 xZR17	180/55 xZR17	1·410	196

Roll of Honor

1947

ITALY
15/2, Viareggio, 55, Recchia Mario, Cucciolo
7/4, Villa Spada-Casaglia, 55, Vitali Bruno, Cucciolo
13/4, Salsomaggiore, 55, Verderi, Cucciolo
13/4, Reggio Emilia, 65, Recchia Mario, Cucciolo
20/4, Naples, 55, Rosati Lorenzo, Cucciolo
11/5, Imola, 55, Muller Bruno, Cucciolo
May, S. Giovanni Valdarno, 40, Luciani Giovanni, Cucciolo
May, Casalecchio di Reno, 50, Pozzi, Cucciolo
29/6, Lucca: 60, Luciani Giovanni, Cucciolo; 100, Santini Angiolo, Cucciolo
24/8, Pesaro, 55, Campanelli Paolo, Cucciolo
31/8, Recanati, 55, Campanelli Paolo, Cucciolo
10/9, Tolentino, 55, Campanelli Paolo, Cucciolo
14/9, Arezzo, 40, Solfanelli Rita, Cucciolo
21/9, Mantua, 50, Battesini Vincenzo, Cucciolo
21/9, Cesena, 55, Campanelli Paolo, Cucciolo
September, Tortoreto, 55, Di Leonardo Claudio, Cucciolo
5/10, Salsomaggiore, 55, Fava Carlo, Cucciolo
5/10, Recanati, 55, Campanelli Paolo, Cucciolo
19/10, Lonato, 50, Zitelli Glauco, Cucciolo
October, Sanremo-Poggio dei Fiori, 50, Lepore Attilio, Cucciolo
9/11, Vermicino-Rocca di Papa, 50, Levantini Romano, Cucciolo
November, Vittorio Veneto, 60, Mayer Italo, Cucciolo
November, Mantua, 60, Battesini Vincenzo, Cucciolo

OFF-ROAD RACING
5/6, Verona, 50, Maragna Arturo, Cucciolo
October, Torricelle, 50, Galbier Giuseppe, Cucciolo
October, Mantua, 50, Gnaccarini Tito, Cucciolo
26/10, Coppa del Pasubio: 50, Benetti, Cucciolo; Benetti-Quaiotti, Cucciolo

1948

ITALY
8/2, Monza, 50, Rossi Umberto, Cucciolo
14/3, Albenga, 50, Ricchieri Mario, Cucciolo
19/3, Salita Monte Mario, 50, Petrucci Franco, Cucciolo
28/3, Villa Spada-Casaglia, 50, Mingotti Giuseppe, Cucciolo
29/3, Florence, 50, Santini Angiolo, Cucciolo
April, Arezzo, 50, Severi Roberto, Cucciolo
25/4, Pontedera, 50, Santini Angiolo, Cucciolo
1/5, Trent, 50, De Jorio Mario, Cucciolo
27/5, Caserta, 50, Russo Luigi, Cucciolo
May, Chieri, 65, Marzani, Cucciolo
6/6, Trent, 50, Zorzan Ivo, Cucciolo
6/6, Mergellina-Posillipo, 50, Lepri Tullio, Cucciolo

13/6, Lomazzo, 50, Baglioni Edoardo, Cucciolo
13/6, Sondrio, 50, Rossi Umberto, Cucciolo
27/6, Montagnana, 50, Scardellato Aldo, Cucciolo
1/7, Conegliano, 50, Scardellato Aldo, Cucciolo
1/7, Mantua, 60, Zitelli Glauco, Cucciolo
4/7, Alassio, 60, Baglioni Edoardo, Cucciolo
11/7, Senigallia, 60, Salvi Alvaro, Cucciolo
25/7, Bologna, 50, Zitelli Glauco, Cucciolo
25/7, Trent-Bondone, 50, Quaiotti Tiziano, Cucciolo
8/8, Coppa della Consuma, 60, Volpi Lino, Cucciolo
8/9, Prato, 50, Tenti Faliero, Cucciolo
5/9, Castiglione delle Stiviere, 50, Zitelli Glauco, Cucciolo
19/9, Dalmine, 50, Bonfanti, Cucciolo
19/9, Belluno: 60, Stringhetto Gino, Cucciolo; 75, Gardellin Tiziano, Cucciolo
26/9, Sassi-Superga, 50, Cannella Salvatore, Cucciolo
3/10, Udine: 50, Stringhetto Gino, Cucciolo; 55, Gardellin Tiziano, Cucciolo
3/10, Milan, 50, Zitelli Glauco, Cucciolo
3/10, Macerata, 50, Valenti Pietro, Cucciolo
3/10, Teramo: 50, Petrucci Franco, Cucciolo; 100, Petrucci Franco, Cucciolo
3/10, Gallarate, 60, Grasselli, Cucciolo
6/10, Roncade, 50, Zampieri Lino, Cucciolo
10/10, Castellucchio, 50, Zitelli Glauco, Cucciolo
10/10, Schio, 60, Falco Renato, Cucciolo
17/10, Vicenza, 50, Gardellin Tiziano, Cucciolo
October, Voltana, 50, Drei Giulio, Cucciolo
17/10, Villaganzerla, 50, Gardellin Tiziano, Cucciolo
1/11, Lido di Genova, 60, Poggi Carlo, Cucciolo
1/11, Lugo di Romagna, 50, Drei Giulio, Cucciolo
1/11, Ravenna, 50, Bacchetta F., Cucciolo
7/11, Lonato, 60, Zampieri Lino, Cucciolo
14/11, Vermicino-Rocca di Papa: 60, Manzari Giuseppe, Cucciolo; 75, Levantini Romano, Cucciolo
21/11, Sanremo-San Romolo, 60, Ricchieri Mario, Cucciolo

OFF-ROAD RACING
March, Voghera, 50, Robotti, Cucciolo
4/4, Ravenna, 60, Drei Giulio, Cucciolo
4/4, Coppa Silla, ex-aequo, 50, Gobbo-Rossi Riboni, Cucciolo
April, Lugo di Romagna, 60, Drei Giulio, Cucciolo
April, Novi Ligure, 65, Foglia Carlo, Cucciolo
April, Targa Colli, Padua, 50, Gardena, Cucciolo
8/5, Milan-Sanremo, ex-aequo, 50, 18 classificati, Cucciolo
22/5, Coppa Busetti, Bergamo, ex-aequo, 50, Riboni-Carlessi-Gobbo-Salvetti-Scariani, Cucciolo
30/5, S. Giovanni in Persiceto, 60, Mattei Giuseppe, Cucciolo
30/5, Siena, ex-aequo, 50, Artini-Vettrino-Celli-Giovannetti, Cucciolo

May, Montalbuccio, Siena, ex-aequo, 60, Artini-Vettrino-Fontani, Giovannetti-Marzi-Danti, Cucciolo
13/6, Turin, 50, Costantini, Cucciolo
25/7, Tre Valli Torinesi, ex-aequo, 50, Actis-Cannella-Zan, Cucciolo
July, Milan, 50, Garofali, Cucciolo
July, Prealpi Vicentine, ex-aequo, 50, Benetti-Quaiotti, Cucciolo
7/11, Coppa Torricelle, 50, Galbier Giuseppe, Cucciolo
November., Cittadella, 60, Berti Mario, Cucciolo

1949

ITALY
1/1, Bologna-Colle Osservanza, 60, Cometti Gino, Cucciolo
27/2, Palermo, 50, La Rosa Giuseppe, Cucciolo
19/3, Villaganzerla, 50, Gardellin Tiziano, Cucciolo
19/3, Ferrara, 50, Giglioli Alberto, Cucciolo
19/3, Monte Mario: 50, Flamini Giuseppe, Cucciolo; 50, Marchino Marcello, Cucciolo; 100, Levantini Romano, Cucciolo
20/3, Ferrara, 50, Giglioli Alberto, Cucciolo
March, Viareggio, 50, Grossi Ugo, Cucciolo
27/3, Lugo di Romagna, 50, Recchia Mario, Cucciolo
27/3, Gradisca, 50, Zippo-Marcoratti, Cucciolo
17/4, Voghera, 50, Baglioni Edoardo, Cucciolo
17/4, Ravenna, 50, Mattei Giuseppe, Cucciolo
25/4, Castellanza, 50, Fiorani Giordano, Cucciolo
1/5, Siena, 50, Sani Ferruccio, Cucciolo
8/5, Trent-Ponte Alto, 50, Zorzan Ivo, Cucciolo
22/5, Riccione, 50, Mattei Giuseppe, Cucciolo
22/5, Marmirolo, 50, Giglioli Alberto, Cucciolo
26/5, Monte Berico, 50, Stringhetto Gino, Cucciolo
26/5, Casalecchio di Reno, 50, Mattei Giuseppe, Cucciolo
26/5, Naples, 50, Tipaldi Armando, Cucciolo
May, Tigli, 60, Giglioli Alberto, Cucciolo
29/5, Alfonsine, 50, Drei Giulio, Cucciolo
5/6, Broni, 50, Carchini Ferruccio, Cucciolo
12/6, Correggio, 50, Giglioli Alberto, Cucciolo
16/6, San Donà, 50, Stringhetto Gino, Cucciolo
16/6, Monsummano, 50, Cometti Gino, Cucciolo
19/6, Lonato Pozzolo, 50, Zitelli Glauco, Cucciolo
26/6, Cormons, 50, Zampieri Lino, Cucciolo
June, Riva del Garda, 50, Gardellin Tiziano, Cucciolo
10/7, Trent, 50, Galasso, Cucciolo
10/7, Poggibonsi, 50, Stendardi Otello, Cucciolo
24/7, Pesaro, 50, Marchetti Guerrino, Cucciolo
15/8, Cingoli, 50, Zitelli Glauco, Cucciolo
August, Monfalcone, 50, Stringhetto Gino, Cucciolo
September, Roncade, 60, Scardellato Aldo, Cucciolo
25/9, Pistoia, 50, Stendardi Otello, Cucciolo

16/10, Vermicino-Rocca di Papa, 50, Organtini Alberto, Cucciolo
16/10, Treviso, 50, Giglioli Alberto, Cucciolo
16/10, Arezzo, 50, Tenti Faliero, Cucciolo
20/10, Borgo di Trent, 50, Recchia Mario, Cucciolo
23/10, Riva del Garda, 50, Feller Giuseppe, Cucciolo
23/10, Alessandria, 50, Baglioni Edoardo, Cucciolo
October, Turin, 50, Conti Mario, Cucciolo
October, Caldaie (AP), 50, Di Leonardi Claudio, Cucciolo
25/10, Pistoia, 50, Stendardi Otello, Cucciolo
30/10, Verona, 75, Recchia Mario, Cucciolo
30/10, Trieste, 50, Sila Carlo, Cucciolo
3/11, Riva Traiana, 50, Sila Carlo, Cucciolo
November, Foggia, 50, Petrozzi R., Cucciolo
27/11, 50, Moro Luigi, Cucciolo
27/11, Sanremo-Poggio dei Fiori, 75, Ricchieri Mario, Cucciolo

OFF-ROAD RACING
Vicenza Championship, 75, Faggi Franco, Ducati 60
Veronese Championship, 60, Benetti Guido, Ducati 60
27/2, Trieste-Monfalcone-Trieste, 60, Sila Carlo, Cucciolo
19/3, Colli, Padua, 65, Carraro Silvano, Cucciolo
27/3, Trieste, 60, Zippo-Macoratti, Cucciolo
3/4, Primi Passi, Milan, 60, Rivolta Giordano, Cucciolo T
3/4, Trofeo Emiliano, ex aequo, 60, Benetti-Farné A., Cucciolo
10/4, Coppa Silla, ex-aequo, 60, Sozzani-Gobbo-Rivolta, Cucciolo
8/5, Milan-Sanremo, ex-aequo, 50, 11 competitors, Cucciolo
15/5, Giro della Campania, ex-aequo, 60, Aulicino-Carrano-Della Valle, Cucciolo
May, Trofeo Mosquito Club, ex-aequo, 60, Boano-Druetta-Danieli-Farinelli E.F.-Grasso, Cucciolo
May, Casalecchio di Reno, ex-aequo, 60, Farné Alberto, Cucciolo
29/5, Coppa Pasubio, 60, Benetti Guido, Cucciolo
June, Dalle Alpi al Mare, ex-aequo, 60, Actis-Druetta-Conti-Ordano-Boano-Danieli-Lanfranco-Farinelli, Cucciolo
10/6, Monti Berici, 50, Lunardi Rino, Cucciolo
June, Arezzo, ex-aequo, 50, Zelli-Tenti-Salvi-Parnetti, Cucciolo
2-3/7, 24 Ore di Milano, ex-aequo, 75, Farné A.-Cremonese-Gardellin-Benetti, Cucciolo
10/7, Otto delle Langhe, ex-aequo, 60, Actis-Como-Danieli, Cucciolo
10/7, Campi di Battaglia, ex-aequo, 60, Farné A.-Faggi-Lodi-Pola-Benetti-Galbier-Bortolan-Tonellato, Ducati 60
17/7, Campi di Battaglia, 60, Faggi-Pola-Lodi, Ducati 60
17/7, Trieste-Lignano, 50, Sila Carlo, Cucciolo
7/8, Savona, 50, Moro Luigi, Cucciolo
7/8, Rovereto, 125, Galasso Romano, Cucciolo 48
September, Voghera, 50, Marconi M., Cucciolo

9/10, Trofeo Piodelli, ex-aequo, 60, Fiorani-Tamarozzi, Cucciolo
9/10, Vicenza, 60, Faggi Franco, Cucciolo
16/10, Giro Tre Provincie, ex-aequo, 60, Nardi N.-Ruberti A.-Salani A.-Merico P., Ducati 60
16/10, Monte Berico, 50, Faggi Franco, Ducati 60
13/11, Trofeo Due Laghi, 50, Pala Italo, Cucciolo
20/11, Melfi, 60, Tamarozzi Ugo, Cucciolo
November, Arezzo, 60, Tenti Faliero, Cucciolo
November, Verona, 50, Pala Italo, Cucciolo

1950

ITALY

6/1, Bologna-Colle Osservanza: 50, Orfei Giuseppe, Cucciolo; 75, Vighi Gualtiero, Cucciolo
12/3, Cesena, 50, Bernacchi Giorgio, Cucciolo
19/3, Trieste, 50, Sila Carlo, Cucciolo
19/3, Forlì, 50, Recchia Mario, Cucciolo
March, Trieste, 50, Sila Carlo, Cucciolo
26/3, Villaganzerla, 50, Carraro Silvano, Cucciolo
August, Cingoli, 50, Marchetti Guerrino, Cucciolo
6/8, Sanremo-MonteBignone: 50, Moro Luigi, Cucciolo; 75, Richieri Mario, Cucciolo
20/8, Savigliano, 50, Boano Adolfo, Cucciolo

OFF-ROAD RACING
19/3, Tre Valli, Gavirate, ex-aequo, 75, Maggi-Bonati, Cucciolo
26/3, Primi Passi (MI), ex-aequo, 75, Maggi-Bonati, Ducati 60
March, Verona, 75, Sartori Luigi, Ducati 60
March, Tre Valli Varesine, ex-aequo, 75, Maggi-Donati-Junco-Manara, Minacci-Parvanoni-Adilbi-Tamarozzi, Ducati 60
2/4, Trofeo Monti, ex-aequo: 50, Galbier-Zin, Cucciolo; 75, Graziani-Leonardi-Tedeschi Ducati 60
10/4, Valli Fiorentine, 60, Tansini Silvio, Ducati 60
25/4, Genoa, ex-aequo, 75, Lolli-Farné A.-Miani, Ducati 60
30/4, Cinque Laghi: 50, Galbier Giuseppe, Cucciolo; 75, Tonellotto Pietro, Ducati 60
14/5, Casalecchio di Reno, ex-aequo, 60, Farné A.-Miani-Orfei-Montagutti, Ducati 60
21/5, Trofeo Piodelli, ex-aequo, 50, Tamarozzi Ugo, Cucciolo
28/5, Campi di Battaglia, ex-aequo, 60, Tonellotto-Graziani-Cremonese, Ducati 60
May, Crevalcore, 60, Farné Alberto, Ducati 60
1/6, Tr.Emiliano-Romagnolo, ex-aequo, 75, Farné A.-Orfei, Ducati 60
2/6, Messina, ex-aequo, 75, Broccio-loculando, Ducati 60
4/6, Due Valli, Sanremo: ex-aequo, 50, Moro Luigi, Cucciolo; 75, Richieri Mario, Ducati 60
11/6, Trieste, 125, Demanis Ferruccio, Cucciolo
11/6, Fiera di Roma, ex-aequo, 60, Petrucci-Volpini-Ciai M.-Alberti R., Cucciolo 60
14/6, Coppa Pasubio, 75, Sartori Luigi, Ducati 60
18/6, Trofeo Laghi, ex-aequo, 75, Tamarozzi-Farné A.-Zitelli, Ducati 60
18/6, Genoa, 75, Cavaliere S., Ducati 60
18/6, Rome, ex-aequo, 75, Alberti R.-Ciai R.-Ciai L.-Ciai M., Ducati 60
June, 24 Ore Milano-Gorizia, 75, Zitelli Glauco, Ducati 60
June, Bologna, 75, Odorici Franco, Cucciolo
28/6, Campi di Battaglia, ex-aequo, 75, Tonellotto-Cremonese, Ducati 60
29/6, Trofeo "Fiorina", 75, Farinelli Ezio Furio, Cucciolo
9/7, Otto delle Langhe, ex-aequo, 50, Boano A.-Boano T.-Orano, Ducati 60
16/7, Brescia, ex-aequo, 98, Farné A.-Miani E.-Zitelli-Tamarozzi, Ducati 60
23/7, Tre Valli Piemontesi, ex-aequo, 60, Boano Adolfo, Cucciolo

3/9, Trent, ex-aequo, 75, Degasperi-Pegoretti, Cucciolo
1/10, Tre Valichi, Sanremo, 60, Richeri Mario, Ducati 60
12-13/10, Rome-Nice-Paris, 60, Richeri Mario, Ducati 60
13-15/10, Giro di Sicilia, ex-aequo, 75, Farné A.-Zitelli-Angeleri-Sanzo-Visioli-Tamarozzi, Ducati 60
October, La Spezia, 50, Lavagnini, Cucciolo

SPAIN

March, Subida Montserrat, 50, Sutrac, Cucciolo
November, Subida Rabassada, 50, Sutrac, Cucciolo

1951

ITALY

OFF-ROAD RACING
4/3, Trapani, 65, Ciotta Orazio, Cucciolo
19/3, Tre Valli Varesine, ex-aequo, 100, Sozzani-Visioli-Tamarozzi-Aulicino, Ducati 60
19/3, Lugo di Romagna, 125, Capineri Goffredo, Ducati 60
1/4, Primi Passi (Milan), ex-aequo, 75, Farné A.-Tamarozzi-Pennati-Miani-Sozzani, Ducati 60
8/4, Valli Fiorentine, ex-aequo, 75, Salani-Cliti, Ducati 60
3/5, Pavia, ex-aequo, 75, Pennati-Tamarozzi-Sozzani-Corolli, Cucciolo
3/5, Verona, ex-aequo, 125, Alverà L.-Cremonese-Cacciavillani-Peruzzi, Ducati 60
May, Scudo del Sud, 75, Zitelli Glauco, Ducati 60
2/6, Rome, ex-aequo, 75, Roccardi-Aballe-Alberti-Caproni-Pisanecchi-Nardi, Ducati 60
3/6, Brescia, ex-aequo, 75, Tamarozzi-Visioli-Zitelli-Sozzani, Ducati 60
23/6, Sanremo-Trieste-Sanremo, ex-aequo, 75, Zitelli-Farné A.-Sozzani-Visioli-Miani-Carolo-Cacciavillani, Ducati 60
July, Trofeo del Garda, ex-aequo, 75, Cremonese Bruno, Ducati 60
15/7, Civitavecchia, 75, Petrucci Franco, Ducati 60
July, Voghera, ex-aequo, 75, Valle Spartaco, Ducati 60
29/7, Borgolavezzaro, ex-aequo, 75, Pennati-Sozzani-Tamarozzi, Ducati 60
5/8, Cavalcata delle Dolomiti ex-aequo, 75, Tamarozzi Ugo, Ducati 60
5/8, Monte Bignone, 100, Moro Luigi, Ducati 60
15/8, Palermo-Partinico, 75, Mauthe Ugo, Ducati 60
15/16-8, Coppa Vischia, ex-aequo, 75, Visioli-Farné A.-Miani-Tamarozzi-Petrucci, Ducati 60
16/9, Padua, ex-aequo, 75, Alverà-Sartori-Cacciavillani Ducati 73
30/9, Sanremo, 100, Moro Luigi, Ducati 60
30/9, Cesena, 75, Bernacchi Giorgio, Ducati 60
October, Rosa dell'Appennino, ex-aequo, 75, Farné A.-Zitelli-Miani-Travaglini, Ducati 60
21/10, Verona, ex-aequo, 75, Cremonese Bruno, Ducati 73

1952

ITALY

OFF-ROAD RACING
27/1, Verona, ex-aequo, 75, Pala Italo, Ducati 73
February, Trofeo Zecchini, ex-aequo, 75, Tamarozzi-Pennati-Sozzani, Ducati 60
2/3, 100 km, Rome, ex-aequo, 75, Venturi-Barchesi-Graffi-Bonserio-Mencaglia, Ducati 60
16/3, Castelli Romani: 60, Graffi Antonio, Ducati 60; 100, Bonserio, Ducati 60
16/3, Lugo di Romagna, 50, Emaldi Romano, Cucciolo

30/3, Primi Passi, 75, Pennati-Sozzani-Tamarozzi, Ducati 75
23/4, Coppa della Raticosa: ex-aequo, 75, Miani-Tamarozzi-Balduini-Travaglini-Farné A.-Zitelli, Ducati 73; 1st team, Farné-Miani-Tamarozzi, Ducati 73
May, Genoa, ex-aequo, 75, Maxema Giobatta, Ducati 60
6-11/5, Scudo del Sud, ex-aequo, 75, Farné A.-Miani-Zitelli, Ducati 73
11/5, Milan, ex-aequo, 60, Rovatti A., Cucciolo
11/5, Ferrara, ex-aequo, 60, Scaramelli-Fagioli, Ducati 60
May, Rosa dell'Appennino, ex-aequo, 75, Bevilacqua Pietro, Ducati
25/5, Coppa Tosco-Umbra, 100, Mariotti Luciano, Ducati 98
1-2/6, Valli Bergamasche, ex-aequo, 100, Miani-Zitelli-Farné A., Ducati 98
8/6, Sanremo, ex-aequo, 60, Modolo-Barsi-Moro-Moraglia, Ducati 60
June, Giro Brianteo, ex-aequo, 75, Pennati-Sozzani-Testa-Bazzanti-Barbieri, Ducati 65
15/6, Trifoglio di Toscana, ex-aequo, 75, Farné A.-Zitelli-Miani, Ducati 73
27/7, Tre Valli Torinesi, ex-aequo, 75, Tamarozzi-Miani-Zitelli-Farné A., Ducati 60
July, Brisighella, 75, Tassinari Walter, Ducati 60
August, Giro della Lucania, ex-aequo, 75, Farné Alberto, Ducati 60
August, Sanremo, 100, Moro Luigi, Ducati 98
August, Trofeo Fiera di Trent, ex-aequo, 75, Farné A.-Miani, Ducati 75
October, Sanremo, 100, Damiano Roberto, Ducati 60
December, Chiavari, 75, Bacigalupo Guido, Ducati

1953

ITALY

1st MOTOGIRO D'ITALIA: 30 March/5 April
30/3, 1st Lap: Bologna-Rome, 50, Malaguti Silvio, Ducati 48
31/3, 2nd Lap: Rome-Bari, 50, Giglioli Alberto, Ducati 48
1/4, 3rd Lap: Bari-Riccione, 50, Bortolotti Giancarlo, Ducati 48
2/4, 4th Lap: Riccione-Trieste, 50, Saccomandi Sergio, Ducati 48
2/4, 6th Lap: Milan-Bologna, 50, Saccomandi Sergio, Ducati 48

OFF-ROAD RACING
March, Coppa Val Bisagno, ex-aequo, 75, Cantarini Guido, Ducati 65
19/4, Trofeo Gianferrari, ex-aequo, 75, Farné A.-Miani-Bartoletti, Ducati
March, Iseo, 60, Garattini R., Ducati
April, Genoa, ex-aequo, 60, Cantarelli Guido, Ducati 65
26/4, Audax del Lario, ex-aequo, 75, Beretta-Zitelli, Ducati 65
14/5, Trofeo FMI, ex-aequo, 75, Farné Alberto, Ducati
June, Cuneo, ex-aequo, 65, Dutto-Reineri, Ducati
28/6, Milan-Misurina, ex-aequo, 100, Orsini-Peccati-Mauri-Di Billio, Ducati 98
28/6, Trofeo Massantini, ex-aequo, 100, Calevi Osvaldo, Ducati 98
3-5/7, Scudo del Sud, ex-aequo, 75, Farné A.-Zitelli-Recchia-Miani-Petrozzi, Ducati
18-19/7 24 Ore Trofeo FMI, ex-aequo, 100, Zitelli Glauco, Ducati 65
27/9, Seregno, 100, Lini Franco, Ducati 98
October, Macerata, ex-aequo, 75, Palmieri-Foglia, Ducati 98
November., Giro Provincia di Firenze, ex-aequo, 60, Milani Bruno, Ducati 60

1954

ITALY

17/10, Ariccia-Madonna del Tufo, 100, Poeti Gianfranco, Ducati 98

2nd MOTOGIRO D'ITALIA: 3 April/11 April
9/4, 6th Lap: Mestre-Bolzano, 100, Gandossi Alberto, Ducati 98
11/4, 8th Lap: Verbania-Bologna, 100, Gandossi Alberto, Ducati 98

OFF-ROAD RACING
February, Lombard Championship, ex-aequo, 75, Pennati Gaetano, Ducati 73
26/2, Città di Aprilia, ex-aequo, 100, Patria, Ducati 98
7/3, Trofeo Aldrighetti, ex-aequo, 75, Messina Tullio, Ducati 75
7/3, Trofeo Agipgas, Florence, ex-aequo, 75, Milani-Carrani-Mariotti, Ducati 75
14/3, Primi Passi, ex-aequo, 75, Ossola-Messina, Ducati 73
21/3, Criterium Primavera, ex-aequo, 75, Di Giorgi W., Ducati 60
16/5, 12 Ore di S. Giuliano, ex-aequo, 100, Zitelli-Farné A.-Farné F.-Bortolotti-Recchia-Malaguti, Ducati 98
16/5, Criterium del Lario, ex-aequo, 75, Messina Tullio, Ducati 75
23/5, Savona, 75, Siccardi Giuseppe, Ducati 75
28-30/5, Scudo del Sud, ex-aequo, 100, Malaguti-Farné F., Ducati 98
6/6, Giro di Calabria, ex-aequo, Farné A.-De Stofani-Recchia, Timpani-Malaguti-De Marco, Ducati
13/6, Giro Tre Provincie, Bologna, ex-aequo, Gandossi-Vicinelli, Gianstefani-Scamandri, Ducati
13/6, S. Croce Sull'Arno, 50, Morelli Enos, Ducati 48
13/6, S. Croce Sull'Arno, 100, Bonanni-Del Bravo, Ducati 98
13/6, Gardone Valtrompia, ex-aequo, 50, Cremaschini-Papi, Ducati 48
4/7, Vallelunga, 50, Papi Mario, Ducati 48
4/7, Sassuolo, 100, Colliva Romano, Ducati 98
4/7, Empoli, ex-aequo, Magnani-Fabbri-Milani, Cacciolli-Ceccherelli, Ducati
18/7, Giro della Sila, ex-aequo, 100, Miranda Raffaele, Ducati 98
25/7, Coppa Tosco-Umbra, ex-aequo, 100, Cipriani Guido, Ducati 98
1/8, Sanremo, ex-aequo, 75, Patria-Grossi, Ducati 65
1/8, Arona, 100, Lini Franco, Ducati 98
5/9, Rovereto, ex-aequo, 75, Bubbole Iles, Ducati 75
September, Rho, ex-aequo, 100, Battaglia G.C., Ducati 98
4/11, Macerata, ex-aequo, Pesenti-Gorini-Perugini-Messina, Ducati

1955

ECUADOR

10/10, Guayaquil, 100, Garcia C.Alberto, Ducati 98

ITALY

Junior Italian Championship: 100, Villa Francesco, Ducati 98

8/5, Imola, 100, Degli Antoni Giovanni, Ducati 98
15/5, Lugo di Romagna, 100, Villa Francesco, Ducati 98
19/5, Rimini, 100, Villa Francesco, Ducati 98
19/5, Rome-Ostia, 100, Danna Marcello, Ducati 98
25/5, Messina-Colle S.Rizzo, 125, Mandini Amedeo, Ducati 125
29/5, Carpi, 100, Degli Antoni Giovanni, Ducati 98
9/6, Turin, 100, Bonaventura Ernesto, Ducati 98
9/6, Teramo, 100, Degli Antoni Giovanni, Ducati 98
12/6, Lugo di Romagna, 100, Degli Antoni Giovanni, Ducati 98
June, Riccione, 100, Geminiani Domenico, Ducati 98
29/6, Thiene, 100, Degli Antoni Giovanni, Ducati 98

3/7, Perugia, 100, Villa Francesco, Ducati 98
10/7, Brescia, 125, Dall'Ara Franco, Ducati 125
10/7, Faenza, 100, Degli Antoni Giovanni, Ducati 98
August, Fermo, 125, Degli Antoni Giovanni, Ducati 125
7/8, Messina, 100, Artusi Alessandro, Ducati 98
21/8, Abbadia San Salvatore, 125, Maranghi Paolo, Ducati 125
28/8, Castellammare di Stabia, 125, Graziano Antonio, Ducati 125
11/9, Montebelluna, 125, Villa Francesco, Ducati 125
11/9, Cosenza: 100, Spaggiari Bruno, Ducati 98; 125, D'Angelo Benito, Ducati 125
14/9, Carini, 125, Mandini Amedeo, Ducati 125

19/6, Milan-Taranto: 100, Degli Antoni Giovanni, Ducati 98; 125, Maoggi Giuliano, Ducati 125

3rd MOTOGIRO D'ITALIA: 17 April/25 April
17/4, 1st Lap: Bologna-Trieste, 100, Villa Francesco, Ducati 98
18/4, 2nd Lap: Trieste-Padua, 100, Degli Antoni Giovanni, Ducati 98
19/4, 3rd Lap: Padua-Riccione, 100, Degli Antoni Giovanni, Ducati 98
20/4, 4th Lap: Riccione-Pescara, 100, Tartarini Leopoldo, Ducati 98
21/4, 5th Lap: Pescara-Taranto, 100, Villa Francesco, Ducati 98
22/4, 6th Lap: Taranto-Cosenza, 100, Degli Antoni Giovanni, Ducati 98
23/4, 7th Lap: Cosenza-Naples, 100, Graziano Antonio, Ducati 98
24/4, 8th Lap: Naples-Perugia, 100, Degli Antoni Giovanni, Ducati 98
25/4, 9th Lap: Perugia-Bologna, 100, Degli Antoni Giovanni, Ducati 98
Final first place: 100, Degli Antoni Giovanni, Ducati 98

OFF-ROAD RACING
22/5, Savona, ex-aequo, 75, Ballestrieri-Siccardi, Ducati 75
May, Bergamo, 100, Gorini Luigi, Ducati 98
September, Cesaro Romano, 125, Strappetti Flavio, Ducati 125

UNITED STATES
16/5, Catalina, 100, D'Alo Allen, Ducati 98

1956

GREAT BRITAIN
May, Blandford, 50, Dendy, Ducati 48
June, Rhydymwyn, 50, Dendy, Ducati 48

HOLLAND
27/5, Zandvoort, 125, Scheidhauer Willy, Ducati 125

ITALY
Junior Italian Championship: 100, Farné Franco, Ducati 98

13/5, Lugo di Romagna: 100, Gandossi Alberto, Ducati 98; 125, Spaggiari Bruno, Ducati 125
20/5, Camerino, 125, Gandossi Alberto, Ducati 125
31/5, Teramo, 125, Villa Francesco, Ducati 125
3/6, Grosseto, 100, Farné Franco, Ducati 98
17/6, Macerata, 125, Spaggiari Bruno, Ducati 125
24/6, Modena : 100, Scorza Vittorio, Ducati 98; 125, De Santis Quintilio, Ducati 125
8/7, Florence, 125, Gandossi Alberto, Ducati 125
15/7, Colleferro-Segni, 100, Forcinelli Aldo, Ducati 98
22/7, Dezzo-Presolana: 100, Farné Franco, Ducati 98; 125, Villa Francesco, Ducati 125
29/7, Tavarnuzze-Impruneta: 100, Spaggiari Bruno, Ducati 98; 125, Maranghi Paolo, Ducati 125

5/8, Coppa della Consuma: 100, Artusi Alessandro, Ducati 98: 125, Maranghi Paolo, Ducati 125
12/8, Fermo, 100, Gandossi Alberto, Ducati 98
12/8, Cuneo, 125, Zito Vittorio, Ducati 125
19/8, Trent-Bondone, 100, Bovolenta Oscar, Ducati 98
26/8, Castellammare di Stabia, 125, Graziano Antonio, Ducati 125
26/8, Mazara del Vallo: 100, Spaggiari Bruno, Ducati 98; 125, Spaggiari Bruno, Ducati 125
2/9, Macerata, 125, Spaggiari Bruno, Ducati 125
23/9, San Cesareo-Montecompatri, 100, Forcinelli Aldo, Ducati 98
30/9, Modena, 100, Ciceri Santo, Ducati 98
7/10, S. Maria Capua Vetere, 125, Graziano Antonio, Ducati 125
7/10, Morciano di Romagna, 125, Gandossi Alberto, Ducati 125
14/10, Modena, 100, Farné Franco, Ducati 98

10/6, Milan-Taranto: 100, Gandossi Alberto, Ducati 98; 125, Degli Antoni Giovanni, Ducati 125

4th MOTOGIRO D'ITALIA: 18 April/25 April
18/4, 1st Lap: Bologna-Udine; 100, Villa Francesco, Ducati 98; 125, Fantuzzi Italo, Ducati 125
19/4, 2nd Lap: Udine-Padua; 100, Gandossi Alberto, Ducati 98; 125, Maoggi Giuliano, Ducati 125
20/4, 3rd Lap: Padua-Riccione; 100, Spaggiari Bruno, Ducati 98; 125, Tartarini Leopoldo, Ducati 125
21/4, 4th Lap: Riccione-L'Aquila; 100, Gandossi Alberto, Ducati 98; 125, Maranghi Paolo, Ducati 125
22/4, 5th Lap: L'Aquila-Salerno; 100, Gandossi Alberto, Ducati 98; 125, Tartarini Leopoldo, Ducati 125
23/4, 6th Lap: Salerno-Perugia; 100, Spaggiari Bruno, Ducati 98; 125, Maranghi Paolo, Ducati 125
24/4, 7th Lap: Perugia-Montecatini T.; 100, Gandossi Alberto, Ducati 98; 125, Maranghi Paolo, Ducati 125
25/4, 8th Lap: Montecatini T.-Bologna; 100, Gandossi Alberto, Ducati 98; 125, Maoggi Giuliano, Ducati 125
Final first place: 100, Gandossi Alberto, Ducati 98; 125, Maoggi Giuliano, Ducati 125
Final first place absolute: 125, Maoggi Giuliano, Ducati 125

OFF-ROAD RACING
June, Trieste, 125, Spessot Fabio, Ducati 125
8/5, Florence, ex-aequo, 125, Decca Antonio, Ducati 125

SPAIN
8/7, 24 Horas de Montjuich, 125, Fargas R.-Ralachs, Ducati 125
26/8, Carrera de Villasar: 50, Mari Antonio, Ducati 48; 75, Mari Antonio, Ducati 100; 100, Rodá José Maria, Ducati 98; 125, Fargas Ricardo, Ducati 125

SWEDEN
15/7, Hedemora, 125, Degli Antoni Giovanni, Ducati 125

YUGOSLAVIA
9/6, Opatja, 125, Mandolini Adelmo, Ducati 125

1957

BRAZIL
Brazilian Championship: 125, Latorre Luiz, Ducati 125; 150, Latorre Luiz, Ducati 125

14/7, São Paulo, 125, Latorre Luiz, Ducati 125
15/11, Rio de Janeiro, 150, Latorre Luiz, Ducati 125
15/12, São Paulo, 150, Latorre Luiz, Ducati 125

FRANCE
August, Villefranche, 125, Lesage Jack, Ducati 125

INDONESIA
13/10, 2 Hours of Djakarta Ver.: 125, Wilson Loa, Ducati 125; 175, Gumilar M.A, Ducati 175

HOLLAND
Holland Championship, 125, Van Bockel Gé, Ducati 125

22/4, Assen, 125, Van Bockel Gé, Ducati 125
30/5, Etten, 125, Van Bockel Gé, Ducati 125
9/6, Tubbergen, 125, Van Bockel Gé, Ducati 125
14/7, Zandvoort, 125, Van Bockel Gé, Ducati 125

ITALY
Junior Italian Championship: 100, Farné Franco, Ducati 98

21/4, Riccione, 125, Spaggiari Bruno, Ducati 125
25/4, Pesaro, 125, Spaggiari Bruno, Ducati 125
28/4, Viareggio, 100, Farné Franco, Ducati 98
1/5, Asola, 125, Mandolini Giuseppe, Ducati 125
1/5, Vigevano, 125, Spaggiari Bruno, Ducati 125
1/5, Rome-Ostia, 100, Sestini Marcello, Ducati 98
19/5, Camerino, 125, Spaggiari Bruno, Ducati 125
16/6, Macerata, 125, Spaggiari Bruno, Ducati 125
4/8, Gallarate, 125, Spaggiari Bruno, Ducati 125
4/8, Trent-Bondone, 125, Scamandri Ettore, Ducati 125
11/8, Fasano-Selva, 125, Mancini Franco, Ducati 125
18/8, Siena, 100, Farné Franco, Ducati 98
25/8, Viano-Baiso, 125, Scamandri Ettore, Ducati 125
8/9, Pontedecimo-Giovi, 125, Scamandri Ettore, Ducati 125
29/9, Bolzano, 100, Farné Franco, Ducati 98
6/10, Morciano di Romagna, 125, Gandossi Alberto, Ducati 125
6/10, Coppa del Cimino: 100, Duroni Ermanno, Ducati 98; 125, Vassallo Ferdinando, Ducati 125
10/11, Frascati-Rocca di Papa: 100, Levantini Eugenio, Ducati 98; 125, Spaggiari Bruno, Ducati 125

5th MOTOGIRO D'ITALIA: 6 April/14 April
6/4, 1st Lap: Bologna-Riva del Garda; 100, Farné Franco, Ducati 98; 125, Scamandri Ettore, Ducati 125
7/4, 2nd Lap: Riva del Garda-Abano T.; 100, Farné Franco, Ducati 98; 125, Rippa Vincenzo, Ducati 125
8/4, 3rd Lap: Abano Terme-Riccione; 100, Artusi Alessandro, Ducati 98; 125, Graziano Antonio, Ducati 125
9/4, 4th Lap: Riccione-Arezzo; 100, Carena Gino, Ducati 98; 125, Graziano Antonio, Ducati 125
10/4, 5th Lap: Arezzo-Perugia; 100, Mandolini Giuseppe, Ducati 98
11/4, 6th Lap: Perugia-Teramo; 100, Mandolini Giuseppe, Ducati 98; 125, Graziano Antonio, Ducati 125
12/4, 7th Lap: Teramo-Chianciano Terme; 100, Mandolini Giuseppe, Ducati 98; 125, Pionava Roberto, Ducati 125
13/4, 8th Lap: Chianciano-Montecatini; 100, Sestini Marcello, Ducati 98; 125, Pionava Roberto, Ducati 125
14/4, 9th Lap: Montecatini T.-Bologna; 100, Mandolini Giuseppe, Ducati 98; 125, Pionava Roberto, Ducati 125
Final first place: 100, Mandolini Giuseppe, Ducati 98; 125, Graziano Antonio, Ducati 125

OFF-ROAD RACING
30/6, Cosenza, ex-aequo, Destefanis-Miranda, Ducati
June, S.Severino Marche, 100, Bonifaci Amerigo, Ducati 98
15/9, Sanremo, 125, Bruzzone Santino, Ducati 98

MALAYA
14/7, Singapore, 125, Chan Peter, Ducati 125

SPAIN
2/6, Cordoba, 125, Del Val Carlos, Ducati 125
6-7/7, 24 Horas de Montjuich, absolute, Gandossi-Spaggiari, Ducati 125

SWEDEN
Sweden Championship, 125, Aaltonen Rauno, Ducati 125

14/7, Hedemora, 125, Aaltonen Rauno, Ducati 125
Karlskoga, 125, Nygren Olle, Ducati 125

UNITED STATES
September, Kansas - Big West Rally, 175, Hainer Harold, Ducati 175

VENEZUELA
Venezuelan Championship, 125, Ciccarelli Mario, Ducati 125

Maracay, 125, Ciccarelli Mario, Ducati 125
April, El Limon, 125, Ciccarelli Mario, Ducati 125
26/5, Caracas, 125, Ciccarelli Mario, Ducati 125
June, Caracas, 125, Ciccarelli Mario, Ducati 125
11/8, Valencia, 125, Ciccarelli Mario, Ducati 125

1958

ALGERIA
27/4, Côte Bouzarea, 175, Pacou, Ducati 175
11/5, Des Quais - Algiers, 175, Baldacchino, Ducati 175

ARGENTINA
8/6, Buenos Aires, 175, Galluzzi Roberto, Ducati 175
20/7, Buenos Aires, 175, Galluzzi Roberto, Ducati 175
31/8, Buenos Aires, 175, Galluzzi Roberto, Ducati 175

BELGIUM
6/7, Grand Prix de Belgique-Spa, 125, Gandossi Alberto, Ducati 125

CEYLON
3/8, Katukurunda: 125, Gunawardena W., Ducati 125; 250, Ariyasena Nihal, Ducati 175; 250, Silva David, Ducati 175; 350, Silva David, Ducati 175

CHILE
6/4, Valparaíso: 100, Gabrié Raul, Ducati 98 TL; 125, Riedel Heinz, Ducati 125 T; 175, Fernandez Carlos, Ducati 175 S; 250, Fernandez Carlos, Ducati 175 S
13/4, Santiago, 100, Gabrié Raul, Ducati 98
27/4, Santiago, 100, Gabrié Raul, Ducati 98
23/11, Santiago, 100, Bassi Patricio, Ducati 98

FRANCE
April, 2 Hours di Montlhéry: 125, Boeri, Ducati 125; 175, Bergetzi, Ducati 175
11/5, Race di Laffrey, 125, Lesage Jack, Ducati 125
June, 12 Heures de Chieires, 125, Pamitessa, Ducati 125

GERMANY
4/5, St. Wendel, 125, Taveri Luigi, Ducati 125

GREAT BRITAIN
7/4, Oulton Park, 125, Purslow Fron, Ducati 125
10/5, Aintree, 125, Purslow Fron, Ducati 125
May, Aintree, 200, Purslow Fron, Ducati 125

26/5, Blandford, 125, Purslow Fron, Ducati 125
14/6, Scarborough, 125, Purslow Fron, Ducati 125
15/6, Snetterton, 250, Hailwood Mike, Ducati 125
22/6, Crimond, 200, Smith A, Ducati 125
12/7, Castle Combe, 125, Hailwood Mike, Ducati 125
4/8, Crystal Palace, 125, Hailwood Mike, Ducati 125
17/8, Errol, 200, Smith A, Ducati 125
13/9, Stratford, 200, Tuppen, Ducati
20/9, Snetterton, 125, Hailwood Mike, Ducati 125
September, Silverstone, 125, Hailwood Mike, Ducati 125
September, Crystal Palace, 125, Hailwood Mike, Ducati 125

GUYANA
3/8, Georgetown: 200, Holder Clive, Ducati 175; 350, Holder Clive, Ducati 175

HOLLAND
15/5, Etten, 125, Van Bockel Gé, Ducati 125
15/6, Tubbergen, 125, Scheidhauer Willy, Ducati 125
15/6, Geek, 125, Van Bockel Gé, Ducati 125
31/8, Zandvoort, 125, Scheidhauer Willy, Ducati 125
18/10, Leksteek Motocross Course, 175, Rehorst L, Ducati 175

ITALY
Senior Italian Championship: 125, Spaggiari Bruno, Ducati 125
Senior Italian Championship Constructors: 125, Ducati Meccanica, Ducati 125
Junior Italian Championship, 125, Farné Franco, Ducati 125
Junior Italian Championship Constructors, 125, Ducati Meccanica, Ducati 125
Trofeo Cadetti, 125, Croci Francesco, Ducati 125

16/3, Vallelunga, 125, Duroni Ermanno, Ducati 125
6/4, Riccione, 125, Farné Franco, Ducati 125
20/4, Vallelunga, 125, Vassallo Ferdinando, Ducati 125
25/4, Modena: 125, Croci Francesco, Ducati 125; 125, Gandossi Alberto, Ducati 125
1/5, Rome-Ostia, 125, Farné Franco, Ducati 125
1/5, Doria-Creto, 125, Mandolini Giuseppe, Ducati 125
1/5, Palermo, 125, De Simone Salvatore, Ducati 125
11/5, Marina Romea, 125, Spaggiari Bruno, Ducati 125
15/5, Monte Pellegrino, 125, Anzon Ernesto, Ducati 125
18/5, Camerino, 100, Farné Franco, Ducati 98
5/6, Strada Panoramica, 100, Cremonini Claudio, Ducati 98
5/6, Pontedecimo-Bocchetta, 125, Mandolini Giuseppe, Ducati 125
8/6, Gallarate, 125, Farné Franco, Ducati 125
15/6, Alessandria: 125, Croci Francesco, Ducati 125; 125, Spaggiari Bruno, Ducati 125
22/6, Falconara, 125, Cozza Angelo, Ducati 125
29/6, Ariccia-Madonna del Tufo, 125, Colabona Enrico, Ducati 125
13/7, Bologna-San Luca, 125, Scamandri Ettore, Ducati 125
20/7, Colleferro-Segni, 125, Colabona Enrico, Ducati 125
20/7, Voltri-Turchino, 125, Mandolini Giuseppe, Ducati 125
27/7, Lago dei Ganzirri, 125, Villa Francesco, Ducati 125
3/8, Abbadia San Salvatore, 125, Farné Franco, Ducati 125
3/8, Aosta-Peroulaz, 125, Longo Luigi, Ducati 125

3/8, Fasano-Selva, 125, Rippa Vincenzo, Ducati 125
10/8, Porretta Terme-Castelluccio, 125, Scamandri Ettore, Ducati 125
17/8, Fermo, 125, Farné Franco, Ducati 125
31/8, Varese-Campo dei Fiori, 125, Mandolini Giuseppe, Ducati 125
31/8, San Cesareo-Montecompatri, 125, Rippa Vincenzo, Ducati 125
7/9, Vallelunga, 125, Rippa Vincenzo, Ducati 125
14/9, Monza, Gran Premio Nazioni, 125, Spaggiari Bruno, Ducati 125
14/9, Sorrento-Sant'Agata, 125, Rippa Vincenzo, Ducati 125
14/9, Monza, 175, Villa Francesco, Ducati 175
21/9, Modena, 125, Croci Francesco, Ducati 125
28/9, Coppa del Cimino, 125, Capocci Alberto, Ducati 125
28/9, Paternò: 125, Farné Franco, Ducati 125; 175, Mandolini Giuseppe, Ducati 175
5/10, Morciano di Romagna, 125, Farné Franco, Ducati 125
12/10, Rimini, 125, Necchi Mario, Ducati 125
12/10, Frascati-Rocca di Papa, 125, Colabona Enrico, Ducati 125
15/10, Tavarnuzze-Impruneta, 125, Massa Enzo, Ducati 125
19/10, Vallelunga, 125, Croci Francesco, Ducati 125

OFF-ROAD RACING
2/6, Due Valli, 125, Odisio Lorenzo, Ducati 125
2/6, 12 Ore di Treviso, 125, Bianchin Adalberto, Ducati 125
10/8, Speedway, Rovigo, 125, Brabetz Alessandro, Ducati 125
10/8, Speedway, Rovigo: 125, Brabetz Alessandro, Ducati 125; Rovigo, Finale, 125, Brabetz Alessandro, Ducati 125
15/8, Speedway, Follonica, 125, Brabetz Alessandro, Ducati 125

MALAYA
23/3, Singapore: 125, Chan Peter, Ducati 125; 175, Chia Louis, Ducati 175; 175, Chan Peter, Ducati 175
25/3, Penang Kilo, 100, Cheah Hock San, Ducati 98
8/6, Penang Kilo, 125, Chan Peter, Ducati 125

PORTUGAL
13/7, Vila Real, 125, Farné Franco, Ducati 125

SPAIN
5/6-7, 24 Horas de Montjuich, absolute, Maranghi-Mandolini G. Ducati 125
7/9, Alicante, 125, Fargas Ricardo, Ducati 125

SWEDEN
Hedemora, 125, Aaltonen Rauno, Ducati 125
Karlskoga, 125, Aaltonen Rauno, Ducati 125

UNITED STATES
18/5, California Cup: 125, Attele Lyle, Ducati 125; 175, Attele Lyle, Ducati 175
8/6, California - T.T. Scrambles, 125, Watkins Don, Ducati 125

VENEZUELA
March, Caracas: 125, Milano Giuseppe, Ducati 125; 125, Giovannetti Augusto, Ducati 125; 175, Fernandez Otto, Ducati 175
16/3, Valencia: 125, Ciccarelli Mario, Ducati 125; 175, Ciccarelli Mario, Ducati 175
20/4, Maracay, 125, Ciccarelli Mario, Ducati 125
11/5, Maiquetia-P.Garcia: 125, Ciccarelli Mario, Ducati 125; 175, Ciccarelli Mario, Ducati 175
15/6, Barquisimeto, 125, Ciccarelli Mario, Ducati 125
20/7, Los Proceres-Caracas, 125, Ciccarelli Mario, Ducati 125
July, 5th Championship race: 125, Ciccarelli Mario, Ducati 125; 175, Dalle Fusine Benigno, Ducati 175

28/9, La Coromoto: 125, Ciccarelli Mario, Ducati 125; 175, Patruno Nicola, Ducati 175
26/10, Maracay: 125, Ciccarelli Mario, Ducati 125; 125, Patruno Nicola, Ducati 125
December, Maracay, 125, Ippolito Andrea, Ducati 125

YUGOSLAVIA
10/6, Opatja, 125, Mandolini Adelmo, Ducati 125
15/6, Opatja, 125, Spinnler Werner, Ducati 125
4/7, Banjica - Beograd, 125, Mandolini Adelmo, Ducati 125

1959

ARGENTINA
Argentinian Championship: 125, Merodio Juan Carlos, Ducati 125; 175, Merodio Juan Carlos, Ducati 175

1/2, Lujan de Cuyo, 100, Boschi Orlando, Ducati 98
1/3, San Rafael, 175, Salazar Juan C, Ducati 175
8/3, San Martin de Mendoza, 100, Boschi Orlando, Ducati 98
8/3, San Martin de Mendoza, 125, Ratto Espean, Ducati 125
22/3, Godey Cruz: 125, Castro Pablo, Ducati 125; 175, Salazar Juan C, Ducati 175
29/3, Rivadavia, 175, Arenas Felipe, Ducati 175
April, Miramar, 175, Drundel Juan, Ducati 175
5/4, Mendoza: 100, Spotti Carlos, Ducati 98; 125, Spotti Carlos, Ducati 125; 175, Arenas Felipe, Ducati 175; 500, Arenas Felipe, Ducati 175
12/4, Lujan de Cuyo, 100, Castro Pablo, Ducati 98
May, Buenos Aires, 175, Galluzzi Roberto, Ducati 175
17/5, Santa Fé, 100, Descano Francisco, Ducati 98
Junio, Tunuyan, 175, Arenas Felice, Ducati 175
24/6, Punta Chica, 100, Martinez Oscar, Ducati 98
5/7, Buenos Aires, 175, Del Rio Malta, Ducati 175
July, Ciudad de Rafaela: 100, Gilli Antonio, Ducati 98; 175, Gilli Antonio, Ducati 175
July, Mar de Plata, 175, Gunden Juan, Ducati 175
July, Miramar, 175, Gunden Juan, Ducati 175
9/8, Necocea, 175, Merodio J.Carlos, Ducati 175
18/10, Mar del Plata: 100, "Bunny". Ducati 98; 125, Merodio J.Carlos, Ducati 125; 175, Merodio J.Carlos, Ducati 175
7/12, Ciudad de Miramar: 100, "Bunny", Ducati 98; 125, Merodio J.Carlos, Ducati 125

AUSTRALIA
May, Port Wakefield, 125, Walter Jack, Ducati 125
1/11, Darley, 250, Phillis Thomas, Ducati 250
17/5, Chimay, 125, Kronmuller Karl, Ducati 125
17/5, Quaregnon Motocross, 175, Bevilacqua Enzo, Ducati 175
August, Flandres Inter. Prix, 125, Vervroegen Pierre, Ducati 125

CANADA
2/5, Ontario, 250, Farné Franco, Ducati 250

CEYLON
10/5, Katukurunda: 125, Herat P.B., Abeysinghe Austin, Ducati 125; 250, De Kretser Ronnie, Ducati 250
12/7, Katukurunda: 125, Wijesori Vimal, Ariyasena Nihal, Ducati 125; 250, De Kretser Ronnie, Ducati 250
November, Nuwara Eliya, 250, Wijesuriya V., Ducati

CHILE
Chilean Championship: 100, Vicuna Ricardo, Ducati 98; 125, Tamayo Juan, Ducati 125

29/6, Viña del Mar: 100, Bassi Patricio, Ducati 98; 125, Fernandez Carlos, Ducati 125
30/8, Santiago, 100, Medel Alfonso, Ducati 98
27/9, Santiago, 100, Vicuna Ricardo, Ducati 98
4/10, Santiago, 100, Vicuna Ricardo, Ducati 98
11/10, Santiago, 100, Medel Alfonso, Ducati 98
12/10, Santiago: 125, Tamayo Juan, Ducati 125; 175, Fiorito Gino, Ducati 175
22/11, Quilpué: 100, Medel Alfonso, Ducati 98; 125, Tamayo Juan, Ducati 125; 175, Vicuna Jaime, Ducati 175
6/12, Valparaíso: 100, Vicuna Ricardo, Ducati 98; 125, Tamayo Juan, Ducati 125; 175, Honorato René, Ducati 175
20/12, Puente Alto: 100, Marfil Patricio, Ducati 98; 125, Tamayo Juan, Ducati 125; 175, Honorato René, Ducati 175

DENMARK
13/9, Roskilde Course, 125, Brening Jan, Ducati 125

FINLAND
11/5, Finland Grand Prix, 125, Kavanagh Kenrick, Ducati 125
17/5, Turku, 125, Ruissalont, Ducati 125
13/9, Turku, 125, Kavanagh Kenrick, Ducati 125

FRANCE
14/4, 2 Hours di Montlhéry, 125, Lesage Jack, Ducati 125

GERMANY
German Championship, 125, Scheidhauer Willy, Ducati 125

21/7, Solitude, 125, Bickel, Ducati 125

GREAT BRITAIN
English Championship Golden Star ACU, 125, Hailwood Mike, Ducati 125

29/3, Snetterton, 125, Hailwood Mike, Ducati 125
30/3, Oulton Park, 125, Purslow Fron, Ducati 125
30/3, Thruxton, 125, Hailwood Mike, Ducati 125
18/4, Silverstone, 125, Hailwood Mike, Ducati 125
27/4, Castle Combe, 125, Hailwood Mike, Ducati 125
9/5, Rhydymwyn: 150, Dugdale Alan, Ducati 125; 200, Dugdale Alan, Ducati 175; 250, Wallwork L, Ducati 204
10/5, Errol, 125, Carr L, Ducati 125
16/5, Aberdare Park, 125, Hailwood Mike, Ducati 125
17/5, Howle Hill Race, 200, Cheshire, Ducati 125
18/5, Brands Hatch, 125, Cambridge M J, Ducati 125
18/5, Blandford, 125, Robb Tommy, Ducati 125
18/5, Cyfarthfa Park, 200, Cheshire T, Ducati 125
23/5, Cukoo Park/Oxenhope, 200, Cheshire, Ducati 125
14/6, Errol, 125, Carr P, Ducati 125
27/6, Rhydymwyn, 125, Dugdale Alan, Ducati 125
11/6, Castle Combe, 125, Hailwood Mike, Ducati 125
18/7, Snetterton, 125, Hailwood Mike, Ducati 125
3/8, Oulton Park, 125, Hailwood Mike, Ducati 125
3/8, Thruxton, 125, Wheeler Arthur, Ducati 125
15/8, Aberdare Park, 125, Hailwood Mike, Ducati 125

23/8, Silverstone, 125, Hailwood Mike, Ducati 125
August, Brands Hatch, 125, Shorey Daniel, Ducati 125
August, Aberdare Park, 125, Hailwood Mike, Ducati 125
August, Biggin Hill, 125, Shorey Daniel, Ducati 125
29/8, Oulton Park, 125, Purslow Fron, Ducati 125
20/9, Snetterton, 125, Hailwood Mike, Ducati 125
26/9, Aintree, 125, Hailwood Mike, Ducati 125
September, Mallory Park, 125, Hailwood Mike, Ducati 125
September, Silverstone, 125, Hailwood Mike, Ducati 125
4/10, Biggin Hill, 200, Hailwood Mike, Ducati 125
October, "A-Cu" Race, 125, Hailwood Mike, Ducati 125

GUYANA
29/3, Atkinson Field: 150, Ten-Pow Errol, Ducati 125; 200, Holder Clive, Ducati 175; 350, Holder Clive, Ducati 175

IRELAND
9/5, North West "200", 125, Robb Tommy, Ducati 125
9/5, Rhydymwyn Wirral "100": 150, Dugdale Alan, Ducati 125; 200, Dugdale Alan, Ducati 175
10/5, Errol - North West "200", 125, Carr P., Ducati 125
8/8, Ulster Grand Prix - Belfast, 125, Hailwood Mike, Ducati 125

HOLLAND
Holland Championship, 125, Swart Gasper, Ducati 125

25/4, Overjissel Motocross, 175, Broker Hans, Ducati 175
26/4, Zandvoort, 125, Swart Gasper, Van Marle Henk, Ducati 125
1/5, Assen, 125, Conswart, Ducati, Van Marle Henk, Ducati 125
10/5, Zandvoort, 125, Pesl Hans, Ducati 125
19/5, Tubbergen, 125, Pesl Hans, Ducati 125
14/6, Atten, 125, Van Marle Henk, Ducati 125
17/6, Beek, 125, Swart Gasper, Vink H., Ducati 125
21/6, Motocross Zandvoort, 175, Steman H., Leyboer J., Ducati 175

ITALY
Junior Italian Championship: 125, Cozza Angelo, Ducati 125
Junior Italian Championship Constructors: 125, Ducati Meccanica, Ducati 125; 175, Ducati Meccanica, Ducati 175
Trofeo Cadetti, 125, Marcaccini Getullio, Ducati 125
Mountain Italian Championship: 100, Carena Gino, Ducati 98; 125, Mandolini Giuseppe, Ducati 125

8/3, Agnano-Cappella Cangiani, 125, Mencaglia Pietro, Ducati 125
29/3, Riccione, 125, Balboni Alfredo, Ducati 125
30/3, Modena: 125, Gandossi Alberto; 125, Croci Francesco, Ducati 125
12/4, Imola - Coppa d'Oro Shell, 125, Scamandri Ettore, Ducati 125
19/4, Frascati-Tuscolo, 125, Colabona Enrico, Mencaglia Pietro, Mancone Bruno, Ducati 125
25/4, Cesenatico, 125, Fallavena Guido, Ducati 125
1/5, Rome-Ostia, 125, Mencaglia Pietro, Colabona Enrico, Ducati 125
1/5, Palermo, 125, Balboni Alfredo, Ducati 125
3/5, Velletri-Pratone: 125, Mancone Bruno, Corsetti Luigi, Ducati 125
7/5, Monza, 125, Lasagni Pio, Ducati 125

24/5, Camerino, 125, Cozza Angelo, Ducati 125
24/5, Rimini, 125, Mandolini Giuseppe, Ducati 125
24/5, Sondrio-Gualtieri, 125, Sciaresa Abbondio, Ducati 125
28/5, Vallelunga, 125, Mancone Bruno, Mencaglia Pietro, Ducati 125
31/5, Bologna-San Luca, 125, Fallavena Guido, Balboni Alfredo, Ducati 125
28/6, Viano-Baiso, 100, Carena Gino, Ducati 98
28/6, Ariccia-Madonna del Tufo, 125, Mencaglia Pietro, Colabona Enrico, Mancone Bruno, Ducati 125
12/7, Vallelunga, 125, Mencaglia Pietro, Ducati 125
19/7, Colleferro-Segni, 125, Mancone Bruno, Ducati 125
19/7, Trent-Bondone: 100, Carena Gino, Ducati 98; 125, Mandolini Giuseppe, Ducati 125
2/8, Fasano-Selva, 125, Mandolini Giuseppe, Ducati 125
2/8, Fasano-Selva, 125, Marcaccini Getullio, Ducati 125
9/8, Porretta-Castelluccio, 125, Fallavena Guido, Scamandri Ettore, Ducati 125
16/8, Lago dei Ganzirri: 125, Cozza Angelo, Ducati 125; 175, Farné Franco, Ducati 175
16/8, Fermo, 125, Mandolini Giuseppe, Ducati 125
August, Salita Gallarate, 175, Mascheroni Ezio, Ducati 175
23/8, Fornaci di Barga-Barga, 125, Sestini Marcello, Ducati 125
30/8, Varese-Campo dei Fiori: 100, Carena Gino, Ducati 98; 125, Mandolini Giuseppe, Ducati 125
6/9, Monza: 125, Villa Francesco, Ducati 125; 175, Villa Francesco, Ducati 175
13/9, Modena, 125, Tirri Franco, Ducati 125
13/9, Pontedecimo-Giovi, 100, Carena Gino, Ducati 98
27/9, Morciano di Romagna, 125, Villa Francesco, Ducati 125
27/9, Sassi-Superga: 100, Carena Gino, Ducati 98; 125, Mandolini Giuseppe, Ducati 125
27/9, Coppa del Cimino, 125, Paolucci Emidio, Ducati 125
4/10, Florence: 125, Villa Francesco, Ducati 125; 175, Villa Francesco, Ducati 175
4/10, Squarciarelli-Rocca di Papa, 125, Mancone Bruno, Mandolini Giuseppe, Ducati 125
11/10, Strettura-Passo della Somma, 125, Capocci Alberto, Ducati 125
18/10, Vallelunga, 125, Marcaccini Getullio, Ducati 125
18/10, Recco-Uscio, 100, Carena Gino, Ducati 98
25/10, S. Maria Capua Vetere, 125, Balboni Alfredo, Ducati 125
25/10, Catania-Etna: 125, Ardini Carmelo, Ducati 125; 175, Faro Carmelo, Ducati 175
8/11, Palermo: 125, Farné Franco, Ducati 125; 175, Farné Franco, Ducati 175
31/12, Monte Pellegrino: 125, Cucina Pietro, Ducati 125; 175, Monreale Salvatore, Ducati 175

OFF-ROAD RACING
July, Bologna, 125, Zacchiroli Silvio, Ducati 125
August, Terni, 125, Cimarelli Franco, Ducati 125

MALAYA
14/6, Sembawang Speed Circuit: 175, Ng Yang Heng, Ducati 175; 250, Hall A.E., Ducati 175

PORTUGAL
22/2, Rally Lisboa-Benfica, 250: Rodriguez Alfredo, Ducati 125 S; Costa Louis Alberto, Ducati 175 S

26/4, Rally do Alenquer-Lisboa, 250, Nuñes Diniz Angelo, Ducati 250
21/6, Rally do Averio, 175, Correia M.Marquez, Ducati 175
July, Stadium Lisboa, 175, Nuñes Diniz Angelo, Ducati 175
7/7, Festival do Lisboa, 175, Nuñes Diniz Angelo, Ducati 175
December, Rally do Benfica, Delinger Heinz, Ducati

RHODESIA
28/6, Belvedere - Salisbury, 175, Lindsay W.T, Ducati 175
2/11, Belvedere - Mem. Ray Amm, Elliott C., Ducati

SPAIN
19/4, Grand Prix de Espana, 125, Fargas Ricardo, Ducati 125
26/4, Subida de Galapagar, 100, Ruiz Joaquim, Ducati 98
24/5, Sevilla: 350, Nuñes Diniz Angelo, Ducati; 500, Nuñes Diniz Angelo, Ducati
5-6/7, 24 Horas de Montjuich, 125, Flores-Carrero, Ducati 125

SWITZERLAND
Junior Switzerland Championship, 125, Piller Michel, Ducati 125

13/9, Locarno, 125, Villa Francesco, Ducati 125
October, Swiss Road Championship, 125, Piller Michel, Ducati 125

UNITED STATES
June, Norfolk - VA Scrambles, 350, Givens Gerald, Ducati 350
5/3, Daytona Beach FL, 250, Farné Franco, Ducati 250
5/4, Petersburg VA, 250, Givens Gerald, Ducati 250
26/4, Yakima WA - Scrambles: 200, Budschat Bob, Ducati 175; 250, Budschat Bob, Ducati
26/4, Malboro Race, 175, Farné Franco, Ducati 175
10/5, Bellingham WA - Short Track, 200, Barclay Allen, Ducati
30/5, Thompson CT, 175, Farné Franco, Ducati 175
21/6, Bremerton WA, 200, Budschat Bob, Ducati
22/6, Laconia NH, 175, Farné Franco, Ducati 175
July, Laconia NH - Motocross, 125, Beach Leslie, Ducati 125
9/8, Watkins Glen NY: Seniors, 175, Burkholder William, Ducati 175; Juniors, 175, Richardson Steve, Ducati 175
7/9, Dodge City KS, 175, Burkholder William, Ducati 175
September, Caroline, 125, Hawkins Robert, Ducati 125
20/9, Fineland NJ, 200, Varnes James, Ducati
November, Dodge City KS - 100 Miles, 175, Burkholder William, Ducati 175
November, Bonneville Salt, 175, Lewis Joe, Ducati 175

VENEZUELA
26/4, Valencia, 175, Ippolito Andrea, Ducati 175
September, Valencia: 175, Ippolito Andrea, Ducati 175; 350, Agilar, Ducati 175

1960

ALGERIA
3/10, Algiers, 250, Barone Michel, Ducati 250

ARGENTINA
Argentinian Championship: 125, Merodio Juan Carlos, Ducati 125; 175, Herceg Miguel, Ducati 175

17/1, Buenos Aires: 125, Merodio J.Carlos, Ducati 125; 175, Galluzzi Roberto, Ducati 175
14/2, Cordoba, 100, Borsi Jorge, Ducati 98
21/2, Mendoza: 125, Spotti Carlos A., Ducati 125; 175, Arenas Felipe, Ducati 175
March, Buenos Aires, 125, Merodio Juan Carlos, Ducati 125
April, Cordoba, 100, Borsi Jorge, Ducati 98
April, Mendoza: 100, Deliberto José, Ducati 98; 125, Parra Antonio, Ducati 125; 175, Arenas Felipe, Ducati 175
8/5, Cordoba, 175, Herceg Miguel, Ducati 175
15/5, Ciudad de Quilmes, 125, Merodio Juan Carlos, Ducati 125
10/7, Cordoba, 100, Borsi Jorge, Ducati 98
24/7, Argentinian Championship: 125, Merodio Juan Carlos, Ducati 125; 175, Herceg Miguel, Ducati 175
28/8, Buenos Aires, 100, Diaz Ricardo, Ducati 98
11/9, Guilmes, 125, Merodio Juan Carlos, Ducati 125
18/9, Buenos Aires: 125, Merodio Juan Carlos, Ducati 125; 175, Pochettino Hector, Pochettino Hector, Ducati 175
2/10, Mar de La Plata: 125, Merodio J.Carlos, Ducati 125; 175, Herceg Miguel, Ducati 175
9/10, San Martin Park, 175, Merodio Juan Carlos, Ducati 175
11/10, Ciudad de Quilmes, 125, Merodio Juan Carlos, Ducati 125
12/10, Buenos Aires, 125, Merodio Juan Carlos, Ducati 125
16/10, San Martin Park, 175, Arenas Felipe, Ducati 175
18/10, Buenos Aires,: 125, Merodio Juan Carlos, Ducati 125; 175, Pochettino Hector, Ducati 175
30/10, Buenos Aires, 175, Herceg Miguel, Ducati 175
7/11, Buenos Aires, 175, Pochettino Hector, Ducati 175
12/11, Mar de La Plata, 125, Masetti Umberto, Ducati 125
26/11, Buenos Aires, 125, Masetti Umberto, Ducati 125

AUSTRALIA
1/1, Phillip Island, 125, Kavanagh Kenrick, Ducati 125
14/2, Fisherman Bend: 125, Kavanagh Kenrick, Ducati 125; 250, Kavanagh Kenrick, Ducati 250
6/3, Langford: 125, Kavanagh Kenrick, Ducati 125; 250, Hinton Eric, Ducati 250
13/3, Symmonds Plains - Tasmania: 125, Kavanagh Kenrick, Ducati 125; 250, Kavanagh Kenrick, Ducati 250

CANADA
2/7, Ontario: 175, Dahler Ronnie, Ducati 175; 250, Johnston Don, Ducati 250

CHILE
6/3, Santiago: 100, Jarpa Ivan, Ducati 98; 125, Gamberini Pablo, Ducati 125; 175, Vicuna Jaime, Ducati 175; 200, Vicuna Jaime, Ducati 175; 350, Vicuna Jaime, Ducati 175; 500, Vicuna Jaime, Ducati 175
25/9, San Filipe, 125, Scherz Adolfo, Ducati 125
25/9, Santiago, 100, Robert Antonio, Ducati 98 S
12/12, Tajmar: 125, Masetti Umberto, Ducati 125; 175, Masetti Umberto, Ducati 175

FRANCE
French Championship, 250, Barone Michel, Ducati 250

3/5, Côte-Lapize, 125, Cecco Hillmar, Ducati 125
May, Course La Ginestre: 175, Barone René, Ducati 175; 250, Barone Michel, Ducati 250
May, Saint-Antonin: 175, Barone René, Ducati 175; 250, Barone Michel, Ducati 250
11/5, Côte de Grenoble, 125, Perret, Ducati 125
May, Course de Laffrey, 250, Barone Michel, Ducati 250

GREAT BRITAIN

English Championship Golden Star ACU:
125, Hailwood Mike, Ducati 125; 250,
Hailwood Mike, Ducati 250

9/4, Silverstone: 125, Hailwood Mike, Ducati
125; 250, Hailwood Mike, Ducati 250
April, Castle Combe, 125, Hailwood Mike,
Ducati 125
15/4, Brands Hatch: 200, Hailwood Mike,
Ducati 125; 250, Hailwood Mike,
Ducati 250
17/4, Snetterton, 125, Hailwood Mike,
Ducati 125
18/4, Oulton Park, 125, Shorey Daniel,
Ducati 125
23/4, Castle Combe, 125, Hailwood Mike,
Ducati 125
30/4, Aberdare Park, 125, Hailwood Mike,
Ducati 125
14/5, Aintree: 125, Hailwood Mike, Ducati
125; 250, Hailwood Mike, Ducati 250
15/5, Brands Hatch, 200, Hailwood Mike,
Ducati 125
28/5, Silverstone: 125, Hailwood Mike,
Ducati 125; 250, Hailwood Mike, Ducati
250; 175/500, Griffith, Ducati 250
6/6, Blandford, 125, Shorey Daniel,
Ducati 125
19/6, Houston Race, 125, Martin Ken,
Ducati 125
25/6, Errol, 125, Martin Ken, Ducati 125
3/7, Aintree, 150, Shorey Daniel, Ducati 125
3/7, Charterthall, 200, Clark Brian, Ducati 125
9/7, Brands Hatch: 125, Hailwood Mike, Ducati
125; 250, Hailwood Mike, Ducati 250
16/7, Castle Combe: 125, Hailwood Mike,
Ducati 125; 250, Hailwood Mike, Ducati 250
17/7, Mallory Park, 250, Hailwood Mike,
Ducati 250
24/7, Snetterton: 125, Hailwood Mike, Ducati
125; 250, Hailwood Mike, Ducati 250
1/8, Oulton Park: 125, Hailwood Mike, Ducati
125; 250, Hailwood Mike, Ducati 250
1/8, Cadwell Park, 250, Crowder H, Ducati
1/8, Thruxton, 125, Budgen P, Ducati 125
August, Castle Combe, 125, Hailwood
Mike, Ducati 125; 250, Hailwood Mike,
Ducati 250
13/8, Oulton Park: race 1, 250, Wallwork L,
Ducati 204; race 2, 250, Crowder H, Ducati
20/8, Silverstone, 200, Hailwood Mike,
Ducati 125
20/8, Barbon Manor, 200, Udall R, Ducati
20/8, Brands Hatch, 200, Hailwood Mike,
Ducati 125
4/9, Errol, 125, Gow J, Ducati 125
4/9, Snetterton, 175/250, Hailwood Mike,
Ducati 250
10/9, Wallasey, 125, Martin Ken, Ducati 125
25/9, Charterhall, 200, Clark Brian,
Ducati 175
October, Wallasey: race 1, 125, Martin Ken,
Ducati 125; race 2, 125, Martin Ken,
Ducati 125; 250, Wallwork L, Ducati 204
October, Silverstone, 125, Munday,
Ducati 125
27/12, Brands Hatch, 200, Shorey Daniel,
Ducati 125

HOLLAND

8/6, Tubbergen, 125, Scheidhauer Willy,
Ducati 125

ITALY

Junior Italian Championship, 125,
Marcaccini Getullio, Ducati 125
Junior Italian Championship Constructors,
125, Ducati Meccanica, Ducati 125
Trofeo Cadetti, 125, Accorsi Sisto, Ducati 125
Trofeo "P.Negri" Challenge triennale, 125,
Ducati Meccanica, Ducati 125
Trofeo Bracciale d'Oro FMI Cadetti, 125,
Garagnani Luciano, Ducati 125
Trofeo Bracciale d'Oro FMI Cadetti, 175,
Vanni Vincenzo, Ducati 175
Mountain Italian Championship, 125, Imola
Elio, Ducati 125

Mountain Latian Championship, 125 F/3,
Colabona Enrico, Ducati 125
Mountain Latian Championship, 125 F/2,
Mencaglia Pietro, Ducati 125

27/3, Agnano-Cappella Cangiani, 125,
Gagliotta Giovanni, Ducati 125
10/4, Frascati-Tuscolo, 125, Colabona
Enrico, Ducati 125
18/4, Doria-Creto, 100, Carena Gino,
Ducati 98
18/4, Cesenatico, 125, Garagnani Luciano,
Ducati 125
1/5, Rome-Ostia, 125, Colabona Enrico,
Mencaglia Pietro, Morgia Giovanni,
Ducati 125
1/5, Palermo: 125, Balboni Alfredo, Ducati
125; Motta Carmelo, Ducati 125
8/5, Monza, 125, Rinaudo Luigi, Ducati 125
8/5, Velletri-Pratone: 125, Colabona Enrico,
Ducati 125; 175, Colabona Enrico,
Ducati 175
15/5, Rimini, 125, Mandolini Giuseppe,
Ducati 125
15/5, Monte Pellegrino, 125, Cucina Pietro,
Ducati 125
22/5, Bologna-San Luca, 125, Cava Pietro,
Balboni Alfredo, Ducati 125
26/5, Florence, 125, Balboni Alfredo,
Ducati 125
26/5, Vallelunga: 125, Necchi Mario, Ducati
125; 175, Paolucci Emidio, Ducati 175
5/6, Pegazzano-Biassa, 125, Ascari Dante,
Ducati 125
12/6, Teramo, 125, Accorsi Sisto, Ducati 125
19/6, Strettura-Passo della Somma, 125,
Mencaglia Pietro, Colabona Enrico,
Ducati 125
26/6, Vallelunga: 125, Gagliotta Giovanni,
Ducati 125; 175, Motta Carmelo,
Ducati 175
29/6, Predappio-Rocca Caminate, 125,
Santarelli Giancarlo, Ducati 125
3/7, Targa Vesuvio, 125, Gagliotta
Giovanni, Ducati 125
3/7, Garessio-San Bernardo, 125, Imola
Elio, Ducati 125
10/7, Ariccia-Madonna del Tufo, 125,
Colabona Enrico, Mancone Bruno,
Ducati 125
10/7, Cernobbio-Bisbino, 125, Imola Elio,
Ducati 125
17/7, S. Maria Capua Vetere, 125, Balboni
Alfredo, Ducati 125
17/7, Colleferro-Segni, 125, Colabona
Enrico, Ducati 125
24/7, Aosta-Peroulaz, 125, Piana Italo,
Ducati 125
24/7, Fermo, 125, Marcaccini Getullio,
Ducati 125
31/7, Gallarate, 125, Villa Francesco,
Ducati 125
7/8, Castell'Arquato-Vernasca, 125, Accorsi
Sisto, Mandolini Giuseppe, Ducati 125
7/8, Fasano-Selva, 125, Farné Franco,
Garagnani Luciano, Ducati 125
21/8, Fornaci di Barga-Barga, 125,
Mandolini Giuseppe, Ducati 125
28/8, Coppa della Consuma: 100, Maffucci
Mauro, Ducati 98; 125, Cava Pietro,
Maoggi Giuliano, Ducati 125
4/9, Modena, 125, Bindini Luciano,
Garagnani Luciano, Ducati 125
4/9, Modena, 125, Cava Pietro, Ducati 125
11/9, Monza : 125, Farné Franco, Ducati
125; 175, Villa Francesco, Ducati 175
18/9, Modena, 125, Ascari Dante,
Ducati 125
18/9, Catania, 125, Cucina Pietro, Ducati 125
25/9, Morciano di Romagna: 125, Farnè
Franco, Ducati 125; 175, Villa Francesco,
Ducati 175
25/9, Coppa del Cimino: 100, Daniele
Vincenzo, Ducati 98; 125, Picca Alberto,
Mencaglia Pietro, Ducati 125
2/10, Misano Mare, 125, Santarelli
Giancarlo, Ducati 125

2/10, Squarciarelli-Rocca di Papa, 125, Colabona
Enrico, Mencaglia Pietro, Ducati 125
9/10, Monza: 125, Garagnani Luciano, Ducati
125; 175, Vanni Vincenzo, Ducati 175
16/10, Vallelunga, 125, Ribuffo Giovanni,
Ducati 125
13/11, San Cesareo-Montecompatri, 125,
Colabona Enrico, Mencaglia Pietro,
Ducati 125
20/11, Siracusa: 125, Cozza Angelo, Ducati
125; 175, Garagnani Luciano, Ducati 175
23/11, Catania-Etna: 100, Leotta Giuseppe,
Ducati 98; 125, Cucina Pietro, Ducati
125; 175, Motta Carmelo, Ducati 175

OFF-ROAD RACING
rofeo FMI Speedway, 125, Brabetz
Alessandro, Ducati 125

May, Speedway, Udine, 125, Brabetz
Alessandro, Ducati 125
June, Speedway, Vallelunga, Finale, 125,
Brabetz Alessandro, Ducati 125
10/7, Speedway, Lonigo, 125, Brabetz
Alessandro, Ducati 125
4/9, Speedway, Rovigo, 125, Brabetz
Alessandro, Ducati 125
October, Speedway, Udine, 125, Brabetz
Alessandro, Ducati 125

PORTUGAL

7/7, Festival Stadium Lisboa, 175, Nuñes
Diniz Angelo, Vieira Alvaro, Delinger Heinz,
Ducati 175

SPAIN

18/4, Subida en Montserrat, 125, Fargas
Ricardo, Ducati 125
24/4, Subida en San Miguel, 125, Fargas
Ricardo, Ducati 125
24/4, San Prudencio - Vitoria, 125, Fargas
Ricardo, Ducati 125
15/5, Sevilla, 175, Nuñes Diniz Angelo,
Ducati 175
6-7/7, 24 Horas de Montjuich, 175, Villa F.-
Balboni A., Ducati 175
17/7, Carrera de Santa Cruz, 125, Fargas
Ricardo, Ducati 125
2/9, Vuelta de Montserrat, 125, Gonzales
Juan, Ducati
16/10, Saragossa, 125, Hailwood Mike,
Ducati 125
1/12, Gerona, 125, Fargas Ricardo,
Ducati 125

SWITZERLAND

Swiss Championship, 125, Cecco Hillmar,
Ducati 125

August, Châtel Saint-Les-Paccots, 125,
Cecco Hillmar, Ducati 125

UNITED STATES

January, Baltimore, 250, Barnes Jim,
Ducati 250
January, Scramble Race - Jeep Bowl, 200,
Budschat Bob, Ducati
10/1, Californian Mojave Desert, 200,
Griffin Moe, Ducati
20/3, Daytona Beach FL, 200, Blanchard,
Ducati
20/4, Thompson CT, 175, Theime Rank,
Ducati 175; 200, Villa Francesco, Ducati
May, West Richland, 250, Ershig Bill, Ducati
May, Willow Springs CA, 125, Barker Bob,
Ducati
15/5, Vineland NJ: 125, Varnes Eddie, Ducati
125; 175, Thieme Frank, Ducati 175
15/5, Vineland NJ, 200, Villa Francesco,
Ducati
22/5, Marlboro Maryland Race: 125,
Varnes Eddie, Ducati 125; 175, Villa
Francesco, Ducati 175; 200, Burkholder
Bill, Ducati
20/6, Laconia NH: 175, Barber Terry,
Ducati 175; Experts Class, 175, Villa
Francesco, Ducati 175; 200, Burkholder
William, Ducati
July, Santa Monica CA: 125, Barker Bob, Ducati
125; 175, Scurria Frank, Ducati 175

16/10, Vaca Race Way CA: 125, Kohli Jim,
Ducati 125; 200, Murray Roy, Ducati;
250, Budschat Bob, Ducati
20/11, Willow Springs CA, 200, Scurria
Frank, Ducati

VENEZUELA

February, Maracaibo, 175, Dalle Fusine
Benigno, Ducati 175

YUGOSLAVIA

11/9, Banjica - Beograd, 125, Wunsche
Erich, Ducati 125

1961

ARGENTINA

15/1, Madariaga, 125, Merodio Juan
Carlos, Ducati 125

BELGIUM

11/6, 24 Heures de Warsage, 175, Fargas
R.-Rippa V., Ducati 175

CANADA

Canadian Championship, 175, Liebmann
Kurt, Ducati 175

1/7, Ontario, 200, Johnston A., Ducati
26/7, Mosport, 175, Liebmann Kurt, Ducati 175

CHILE

2/4, Valparaíso: 125, Merodio Juan Carlos,
Ducati 125; 175, Herceg Miguel, Ducati 175
30/4, Quintrala: 100, Andrade Alberto, Ducati
98; 125, Baylli Rolando, Ducati 125
20/8, Timed Race Championship, 175,
Avedano Sergio, Ducati 175
8/10, Santiago: 100, Pelaez H., Ducati 98;
175, Vicuna Jaime, Ducati 175

FRANCE

17/9, Côte de Limonest-Lyon, 175, Barone
Michel, Ducati 175

GERMANY

German Championship: 125, Scheidhauer
Willy, Ducati 125; 125 Juniores,
Schoppner L., Ducati 125

13/8, Flughafen Rennen-Munich, 125,
Durr Peter, Ducati 125

GREAT BRITAIN

2/4, Snetterton, 125, Hailwood Mike,
Ducati 125
24/4, Blackpool, 125, Wilkinson D,
Ducati 125
21/5, Charterhall: 125, Dickinson Gary,
Ducati 125; 126/200, Clark Brian, Ducati
125; 200, Clark Brian, Ducati
22/5, Aintree, 125, Tait Percy, Ducati 125
28/5, Prees Heath, 125, Dugdale Alan,
Ducati 125
18/6, Ouston: 125, Dickinson Gary, Ducati
125; Clark Brian, Ducati
25/6, Cadwell Park, 250, Manley Mick,
Ducati 203
2/7, Charterhall,: 125, Dickinson Gary,
Ducati 125; 200, Clark Brian, Ducati, Gow
J, Ducati
July, Oulton Park, 250, Manley Mick,
Ducati 203
August, Cadwell Park, 250, Crowder H,
Ducati 204
August, Prees Heath, 125, Purslow Fron,
Ducati 125
August, Oulton Park, 125, Tait Percy,
Ducati 125
3/9, Snetterton, 250, Surtees Normann,
Ducati
9/9, Wallasey, 150, Dugdale Alan, Ducati 125
23/9, Rhydymwyn: 200, Trick I, Ducati
175; 250, Watton I, Ducati
September, Charterhall, 200, Clark Brian,
Ducati
14/10, Warwickshire, 175, Keyes Basil E,
Ducati 175
15/10, Snetterton, 125, Wheeler Arthur,
Ducati 125
November, Scotland: 125, Dickinson Gary,
Ducati 125; 200, Clark Brian, Ducati

ITALY

Junior Italian Championship, 125, Cozza Angelo, Ducati 125

Constructors Italian Championship, 125, Ducati Meccanica, Ducati 125

Mountain Italian Championship, 100, Maffucci Mauro, Ducati 98

Trofeo "P.Negri" Challenge Constructors, 125, Ducati Meccanica, Ducati 125

12/3, Agnano-Cappella Cangiani, 125, Mencaglia Pietro, Ducati 125

19/3, Modena, 125, Farné Franco, Ducati 125

2/4, Misano Mare, 125, Garagnani Luciano, Marcaccini Getullio, Ducati 125

3/4, Cesenatico, 125, Farné Franco, Ducati 125

9/4, Frascati-Tuscolo, 125, Mancone Bruno, Colabona Enrico, Ducati 125

16/4, Imola - Coppa d'Oro Shell, 125, Farné Franco, Ducati 125

25/4, Pesaro, 125, Villa Francesco, Ducati 125

1/5, Vallelunga, 175, Vassallo Ferdinando, Ducati 175

7/5, Bologna-San Luca, 125, Garagnani Luciano, Cava Pietro, Ducati 125

7/5, Velletri-Pratoni, 125, Corsetti Luigi, Mancone Bruno, Ducati 125

11/5, Modena, 125, Villa Francesco, Ducati 125

14/5, Pegazzano-Biassa, 125, Mencaglia Pietro, Ducati 125

4/6, Gallarate: 125, Villa Francesco, Ducati 125; 175, Villa Francesco, Ducati 175

11/6, Castell'Arquato-Vernasca: 100, Maffucci Mauro, Ducati 98; 125, Arcoletti Luigi, Ducati 125

25/6, Predappio-Rocca Caminate, 125, Santarelli Giancarlo, Santarelli Giancarlo, Ducati 125

25/6, Ariccia-Madonna del Tufo, 125, Mancone Bruno, Ducati 125

29/6, S. Maria Capua Vetere, 125, Garagnani Luciano, Ducati 125

29/6, Campomorone-Bocchetta, 125, Arcoletti Luigi, Ducati 125

9/7, Manasuddas-Nuoro: 125, Cocco Mariano, Ducati 125; 175, Podda Giuseppe, Ducati 175

16/7, Colleferro-Segni, 125, Mancone Bruno, Ducati 125

16/7, Toirano-Bardinato, 125, Visenzi Giuseppe, Arcoletti Luigi, Ducati 125

23/7, Bobbio-Passo Penice, 125, Visenzi Giuseppe, Ducati 125

23/7, Vinci-San Baronto: 100, Maffucci Mauro, Ducati 98; 125, Santarelli Giancarlo, Ducati 125

30/7, Trent-Bondone, 125, Visenzi Giuseppe, Ducati 125

13/8, Fermo, 125, Cozza Angelo, Ducati 125

27/8, Marina di Carrara: 125, Villa Francesco, Ducati 125; 175, Villa Francesco, Ducati 175

27/8, Montecompatri-Rocca Priora, 125, Mancone Bruno, Ducati 125

3/9, Monza, 125, Villa Francesco, Ducati 125

10/9, Pontedecimo-Giovi, 125, Burlando Giovanni, Ducati 125

10/9, Coppa del Cimino, 125, Capocci Alberto, Ducati 125

24/9, Ballabio-Resinelli, 125, Cresta Maurilio, Ducati 125

8/10, Coppa della Consuma, 125, Burlando Giovanni, Ducati 125

OFF-ROAD RACING

May, Speedway, Rovigo, 125, Brabetz Alessandro, Ducati 125

June, Speedway, Rovigo, 125, Brabetz Alessandro, Ducati 125

24/10, Cross di Menzago: 125, Realini Giuseppe, Ducati 125; 175, Realini Giuseppe, Ducati 175

29/10, Trofeo Italia 1961: 100, Tramontana Franco, Ducati 98; 125, Ferrazza Claudio, Ducati 125

MALAYA

26/11, Singapore, 250, Ng Yang Heng, Ducati 200

MOROCCO

August, Mohammedia, 175, Calatayoud, Ducati 175

SPAIN

30/6, Cataluña, 125, Gonzales Juan, Ducati 125

1/10, Subida de Rabassada: 125, Quintas M, Ducati 125; 250, Fargas Ricardo, Ducati 250

1/10, Subida de Rabassada, Sidecars, Sagnier-Quinovart, Ducati 250

15/10, Saragossa, 125, Villa Francesco, Ducati 125

UNITED STATES

23/4, Hillsboro NC, 250, Hoyes Jim, Ducati

18/6, Laconia NH, Cl. 3, Varnes James, Ducati, Nelson Richard, Ducati

22/6, Northwest Scrambles, 200, Budschat Bob, Ducati

2/6, Daytona Beach FL - 25 Miles, 250, Hayes Jim, Ducati

October, Los Angeles CA, 200, Leim Jim, Ducati

October, Tobacco Trail Classic, Cl.III, Varnes James, Ducati

7/10, Savannah GA, 125, Hayes Jim, Ducati 125

14/10, Riverside CA: 175, Murphy Bill, Ducati 175; 200, Wallace, Ducati

November, Lorain OH, Cl.Senior, Bergman Carl, Ducati

November, Dodge City KS, 175, Bridgewater Jim, Ducati

5/11, Rosamond CA, 175, Murphy Bill, Ducati

URUGUAY

Uruguay Championship, 175, Tassoni Aldobrando, Ducati 175

21/5, Motor Racing "El Pinar", 175, Tassoni Aldobrando, Ducati 175

18/6, Montevideo, 175, Moreira Limberg, Tassoni Aldobrando, Ducati 175

YUGOSLAVIA

June, Portoroz, 125, Rinaudo Luigi, Ducati 125

1962

ARGENTINA

22/7, Buenos Aires: 125, Geromini Juan, Ducati 125; 175, Catania Pancrazio, Ducati 175

21/10, Mondoza, 125, Parra Antonio, Ducati 125

21/10, Buenos Aires: 125, Geromini Juan C, Ducati 125; 175, Catania Pancrazio, Ducati 175

2/12, Buenos Aires, 125, Jeromini Juan, Ducati 125

23/12, Buenos Aires, 175, Catania Pancrazio, Ducati 175

AUSTRALIA

1/1, Phillip Island, 125, Phillis Thomas, Ducati 125

CANADA

Canadian Championship, 250, Budschat Bob, Ducati 250

20/5, Westwood – Vancouver, 250, Budschat Bob, Ducati 250

July, Westwood - Vancouver, 250, Budschat Bob, Ducati 250

7/9, Mosport, 250, Andrews Charles, Ducati 250

FRANCE

July, Roches Faron, 175, Barone Michel, Ducati 175

October, Coupe Salon Montlhéry, 125, Offenstadt Eric, Ducati 125

GERMANY

German Championship, 125, Eser Peter, Ducati 125

November, Avus-Berlin, 125, Thomas, Ducati 125

GREAT BRITAIN

14/4, Kirkcaldy, 200, Gow J, Ducati

23/4, Thruxton, 125, Wheeler Arthur, Ducati 125

13/5, Aberdare Park, 125, Hardy Fred, Ducati 125

17/6, Snetterton, 250, Manley Mick, Ducati 220

1/7, Charterhall, 200, Gow J, Ducati

1/7, Cadwell Park, Smith A, Ducati

7/7, Oulton Park: 125, Bottomley I, Ducati 125; 250, Manley Mick, Ducati 220

11/7, Douglas, Isle of Man, 125, Dickinson Gary, Ducati 125

6/8, Crystal Palace, 250, Manley Mick, Ducati 220

2/9, Malborough Stadium, 250, Whyte J, Ducati

9/9, Snetterton, 250, Surtees Normann, Ducati 250

September, Gask, Scotland, 125, Wilkinson, Ducati 125

23/9, Silverstone, 250, Rawnsley, Ducati

IRELAND

8/9, Carrowdore 100, 250, Donaghy C, Ducati 250

September, County Down Race – Ulster, 250, Donaghy C, Ducati 250

ITALY

11/3, Agnano-Cappella Cangiani, 125, Gagliotta Giovanni, Ducati 125

25/4, Pesaro, 125, Accorsi Sisto, Ducati 125

20/5, Voltri-Turchino, 125, Spinello Luciano, Burlando Giovanni, Ducati 125

20/5, Velletri-Pratoni, 125, Mancone Bruno, Colabona Enrico, Ducati 125

27/5, Bologna-San Luca, 125, Garagnani Lucaino, Ducati 125

2/6, Modena, 125, Garagnani Luciano, Ducati 125

3/6, Sassi-Superga, 125, Burlando Giovanni, Ducati 125

10/6, Castell'Arquato-Vernasca: 100, Salotti Pietro, Ducati 98; 125, Ceré Ernesto, Ducati 125

17/6, Marreri-Salotti, 175, Podda Giuseppe, Ducati 175

21/6, Gallarate, 125, Accorsi Sisto, Ducati 125

21/6, Campomorone-Bocchetta, 125, Burlando Giovanni, Mion Orlando, Ducati 125

24/6, Fornaci di Barga-Barga, 100, Salotti Pietro, Ducati 98

28/6, S. Maria Capua Vetere, 125, Garagnani Luciano, Ducati 125

1/7, Cernobbio-Bisbino, 125, Spinello Luciano, Burlando Giovanni, Ducati 125

1/7, Ariccia-Quattro Strade, 125, Tintisona Virgilio, Ducati 125

15/7, Colleferro-Segni: 125, Vassallo Ferdinando, Ducati 125; 175, Vassallo Ferdinando, Ducati 175

22/7, Trent-Bondone, 125, Spinello Luciano, Ducati 125

29/7, Bobbio-Passo Penice, 100, Villa Walter, Ducati 98

5/8, Fasano-Selva, 100, Cavaliere Domenico, Ducati 98

19/8, Fermo, 125, Spinello Luciano, Ducati 125

26/8, Ponte Oliena-Nuoro: 50, Seddone Graziano, Ducati 48; 125, Amatori Massimiliano, Ducati 125

2/9, Pontedecimo-Giovi, 125, Burlando Giovanni, Mion Orlando, Ducati 125

16/9, Coppa del Cimino, 175, Villa Walter, Ducati 175

18/9, Carini, 125, Chinnici Salvatore, Ducati 125

14/10, Recco-Uscio, 125, Burlando Giovanni, Ducati, Mion Orlando, Ducati 125

4/11, Catania-Etna, 125, Galliano Salvatore, Ducati 125

MALAYA

18/3, Singapore, 250, Ng Yang Heng, Ducati 200

22/7, Singapore: 250, Ng Yang Heng, Ducati 200; 350, Ng Yang Heng, Ducati 350

MOROCCO

2/9, El-Jadida, 175, Calatayoud, Ducati 175

30/9, Rabat, 175, Guarnieri Giancarlo, Ducati 175

SPAIN

January, Carrera en Valvidrera: 175, "Tiger", Ducati 175; 250, Arenas José M., Ducati 250; Sidecars, Sagnier L., Ducati 250

8/4, Subida de Montserrat: 125, Fargas Ricardo, Ducati 125; 250, Fargas Ricardo, Ducati 250

June, Carrera en Valvidrera: 125, Fargas Ricardo, Ducati 125; 250, Fargas Ricardo, Ducati 250

17/6, Carrera en Rabassada, 125, Fargas Ricardo, Ducati 125

7-8/7, 24 Horas de Montjuich, absolute, Fargas R.-Rippa V., Ducati 255

9/9, Tarragona: Sport, Farné Franco, Ducati; Comp., Farné Franco, Ducati

9/9, S.Feliu de Codinas, 250, "Panocha", Ducati 250

16/9, Comarruga: 125S, Quintas Miguel, Ducati 125; 125, Quintas Miguel, Ducati 125

SWITZERLAND

Switzerland Mountain Championship, 125, Zurfluf Heinz, Ducati 125

UNITED STATES

June, Fayetteville NC, 250, Hayes Ken, Ducati

24/6, Riverside, 175, Hamilton Dave, Ducati 175

August, Light Weight, 250, Andrews Charles, Ducati

11/8, Watkins Glen, 250, Andrews Cuck, Ducati

19/8, Greensboro NC, 175, Kennedy Sherril, Ducati 175

September, Ashville NC, 3nd Heat, McDonald Bob, Ducati

September, Dade City FL, 250, Hempstead Ray, Ducati

6/9, Newport TN, Hayes Kenneth, Ducati

16/9, Gastonia, Bootle Benny, Ducati

16/9, Bangor MA, 250, Ashmore Colby, Ducati

22/9, Gastonia, Hayes Kenneth, Ducati

23/9, Rocky Creek NY, Senior, Bergman Carl, Ducati

October, 25 Miles Novice Final, Expert, Andrews Charles, Ducati

14/10, Clewiston FL, 250, Sherbert Royal, Ducati

14/10, Clewiston FL, Ream Roy, Ducati

28/10, St. Pete FL, 250, Hempstead Ray, Ducati

25/11, Flo. West Coast Scrambles: 250, Hempstead Ray, Ducati; G.F., Hempstead Ray, Ducati

2/12, Maybrook NC, Clas III, Clausson Charles, Ducati

YUGOSLAVIA

4/6, Portoroz, 125, Visenzi Giuseppe, Ducati 125

1963

ARGENTINA

Argentinian Standard Championship: 125, Geromini Juan Carlos, Ducati 125; 175, Amoroso Eduardo, Ducati 175

3/3, Buenos Aires, 125, Geromini Juan C., Ducati 125

12/5, Buenos Aires: 125, Geromini Juan C., Ducati 125; 175, Amoroso Eduardo, Ducati 175

June, Chascomus, 175, Catania Pancrazio, Ducati 175

20/6, Buenos Aires, 125, Geromini Juan C., Ducati 125

July, Chascomus, 175, Catania Pancrazio, Ducati 175
17/11, Buenos Aires, 175, Iglesias Luis, Ducati 175
22/12, Rosario, 175, Amoroso Eduardo, Ducati 175

BELGIUM
17/3, Hechtel Motocross, 250: gara 1, Van der Becken Roger, Ducati 250; race 2, Van der Becken Roger, Ducati 250

CANADA
Canadian Championship, 175, Fernandez Bud, Ducati 175

10/2, Québec, 175, Fernandez Bud, Ducati 175

GREAT BRITAIN
23/3, Oulton Park, 200: race 1, Whittaker A., Ducati; race 2, Scully B., Ducati
31/3, Mallory Park, 250: race 1, Hailwood Mike, Ducati 250; Final, Hailwood Mike, Ducati 250
1/4, Cadwell Park, 175, Chatterton Derek, Ducati 175
27/4, Prees Heath: 125, Trick I, Ducati 125; 250, Pladdys R., Ducati
28/4, Charterhall, 200, Gow J, Ducati
11/5, Aberdare Park, 125, Trick I, Ducati 125
June, Prees Heath, 250, Pladdys B., Ducati 250
27/7, Prees Heath, 125, Dugdale Alan, Ducati 125

ITALY
Junior Italian Championship, 125, Accorsi Sisto, Ducati 125
Constructors Italian Championship, 125, Ducati Meccanica, Ducati 125

31/3, Riccione, 125, Villa Walter, Ducati 125
7/4, Targa Vesuvio, 125, Rippa Vincenzo, Ducati 125
15/4, Cesenatico, 125, Accorsi Sisto, Ducati 125
15/4, Frascati-Tuscolo, 125, Marini Paolo, Ducati 125
21/4, Doria-Creto, 125, Burlando Giovanni, Ducati 125
24/4, Imola, 125, Villa Walter, Ducati 125
19/5, Campomorone-Bocchetta, 125, Burlando Giovanni, Ducati 125
23/5, Castell'Arquato-Vernasca, 125, Ceré Ernesto, Ducati 125
26/5, Fola-Cavazzone: 100, Villa Walter, Ducati 98; 125, Giovanardi Carlo, Ducati 125
2/6, Sassi-Superga: 100, Cresta Maurilio, Ducati 98; 125, Burlando Giovanni, Ducati 125
13/6, Bobbio-Passo Penice: 100, Cresta Maurilio, Ducati 98; 125, Bertarelli Silvano, Orsenigo Angelo, Ducati 125
16/6, Coppa della Consuma: 100, Cresta Maurilio, Ducati 98; 125, Burlando Giovanni, Ducati 125
23/6, Bologna-San Luca, 125, Ceré Ernesto, Zacchiroli Vittorio, Ducati 125
7/7, Cernobbio-Bisbino, 125, Raffi Giancarlo, Ducati 125
7/7, Ariccia-Quattro Strade, 125, Marini Paolo, Ducati 125
21/7, Bogliasco-Sessarego: 100, Polenghi Giovanni, Ducati 98; 125, Orsenigo Angelo, Ducati 125
28/7, Trent-Bondone, 125, Burlando Giovanni, Ducati 125
4/8, Fasano-Selva, 125, Tondo Luigi, Ducati 125
11/8, Colleferro-Segni, 125, Marini Paolo, Ducati 125
18/8, Anagnina-Rocca Priora, 125, Marini Paolo, Ducati 125
25/8, Caniparola-Fosdinovo, 125/2, Mion Orlando, Ducati 125; 125/3, Gentili Giorgio, Ducati 125
8/9, Targa Vesuvio, 125, Santaniello Alfonso, Ducati 125
22/9, Pontedecimo-Giovi, 125, Burlando Giovanni, Ducati 125

29/9, Chivasso-Castagneto, 125, Cresta Burlando Giovanni, Ducati 125
6/10, Signorino-Collina Pistoiese, 125, Mandolini Giuseppe, Ducati 125
13/10, Recco-Uscio, 125, Mion Orlando, Ducati 125

OFF-ROAD RACING
19/3, Brunico, 125, Botter Hans, Ducati 125
12/5, Cross di Priabona, Over 125, Battilana Bruno, Ducati 250
9/6, Savona, 125, Bresolin F, Ducati 125
July, Turri, Over 125, Battilana Bruno, Ducati 250
Sett., Lendinara, 125, Boaretti Ottavio, Ducati 125
October, Aprilia, ex-aequo, 125, Pellegrini-Bianchi-Sebastianelli, Ducati 125

MALAYA
1/12, Singapore: 250, Curran A.D, Ducati; 350, Curran A.D, Ducati 250

MOROCCO
24/3, Kasba Tadla, 175, Brignone, Ducati 175
14/4, Marrakesh, 175, Brignone, Ducati 175

RUMANIA
29/9, Bucarest: 125, Garagnani Luciano, Ducati 125; 250, Garagnani Luciano, Ducati 250; 350, Garagnani Luciano, Ducati 350

SPAIN
31/3, Carrera de Montserrat, 250, Fargas Ricardo, Ducati 250
May, Preliminary Competition, 125 S, Aguilar J. L, Ducati 125
5/5, Grand Prix de Espana, 250, Fargas Ricardo, Ducati 250
12/5, 12 Horas de Las Palmas, 200, Artigas-San Juan, Ducati
June, Cartagena, 250, Fargas Ricardo, Ducati 250
26/8, Almeria, 250, Fargas Ricardo, Ducati 250
3/9, Santander, 250, Fargas Ricardo, Ducati 250
9/9, Albacete, 125, Farné Franco, Ducati 125
September, Valladolid, 125, Farné Franco, Ducati 125
September, Valladolid, 250, Farné Franco, Ducati 250
22/9, Jerez de La Frontera, 125, Farné Franco, Ducati 125
22/9, Subida al Puig Mayor, 125, Fargas Ricardo, Ducati 125
22/9, Subida al Puig Mayor, 250, Fargas Ricardo, Ducati 250
1/11, Ferias de Gerona: 125, Fargas Ricardo, Ducati 125; 250, Fargas Ricardo, Ducati 250
3/11, Barcelona, 125 S, Domingo Rafael, Ducati 125
17/11, Fiesta de Olot Gerona, Fargas Ricardo, Ducati

SWITZERLAND
Swiss Championship, 125, Marti, Ducati 125

UNITED STATES
20/1, Clewiston FL: 50, Gill Bob, Ducati; 175, Hempstead Ray, Ducati 175; 250, Sherbet Royal, Ducati
27/1, Tampa FL: 50, Gill Bob, Ducati; 175, Hempstead Ray, Ducati 175; 250, Sherbet Royal, Ducati
17/2, Lakeland FL - Motocross, 175, Sherbet Royal, Ducati 175
24/2, Dade City FL: 175, Hempstead Ray, Ducati; 250, Robinson Steve, Ducati
17/3, Pinellas Park, 50, Gill Bob, Ducati
27/3, Daytona Beach FL: 250, Hempstead Ray, Ducati; Class V, Hempstead Ray, Ducati; Class III, Varnes Bill, Ducati
April, Florida: 125, Varnes Bill, Ducati 125; 250, Hempstead Ray, Ducati
April, Ice Championship Trophy, 175, Ferandez Buddy, Ducati 175
14/4, Punta Gorda, 250, Hempstead Ray, Ducati

21/4, Pinellas Park, Sweepst., Hempstead Ray, Ducati
21/4, Tennessee, 250, Hayes Ken, Ducati
27/4, Tennessee, 250, Hayes Ken, Ducati
28/4, Gate City: 125, Kennedy Sherrill, Ducati 125; 175, Kennedy Sherrill, Ducati
28/4, Monson MS, 175, Morell Gary, Ducati
5/5, Buckingham Airport, 250, Hempstead Ray, Ducati
5/5, Alden Wightman, 250, Marvin Chuck, Ducati
5/5, Daytona Stadium FL, Hayes Jim, Ducati
18/5, Drag Races, 250, Hardy Sim, Ducati
19/5, Fishkill NY, Class III, Merle Stevens, Ducati
26/5, Danville, 200, Kennedy Sherrill, Ducati
26/5, Marlow, 250, Trombley Mike, Ducati
June, Lightweight Road Races, Class III, Varnes William, Ducati
June, Lightweight Road Races, Class V, Hempstead Ray, Ducati
June, A.M.A., Class V: Gardner Chas, Ducati; Class V, Hempstead Ray, Ducati
9/6, Road Knights, 250, Pelotte Roger, Ducati
9/6, Davie Speedway in Advance, Hayes Ken, Ducati
16/6, Kresgeville, Class V, Nothstein Richard, Ducati
23/6, Montourville, 250, Lyons Richard, Ducati
30/6, Randleman Scramble: 125, Kennedy Sherrill, Ducati 125; 175, Kennedy Sherrill, Ducati
2/8, Piedmont Gypsy Tour: Hayes Ken, Ducati; Hayes Jim, Ducati
August, Turnout: 250, Gardner Charles, Ducati; Experts, 250, Hempstead Ray, Ducati
August, South Newbury, 250, Trombley Mike, Ducati
August, "The Day That the Rains Came", 250, Wendell Poggie, Ducati
18/8, Skippack, White White, Ducati
18/8, Nelson NH, 250, Houghton Brian, Ducati
25/8, Vineland NJ, 175, Pearce William, Ducati
25/8, Championship T.T., 250, Fox Robert, Ducati
25/8, Tri-State Scrambles, 250, Peacock Robert, Ducati
25/8, Arcadian Activity, 250, Colby Ashmore, Ducati
September, Big Week End at, 250, Razee Gordon, Ducati
September, Rain Fellow Edgewood, Bobino Edson, Ducati
September, Cattaraugus County Fairgrouns, 250, Henderson Dave, Ducati
September, Arkansas, 250, Neighbors John, Ducati
September, Johnson City, 200, Hayes Ken, Ducati
8/9, Georgia Championship, 250, Fox Robert, Ducati
15/9, Parkesburg PA, Gottschall, Ducati
21/9, North Sportsmen Shortracking: 175, Gardner Charles, Ducati; 250, Gardner Charles, Ducati
22/9, Scirpo Wins - 150 Miles Enduro, Bergman Carl, Ducati
October, Advance Short Track, Verse Brow, Ducati
October, Lightweight Championship, Williams David, Ducati
6/10, Middlesborough, Henderson Dave, Ducati
6/10, District 6 Championship, 48, Miller Lester, Ducati
13/10, Race Baird Wins Sea Shell Too, 250, Bitter W, Ducati
20/10, Baltimore Rambles, 250, Dougherty B, Ducati
20/10, Piston Poppers Pleased: Phipps Fred, Ducati; Hall Barry, Ducati
November, Edgewood, Hayes Ken, Ducati

November, Barnes Wins Little Bone, 150/175, Burr Frank, Ducati
November, Whitt Wins, Kennedy Sherrill, Ducati
3/11, Walden NY, Holas Lew, Ducati
15/12, Tampa FL, 250, Robinson Steve, Ducati

1964

CHILE
8/3, Santiago, 125, Masetti Umberto, Ducati 125
15/3, San Bernardo, 125, Masetti Umberto, Ducati 125
20/3, Conchali, 125, Masetti Umberto, Ducati 125

HONG KONG
September, Autumn Sprint Meeting, 250, Ho Hon-Kah, Lew Kwan, Ducati Mach/1

ITALY
Junior Italian Championship, 125, Giovanardi Carlo, Ducati 125
Constructors Italian Championship, 125, Ducati Meccanica, Ducati 125
Mountain Italian Championship, 125, Burlando Giovanni, Ducati 125

19/4, Modena, 125, Ceré Ernesto, Ducati 125
5/4, Doria-Creto, 125, Burlando Giovanni, Ducati 125
1/5, Frascati-Tuscolo, 125, Burlando Giovanni, Ducati 125
7/5, Sondrio-Gualtieri, 125, Burlando Giovanni, Ducati 125
31/5, Campomorone-Bocchetta, 125, Burlando Giovanni, Ducati 125
14/6, Trent-Bondone, 125, Burlando Giovanni, Ducati 125
28/6, Ballabio-Resinelli, 125, Burlando Giovanni, Ducati 125
5/7, Cernobbio-Bisbino, 125, Burlando Giovanni, Ducati 125
12/7, Bobbio-Passo Penice, 125, Mion Orlando, Burlando Giovanni, Ducati 125
26/7, Camucia-Cortona, 125, Ceré Ernesto, Ducati 125; 250, Villa Walter, Ducati 250
2/8, Lago Bolsena-Montefiascone, 125, Ceré Ernesto, Ducati 125
9/8, Colleferro-Segni, 125, Paolucci Emidio, Ducati 125
23/8, Caniparola-Fosdinovo, 125, Burlando Giovanni, Ducati 125
20/9, Sei Ore di Monza, 125, Polenghi-Orsenigo
20/9, Pontedecimo-Giovi, 125, Burlando Giovanni, Ducati 125
20/9, Targa Vesuvio, 125, De Rosa Achille, Ducati 125
11/10, Sassi-Superga, 125, Burlando Giovanni, Ducati 125
18/10, Recco-Uscio, 125, Burlando Giovanni, Ducati 125
1/11, San Cesareo-Montecompatri, 125, Paolucci Emidio, Ducati 125

MALAYA
8/11, Singapore: 250, Ng Yang Heng, Ducati; 350, Ng Yang Heng, Ducati; 350 on, Ng Yang Heng, Ducati
13/12, Batu Tika: 250, Seng Kieu Kang, Ducati; 350, Seng Kieu Kang, Ducati

RUMANIA
22/10, Ploesti: 125, Farné Franco, Ducati 125; 175/250, Garagnani Luciano, Ducati 250; 350/500, Garagnani Luciano, Ducati 350

SPAIN
1/3, Las Mayolas-Igualads: 125, Domingo Rafael, Ducati 125; 250, Fargas Ricardo, Ducati 250; 250 J, Segnier Luis, Ducati 250
12/4, Subida de Montserrat: 125, Domingo Rafael, Ducati 125; 175, Fargas Ricardo, Ducati 175; 250, Fargas Ricardo, Ducati 250

277

10/5, Grand Prix de Espana, 125 S, Aguilar José L, Ducati 125

17/5, Puerto de La Morcuera, 250, Fargas Ricardo, Ducati 250

24/5, Subida de Valvidrera: 125 S, Escualo Alberto, Ducati 125; 125 C, Domingo Rafael, Ducati 125; 175, Fargas Ricardo, Ducati 175; 250, Fargas Ricardo, Ducati 250; 250 S, Sagnier Luis, Ducati 250

12/7, 24 Horas de Montjuich, absolute, Spaggiari-Mandolini G.Ducati 285

23/8, Bages-Barcelona, 250, Fargas Ricardo, Ducati 250

30/9, Subida al Sotillo, 175, Fargas Ricardo, Ducati 175

SWITZERLAND
September, Châtel-St-Dedis, 125, Stadelmann Hans, Ducati 125

UNITED STATES
26/1, Short Track Twin Bill, 175, Gill Bob, Ducati

March, Daytona Sebring CA, 250, Hempstead Ray, Ducati

19/3, Sebring CA: 175, Tunstall Sid, Ducati; 250, Gill Bob, Ducati

April, Clearwater Swings, 250, Hempstead Ray, Ducati

5/4, Punta Gorda, 175, Tampa Nicks, Ducati

26/4, Emmaus T.T., Varnes William, Ducati

3/5, Piston Poppers Opener, Hall Barry, Ducati

3/5, Walden NY, Bigelow Richard, Ducati

10/5, Walden NY, Bigelow Richard, Ducati

17/5, Crotona - Fishkill NY, Nelson Richard, Ducati

17/5, Tough Trock, 250, Murray Charles, Ducati

23/5, Durham Wins Again NC, Hayes Jim, Ducati

24/5, Blue Comet M.C., Wayne White, Varnes William, Ducati

24/5, Race Hot Dry and Dusty, Bigalow Robert, Ducati

27/5, Blue Hen Opener, Dougherty Bill, Ducati

June, Keystone, 250, Varnes William, Ducati

June, Road Rebels Rally, Pierce William, Ducati

June, Vineland NJ: 175, Nelson John, Ducati; 250, Druding James, Ducati

13/6, Parkesburg - Scramble, Dougherty Bill, Ducati

23/8, Clearwater M.C., 250, Hemstead Ray, Ducati

October, Florida in Focus, 175, Thompson Charles, Ducati

October, Tri-State Championship, 250, Bootle Benny, Ducati

1965

ITALY
4/4, Frascati-Tuscolo, 125, Bertarelli Silvano, Ducati 125

23/5, Modena, 125, Lazzarini Eugenio, Ducati 125

30/5, Marina di Carrara, 125, Lazzarini Eugenio, Ducati 125

6/6, Sei Ore di Monza, 125, Tosolini-Mondani, Ducati 125

29/6, Ballabio-Resinelli, 125, Bongiovanni Sergio, Ducati 125

18/7, Castell'Arquato-Vernasca, 125, Burlando Giovanni, Ducati 125

18/7, Catania-Etna, 125, Motta Carmelo, Ducati 125

OFF-ROAD RACING
9/3, Fara, 125, Battilana Bruno, Ducati 125

23/5, Messina, 100, Bianca Salvatore, Ducati 98

13/6, Cornedo, 250, Battilana Bruno, Ducati 250

15/8, Monastier, 50, Spinazze Guido, Ducati 48

29/8, Riva, 250, Battilana Bruno, Ducati 250

5/9, Cornedo, 250, Battilana Bruno, Ducati 250

MALAYA
Singapore: 250, Ng Yang Heng, Ducati; 350, Ng Yang Heng, Ducati 350; over 350, Ng Yang Heng, Ducati 350

PERU
Monterrico, Lima, 250, Barbacci Carlo, Ducati 250

SPAIN
July, La Coruña, 125, Spaggiari Bruno, Ducati 125

July, La Coruña, 250, Spaggiari Bruno, Ducati 250

August, Bilbao, 125, Spaggiari Bruno, Ducati 125

August, Valladolid, 125, Spaggiari Bruno, Ducati 125

SWITZERLAND
Swiss Championship, 250, Stadelmann Hans, Ducati 250

UNITED STATES
A.M.A. CHAMPIONSHIP
8/8, Des Moines, IA, Novice Final, Tacchi Torello, Ducati

15/8, Carpentersville, IL, Nov. Fin., Tacchi Torello, Ducati

5/9, Marlboro, MD, Nov. Fin., Russell J.Robert, Ducati

1966

AUSTRALIA
June, Victoria Park, 250, Dillion Mick, Ducati, Bull Lindsay, Ducati Mach/1

FRANCE
French International Championship, 350, Roca Jacques, Ducati 350

French National Championship, 250, Ravel Christian, Ducati 250

13/3, Côte Lapize, 350, Roca Jacques, Ducati 350

27/3, Côte de Meru, 350, Roca Jacques, Ducati 350

24/4, Montlhéry, 350, Roca Jacques, Ducati 350

19/5, Côte Falicon-Nice, 350, Roca Jacques, Ducati 350

3/7, Côte Du Mont Chauve, 350, Roca Jacques, Ducati 350

14/8, Côte Du Peillon, 350, Roca Jacques, Ducati 350

25/9, Coupes de Paris Montlhéry: 350, Roca Jacques, Ducati 350; 500, Roca Jacques, Ducati 350

16/10, Coupes du Salon Montlhéry: 250 Sport, Gey Daniels, Ducati 250; 350, Roca Jacques, Ducati 350

GREAT BRITAIN
August, Crystal Palace, 250, Bunting G. R. Ducati 250

ITALY
22/5, Marina di Carrara, 125, Lazzarini Eugenio, Ducati 125

2/6, Sei Ore di Imola: 125, Accorsi-Barabaschi, Ducati 125; 250, Ceré-Giovanardi, Ducati 250; 350, Farné-Garagnani, Ducati 350

12/6, Crema, 125, Barabaschi Giovanni, Ducati 125

14/8, Lecco, 125, Barabaschi Giovanni, Ducati 125

OFF-ROAD RACING
Timed Race Italian Championship, 250, Reggioli Walter, Ducati 250

Junior Cross-Country Italian Championship, 250, Battilana Bruno, Ducati 250

19/3, Fara, 250, Battilana Bruno, Ducati 250

24/4, Bressanone, 75, Urthaler Hubert, Ducati

24/25-4, Due Giorni di Bologna, 250, Reggioli Walter, Ducati 250

15/5, Priabona, 250, Battilana Bruno, Ducati 250

19/5, Cornedo, 250, Battilana Bruno, Ducati 250

12/6, Chianti, 250, Reggioli Walter, Ducati 250

9/10, Perugia, 250, Battilana Bruno, Ducati 250

October, Pergine, 175, Vicentini Mario, Ducati 175

27/11, Rally Due Province, 250, Motta Carmelo, Ducati 250

PERU
Campo de Marte, 250, Barbacci Carlo, Ducati 250

SPAIN
20/3, Subida de Montserrat: 125, Fargas Ricardo, Ducati 125; 250, Fargas Ricardo, Ducati 250

VENEZUELA
27/10, Caracas, 250, Ursini Adamo, Ducati

1967

FRANCE
Sport 250 French Championship, Gey Daniels, Ducati 250

March, Côte Lapize, 250 Sport, Prandi, Ducati 250

18/6, Côte du Mont Ventoux, 250, Viura Pierre, Ducati 250

8/10, Coupes Du Salon Montlhéry, 250 Sport, Pogolotti André, Ducati 250

GREAT BRITAIN
26/7, Brands Hatch, 350, Williams John, Ducati 350

HOLLAND
Holland Championship, 250, Van der Lugt Frans, Ducati 250

6/4, Noord-Brabant, 250, Van der Lugt Frans, Ducati 250

15/5, Oss/North Brabant, 250, Van der Lugt Frans, Ducati 250

17/6, 250, Val Charles, Ducati 250

19/6, Etten, 250, Van der Lugt Frans, Ducati 250

23/7, Dremt, 250, Van der Lugt Frans, Ducati 250

17/9, Nijmegen, 250, Van der Lugt Frans, Ducati 250

ITALY
5/6, Velletri-Pratoni, 250, Tintisona Virgilio, Ducati 250

29/6, Frascati-Tuscolo, 250, Tintisona Virgilio, Ducati 250

2/7, Monza, 125, Tarlazzi Renato, Ducati 125

20/8, Consonno, 250, Rossi Luciano, Ducati 250

24/8, Anagnina-Rocca Priora, 250, Tintisona Virgilio, Ducati 250

OFF-ROAD RACING
Cross-Country Tuscan Championship, 175, Cozzi Paolo, Ducati 175

9/7, Speedway, Lonigo, 250, Rupil Mario, Ducati 250

Speedway, Udine, 250, Rupil Mario, Ducati 250

8/10, Valli Verdi, Florence, 250, Cozzi Paolo, Ducati 250

UNITED STATES
A.M.A. CHAMPIONSHIP
18/6, Loudon, NH, Nov. Fin, Cromer Leon, Ducati

YUGOSLAVIA
11/6, Ljubljana, 250, Palikovic Jovica, Ducati 250

27/8, Nova Gorica, 250, Parlotti Gilberto, Ducati 250

1968

FRANCE
French National Championship, 250, Pogolotti André, Ducati 250

14/4, Nogaro, 250, Pogolotti André, Ducati 250

28/4, Montlhéry, 250, Pogolotti André, Ducati 250

28/4, Côte de Hébecrévon, 250, Caignart, Ducati 250

22/9, Montlhéry, 350, Gallottini, Ducati 350

22/9, Côte du Mont Ventoux: 350, Fargas Ricardo, Ducati 350; 500, Fargas Ricardo, Ducati

HOLLAND
3/5, Schijndel, 250, Van der Lugt Frans, Ducati 250

12/5, Venhuizen, 250, Van der Lugt Frans, Ducati 250

3/6, Oss, 250, Van der Lugt Frans, Ducati 250

14/7, Uden, 350, Smeets, Ducati Mark/3

17/8, Zandvoort, 250, Naber Henk, Ducati 250

15/9, Gulpen, 250, Van der Lugt Frans, Ducati 250

12/10, Zandvoort, 250, Van der Lugt Frans, Ducati 250

INDONESIA
27/1, Surabaya: 50, Effendi Usman, Ducati 48; 60, Effendi Usman, Ducati 48; 250, Gumilar M.A., Ducati Mark/3

ITALY
Mountain Tuscan Championship, 250, Brettoni Augusto, Ducati 250

13/6, Vergato-Cerelia, 250, Ribuffo Giovanni, Ducati 250

23/6, Giulianova, 125, Tarlazzi Renato, Ducati 125

30/6, Pesaro, 250, Faga Nino, Ducati 250

30/6, Treviso: 125, Tarlazzi Renato, Ducati 125; 250, Baroncini Sergio, Ducati 250

30/6, Trent-Bondone, 250, Gallina Roberto, Ducati 250

28/7, Lugagnano-Vernasca, 250, Gallina Roberto, Ducati 250

11/8, Colleferro-Segni, 250, Tintisona Virgilio, Ducati 250

18/8, Nicolosi-Etna: 175, Curia Luigi, Ducati 175; 250, Di Dio Orazio, Ducati 250

18/8, Poggibonsi-Castellina: 250, Gallina Roberto, Ducati 250; 500, Gallina Roberto, Ducati 450

25/8, Pescara, 250, Di Dio Orazio, Ducati 250

22/9, Castelnuovo-Albugnano, 250, Mandracci Guido, Ducati 250

29/9, Molin del Piano-Olmo, 250, Brettoni Augusto, Ducati 250

6/10, Frascati-Tuscolo, 250, Tintisona Virgilio, Ducati 250

OFF-ROAD RACING
14/7, Speedway, Lonigo, 250, Rupil Mario, Ducati 250

28/4, Valli Fiorentine, 250, Ceccarelli Leandro, Ducati 250

1/5, Pontedera, Trofeo FMI, 250, Ceccarelli Leandro, Ducati 250

12/5, Chianti, Trofeo FMI, 250, Ceccarelli Leandro, Ducati 250

SPAIN
March, Begas de Barcelona, 250, Fargas Ricardo, Ducati 250

Col de Estenalles, 250, Fargas Ricardo, Ducati 250

9/6, Castellan, 250, Fargas Ricardo, Ducati 250

13/6, Trofeo Corpus, 250, Fargas Ricardo, Ducati 250

September, Barcelona, 250, Smart Paul, Ducati 250

20/10, Subida de la Rabassa, 250, Fargas Ricardo, Ducati 250

UNITED STATES
1/9, Dade City FL, 500, Rockett George, Ducati 350

1/9, 5 Hour Production Race VA, 250, Gebb Albert-Finnegan Walter, Ducati

YUGOSLAVIA
4/6, Murska Sobota, 350, Parlotti Gilberto, Ducati 350
25/8, Nuova Gorica, 350, Parlotti Gilberto, Ducati 350
6/10, Zenica, 175, Parlotti Gilberto, Ducati 175
15/10, Zenica, 250, Parlotti Gilberto, Ducati 250

1969

GREAT BRITAIN
June, T.T. - Isle of Man, 250, Rogers A. M., Ducati 250

ITALY
Mountain Tuscan Championship, 250, Brettoni Augusto, Ducati 250

16/3, Rimini, 250, Ribuffo Giovanni, Ducati 250
20/4, Pesaro, 250, Tarlazzi Renato, Ducati 250
1/5, Frascati-Tuscolo, 250, Nicoli Benito, Ducati 250
4/5, Camucia-Cortona: 250, Gallina Roberto, Ducati 250; 500, Gallina Roberto, Ducati 450
11/5, Cuorgné-Alpette, 250, Gallina Roberto, Ducati 250
5/6, Vergato-Cerelia, 250, Gallina Roberto, Ducati 250
29/6, Treviso, 250, Ribuffo Giovanni, Ducati 250
5/7, Modena, 250, Baroncini Sergio, Ducati 250
27/7, Molin del Piano-Olmo, 250, Brettoni Augusto, Ducati 250
3/8, Castiglione del Lago, 250, Brettoni Augusto, Ducati 250
3/8, Velletri-Pratoni, 250, Gallina Roberto, Ducati 250
10/8, Poggibonsi-Castellina, 250, Brettoni Augusto, Ducati 250
31/8, Nicolosi-Etna: 175, Curia Luigi, Ducati 175; 250, Di Dio Orazio, Ducati 250

OFF-ROAD RACING
16/3, Ragusa, 175, Motta Carmelo, Ducati 175
20/4, Catania, Trofeo FMI, 175, Grasso Vito, Ducati 175
25/4, Motogiro dei Monti Prenestini, 175, Antonioli, Ducati 175
May, Due Giorni Esso Fiorentina, 175, Focardi Valerio, Ducati 175
7/12, Giro dei Due Laghi, 250, Marcucci Roberto, Ducati 250

YUGOSLAVIA
3/8, Murska Sobota, 250, Parlotti Gilberto, Ducati 250
28/9, Zenica, 175, Parlotti Gilberto, Ducati 175

1970

GREAT BRITAIN
June, T.T. - Isle of Man, 250, Mortimer Charles, Ducati 250
500 Miles of Thruxton, 250, Mortimer-Browning, Ducati 250

ITALY
Mountain Tuscan Championship, 250, Brettoni Augusto, Ducati 250
Mountain Latian Championship, 250, Tintisona Virgilio, Ducati 250

10/5, Saline-Volterra, 250, Brettoni Augusto, Ducati 250
24/5, Camucia-Cortona, 250, Brettoni Augusto, Ducati 250
28/5, Frascati-Tuscolo, 250, Tintisona Virgilio, Ducati 250
2/6, Sassi-Superga, 250, Giuliano Ermanno, Ducati 250
14/6, Velletri-Pratoni, 250, Tintisona Virgilio, Ducati 250

5/7, Sillano-Ospedaletto, 250, Agostini Maurizio, Ducati 250
26/7, Molin del Piano-Olmo, 250, Brettoni Augusto, Ducati 250
23/8, Poggibonsi-Castellina, 250, Bianchin Anzio, Ducati 250
30/8, Grosseto, 250, Bianchin Anzio, Ducati 250
20/9, Imola, 250, Tarlazzi Renato, Ducati 250
27/9, Castelnuovo-Albugnano, 250, Giuliano Ermanno, Ducati 250
11/10, S.Polo-S.Polo Cavalieri, 250, Tintisona Virgilio, Ducati 250
15/11, Nicolosi-Etna, 250, Curia Luigi, Ducati 250

OFF-ROAD RACING
Roman Winter Championship, Over 250, Marcucci Roberto, Ducati 250
8/3, Giro Bassa Sabina, 250, Spitoni Davide, Ducati 250
8/3, Giro Bassa Sabina, Over 250, Marcuci Roberto, Ducati
22/3, Lago di Bracciano, 250, Spitoni Davide, Ducati 250
Due Giorni Esso Fiorentina, Over 175, Focardi Valerio, Ducati 175
5/4, Seriate, Over 250, Dall'Ara Franco, Ducati 450

YUGOSLAVIA
14/6, Zenica, 250, Parlotti Gilberto, Ducati 250

1971

ITALY
Mountain Tuscan Championship, 250, Marchetti Piramo, Ducati 250

18/4, Saline-Volterra, 250, Marchetti Piramo, Ducati 250
25/4, Pesaro, 250, Loigo Claudio, Ducati 250
20/5, Pieve S.Stefano-Passo Spino, 250, Cresta Giovanni, Ducati 250
30/5, Molin del Piano-Olmo, 250, Marchetti Piramo, Ducati 250
2/6, Sassi-Superga, 250, Cresta Giovanni, Ducati 250
6/6, Grosseto, 250, Loigo Claudio, Ducati 250
27/6, Treviso, 500, Cocchi Adriano, Ducati 450
29/6, Signorino-Collina Pistoiese, 250, Toracca Armando, Ducati 250
22/8, Poggibonsi-Castellina, 250, Brettoni Augusto, Ducati 250
5/9, Isola Liri-Arpino: 250, Piccirilli Tommaso, Ducati 250; 500, Paolucci Emidio, Ducati 450

OFF-ROAD RACING
21/2, Motogiro della Sabina, 250, Spitoni Davide, Ducati 250
4/4, Varese, Over 250, Dall'Ara Franco, Ducati 450
25/4, Motogiro dei Due Laghi, 250, Spitoni Davide, Ducati 250

YUGOSLAVIA
30/5, Skopia Locka, 500, Parlotti Gilberto, Ducati 500

1972

GREECE
October, Corfu, 750, Smart Paul, Ducati 750

ITALY
Mountain Tuscan Championship, 500, Peruzzi Marcello, Ducati 450

26/3, Doria-Creto, 500, Marchetti Piramo, Ducati 450
23/4, Imola - 200 Miglia, 750, Smart Paul, Ducati 750
23/4, Saline-Volterra, 250, Marchetti Piramo, Ducati 250
1/5, Ballabio-Resinelli, 500, Marchetti Piramo, Ducati 450

11/5, Limoncino-Valle Benedetta: 250, Rossi Luciano, Ducati 250; 500, Marchetti Piramo, Ducati 450
2/6, Certaldo-Gambassi, 250, Marchetti Piramo, Ducati 250
2/6, Certaldo-Gambassi: 500, Marchetti Piramo, Ducati 450; Sidecars, Pedrini-Mignani, Ducati 450
11/6, Vergato-Cerelia, 500, Latteri Mario, Ducati 450
29/6, Figline Valdarno-4 Strad: 250, Giamboni Rinaldo, Ducati 250; 500, Checchi Sergio, Ducati 450
6/8, Nicolosi-Etna, 250, Bonfardeci Francesco, Ducati 250
10/9, Pieve S.Stefano-Passo Spino, 500, Latteri Mario, Ducati 450
10/9, Pieve S.Stefano-Passo Spino, Sidecars, Pedrini-Mignani, Ducati 750
1/10, Valdobiadene-Pianezze: 250, Cresta Giovanni, Ducati 250; 500, Bianchin Anzio, Ducati 450
22/10, Vallelunga, Sidecars, Pedrini-Mignani, Ducati 750

OFF-ROAD RACING
9/4, 12 Ore di Brescia, Over 175, Dall'Ara F.-Consonni Ducati 450

1973

AUSTRIA
Arauch, Over 500, Zach, Braumandl, Ducati 750 SS

ITALY
13/5, Vergato-Cerelia: 500, Latteri Mario, Ducati 450; Sidecars, Pedrini-Mignani, Ducati 750
20/5, Monza, 250, Tosolini Ettore, Ducati 250
31/5, Figline Valdarno-4 Strade, 500, Neri Riccardo, Ducati 450
16/9, Alberi-Montaione, 250, Rossi Antonio, Ducati 250
7/10, Certaldo-Gambassi, Sidecars, Pedrini-Mignani, Ducati 750

SPAIN
7-8/7, 24 Horas de Montjuich, absolute, Cañellas S.-Grau B., Ducati 900

1974

ITALY
Mountain Tuscan Championship, 250, Rossi Antonio, Ducati 250

30/6, Certaldo-Gambassi, Side, Pedrini-Mignani, Ducati 750
1/9, Fontepetri-Montalcino: 250, Rossi Antonio, Ducati 250; Sidecars, Pedrini-Mignani, Ducati 750
15/9, Alberi-Montaione, 250, Rossi Antonio, Ducati 250
20/10, Vallelunga, 750, Sabattini Giulio, Ducati 750

1975

ITALY
31/3, Misano, 750, Saltarelli Carlo, Uncini Franco, Ducati 750
25/4, Vallelunga, 750, Uncini Franco, Ducati 750
1/5, Vallelunga, 750, Uncini Franco, Faccioli Adelio, Sabattini Giulio, Ducati 750
2/6, Misano, 750, Uncini Franco, Ducati 750
3/9, Vallelunga, 750, Perugini Carlo, Sabattini Giulio, Ducati 750
14/9, Misano, 750, Uncini Franco, Ducati 750
28/9, Vallelunga, 750, Uncini Franco, Sabattini Giulio, Ducati 750
19/10, Misano, 750, Uncini Franco, Perugini Carlo, Ducati 750
9/11, Vallelunga, 750, Venanzi Arturo, Tuzii Corrado, Ducati 750

SPAIN
5-6/7, 24 Horas de Montjuich, absolute, Cañellas S.-Grau B., Ducati 900

1976

AUSTRIA
Salzburgring, Serie Class, Braumandl, Ducati 900 SS
Schwanenstadt, Serie Class, Braumandl, Ducati 900 SS
Eisenstadt, Serie Class, Braumandl, Ducati 900 SS
Grossramming, Serie Class, Braumandl, Ducati 900 SS

ITALY
Trofeo Nazionale Maximoto, 750, Faccioli Adelio, Ducati 750

19/3, Misano - Bol d'Or: absolute, Ferrari-Perugini, Ducati 850; 750, Saltarelli C.-Benini, Ducati 750
11/4, Vallelunga, 750, Saltarelli Carlo, Ducati 750
25/4, Pergusa, 750, Montaldo Sergio, Ducati 750
2/6, Vallelunga: 750, Saltarelli Carlo, Ducati 750
29/6, Misano, 750, Martini Raoul, Saltarelli Carlo, Ducati 750
19/9, Monza: 750, Martini Raoul, Faccioli Adelio, Ducati 750
26/9, Vallelunga: 750, Faccioli Adelio, Martini Raoul, Ducati 750
24/10, Vallelunga: 750, Venanzi Arturo, Faccioli Adelio, Baccante Giorgio, Ducati 750

1977

ITALY
1/5, Pergusa, 500, Parrinelli Giuseppe, Ducati
12/6, Monza, Pelatti Giancarlo, Ducati
10/7, Pergusa, 750, Gaggia Salvatore, Ducati 750

UNITED STATES
A.M.A. CHAMPIONSHIP
11/6, Daytona Beach, FL, SBK, Neilson Cook, Ducati
16/7, Sonoma, CA, SBK, Ritter Paul, Ducati

1978

AUSTRIA
Austrian Championship, Osk Cup Serie Class, Wolfschlucker, Ducati 900 SS
Amstetten, S.C., Wolfschlucker, Ducati 900 SS
Salzburgring, S.C., Wolfschlucker, Ducati 900 SS

GREAT BRITAIN
TT 1 World Championship, Hailwood Mike, Ducati 900
TT 1 Constructors World Championship, Ducati Meccanica, Ducati 900

3/6, T.T. - Isle of Man, F/1, Hailwood Mike, Ducati 900
11/6, Mallory Park, F/1, Hailwood Mike, Ducati 900

SPAIN
21/5, Subida S.Maria de Vilalba, 500, Coronilla José, Ducati

UNITED STATES
A.M.A. CHAMPIONSHIP
15/7, Sonoma, CA, SBK, Ritter Paul, Ducati

1979

ITALY
26/8, Fontepetri-Montalcino, 250, Rossi Antonio, Ducati 250

UNITED STATES
A.M.A. CHAMPIONSHIP
17/6, Loudon, NH, SBK, Schlachter Rick, Ducati

1980

ARGENTINA
Argentinian Championship, Maximoto, Garcia Ricardo Camillo Ducati 900 SS

279

ITALY

Junior Italian Championship Formula, TT/2, Del Piano Guido, Ducati 600
Mountain Tuscan Championship, TT/2, Bertoni Mauro, Ducati 600
Trofeo delle Regioni Formula TT, TT/1, Francini Vanes, Ducati 900

23/3, Misano, TT/2, Menchini Pietro, Ducati 600
20/4, Vallelunga, TT/2, Francini Vanes, Ducati 600
20/4, Fontepetri-Montalcino, TT/2, Piano Mauro, Ducati 600
4/5, Mugello, TT/1, Francini Vanes, Ducati 600
8/6, Misano, TT/1, Francini Vanes, Saltarelli Amerigo, Ducati 900
29/6, Gubbio-Madonna della Cima, TT/2, Rogari Fausto, Ducati 600
29/6, Vallelunga, TT/1, Francini Vanes, Saltarelli Amerigo, Ducati 900
6/7, Sarnano-Sassotetto, TT/2, Piano Mauro, Ducati 600
6/7, Misano, TT/1, Francini Vanes, Ducati 900
14/7, Adrara-San Rocco, TT/2, Piano Mauro, Ducati 600
20/7, Trent-Bondone, TT/2, Piano Mauro, Ducati 600
3/8, Misano, TT/2, Francini Vanes, Ducati 600
3/8, Sillano-Ospedaletto, TT/2, Piano Mauro, Ducati 600
7/9, Alberi-Montaione, TT/2, Piano Mauro, Ducati 600
28/9, Massa-San Carlo, TT/2, Piano Mauro, Ducati 600

SPAIN

11/5, 6 Horas de Calafat: TT/2, Duran-Rejes, Ducati 500; TT/1, Herrera-Rapizarda, Ducati 900
15/6, 12 Horas de Jarama: TT/2, Duran-Rejes, Ducati 500; TT/1, Mallol J.-Tejedo A., Ducati 900
5-6/7, 24 Horas de Montjuich, absolute, Mallol J.-Tejedo A., Ducati 900

1981

GREAT BRITAIN
TT 2 World Championship, Rutter Anthony, Ducati 600
TT 2 Constructors World Championship, Ducati Meccanica, Ducati 600

5-12/6, T.T. - Isle of Man, F/2, Rutter Anthony, Ducati 600

ITALY
Junior Italian Championship Formula, TT/2, Broccoli Massimo, Ducati 600
Constructor Italian Championship Formula, TT/2, Ducati Meccanica, Ducati 600
Trofeo Junior Formula TT, TT/2, Saltarelli Amerigo, Ducati 600
Mountain Italian Championship, TT/2, Piano Mauro, Ducati 600
Endurance Italian Championship, TT/2, Perugini-Ricci M., Ducati 600
Endurance Constructors Italian Championship, TT/2, Ducati Meccanica, Ducati 600

22/3, Magione, TT/2, Saltarelli Amerigo, Ducati 600
29/3, Misano, TT/2, Broccoli Massimo, Ducati 600
29/3, Vallelunga, TT/2, Saltarelli Amerigo, Ducati 600
19/4, Misano, TT/2, Broccoli Massimo, Ducati 600
26/4, Buonconvento-Montalcino, TT/2, Piano Mauro, Ducati 600
17/5, Magione, TT/2, Becchetti Ugo, Ducati 600
31/5, Magione, TT/2, Colucci Michele, Ducati 600
31/5, Issiglio-Castelnuovo, TT/2, Piano Mauro, Ducati 600

21/6, Magione, TT/2, Becchetti Ugo, Ducati 600
28/6, Mugello, TT/2, Broccoli Massimo, Ducati 600
12/7, Magione, TT/2, Rossi Maurizio, Ducati 600
12/7, Trent-Bondone, TT/2, Piano Mauro, Ducati 600
19/7, Monza - Endurance, TT/2, Perugini-Ricci M., Ducati 600
26/7, Fasano-Selva, TT/2, Tondo Luigi, Ducati 600
6/9, Alberi-Montaione, TT/2, Limberti Paolo, Ducati 600
13/9, Massa-San Carlo Terme, TT/2, Piano Mauro, Ducati 600
13/9, Massa-San Carlo Terme, TT/1, Favero Paolo, Ducati 600
13/9, Vallelunga, TT/2, Rossi Maurizio, Ducati 600
20/9, Magione, TT/2, Rossi Maurizio, Ducati 600
4/10, Monza, TT/2, Cussigh Walter, Ducati 600

SPAIN
11-12/7, 24 Horas de Montjuich, absolute, Grau B.-De Juan E., Ducati

1982

GREAT BRITAIN
TT 2 World Championship, Rutter Anthony, Ducati 600
TT 2 Constructors World Championship, Ducati Meccanica, Ducati 600

5-11/6, T.T. - Isle of Man, F/2, Rutter Anthony, Ducati 600

IRELAND
21/8, Ulster Grand Prix - Ulster, F/2, Rutter Anthony, Ducati 600

ITALY
Junior Italian Championship Formula, TT/2, Cussigh Walter, Ducati 600
Constructors Italian Championship Formula, TT/2, Ducati Meccanica, Ducati 600
Mountain Italian Championship, TT/2, Piano Mauro, Ducati 600
Endurance Italian Championship, TT/2, Tardozzi-Rossi M., Ducati 600

28/3, Monza, TT/2, Cussigh Walter, Ducati 600
11/4, Misano, TT/2, Cussigh Walter, Ducati 600
25/4, Vallelunga-Endurance, TT/2, Tardozzi-Rossi M., Ducati 600
2/5, Mugello, TT/2, Cussigh Walter, Ducati 600
9/5, Biella-Oropa, TT/2, Piano Mauro, Ducati 600
30/5, Fontepetri-Montalcino, TT/2, Limberti Paolo, Ducati 600
20/6, Vallelunga, TT/2, Cussigh Walter, Ducati 600
27/6, Fasano-Selva, TT/2, Tondo Luigi, Ducati 600
4/7, Misano, TT/2, Cussigh Walter, Ducati 600
8/8, Sillano-Ospedaletto, TT/2, Piano Mauro, Ducati 600
29/8, Gubbio-Madonna della Cima, TT/2, Piano Mauro, Ducati 600
5/9, Lanzo-Coassolo, TT/2, Piano Mauro, Ducati 600
19/9, Alberi-Montaione, TT/2, Piano Mauro, Ducati 600
26/9, Magione, TT/2, Tardozzi Davide, Ducati 600
24/10, Misano - Endurance, TT/2, Matteoni-Vitali M., Ducati 600
7/11, Trofeo Valle dei Templi, TT/2, Barone Domenico, Ducati 600

PORTUGAL
4/7, Vila Real, F/2, Rutter Anthony, Ducati 600

UNITED STATES

A.M.A. CHAMPIONSHIP
American Championship Battle of the Twins Modified, Mills Joey III, Ducati

14/3, Talladega, AL, B.ot T.M., Mills Joey III, Ducati
23/5, Elkhart Lake, WI, B.ot T.M., Bracken Kevin, Ducati
20/6, Loudon, NH, B.ot T.M., Hopp Winfried, Ducati
11/7, Monterey, CA, B.ot T.M., Hopp Winfried, Ducati
8/8, Mt. Pocono, PA, B.ot T.M., Mills Joey III, Ducati
22/8, Sonoma, CA, B.ot T.M., Hopp Winfried, Ducati
12/9, Kent, WA, B.ot T.M., Mills Joey III, Ducati
3/10, Daytona Beach, FL, B.ot T.M., Sbordone Ron, Ducati
10/10, W. Palm Beach, FL, B.ot T.M., Mills Joey III, Ducati

American Championship Battle of the Twins G.P., Adamo James, Ducati

5/3, Daytona Beach, FL, B.ot T.GP, Adamo James, Ducati
14/3, Talladega, AL, B.ot T.GP, Adamo James, Ducati
23/5, Elkhart Lake, WI, B.ot T.GP, Tunstall Malcolm, Ducati
20/6, Loudon, NH, B.ot T.GP, Adamo James, Ducati
11/7, Monterey, CA, B.ot T.GP, Adamo James, Ducati
8/8, Mt. Pocono, PA, B.ot T.GP, Adamo James, Ducati
22/8, Sonoma, CA, B.ot T.GP, Adamo James, Ducati
12/9, Kent, WA, B.ot T.GP, Williams John, Ducati
3/10, Daytona Beach, FL, B.ot T.GP, Adamo James, Ducati
10/10, Palm Daytona, FL, B.ot T.GP, Adamo James, Ducati

1983

GREAT BRITAIN
TT 2 World Championship, Rutter Anthony, Ducati 600
TT 2 British Championship, McGregory Graham, Ducati 600

9/6, T.T. - Isle of Man, F/2, Rutter Anthony, Ducati 600

ITALY
Junior Italian Championship, TT/2, Cussigh Walter, Ducati 600
Constructors Italian Championship, TT/2, Ducati Meccanica, Ducati 600
Endurance Italian Championship, TT/1, Cussigh-La Ferla, Ducati 750
Endurance Italian Championship, TT/2, Becchetti-De Cecco, Ducati 600
Trofeo FMI Formula TT, TT/2, Becchetti Ugo, Ducati 600
Mountain Tuscan Championship, TT/2, Maccari Mario, Ducati 600
Trofeo Moto di Serie, 500, Casarino, Ducati

10/4, Magione, TT/2, De Bortoli Tiziano, Ducati 600
17/4, Magione, TT/2, Leandrini Luciano, Ducati 600
8/5, Mugello, TT/2, Becchetti Ugo, Ducati 600
29/5, Orvieto-La Castellana, TT/2, Federiconi Franco, Ducati 600
29/5, Torrazzo-Mongardino, TT/2, Magliano, Ducati 600
29/5, Mugello - Endurance, TT/2, Cussigh-La Ferla, Ducati 600
5/6, Misano, TT/1, La Ferla Oscar, Ducati 750
19/6, Menfi-Marina Porto, TT/2, Barone Domenico, Ducati 600

3/7, Magione, TT/2, Federiconi Franco, Ducati 600
10/7, La Rocca-Coiro, TT/2, Luzzuati Sergio, Ducati 600
24/7, Casteldelpiano-Macinaie, TT/2, Federiconi Franco, Ducati 600
31/7, Misano, TT/2, Becchetti Ugo, Ducati 600
31/7, La Pace-Valico Scopetone, TT/2, Maccari Mario, Ducati 600
7/8, Sillano-Ospedaletto, TT/2, Maccari Mario, Ducati 600
27/8, Misano Endurance: TT/1, La Ferla-Cussigh, Ducati 750; TT/2, Becchetti-De Cecco, Ducati 600
4/9, Rigaiolo-Collalto, TT/2, Maccari Mario, Ducati 600
2/10, Monza, TT/2, De Cecco Ferdinando, Ducati 600
2/10, Vallelunga, TT/1, Cussigh Walter, Ducati 750
9/10, Magione, TT/2, Guercini Massimo, Ducati 600
23/10, Vallelunga - Endurance: TT/1, Cussigh-La Ferla, Ducati 750; TT/2, Sakamoto-Brutti, Ducati 600

UNITED STATES

A.M.A. CHAMPIONSHIP
American Championship Battle of the Twins Modified, Mills Joey III, Ducati

11/3, Daytona Beach, FL, B.ot T.M., Mills Joey III, Ducati
21/3, Talladega, AL, B.ot T.M., Cox Madison, Ducati
21/5, Lexington, CH, B.ot T.M., Mills Joey III, Ducati
5/6, Elkhart Lake, WI, B.ot T.M., Mills Joey III, Ducati
19/6, Loudon, NH, B.ot T.M., Church, Ducati
26/6, Mt. Pocono, PA, B.ot T.M., Cox Madison, Ducati
17/7, Monterey, CA, B.ot T.M., Church, Ducati
21/8, Sonoma, CA, B.ot T.M., Mills Joey III, Ducati
3/9, Brainerd, MN, B.ot T.M., Mills Joey III, Ducati
11/9, Kent, WA, B.ot T.M., Mills Joey III, Ducati
2/10, Daytona Beach, FL, B.ot T.M., Mills Joey III, Ducati

American Championship Battle of the Twins G.P., Adamo James, Ducati

21/3, Talladega, AL, B.ot T.GP, Adamo James, Ducati
21/5, Lexington, OH, B.ot T.GP, Adamo James, Ducati
5/6, Elkhart Lake, WI, B.ot T.GP, Tunstall Malcolm, Ducati
19/6, Loudon, NH, B.ot T.GP, Adamo James, Ducati
26/6, Mt. Pocono, PA, B.ot T.GP, Adamo James, Ducati
21/8, Sonoma, CA, B.ot T.GP, Adamo James, Ducati
3/9, Brainerd, MN, B.ot T.GP, Adamo James, Ducati
21/9, Kent, WA, B.ot T.GP, Adamo James, Ducati

1984

GREAT BRITAIN
World Championship Formula 2, Rutter Anthony, Ducati

23/4, Oulton Park: Four Strokes F/1, Rutter Anthony, Ducati 750; B.ot T., Nation Trevor, Ducati 750
6/5, Snetterton, B.ot T., Nation Trevor, Ducati 750
7/5, Brands Hatch, B.ot T., Rutter Anthony, Ducati 750
17/6, Mallory Park, B.ot T., Rutter Anthony, Ducati 750

8/7, Oliver's Mount, B.ot T., Rutter Anthony, Ducati 750
22/7, Snetterton, B.ot T., Rutter Anthony, Ducati 750
29/7, Donington Park, B.ot T., Rutter Anthony, Ducati 750
15-16/9, Oliver's Mount, B.ot T., Nation Trevor, Ducati 750
6/10, Oulton Park, B.ot T., Rutter Anthony, Ducati 750
20-21/10 Brands Hatch, B.ot T., Nation Trevor, Ducati 750

ITALY
Junior Italian Championship, TT/2, Barchitta Fabio, Ducati 600
Italian Championship TT/1, Tardozzi Davide, Ducati 750
Mountain Tuscan Championship, TT/2, Maccari Mario, Ducati 600
11/3, Misano, TT/2, Barchitta Fabio, Duacti 600
22/4, Trofeo Città di Favara, 500, Grasso Santo, Ducati 500
22/4, Trofeo Città di Favara, TT/3, Bonaccorsi Claudio, Ducati
29/4, Mugello, TT/2, Barchitta Fabio, Ducati 600
20/5, Monza, TT/2, Leandrini Luciano, Ducati 600
27/5, Vallelunga, TT/2, Muratori Maurizio, Ducati 600
10/6, La Pace-Valico Scopetone, TT/2, Maccari Mario, Ducati 600
10/6, Issiglio-Castelnuovo, TT/2, Rolfo Angelo, Ducati 600
29/7, Casteltermini, 500, Siciliano Cateno, Ducati
12/8, Casteldelpiano-Macinaie, TT/2, Maccari Mario, Ducati 600
19/8, Misano, TT/2, Leandrini Luciano, Ducati 600
9/9, Alberi-Montaione, TT/2, Maccari Mario, Ducati 600
9/9, Vallelunga - Endurance, TT/2, Muratori-Barchitta, Ducati 600
9/9, Varano Melegari, 600, Brusini, Ducati 600
9/9, Varano Melegari, Special, Preziosa Giovanni, Ducati
30/9, Misano- Endurance, TT/2, Barchitta-Muratori, Ducati 600
14/10, Vallelunga, TT/1, Tardozzi Davide, Ducati 750
11/11, Randazzo-Sciarone, TT/2, Maratorana, Ducati

PORTUGAL
15/7, Vila Real, F/2, Rutter Anthony, Ducati 600

SPAIN
14-15/7, 24 Horas de Montjuich, absolute, Grau-De Juan-Garriga, Ducati

UNITED STATES
A.M.A. CHAMPIONSHIP
10/6, Elkhart Lake, WI, B.ot T.M., Guest Tony, Ducati
18/8, Sonoma, CA, B.ot T.M., Smith Simon, Ducati
4/10, Daytona Beach, FL, B.ot T.M., Liebrecht Dennis, Ducati
10/6, Elkhart Lake, WI, B.ot T.GP, Adamo James, Ducati
17/6, Loudon, NH, B.ot T.GP, Roper David, Ducati
22/6, Monterey, CA, B.ot T.GP, Williams John, Ducati
4/8, Mt. Pocono, PA, B.ot T.GP, Adamo James, Ducati
18/8, Sonoma, CA, B.ot T.GP, Adamo James, Ducati
1/9, Brainerd, MN, B.ot T.GP, Adamo James, Ducati
4/11, Daytona Beach, FL, B.ot T.GP, Adamo James, Ducati

1985

GREAT BRITAIN
1-7/6, T.T. - Isle of Man, F/2, Rutter Anthony, Ducati 600
31/8, Isle of Man, Man Grand Prix, 600, Knight Tom, Ducati 600
14/9, Olver's Mount, TT/2, Nation Trevor, Ducati 600

ITALY
Italian Championship F/1, Ferrari Virginio, Ducati 750
Constructors Italian Championship, F/1, Ducati Meccanica, Ducati 750
Endurance Italian Championship, F/1, Cussigh Walter, Ducati 750
Endurance Constructors Italian Championship, F/1, Ducati Meccanica, Ducati 750
Mountain Sicily Championship, F/1, Maltacesare Marco, Ducati 750

17/3, Misano - Endurance, F/1, Villa W.-Cussigh, Ducati 750
14/4, Imola, F/1, Lucchinelli Marco, Ducati 750
5/5, Fontepetri-Montalcino, TT/2, Bertoni Mario, Ducati 600
19/5, Vallelunga, F/1, Cussigh Walter, Ducati 750
9/6, Monza, F/1, Ferrari Virginio, Ducati 750
23/6, Salita a Catania, F/1, La Tona Adolfo, Ducati 750
30/6, Salita a Menfi, 500, Siciliano Cateno, Ducati 500
14/7, Mugello, F/1, Ferrari Virginio, Ducati 750
27/7, Misano: F/1, Matteoni Massimo, Ducati 750; Endurance, F/1, Cussigh-Caracchi, Ducati 750
17/8, Misano, F/1, Lucchinelli Marco, Ducati 750
15/9, Misano - Endurance, F/1, Cussigh-Caracchi, Ducati 750
22/9, Randazzo-Sciarone: F/1, Maltacesare Marco, Ducati 750; 500, Siciliano Cateno, Ducati 500
6/10, Linguaglossa-Provenzano: F/1, Maltacesare Marco, Ducati 750; 500, Siciliano Cateno, Ducati 500
13/10, Vallelunga, F/1, Lucchinelli Marco, Ducati 750

SPAIN
13-14/7, 24 Horas de Montjuich, absolute, Grau-De Juan-Garriga, Ducati

UNITED STATES
A.M.A. CHAMPIONSHIP
20/10, Daytona Beach, FL, B.ot T.M., Liebrecht Dennis, Ducati
9/6, Elkhart Lake, WI, B.ot T.GP, Williams John, Ducati
16/6, Loudon, NH, B.ot T.GP, Adamo James, Ducati
14/7, Monterey, CA, B.ot T.GP, Adamo James, Ducati
20/10, Daytona Beach, FL, B.ot T.GP, Tunstall Malcolm, Ducati

1986

ITALY
Trofeo Grand Prix Velocità, F/1, Leandrini Luciano, Ducati 750

6/4, Misano, F/1, Lucchinelli Marco, Matteoni Massimo, Ducati 750
24/8, Rigaiolo-Collalto, 250, Rossi Antonio, Ducati 250

SPAIN
13/7, Jerez, F/2, McGregor Graham, Ducati 600
25-26/10 24 Horas de Montjuich, absolute, Grau-Garriga-Cardus, Ducati

UNITED STATES
A.M.A. CHAMPIONSHIP
American Championship Battle of the Twins Modified, Gross Doug, Ducati

31/5, Brainerd, MN, B.ot T.M., Holland Chris, Ducati
6/6, Elkhart Lake, WI, B.ot T.M., Gross Doug, Ducati
22/6, Pocono, PA, B.ot T.M, Gross Doug, Ducati
2/8, Lexington, OH, B.ot T.M., Gross Doug, Ducati
10/8, Atlanta, GA, B.ot T.M., Gross Doug, Ducati
7/3, Daytona Beach, FL, B.ot T.GP, Lucchinelli Marco, Ducati 750 F1
8/6, Elkhart Lake, WI, B.ot T.GP, Adamo James, Ducati
13/7, Monterey, CA, B.ot T.GP, Lucchinelli Marco, Ducati 750 F1
2/8, Lexington, OH, B.ot T.GP, Adamo James, Ducati
9/8, Atlanta, GA, B.ot T.GP, Adamo James, Ducati

1987

ITALY
Mountain Italian Championship, B.ot T., Cerrini Libertario, Ducati 750
Mountain Tuscan Championship, B.ot T., Di Paolo Walter, Ducati 750

5/4, Orvieto-La Castellana, B.ot T., Cerrini Libertario, Ducati 750
12/4, Magione, B.ot T., Monti Baldassare, Ducati 750
10/5, Forno Canavese-Milani, B.ot T., Giona Manlio, Ducati 750
31/5, Cesi Scalo-Cesi, B.ot T., Cerrini Libertario, Ducati 750
7/6, Ballabio-Resinelli, B.ot T., Giona Manlio, Ducati 750
21/6, Monza, Trophy SBK, Lucchinelli Marco, Ducati 851
21/6, Romanina-Veglio, B.ot T., Giona Manlio, Ducati 750
28/6, Sassi-Superga, B.ot T., Merla Giampiero, Ducati 750
18/7, Colleferro-Segni, B.ot T., Giona Manlio, Ducati 750
26/7, Sillano-Ospedaletto: B.ot T., Badiali Alberto, Ducati 750; 500, Bertoni Mario, Ducati 500
9/8, Linguaglossa-Provenzana, B.ot T., Cerrini Libertario, Ducati 750
15/8, Misano, Trophy SBK, Lucchinelli Marco, Ducati 851
23/8, Rigaiolo-Collalto, B.ot T., Badiali Alberto, Ducati 750
30/8, Massa-San Carlo Terme, B.ot T., Di Paolo Walter, Ducati 750
20/9, Montichiello-Cerrone: B.ot T., Badiali Alberto, Ducati 750; 500, Bertoni Mario, Ducati 500

UNITED STATES
A.M.A. CHAMPIONSHIP
American Championship Battle of the Twins Modified, Johnson Pete, Ducati

6/3, Daytona Beach, FL, B.ot T.M., Johnson Pete, Ducati
14/5, Gainesville, GA, B.ot T.M., Johnson Pete, Ducati
21/6, Loudon, NH, B.ot T.M., Johnson Pete, Ducati
28/6, Elkhart Lake, WI, B.ot T.M., Johnson Pete, Ducati
9/8, Memphis, TN, B.ot T.M., Johnson Pete, Ducati
30/8, Sonoma, CA, B.ot T.M., Johnson Pete, Ducati
6/3, Daytona Beach, FL, B.ot T.GP, Lucchinelli Marco, Ducati
17/5, Gainesville, GA, B.ot T.GP, Adamo James, Ducati
7/6, Brainerd, MN, B.ot T.GP, Adamo James, Ducati
12/7, Monterey, CA, B.ot T.GP, Lucchinelli Marco, Ducati
2/8, Lexington, OH, B.ot T.GP, Adamo James, Ducati
9/8, Memphis, TN, B.ot T.GP, Adamo James, Ducati

1988

GREAT BRITAIN
British Championship Battle of the Twins, Mitchell Wayne, Ducati 750

13/3, Cadwell Park, B.ot T., Brown David, Ducati 600
25/6, Aberdare Park, B.ot T., Mitchell Wayne, Ducati 750
3/7, Scarborough, B.ot T., Ward Mark, Ducati 600
14/8, Knockhill, B.ot T., Mitchell Wayne, Ducati 750
29/8, Darley Moor, B.ot T., Mitchell Wayne, Ducati 750

ITALY
Italian Championship, B.ot T., Monti Baldassare, Ducati 851
Constructors Italian Championship, B.ot T., Ducati Meccanica, Ducati 851
Mountain Italian Championship, B.ot T., Merla Giampiero, Ducati 851
Mountain Ligurian Championship, B.ot T., Salvioli Claudio, Ducati 851

20/3, Magione, B.ot T., Zucchetta Claudio, Ducati 851
4/4, Vallelunga, F/1, Caracchi Stefano, Ducati 851
4/4, Mugello, B.ot T., Monti Baldassare, Ducati 851
10/4, Doria-Creto, B.ot.T., Malfatto Massimo, Ducati 851
17/4, Monza, B.ot T., Monti Baldassare, Ducati 851
24/4, Orvieto-La Castellana, B.ot T., Merla Giampiero, Ducati 851
24-25/4, Varano Melegari, B.ot T., Garattini Tiberio, Ducati 851
8/5, Forno Canavese-Milani, B.ot T., Gilardi Roberto, Ducati 851
15/5, Vallelunga, B.ot T., Zucchetta Claudio, Ducati 851
15/5, Varano Melegari, B.ot T., Monti Baldassare, Ducati 851
29/5, Mossini-Triangia, B.ot T., Merla Giampiero, Ducati 851
5/6, Misano, B.ot T., Monti Baldassare, Ducati 851
5/6, Cesi Scalo-Cesi, B.ot T., Merla Giampiero, Ducati 851
19/6, Magione, B.ot T., Molteni Giuseppe, Ducati 851
19/6, Montichiello-Cerrone, B.ot T., Malfatto Massimo, Ducati 851
19/6, Montichiello-Cerrone, 500, Bertoni Mario, Ducati
26/6, Sassi-Superga, B.ot T., Gilardi Roberto, Ducati 851
26/6, Mugello, B.ot T., Monti Baldassare, Ducati 851
3/7, Mugello, B.ot T., Carpinelli Alberto, Ducati 851
17/7, Varano, F/1, Monti Baldassare, Ducati 851
7/8, Sillano-Ospedaletto, B.ot T., Merla Giampiero, Ducati 851
8/8, Misano, B.ot T., Monti Baldassare, Ducati 851
28/8, Massa-S. Carlo Terme, B.ot T., Salvioli Claudio, Ducati 851
4/9, Rigaiolo-Collalto, B.ot T., Salvioli Claudio, Ducati 851
Sett., Doria-Creto, B.ot T., Salvioli Claudio, Ducati 851
18/9, Vallelunga, B.ot T., Garattini Tiberio, Ducati 851
25/9, Mugello, B.ot T., Monti Baldassare, Ducati 851
25/9, Intra-Premeno, B.ot.T., Merla Giampiero, Ducati 851
9/10, Mugello, B.ot T., Marsigli Wilmer, Monti Baldassare, Ducati 851

SPAIN
17/4, Calafat, SBK, Amatriain Daniel, Ducati 851
9/10, Calafat, SBK, Amatriain Daniel, Ducati 851

UNITED STATES

A.M.A. CHAMPIONSHIP
American Championship Pro Twins
Modified, Erion Kevin, Ducati

4/3, Daytona Beach, FL, P.T.M., Erion Kevin,
Ducati
14/5, Gainesville, GA, P.T.M., Erion Kevin,
Ducati
18/6, Loudon, NH, P.T.M., Stas Gary, Ducati
25/6, Elkart Lake, WI, P.T.M., Shambaugh
Craig, Ducati
9/7, Monterey, CA, P.T.M., Johnson Pete, Ducati
6/8, Lexington, OH, P.T.M., Johnson Pete,
Ducati
1/10, Sonoma, CA, P.T.M., Erion Kevin, Ducati

American Championship Pro Twins Grand
Prix, Quarterley Dale, Ducati

15/5, Gainesville, GA, P.T.G.P., Long John,
Ducati
19/6, Loudon, NH, P.T.G.P., Quarterley Dale,
Ducati
26/6, Elkart Lake, WI, P.T.G.P., Quarterley
Dale, Ducati
10/7, Monterey, CA, P.T.G.P., Quarterley
Dale, Ducati
2/10, Sonoma, CA, P.T.G.P., Quarterley Dale,
Ducati

SBK WORLD CHAMPIONSHIP
3/4, Donington Park, GB, race 2, Lucchinelli
Marco, Ducati 851
3/7, Zeltweg, A, race 1, Lucchinelli Marco,
Ducati 851

1989

ITALY
SBK Italian Championship, Monti
Baldassare, Ducati 851
SBK Constructors Italian Championship,
Meccanica Ducati, Ducati 851
Italian Championship, B.ot T., Brunotti
Andrea, Ducati 851
Constructors Italian Championship, B.ot T.,
Ducati Meccanica, Ducati 851
Mountain Italian Championship, 750, Truffa
Claudio, Ducati 750
Mountain Italian Championship, B.o.T.,
Carpinelli Alberto, Ducati 851

19/3, Magione: B.ot T., Molteni Giuseppe, Ducati
851; 750, Mattera Andrea, Ducati 851
26/3, Misano, B.ot T., Colombari
Massimiliano Ducati 851
2/4, Pergusa, B.ot T., Coresi Francesco,
Ducati 851
30/4, Magione: B.ot T., Brunotti Andrea,
Ducati 851; 750, Mattera Andrea,
Ducati 851
21/5, Vallelunga: B.ot T., Canatalupo
Giorgio, Ducati 851; 750, Mattera
Andrea, Ducati 851
May, Testico-Colle Ginestro, B.ot T., Malfatto
Massimo, Ducati 851
May, Testico-Colle Ginestro, F/1, Bottazzi
Gianni, Ducati 750
4/6, Monza, B.ot T., Brunotti Andrea,
Ducati 851
18/6, Vallelunga, B.ot T., Brunotti Andrea,
Ducati 851
25/6, Imola, SBK, Broccoli Massimo,
Ducati 851
June, Riva Tricoso-Bracco, B.ot T., Malfatto
Massimo, Ducati 851
8-9/7, Monza: B.ot T., Toschi Danilo, Ducati
851; SBK, Broccoli Massimo, Ducati 851
23/7, Mignego-Badalucco, B.ot T., Piombo
Claudio, Ducati 851
30/7, Montichiello-Cerrone, B.ot T., Merla
Giampiero, Ducati 851
6/8, Sillano-Ospedaletto, B.ot T., Peroni
Gianni, Ducati 851
27/8, Rigaiolo-Collalto, B.o.t T., Carpinelli
Alberto, Ducati 851
10/9, La Castellana: B.ot T., Carpinelli Alberto,
Ducati 851; 750, Truffa Claudio, Ducati

24/9, Vallelunga: 750, Bellini Oscar, Ducati;
B.ot T., Brunotti Andrea, Ducati 851
14-15/10 Vallelunga, SBK, Roche
Raymond, Ducati 851
22/10, Monza, B.o.t T., Brunotti Andrea,
Ducati 851

UNITED STATES

A.M.A. CHAMPIONSHIP
10/3, Daytona Beach, FL, P.T.G.P.,
Quarterley Dale, Ducati
6/5, Atlanta, GA, P.T.G.P., Shambaugh Craig,
Ducati
26/6, Elkart Lake, WI, P.T.G.P., Quarterley
Dale, Ducati
6/8, Lexington, OH, P.T.G.P., Quarterley
Dale, Ducati

SBK WORLD CHAMPIONSHIP
11/6, Brainerd, USA: race 1, Roche
Raymond, Ducati 851; race 2, Roche
Raymond, Ducati 851
17/9, Hockenheim, D: race 1, Roche
Raymond, Ducati 851; race 2, Roche
Raymond, Ducati 851
24/9, Pergusa, I, race 2, Roche Raymond,
Ducati 851

1990

BELGIUM
17/6, Zolder, SBK, Monaco Francesco,
Ducati 851

GREAT BRITAIN
28/10, Donington Park, B.ot T., Haslam
Ronald, Ducati 750

ITALY
Italian Championship, B.ot.T, Toschi Danilo,
Ducati 851
Mountain Italian Championship, B.o.T.T.,
Truffa Claudio, Ducati 851

4/3, Vallelunga, B.ot T., Pedercini Lucio,
Ducati 851
11/3, Magione, Open, Balbi Romolo,
Ducati 851
25/3, Misano: SBK, Tardozzi Davide, Ducati
851; B.ot T., Maestri Massimo, Ducati 851
1/4, Pergusa, B.ot T., Prudente, Ducati
22/4, Vallelunga: 2 V., Carotenuto Mario,
Ducati; 4 V., Bastianini Ermanno, Ducati
22/4, Varano Melegari, 750, Bellini Oscar,
Ducati 750
22/4, Alto-Caprauna, B.ot T., Malfatto
Massimo, Ducati 851
29/4, Misano, Balbi Romolo, Ducati 851
6/5, Monza, 750, Bellini Oscar, Ducati 750
27/5, Varano Melegari, 750, Pedercini
Lucio, Ducati 750
3/6, Magione, B.ot T., Toschi Danilo,
Ducati 851
10/6, Vallelunga, B.ot T., Molteni Giuseppe,
Ducati 851
17/6, Magione, B.ot T., Maestri Massimo,
Ducati 851
7/7, Monza, B.ot T., Toschi Danilo, Ducati 851
29/7, Pontremoli, B.ot T, Truffa Claudio,
Ducati 851
5/8, Sillano-Ospedaletto, B.ot T., Merla
Giampiero, Ducati 851
11/8, Misano: SBK, Tardozzi Davide, Ducati
851; B.ot T., Toschi Danilo, Ducati 851
26/8, Massa-San Carlo, B.ot T., Salvioli
Claudio, Ducati 851
16/9, Vallelunga: B.ot T., Coresi Francesco,
Ducati 851; Open, Maddaluno Angelo,
Ducati
30/9, Misano, B.ot.T., Toschi Danilo, Ducati 851
30/9, Vallelunga, B.ot T., Marras, Ducati 851

UNITED STATES

A.M.A. CHAMPIONSHIP
American Championship Pro Twins GP2,
Cortez Fabian III, Ducati 851

9/3, Daytona Beach, FL, P.T.GP2, Cortez
Fabian III, Ducati 851

6/5, Atlanta, GA, P.T.GP2, Cortez Fabian III,
Ducati 851
17/6, Loudon, NH, P.T.GP2, Cortez Fabian
III, Ducati 851
22/6, Miami, FL, P.T.GP2, Cortez Fabian III,
Ducati 851
2/8, Lexington, OH, P.T.GP2, Shambaugh
Craig, Ducati 851
9/9, Topeka, KS, P.T.GP2, Cortez Fabian III,
Ducati 851

American Championship Pro Twins GP1,
James Jamie, Ducati 851

9/3, Daytona Beach, FL, P.T.GP1, James
Jamie, Ducati 851
6/5, Atlanta, GA, P.T.GP1, James Jamie,
Ducati 851
17/6, Loudon, NH, P.T.GP1, James Jamie,
Ducati 851
1/7, Elkart Lake, WI, P.T.GP1, James Jamie,
Ducati 851
22/7, Miami, FL, P.T.GP1, James Jamie,
Ducati 851
5/8, Lexington, OH, P.T.GP1, James Jamie,
Ducati 851
9/9, Topeka, KS, P.T.GP1, Adamo James,
Ducati 851
16/9, Rosamond, CA, P.T.GP1, Adamo
James, Ducati 851

SBK WORLD CHAMPIONSHIP
Superbike World Championship, Roche
Raymond, Ducati 851

1/4, Jerez, E: race 1, Roche Raymond, Ducati
851; race 2, Roche Raymond, Ducati 851
16/4, Donington Park, GB, race 2, Falappa
Giancarlo, Ducati 851
30/4, Hungaroring, H, race 2, Roche
Raymond, Ducati 851
3/6, Mosport, CDN,: race 1, Roche
Raymond, Ducati 851; race 2, Roche
Raymond, Ducati 851
26/8, Sugo, J, gara 1, Roche Raymond,
Ducati 851
9/9, Le Mans, F: race 1, Roche Raymond,
Ducati 851; race 2, Roche Raymond,
Ducati 851

1991

AUSTRIA
19/5, Salzburgring, SBK, Tardozzi Davide,
Ducati 888

GREAT BRITAIN
1/4, Donington Park, SBK, Tardozzi Davide,
Ducati 851

ITALY
Italian Championship, B.ot T., Colombari
Massimiliano, Ducati 750
Mountain Italian Championship, B.ot T.,
Truffa Claudio, Ducati 851

3/3, Magione, B.ot T., Colombari
Massimiliano Ducati 750
3/3, Vallelunga, B.ot T., Zucchetta Claudio,
Ducati 888
10/3, Misano: SBK, Tardozzi Davide, Ducati
888; 750, Pedercini Lucio, Ducati 750
17/3, Vallelunga: SBK, Tardozzi Davide,
Ducati 888; B.ot T., Zucchetta Claudio,
Ducati 888
17/3, Magione, B.ot T., Colombari
Massimiliano Ducati 750
7/4, Misano: SBK, Tardozzi Davide, Ducati
888; 750, Pedercini Lucio, Ducati 750
5/5, Magione, B.ot T., Colombari
Massimiliano Ducati 750
19/5, Vallelunga, B.ot T., Molteni Giuseppe,
Zucchetta Claudio, Ducati 888
19-5, Binetto, B.ot T., Brunotti Andrea, Ducati
2/6, Varano Melegari, B.ot T., Colombari
Massimiliano Ducati 750
9/6, Binetto, B.ot T., Molteni Giuseppe, Ducati
9/6, Monza, 750, Amati Davide, Ducati 750
16/6, Romanina-Veglio, B.ot T., Truffa
Claudio, Ducati 851

7/7, Monza, B.ot P.T., Destefanis Valerio,
Ducati 851
21/7, Monza, Over 750, Destefanis Valerio,
Ducati 851
21/7, Due Ponti-Cassingheno, B.ot T., Merla
Giampiero, Ducati 851
4/8, Sillano-Ospedaletto, B.ot T., Malfatto
Massimo, Ducati 600
4/8, Misano, SBK, Tardozzi Davide,
Ducati 888
10/8, Misano, 750, Pedercini Lucio, Ducati
15/9, Garessio-San Bernardo, B.ot T., Truffa
Claudio, Ducati 851
15/9, Vallelunga, B.ot T., Monaco
Francesco, Ducati 851
22/9, Misano: SBK, Tardozzi Davide, Ducati
888; 750, Destefanis Valerio, Ducati 851,
B.ot T., Veltroni Daniele, Ducati
22/9, Levico-Vetriolo, B.ot T., Rozza Cesare,
Ducati
20/10, Binetto, Paolucci, Ducati

SPAIN
21/4, Calafat, SBK, Tardozzi Davide, Ducati 888
28/4, Jarama, SBK, Tardozzi Davide,
Ducati 888

SWITZERLAND
Superbike Swiss Championship, Imstepf,
Ducati 851

UNITED STATES

A.M.A. CHAMPIONSHIP
8/3, Daytona Beach, FL, P.T.GP2 P.S.,
Shambaugh Craig, Ducati 851
16/6, Loudon, NH, P.T.GP2 P.S., Mathews
Stephen, Ducati 851
30/6, Elkhart Lake, WI, P.T.GP2 P.S.,
Mathews Stephen, Ducati 851
4/8, Lexington, OH, P.T.GP2 P.S., Mathews
Stephen, Ducati 851
8/3, Daytona Beach, FL, Pro Twins GP1,
Polen Doug, Ducati 851
16/6, Loudon, NH, P.T.GP1, Polen Doug,
Ducati 851
30/6, Elkhart Lake, WI, P.T.GP1, Picotte
Pascal, Ducati 851
6/7, Charlotte, NC, P.T.GP1, Adamo James,
Ducati 851
4/8, Lexington, OH, P.T.GP1, Picotte Pascal,
Ducati 851
8/9, Topeka, KS, P.T.GP1, Real Pablo,
Ducati 851
6/10, College Station, TX, P.T.GP1, Real
Pablo, Ducati 851
10/10, Miami, FL, P.T.GP1, Picotte Pascal,
Ducati 851

SBK WORLD CHAMPIONSHIP
Superbike World Championship, Polen
Doug, Ducati 888
Superbike Constructors World
Championship, Ducati Meccanica,
Ducati 888

1/4, Donington Park, GB: race 1, Polen
Doug, Ducati 888; race 2, Mertens
Stephane, Ducati 888
28/4, Jarama, E: race 1, Polen Doug, Ducati
888; race 2, Polen Doug, Ducati 888
9/6, Brainerd, USA: race 1, Polen Doug, Ducati
888; race 2, Polen Doug, Ducati 888
30/6, Zeltweg, A: race 1, Mertens
Stephane, Ducati 888; race 2, Polen
Doug, Ducati 888
4/8, Misano, RSM: race 1, Polen Doug, Ducati
888; race 2, Polen Doug, Ducati 888
11/8, Anderstorp, S: race 1, Polen Doug, Ducati
888; race 2, Polen Doug, Ducati 888
25/8, Sugo, J: race 1, Polen Doug, Ducati
888; race 2, Polen Doug, Ducati 888
1/9, Shal Alam, MAL: race 1, Roche
Raymond, Ducati 888; gara 2, Roche
Raymond, Ducati 888
15/9, Hockenheim, D: gara 1, Polen Doug,
Ducati 888; gara 2, Roche Raymond,
Ducati 888
29/9, Magny Cours, F: race 1, Polen Doug,
Ducati 888; race 2, Polen Doug, Ducati 888

6/10, Mugello, I: race 1, Polen Doug, Ducati 888; race 2, Roche Raymond, Ducati 888
19/10, Phillip Island, AUS, race 2, Polen Doug, Ducati 888

1992

AUSTRIA
Österreichring, SBK, Meklau Andreas, Ducati 888
Salzburgring, SBK, Meklau Andreas, Ducati 888

ITALY
Trofeo Techna Racing 900, Iannetti Domenico, Ducati 900
Sport Production Italian Championship, 750, Destefanis Valerio, Ducati 888

8/3, Vallelunga: 750, Innamorati Mario, Ducati 888; B.ot T., Zucchetta Claudio, Ducati 750
15/3, Misano, 750, Arnoldi Ivo, Ducati 888
12/4, Monza, 750, Destefanis Valerio, Ducati 888
12/4, Vallelunga, Winner Cup, Fugardi Enrico, Duacti 900
26/4, Vallelunga, B.ot T., Tamantini Marco, Ducati
26/4, Varano Melegari, 750, Merlo Davide, Ducati
3/5, Binetto, Winner Cup, Fugardi Enrico, Ducati 900
3/5, Pergusa, 750, Zerbo Sebastiano, Ducati 888
31/5, Vallelunga: B.ot T., Molteni Giuseppe, Ducati 900, Carpinelli Alberto, Ducati 851; Winner Cup, Fugardi Enrico, Ducati 900
7/6, Monza: SBK, Tardozzi Davide, Ducati 888; 750, Bulega Davide, Ducati 888
7/6, Magione, 750, Moroni Mauro, Ducati 888
7/6, Bonvicino-Lovera, B.ot T., Bongiovanni, Ducati
14/6, Binetto, 750, Moroni Mauro, Ducati 888
21/6, Varano Melegari, 750, Destefanis Valerio, Ducati 888
21/6, Due Ponti-Cassangheno: B.ot T., Rozza Cesare, Ducati; 750, Gazzolo, Ducati
28/6, Magione, Winner Cup, Fugardi Enrico, Ducati 900
4/7, Monza, B.ot T., Arnoldi Ivo, Coresi Francesco, Ducati
12/7, Misano: 750, Bellezza Ivo, Ducati 888; Winner Cup, Iannetti Domenico, Ducati 900
23/8, Varano Melegari, 750, Anadaloro Stefano, Ducati 888
23/8, Biassura-Chiesa, B.ot T., Merla Giampiero, Ducati 888
30/8, Chivasso-Castagneto, B.ot T., Parolini, Ducati
6/9, Misano, 750, Arnoldi Ivo, Ducati 888
13/9, Misano: 750, Destefanis Valerio, Ducati 888; Winner Cup, Fugardi Enrico, Ducati 900
13/9, Bollegno-Serra, B.ot T., Rozza Cesare, Ducati
20/9, Vallelunga: SBK, Tardozzi Davide, Ducati 888; 750, Destefanis Valerio, Ducati 888
27/9, Monza, 750, Destefanis Valerio, Ducati 888
18/10, Mugello, Open, Monti Baldassare, Ducati 888
1/11, Binetto, Open, Mattera Andrea, Ducati 888

SPAIN
Superbike European Championship, Amatriain Daniel, Ducati 888

5/4, Albacete, SBK, Amatriain Daniel, Ducati 888

UNITED STATES
26/4, Monterey, CA, Superbike, Polen Doug, Ducati 888
14/6, Brainerd, MN, SBK, Polen Doug, Ducati 888
1/8, Lexington, OH, SBK, Polen Doug, Ducati 888

SBK WORLD CHAMPIONSHIP
Superbike World Championship, Polen Doug, Ducati 888
Superbike Constructors World Championship, Ducati Meccanica, Ducati 888

5/4, Albacete, E, race 2, Polen Doug, Ducati 888
20/4, Donington Park, GB: race 1, Roche Raymond, Ducati 888; race 2, Fogarty Carl, Ducati 888
10/5, Hockenheim, D: race 1, Polen Doug, Ducati 888; race 2, Polen Doug, Ducati 888
24/5, Spa-Francorchamps, B, race 2, Polen Doug, Ducati 888
21/6, Jarama, E, race 2, Polen Doug, Ducati 888
28/6, Zeltweg, A: race 1, Falappa Giancarlo, Ducati 888; race 2, Falappa Giancarlo, Ducati 888
19/7, Mugello, RSM: race 1, Roche Raymond, Ducati 888; race 2, Roche Raymond, Ducati 888
23/8, Johr, MAL: race 1, Roche Raymond, Ducati 888; race 2, Polen Doug, Ducati 888
30/8, Sugo, J, race 1, Polen Doug, Ducati 888
13/9, Assen, NL: race 1, Polen Doug, Ducati 888; race 2, Falappa Giancarlo, Ducati 888
18/10, Phillip Island, AUS, race 2, Roche Raymond, Ducati 888
25/10, Manfeild, NZ: race 1, Polen Doug, Ducati 888; race 2, Falappa Giancarlo, Ducati 888

1993

AUSTRIA
Österreichring, SBK, Meklau Andreas, Ducati 888
Salzburgring, SBK, Meklau Andreas, Ducati 888

BELGIUM
Belgian Championship Battle of the Twins, Orban Patrick, Ducati
Belgian Superbike Championship, Hubin Richard, Ducati

4/4, Richelle, B.ot T., Orban Patrick, Ducati 750
11/4, Presgaux, B.ot T., Orban Patrick, Ducati 750
12/4, Presgaux, B.ot T., Orban Patrick, Ducati 750
2/5, Huy, B.ot T., Orban Patrick, Ducati 750
16/5, Mettet: B.ot T., Orban Patrick, Ducati 750; SBK, Hubin Richard, Ducati 888, K.ot R., Hubin Richard, Ducati
6/6, Ostend: SBK, Hubin Richard, Ducati 888; B.ot T., Wuyts Louis, Ducati 750
20/6, Aalter, B.ot T., Orban Patrick, Ducati 750
27/6, Chimay, SBK, Hubin Richard, Kempener Alain, Ducati 888
8/8, Evergen: SBK, Hubin Richard, Ducati 888; B.ot T., Orban Patrick, Ducati 750
22/8, Gedinne: B.ot T., Orban Patrick, Ducati 750; SBK, Hubin Richard, Ducati 888
29/8, Jehonville, B.ot T., Orban Patrick, Ducati 750
12/9, Mettet: B.ot T., Orban Patrick, Ducati 750; SBK, Hubin Richard, Kempener Alain, Ducati 888

CZECH REPUBLIC
Pro-Superbike Czech Championship, Sale Petr, Ducati 888

13/6, Brno, Pro-SBK, Sale Petr, Ducati 888
6/7, Most, Pro-SBK, Sale Petr, Ducati 888
15/8, Most, Pro-SBK, Sale Petr, Ducati 888
21/8, Brno, Pro-SBK, Weibel Edwin, Ducati 888
22/8, Brno, Pro-SBK, Weibel Edwin, Ducati 888

FRANCE
21/3, Carole, SBK, Orban Patrick, Ducati 888
9/5, Magny Cours, SBK, Hubin Richard, Ducati 888

GERMANY
Pro-Superbike German Championship, Weibel Edwin, Ducati

1/8, Nürburgring, Pro-SBK, Weibel Edwin, Ducati

GREAT BRITAIN
Superbike British Championship, Whitham James, Ducati 888

20/6, Donington Park, TT SBK, Fogarty Carl, Ducati
3/10, Donington Park, Supermono, Coles Owen, Ducati 550

ITALY
Sport Production Italian Championship, 750, Amati Davide, Ducati 888
Supermono Italian Championship, Lucchiari Mauro, Ducati
Winner Cup 900, Fugardi Enrico, Ducati 900
Sport Production Tuscan Championship, 750, Iandolo Francesco, Ducati 888

14/3, Misano: Supermono, Lucchiari Mauro, Ducati; SBK, Monti Baldassare, Ducati 888
21/3, Misano: 750, Panichi Roberto, Ducati 888; Winner Cup, Fugardi Enrico, Ducati 900
12/4, Monza, 750, Andaloro, Ducati 888
18/4, Misano: 750, Panichi Roberto, Ducati 888; Winner Cup, Iannetti Domenico, Ducati 900; SBK, Mertens Stephane, Ducati 888
25/4, Vallelunga: SBK, Monti Baldassare, Ducati 888; Open, Presciutti Aldeo, Ducati; Supermono, Lucchiari Mauro, Ducati
25/4, Pergusa, 750, Ali Davide, Ducati
16/5, Binetto, Winner Cup, Fugardi Enrico, Ducati 900
23/5, Misano, B.ot T., Colombari Massimiliano Ducati 750
30/5, Vallelunga: 750, Innamorati Mario, Ducati 888; Winner Cup, Fugardi Enrico, Ducati 900
6/6, Magione, 750, Innamorati Mario, Ducati 888
6/6, Pergusa, 750, Mancuso Antonio, Ducati
13/6, Binetto, 750, Innamorati Mario, Ducati 888
20/6, Monza, 750, Foti Serafino, Ducati 888
20/6, Pergusa, 750, Mancuso Antonio, Ducati
20/6, Mugello: SBK, Falappa Giancarlo, Ducati 888; Supermono, Lucchiari Mauro, Ducati
4/7, Varano Melegari, 750, Foti Serafino, Ducati 888
11/7, Magione: B.ot T., Castrichini Paolo, Ducati; Winner Cup, Iannetti Domenico, Ducati 900
31/7, Mugello: Open, Caracchi Stefano, Ducati; Winner Cup, Iannetti Domenico, Ducati 900
19/9, Mugello, 750, Foti Serafino, Ducati 888
26/9, Monza, 900, Reina, Ducati 900
3/10, Monza, 750, Amati Davide, Ducati 888
10/10, Vallelunga: SBK, Presciutti Aldeo, Ducati 888; SBK, Presciutti Aldeo, Ducati 888; Open, Innamorati Mario, Ducati 888
14/11, Binetto, B.ot T., Castrichini Paolo, Ducati

SPAIN
30/5, Albacete, SBK, Garriga Juan, Ducati 888

SWITZERLAND
Monobike Swiss Championship, Imstepf, Ducati mono

UNITED STATES
A.M.A. CHAMPIONSHIP
Superbike American Championship, Polen Doug, Ducati 888

15/2, Phoenix, AZ, SBK, Polen Doug, Ducati 888
18/4, Monterey, MN, SBK, Polen Doug, Ducati 888
2/5, Charlotte, NC, SBK, Polen Doug, Ducati 888

13/6, Elkhart Lake, WI, SBK, Polen Doug, Ducati 888
18/7, Atlanta, GA, SBK, Polen Doug, Ducati 888
1/8, Brainerd, MN, SBK, Polen Doug, Ducati 888

SBK WORLD CHAMPIONSHIP
Superbike Constructors World Championship, Ducati Meccanica, Ducati 888

9/4, Brands Hatch, GB: race 1, Falappa Giancarlo, Ducati 888; race 2, Falappa Giancarlo, Ducati 888
9/5, Hockenheim, D, race 1, Falappa Giancarlo, Ducati 888
30/5, Albacete, E: race 1, Fogarty Carl, Ducati 888; race 2, Fogarty Carl, Ducati 888
27/6, Misano, RSM: race 1, Falappa Giancarlo, Ducati 888; race 2, Falappa Giancarlo, Ducati 888
11/7, Zeltweg, A: race 1, Meklau Andreas, Ducati 888; race 2, Falappa Giancarlo, Ducati 888
18/7, Brno, CZE, race 1, Fogarty Carl, Ducati 888
8/8, Anderstorp, S: race 1, Fogarty Carl, Ducati 888; race 2, Fogarty Carl, Ducati 888
22/8, Johr, MAL: race 1, Fogarty Carl, Ducati 888; race 2, Fogarty Carl, Ducati 888
29/8, Sugo, J, race 1, Fogarty Carl, Ducati 888
12/9, Assen, NL: race 1, Fogarty Carl, Ducati 888; race 2, Fogarty Carl, Ducati 888
26/9, Monza, I, race 2, Falappa Giancarlo, Ducati 888
17/10, Estoril, P, race 2, Fogarty Carl, Ducati 888

1994

AUSTRALIA
15/5, Mallala, SBK, Doohan Scott, Ducati 888
24/7, Oran Park, SBK, Doohan Scott, Ducati 888

AUSTRIA
22/5, Salzburgring, Pro-SBK, Mark Udo, Ducati 916
Österreichring, SBK, Meklau Andreas, Ducati 926
Österreichring, SOS, Windhager, Ducatimono

CZECH REPUBLIC
10/7, Most, Pro-SBK, Weibel Edwin, Ducati 888
21/8, Brno, Pro-SBK, Weibel Edwin, Ducati 888
21/8, Brno, Pro-SBK, Weibel Edwin, Ducati 888

GERMANY
7/5, Hockenheim, SBK, Agnoletti Mario, Ducati 916
8/5, Hockenheim, Euro Cup, Fugardi Enrico, Ducati 900
15/5, Nürburgring, Pro-SBK, Mark Udo, Ducati 888
3/9, Hockenheim, Pro-SBK, Mark Udo, Weibel Edwin, Ducati 888

GREAT BRITAIN
4/4, Donington Park, TT SBK, Fogarty Carl, Ducati 916
17/4, Mallory Park, Single C., Carter Alan, Ducati mono
2/5, Donington Park, Euro Cup, Carter Alan, Ducati 900
24/7, Donington Park, SBK, Whitham James, Ducati 916
7/8, Pembrey, Single C., Carter Alan, Ducati mono

HOLLAND
11/9, Assen, Euro Cup, Catchart Alan, Ducati

ITALY
Superbike Italian Championship, Pirovano Fabrizio, Ducati 888
Open Italian Championship, Innamorati Mario, Ducati 916

Sport Production Italian Championship, 750, Pasini Luca, Ducati 916
Sport Production Constructors Italian Championship, 750, Ducati Meccanica, Ducati 916
Superbike Tuscan Championship, Perselli Andrea, Ducati 916
Trofeo Winner Cup 900, Massimi Walter, Ducati 900
Trofeo Inverno Open, Gallina Michele, Ducati 916

6/3, Misano, SBK, Pirovano Fabrizio, Ducati 888
13/3, Vallelunga: SBK, Pirovano Fabrizio, Destefanis Valerio, Ducati 888; Open, Presciutti Aldeo, Ducati 750
20/3, Magione, B.ot T., Agnoletti Mario, Ducati 750
20/3, Misano, 750, Pasini Luca, Ducati 916
27/3, Varano Melegari, 750, Teneggi Roberto, Ducati 916
27/3, Magione, 750, "Snoopy", Ducati 916
4/4, Monza: SBK, Pirovano Fabrizio, Ducati 916; Open, Innamorati Mario, Ducati 916
10/4, Binetto, 750, "Snoopy", Ducati 916
10/4, Mugello: Winner Cup, Marino Stefano, Ducati 900; B.ot T., Molteni Giuseppe, Ducati
17/4, Magione, 750, Veltroni Giuseppe, Ducati 916
24/4, Misano, 750, Marchini Masimiliano, Ducati 916
1/5, Vallelunga, SBK, Colombari Massimiliano Ducati 888
15/5, Misano: Open, Innamorati Mario, Ducati 916; SBK, Pirovano Fabrizio, Ducati 888
15/5, Vallelunga: 750, "Snoopy", Ducati 916; Winner Cup, Massimi Walter, Ducati 900
15/5, Mugello, Open, Diacci Daniele, Ducati 916
22/5, Varano Melegari, 750, Teneggi Roberto, Ducati 916
29/5, Misano, Euro Cup 900, Agnoletti Mario, Ducati 900
12/6, Monza, 750, Marchini Massimiliano, Ducati 916
12/6, Varano Melegari, 750, Tavella Roberto, Ducati
12/6, Vallelunga, B.ot T., Molteni Giuseppe, Ducati
19/6, Mugello, 750, Teneggi Roberto, Ducati 916
June, Magione, Winner Cup 900, Massimi Walter, Ducati 900
25/6, 750, Marchini Massimiliano, Ducati 916
11/9, Varano Melegari, 750, Moretti, Ducati
18/9, Mugello, 750, Teneggi Roberto, Ducati 916
18/9, Binetto: B.ot T., ., Agnoletti Mario, Ducati 916; Winner Cup 900, "Ramardo", Ducati 900
25/9, Mugello: Supermono, Chili Pier Francesco, Ducati; Euro Cup 900, Lopez David, Ducati 900; 750, Marchini Massimiliano, Ducati 916
9/10, Vallelunga, Winner Cup 900, Plenario Pier Giorgio, Ducati 900
16/10, Misano, 750, Pasini Luca, Ducati 916
30/10, Binetto, Open, Gallina Michele, Ducati 916
13/11, Binetto, Open, Gallina Michele, Ducati 916
11/12, Binetto, Open, Gallina Michele, Ducati 916

UNITED STATES
Superbike American Championship, Corser Troy, Ducati 888

27/3, Phoenix, AZ, SBK, Corser Troy, Ducati 888
10/4, Pomona, CA, SBK, Corser Troy, Ducati 888
22/5, Monterey, CA, SBK, Picotte Pascal, Ducati 888
12/6, Elkhart Lake, WI, SBK, Picotte Pascal, Ducati 888
19/6, Loudon, NH, SBK, Corser Troy, Ducati 888

SBK WORLD CHAMPIONSHIP
Superbike World Championship, Fogarty Carl, Ducati 916
Superbike Constructors World Championship, Ducati Meccanica, Ducati 916

2/5, Donington Park, GB, race 1, Fogarty Carl, Ducati 916
29/5, Misano, I, race 2, Falappa Giancarlo, Ducati 916
19/6, Albacete, E: race 1, Fogarty Carl, Ducati 916; race 2, Fogarty Carl, Ducati 916
17/7, Zeltweg, A: race 1, Fogarty Carl, Ducati 916; race 2, Fogarty Carl, Ducati 916
21/8, Sentul, IND: race 1, Whitham James, Ducati 916; race 2, Fogarty Carl, Ducati 916
11/9, Assen, NL: race 1, Fogarty Carl, Ducati 916; race 2, Fogarty Carl, Ducati 916
25/9, Mugello, RSM, race 2, Fogarty Carl, Ducati 916
30/10, Phillip Island, AUS, race 1, Fogarty Carl, Ducati 916

1995

AUSTRALIA
Australian Shell Master Series, Giles Shawn, Ducati 916

5/2, Sandown Park, Shell M.S., McEwen Jason, Ducati 916
21/5, Winton, S.M.S., McEwen Jason, Ducati 916
28/5, Eastern Creek, S.M.S., Giles Shawn, Ducati 916
16/6, Eastern Creek, SBK, Giles Shawn, Ducati 916
9/7, Mallala, S.M.S., Giles Shawn, Ducati 916
13/8, Lakeside, SBK, Giles Shawn, Ducati 916
3/9, Baskerville, SBK, McEwen Jason, Ducati 916

AUSTRIA
Österreichring, SBK, Meklau Andreas, Ducati 916
2/7, Zeltweg, Pro-SBK, Mark Udo, Ducati 916
9/7, Salzburgring: SBK, Innamorati Mario, Ducati 916; S.S., Pacquay Michael, Ducati 748

COLOMBIA
21/5, Yanarcoche, SBK, Irizar Antonio, Ducati

CZECH REPUBLIC
Supersport Czech Championship, Pinz, Ducati 748

30/7, Most: SBK, Innamorati Mario, Ducati 916; S.S.600, Pacquay Michael, Ducati 748
27/8, Most, Pro-SBK, Mark Udo, Ducati 916

GERMANY
30/4, Speyer, Pro-SBK, Weibel Edwin, Ducati
7/5, Hockenheim, SBK, Agnoletti Mario, Ducati 916
6/8, Nürburgring, Pro-SBK, Weibel Edwin, Ducati

GREAT BRITAIN
Superbike British Championship, Hislop Steve, Ducati 888
Superbike British Championship, Llewellyn Matt, Ducati 888

17/4, Donington Park, SBK, Rutter Michel, Whitham James, Ducati 888
30/4, Mallory Park, SBK, Whitham James, Ducati 888
8/5, Oulton Park, SBK, Whitham James, Hislop Steve, Ducati 888
14/5, Brands Hatch, SBK Trophy, Whitham James, Ducati 888
28/5, Donington Park: SBK, Innamorati Mario, Ducati 916; S.S.600, Pacquay Michael, Ducati 748
29/5-9/6 Isle of Man - T.T., Singles TT, Holden Robert, Ducati 888
18/6, Oulton Park, SBK Trophy, Whitham James, Hislop Steve, Ducati 888
25/6, Snetterton, SBK, Whitham James, Hislop Steve, Ducati 888
9/7, Knockhill, SBK, Hislop Steve, Whitham James, Ducati 888
6/8, Brands Hatch, S.S.600, Paquay Michael, Ducati 748
28/8, Cadwell Park, SBK, Hislop Steve, Ducati 888
3/9, Brands Hatch, SBK, Hislop Steve, Ducati 888

HOLLAND
24/6, Assen: SBK, Innamorati Mario, Ducati 916; S.S.600, Pacquay Michael, Ducati 748
10/9, Assen, S.S. 600, Pacquay Michael, Ducati 748

ITALY
Superbike European Championship, Innamorati Mario, Ducati 916
Supersport 600 Italian Championship, Mariottini Camillo, Ducati 748
Sport Production Italian Championship, 750, Teneggi Roberto, Ducati 916
Sport Production Constructors Italian Championship., 750, Ducati Meccanica, Ducati 916
Trofeo Winner Cup 748, 748, Massimi Walter, Ducati 748
Trofeo 600 Nazionale Inverno, Bungaro Stefano, Ducati 748

5/3, Vallelunga, B.ot T., Pisanelli Mariano, Ducati
19/3, Misano, 600 S.P., Teneggi Roberto, Ducati 748
19/3, Magione: 600, Morelli Roberto, Ducati 748; 750, Veltroni Daniele, Ducati 916
26/3, Varano Melegari, 600, Teneggi Roberto, Ducati 748
26/3, Pergusa, 750, Iannuzzo Armando, Ducati
2/4, Mugello: 600 S.P., Teneggi Roberto, Ducati 748; 750 S.P., Mazzali Andrea, Ducati 916
9/4, Misano, 750 S.P., Mazzali Andrea, Ducati 916
17/4, Monza, SBK, Chili Pier Francesco, Ducati 916
23/4, Vallelunga: SBK, Pirovano Fabrizio, Ducati 916; 600 S.P., Mariottini Camillo, Ducati 748; Winner Cup, Massimi Walter, Ducati 748
23/4, Varano Melegari, 750, Cantalupo Giorgio, Ducati 916
30/4, Misano, 750, Arnoldi Ivo, Ducati
14/5, Misano: SBK, Pirovano Fabrizio, Pirovano Fabrizio, Ducati 916; 600 S.P., Teneggi Roberto, Ducati 748
14/5, Magione, 750 S.P., Veltroni Daniele, Ducati 916
21/5, Misano: SBK, Agnoletti Mario, Ducati 916; S.S.600, Mariottini Camillo, Ducati 748
21/5, Binetto, 600, Morelli Roberto, Ducati 748
21/5, Vallelunga: Winner Cup, Massimi Walter, Ducati 748; Trophy B.ot T., Castrichini Paolo, Ducati
21/5, Massa-S. Carlo, Open, Giocoso Antonio, Ducati
28/5, Magione: Winner Cup, Marchetti Dario, Ducati 748; Trophy B.ot T., Coresi Francesco, Ducati
4/6, Monza; 600 S.P., Teneggi Roberto, Ducati 748; 750 S.P., Arnoldi Ivo, Ducati 916
11/6, Varano Melegari, Over 750, Diacci Daniele, Ducati 916
18/6, Monza: SBK, Innamorati Mario, Ducati 916; S.S.600, Pacquay Michael, Ducati 748
18/6, Vallelunga, 750, Arnoldi Ivo, Ducati 916
25/6, Misano: 600 S.P., Teneggi Roberto, Ducati 748; 750 S.P., Teneggi Roberto, Ducati 916; Winner Cup, Biondi Dario, Ducati 748
25/6, Pergusa: 600 S.P., Mancuso Nino, Ducati 748; 750 S.P., Maltacesare Marco, Ducati 916
2/7, Mugello: 600 S.P., Teneggi Roberto, Ducati 748; 750 S.P., Teneggi Roberto, Ducati 748
16/7, Pergusa, 600 S.P. Mancuso Nino, Ducati 748
16/7, Mugello: 750, Diacci Daniele, Ducati 916; Winner Cup, Perselli Andrea, Ducati 748
20/8, Misano, 750, Bosetti, Ducati
27/8, Varano Melegari, 750, Boccelli Massimo, Diacci Daniele, Ducati 916
3/9, Mugello, 750 S.P., Diacci Daniele, Ducati 916
10/9, Misano: 600, Gennari Maurizio, Ducati; 750, Di Giuli Antonio, Ducati
17/9, Vallelunga: B.ot T., Giangiacomo Antonio, Ducati; 750 S.P., Teneggi Roberto, Ducati 916
24/9, Mugello: SBK, Pirovano Fabrizio, Ducati 916; 600 S.P., Teneggi Roberto, Ducati 748
1/10, Misano, 750 S.P., Teneggi Roberto, Ducati 916
22/10, Vallelunga: 750 S.P., Mazzali Andrea, Ducati 916; B.ot T., Giangiacomo Antonio, Ducati
29/10, Binetto: 600, Bungaro Stefano, Ducati 748; B.ot T., Giangiacomo Antonio, Ducati
10/12, Binetto: 600, Bungaro Stefano, Ducati 748; Open, Mastrelli Mauro, Ducati

SPAIN
6/5, Jerez, SBK, Agnoletti Mario, Ducati 916

SWITZERLAND
Elite Supersport Swiss Championship, Blanc, Ducati 748
Superbike Swiss Championship, Blanc, Ducati 916

UNITED STATES
Superbike American Championship, Corser Troy, Ducati 888

1/5, Monterey, CA, SBK, Spencer Freddie, Ducati 916

VENEZUELA
23/4, San Carlos, Open SBK, Baiz Fernando, Ducati
10/9, San Carlos, Open SBK, Baiz Fernando, Ducati

SBK WORLD CHAMPIONSHIP
Superbike World Championship, Fogarty Carl, Ducati 916
Superbike Constructors World Championship, Ducati Meccanica, Ducati 916

7/5, Hockenheim, D: race 1, Fogarty Carl, Ducati 916; race 2, Fogarty Carl, Ducati 916
21/5, Misano, I: race 1, Lucchiari Mauro, Ducati 916; race 2, Lucchairi Mauro, Ducati 916
28/5, Donington Park, GB: race 1, Fogarty Carl, Ducati 916; race 2, Fogarty Carl, Ducati 916
18/6, Monza, RSM: race 1, Fogarty Carl, Ducati 916; race 2, Chili P.Francesco, Ducati 916
25/6, Albacete, E, race 2, Fogarty Carl, Ducati 916
9/7, Salzburgring, A: race 1, Fogarty Carl, Ducati 916; race 2, Corser Troy, Ducati 916
23/7, Laguna Seca, USA, race 2, Corser Troy, Ducati 916
6/8, Brands Hatch, GB: race 1, Fogarty Carl, Ducati 916; race 2, Fogarty Carl, Ducati 916
27/8, Sugo, J: race 1, Corser Troy, Ducati 916; race 2, Fogarty Carl, Ducati 916
10/9, Assen, NL: race 1, Fogarty Carl, Ducati 916; race 2, Fogarty Carl, Ducati 916
15/10, Sentul, IND: race 1, Fogarty Carl, Ducati 916
29/10, Phillip Island, AUS, race 2, Corser Troy, Ducati 916

1996

AUSTRALIA
14/4, Phillip Island, Shell M.S., Giles Shawn, Ducati 916

AUSTRIA
Superbike Austrian Championship, Meklau Andreas, Ducati 955
Österreichring, SBK, Meklau Andreas, Ducati 955
Salzburgring, SBK, Meklau Andreas, Ducati 955
A1 - Ring, SBK, Meklau Andreas, Ducati 955
1/9, Zeltweg, Pro-SBK, Lindholm Christer, Ducati 916

BELGIUM
21/7, Zolder, Pro-SBK, Lindholm Christer, Meklau Andreas, Ducati 916

CZECH REPUBLIC
Supersport Czech Championship, Madera, Ducati 748

23/6, Most, Pro-SBK, Morrison Brian, Lindholm Christer, Ducati 916
30/6, Brno, Open S.S., Lucchiari Mauro, Ducati 748

FRANCE
5/5, Nogaro, SBK, Chambon Stephane, Ducati 916
June, Albi, SBK, Chambon Stephane, Ducati 916
21/7, Le Castelet, SBK, Chambon Stephane, Ducati 916
13/10, Magny Cours, SBK, Sain Oscar, Ducati 916

GERMANY
Superbike German Championship, Lindholm Christer, Ducati 916

21/4, Speyer, Pro-SBK, Lindholm Christer, Ducati 916
25/5, Sachsenring, Pro-SBK, Lindholm Christer, Ducati 916
4/8, Nürburgring, Pro-SBK, Lindholm Christer, Ducati 916
21/9, Hockenheim, Pro-SBK, Lindholm Christer, Ducati 916

GREAT BRITAIN
31/3, Donington Park, SBK, Rymer Terry, Ducati 916
8/4, Thruxton, SBK, Rymer Terry, Ducati 916
28/4, Donington Park, Open S.S., Pirovano Fabrizio, Ducati 748
5/5, Oulton Park, SBK, Rymer Terry, Ducati 916
4/8, Brands Hatch, Open S.S., Korner Thoams, Ducati 748
29/6, Brands Hatch, SBK, Rymer Terry, Ducati 916

HOLLAND
8/9, Assen, Open S.S., Lucchiari Mauro, Ducati 748

INDONESIA
18/8, Sentul, Open S.S., Pirovano Fabrizio, Ducati 748

ITALY
Superbike Italian Championship, Casoli Paolo, Ducati 916
Superbike Constructors Italian Championship, Ducati Motor, Ducati 916
Italian Championship, S.P. 750 2 cyl., Mazzali Andrea, Ducati 916
Sport Production Constructors Italian Championship, 750, Ducati Motor, Ducati 916
Supersport Italian Championship, 600, Lucchiari Mauro, Ducati 748
Italian Championship 600 Sport P., Marchini Massimiliano Ducati 748
Constructors Italian Championship 600 S.P., Ducati Motor, Ducati 748

10/3, Vallelunga: 600 S.P., Marchini Massimiliano, Ducati 748; B.ot T., Giangiacomo Antonio, Ducati

17/3, Magione, 750, Carlacci Antonio, Ducati 916
24/3, Misano: SBK, Chili Pier Francesco, Ducati 916; 600, Lucchiari Mauro, Ducati 748
8/4, Monza, SBK, Chili Pier Francesco, Ducati 916
14/4, Misano, Open S.S., Pirovano Fabrizio, Ducati 748
14/4, Pergusa, 600, Fagone Fausto, Ducati
21/4, Vallelunga: 600 S.P., Marchini Massimiliano Ducati 748; 750 S.P., Carlacci Antonio, Ducati 916
28/4, Misano, 750 S.P., Mazzali Andrea, Ducati 750
28/4, Magione, Super Twins, Coresi Franco, Ducati
28/4, Pergusa, 600, Fagone Fausto, Ducati
19/5, Binetto, 750, Carlacci Antonio, Ducati 916
19/5, Pergusa, 600, Mancuso Nino, Ducati
26/5, Vallelunga, Open, Giangiacomo Antonio, Ducati
9/6, Vallelunga, SBK, Casoli Paolo, Ducati 916
9/6, Monza, 600, Eugeni Enrico, Ducati 748
16/6, Varano Melegari, 750, Boccelli Massimo, Ducati
23/6, Massa-S. Carlo, 600, Bertoni Mario, Ducati
21/7, Mugello, 750 S.P., Marchini Massimiliano, Ducati 916
28/7, Varano Melegari, Open, Gallina Michele, Ducati 916
8/9, Misano: 600, Conti Angelo, Ducati 748; 750, Mazzali Andrea, Ducati 916
15/9, Vallelunga: 600 S.P., Marchini Massimiliano, Ducati 748; 750 S.P., Ruozi Roberto, Ducati 916
21/9, Mugello: SBK, Casoli Paolo, Ducati 916; S.S. 600, Lucchiari Mauro, Ducati 748; 600 S.P., Marchini Massimiliano, Ducati 748; 750 S.P., Marchini Massimiliano, Ducati 916
17/11, Binetto, B.ot T., Bungaro Stefano, Ducati
8/12, Binetto, Open, Sorrentino, Ducati

JAPAN
25/8, Sugo, Open S.S., Pirovano Fabrizio, Ducati 748

SPAIN
10/3, Cartagena, SBK, Vazquez David, Ducati 916
5/5, Albacete, Open S.S., Sainz Oscar, Ducati 916
6/10, Albacete, Open S.S., Pirovano Fabrizio, Ducati 748

UNITED STATES
A.M.A. CHAMPIONSHIP
11/6, Elkhart Lake, WI, SBK, Gramigni Alessandro, Ducati 916
16/7, Brainerd, MN, SBK, Gramigni Alessandro, Ducati 916

SBK WORLD CHAMPIONSHIP
Superbike World Championship, Corser Troy, Ducati 916
Superbike Constructors World Championship, Ducati Motor, Ducati 916

14/4, Misano, RSM: race 1, Kocinski John, Ducati 916; race 2, Kocinski John, Ducati 916
28/4, Donington Park, GB: race 1, Corser Troy, Ducati 916; race 2, Corser Troy, Ducati 916
16/6, Monza, I, race 2, Chili P.Francesco, Ducati 916
30/6, Brno, CZE: race 1, Corser Troy, Ducati 916; race 2, Corser Troy, Ducati 916
21/7, Laguna Seca, USA, race 1, Kocinski John, Ducati 916
4/8, Brands Hatch, GB: race 1, Chili Pier Francesco, Ducati 916; race 2, Corser Troy, Ducati 916
18/8, Sentul, IND: race 1, Kocinski John, Ducati 916; race 2, Kocinski John, Ducati 916
6/10, Albacete, E: race 1, Corser Troy, Ducati 916; race 2, Corser Troy, Ducati 916

1997

AUSTRIA
Superbike Austrian Championship, Meklau Andreas, Ducati 996

A1 - Ring, SBK, Meklau Andreas, Ducati 996
17/8, Zeltweg, S.S., Conti Angelo, Ducati 748

FRANCE
9/3, Le Mans, SBK, Chambon Stephane, Ducati 916
31/3, Magny Cours: SBK, Chambon Stephane, Ducati 916; S.S., Chambon Stephane, Ducati 748
27/4, Carole: SBK, Chambon Stephane, Ducati 916; S.S., Muscat David, Ducati 748
18/5, Albi: SBK, Chambon Stephane, Ducati 916; S.S., Chambon Stephane, Ducati 748
1/6, Nogaro, SBK, Chambon Stephane, Ducati 916
1/6, Nogaro, S.S., Chambon Stephane, Ducati 748
6/7, Paul Richard, S.S., Chambon Stephane, Ducati 748

GERMANY
20/4, Zweibrücken, Pro-SBK, Lavilla Gregorio, Ducati 916
1/6, Sachsenring, Super S., Korner Thomas, Ducati 916
3/8, Nürburgring, Pro-SBK, Lavilla Gregorio, Ducati 916
7/9, Oschersleben, S.S. W.S., Casoli Paolo, Ducati 748

GREAT BRITAIN
27/4, Oulton Park, SBK, Reynolds John, Ducati 916
4/5, Donington Park, S.S.W.S., Casoli Paolo, Ducati 748
22/6, Brands Hatch, SBK, Emmett Sean, Reynolds John, Ducati 916
3/8, Brands Hatch, S.S.W.S., Chambon Stephane, Ducati 748
25/8, Cadwell Park, SBK, Simpson Ian, Ducati 916

ITALY
World Championship Supersport 600 W.S., Casoli Paolo, Ducati 748
Constructors World Championship Supersport 600 W.S., Ducati Motor, Ducati 748
Italian Championship Supersport 600, Casoli Paolo, Ducati 748
Constructors Italian Championship Supersport 600, Ducati Motor, Ducati 748
Italian Championship 600 Sport P., Teneggi Roberto, Ducati 748
Constructors Italian Championship 600 Sport P., Ducati Motor, Ducati 748
Italian Championship Sport P. 750, Gallina Michele, Ducati 916
Constructors Italian Championship Sport P. 750, Ducati Motor, Ducati 916
Superbike Italian Championship, Foti Serafino, Ducati 916
Superbike Constructors Italian Championship, Ducati Motor, Ducati 916
Open Italian Championship, Brugnara Franco, Ducati 916
Open Constructors Italian Championship, Ducati Motor, Ducati 916
Challenge Ducati Cup Monster 900, Massimi Walter, Ducati 900
Trofeo Italiano Super Twins, Senatore Christian, Ducati 750
Trofeo Italiano Over 32 Open, Saracco Valter, Ducati 916
Tuscan Championship Sport Production 600, Cirri Andrea, Ducati 748
Open Tuscan Championship, Nerozzi Stefano, Ducati 916

23/3, Varano Melegari, Open, Saracco Valter, Ducati 916
6/4, Misano: SBK, Foti Serafino, Ducati 916; Open, Brugnara Franco, Ducati 916
20/4, Misano, SBK, Cantalupo Giorgio, Ducati 916

4/5, Misano: 750 S.P., Gallina Michele, Ducati 916; Super Twins, Senatore Christian, Ducati 750
18/5, Varano Melegari: 750, Panella Walter, Ducati 916; Open, Saracco Valter, Ducati 916
18/5, Vallelunga, Monster Cup, Massimi Walter, Ducati 900
25/5, Mugello, Monster Cup, Massimi Walter, Ducati 900
8/6, Misano: 750, Panella Walter, Ducati 916; Open, Saracco Valter, Ducati 916; 750 S.P., Iandolo Francesco, Ducati 916
15/6, Binetto, Super Twins, Senatore Christian, Ducati 750
22/6, Monza, Supersport W.S., Pirovano Fabrizio, Ducati 748
29/6, Misano: 750 S.P., Ruozi Roberto, Ducati 916; Monster Cup, Massimi Walter, Ducati 900
13/7, Mugello: 600 S.P., Conti Angelo, Ducati 748; 750 S.P., Gallina Michele, Ducati 916
27/7, Misano: S.S. 600, Conti Angelo, Ducati 748; SBK, Foti Serafino, Ducati 916
31/8, Misano: 600 S.P., Teneggi Roberto, Ducati 748; 750 S.P., Carlacci Antonio, Ducati 916; Monster Cup, Bosio Samuele, Ducati 900
14/9, Mugello, 750 S.P., Gallina Michele, Ducati 916
14/9, Magione, Monster Cup, Morigi Daniele, Ducati 900
5/10, Vallelunga: 600 S.P., Teneggi Roberto, Ducati 748; 750 S.P., Arnoldi Ivo, Ducati 916; Super Twins, Senatore Christian, Ducati 750
19/10, Varano Melegari: Monster Cup, Collini, Ducati 900; 750, Panella Walter, Ducati 916
26/10, Misano: 600 S.P., Marchini Massimiliano, Ducati 748; 750 S.P., Mazzali Andrea, Ducati 916; 750 Over 32, Panella Walter, Ducati 916; Over 32 Open, Saracco Valter, Ducati 916; Super Twins, Vari Michele, Ducati 750
9/11, Vallelunga, Open, Soppelsa Ivan, Ducati

JAPAN
5/10, Sugo, S.S. W.S., Casoli Paolo, Ducati 748

SPAIN
Supersport Spanish Championship, Torrontegui Herri, Ducati 748

16/3, Albacete, S.S., Rodriguez Javier, Riquelme Francisco, Ducati 748
1/6, Jarama, S.S., Torrontegui Francisco, Ducati 748
23/11, Jerez, S.S., Torrontegui Francisco, Ducati 748

UNITED STATES
16/2, Phoenix, AZ, SBK, Mladin Mathew, Ducati 916
8/6, Elkhert Lake, WI, SBK, Mladin Mathew, Ducati 916
15/6, Loudon, NH, SBK, Mladin Mathew, Ducati 916
5/10, Las Vegas, NV, SBK, Mladin Mathew, Ducati 916

VENEZUELA
14/11, San Carlos, SBK, Irizar Antonio, Ducati
15/11, San Carlos, SBK, Irizar Antonio, Ducati

SBK WORLD CHAMPIONSHIP
20/4, Misano, RSM, race 1, Chili Pier Francesco, Ducati 916
4/5, Donington Park, GB, race 2, Fogarty Carl, Ducati 916
8/6, Hockenheim, D, race 2, Fogarty Carl, Ducati 916
22/6, Monza, I, race 2, Chili Pier Francesco, Ducati 916
3/8, Brands Hatch, GB: race 1, Chili Pier Francesco, Ducati 916; race 2, Fogarty Carl, Ducati 916
17/8, Zeltweg, A, race 1, Fogarty Carl, Ducati 916

31/8, Assen, NL, race 2, Fogarty Carl,
 Ducati 916
12/10, Sentul, IND, race 2, Fogarty Carl,
 Ducati 916

1998

AUSTRALIA
June, Calder Park, SBK, Martin Steve,
 Ducati 996
July, Philip Island: Bayliss Troy, Ducati 996;
 Emmett Sean, Ducati 996

AUSTRIA
May, Salzburg, SBK, Meklau Andreas,
 Ducati 996

GERMANY
Superbike German Championship, Meklau
 Andreas, Ducati 996

GREAT BRITAIN
April, Brands l latch, Graves Peter, Ducati 748
13/4, Donington Park, SS 600, Casoli
 Paolo, Ducati 916
3/8, Brands Hatch, SBK, Corser Troy, Ducati 996
August, Silverstone, SBK, Bayliss Troy,
 Ducati 996

ITALY
Italian Championship Superbike, Blora
 Paolo, Ducati 916
Italian Championship Ducati 900, Morigi
 Davide, Ducati 900SS

8/3, Vallelunga, Open, Blora Paolo, Ducati 916
22/3, Varano Melegari, 600 S.P. Colombo
 Matteo, Ducati 748
29/3, Misano: SBK, Cantalupo Giorgio,
 Ducati 916; S.S.600, Briguet Yves, Ducati
 748; S.Twins, Bastianini Ermanno, Ducati
 916
19/4, Vallelunga: S.Twins, Bastianini
 Ermanno, Ducati 916; Supermono, Baines
 Geoff, Ducati
3/5, Misano: S.P. 600, Migliorati Cristiano,
 Ducati 748; SBK, Cantalupo Giorgio,
 Ducati 916; Trofeo Ducati, Temporali,
 Ducati 900
10/5, Binetto, 600 S.P., Malatesta Michele,
 Ducati 748
31/5, Vallelunga, Trofeo Techns Racing,
 Lucchinelli Marco, Ducati 900 SS;
 S.Twins, Bastianini Ermanno, Ducati 916;
 S.S.600, Pasini Luca, Ducati; SBK,
 Cantalupo Giorgio, Ducati 916
21/6, Varano Melegari, Trofeo Ducati, Viani
 Gianni, Ducati; S.Twins, Ruozi Roberto,
 Ducati; Open, Boccelli Massimo, Ducati
14/6, Misano, 600 S.P., Malatesta Michele,
 Ducati 748; SBK, Blora Paolo, Ducati 916
5/7, Mugello, S.Twins-Supermono,
 Bastianini Ermanno, Ducati 916
12/7, Monza, Open, Boccelli Massimo, Ducati
19/7, Imola, 600 S.P., Carlacci Antonio,
 Ducati 748; Ducati 900, Lucchinelli
 Marco, Ducati 900 SS
20/9, Mugello, Ducati 900, Lucchinelli
 Marco, Ducati 900SS
4/10, Varano Melegari, 600 S.P., Tondini,
 Ducati 748
11/10, Misano, 600 S.P., Malatesta
 Michele, Ducati 748
11/10, Vallelunga, S.Twins, Tirelli Paride,
 Ducati
25/10, Monza, S.Twins, Calasso Antonio,
 Ducati 4 V

UNITED STATES
17/2, Phoenix, AZ, SBK, Gobert Anthony,
 Ducati 996
3/5, Atlanta, SBK, Gobert Anthony,
 Ducati 996

12/7, Laguna Seca, S.S.600, Casoli Paolo,
 Ducati 748

YUGOSLAVIA
27/9, Rijeka, 600 S.S., Furlan Fabrizio,
 Ducati

SBK WORLD CHAMPIOSHIP
Superbike World Championship, Fogarty
 Carl, Ducati 996
Superbike Constructors World
 Championship, Ducati Motor, Ducati 996

22/3, Phillip Island, Aus, race 1, Fogarty
 Carl, Ducati 996
24/5, Albacete, E: race 1 Chili Pier Francesco,
 Ducati 996; race 2, Fogarty Carl, Ducati 996
12/7, Laguna Seca, USA, race 1, Corser,
 Troy, Ducati 996
7,6, Nürburgring, D, race 2, Chili Pier
 Francesco, Ducati 996
5/7 Kyalami, R.S.: race 1, Chili Pier
 Francesco, Ducati 996; race 2 Chili Pier
 Francesco, Ducati 996
6/9, Assen, NL: race 1, Chili Pler
 Francesco, Ducati 996; race 2, Fogarty
 Carl, Ducati 996